THE SACK OF ROME

THE SACK OF ROME

How a Beautiful European Country

with a Fabled History and a Storied Culture

Was Taken Over by a Man Named

Silvio Berlusconi

Alexander Stille

THE PENGUIN PRESS

New York

2006

THE PENGUIN PRESS
Published by the Penguin Group
Penguin Group (USA) Inc., 375 Hudson Street, New York, New York 10014, U.S.A. • Penguin
Group (Canada), 90 Eglinton Avenue East, Suite 700, Toronto, Ontario, Canada M4P 2Y3
(a division of Pearson Penguin Canada Inc.) • Penguin Books Ltd, 80 Strand, London
WC2R 0RL, England • Penguin Ireland, 25 St. Stephen's Green, Dublin 2, Ireland (a division of
Penguin Books Ltd) • Penguin Books Australia Ltd, 250 Camberwell Road, Camberwell, Victoria
3124, Australia (a division of Pearson Australia Group Pty Ltd) • Penguin Books India Pvt Ltd,
11 Community Centre, Panchsheel Park, New Delhi - 110 017, India • Penguin Group (NZ),
Cnr Airborne and Rosedale Roads, Albany, Auckland 1310, New Zealand (a division of Pearson
New Zealand Ltd) • Penguin Books (South Africa) (Pty) Ltd, 24 Sturdee Avenue,
Rosebank, Johannesburg 2196, South Africa

Penguin Books Ltd, Registered Offices:
80 Strand, London WC2R 0RL, England

First published in 2006 by The Penguin Press,
a member of Penguin Group (USA) Inc.

1   3   5   7   9   10   8   6   4   2

LIBRARY OF CONGRESS CATALOGING-IN-PUBLICATION DATA
Stille, Alexander.
The sack of Rome : how a beautiful European country with a fabled history and a
storied culture was taken over by a man named Silvio Berlusconi / Alexander Stille.
p.   cm.
ISBN 1-59420-053-X
1. Berlusconi, Silvio, 1936–   2. Prime ministers—Italy—Biography.   3. Businesspeople—
Italy—Biography.   4. Italy—Politics and government—1994–
5. Political corruption—Italy.   I. Title.

DG583.B47S75 2006
945.092'9092—dc22
[B]   2005056491
Printed in the United States of America
Set in Fournier
Designed by Chris Welch

For Lexi

ACKNOWLEDGMENTS

I received assistance from a number of people in the course of working on on this book. The idea for it was generated by Christine Zeile of Beckverlag in Munich and I owe her very much for her pushing and encouraging me in all my work over the years. The work I did for Robert Silvers at the *New York Review of Books* helped me a great deal in thinking through some of the material. Sarah Chalfant at the Wylie Agency helped greatly in actually making the project happen and in coordinating the actions of different publishers in the United States and Europe. Scott Moyers at Penguin did a superb job of editing; his comments were always intelligent, thoughtful, and helpful and his editing pencil respectful but incisive. His assistant, Jane Fleming, was patient and tireless in helping to iron out many of the wrinkles in a book written under deadline pressure with a rushed production schedule. In the course of research, I had help with research from Emily Backus, interview transcription from Nadia Zonis, and fact-checking from Emilia Casella—all of which made it possible to write a longish and complex book in a concentrated time. My wife, Lexi, along with giving me so much happiness, was a superb, reliable, and conscientious reader. The careful and painstaking reading and editing of my good friend Catherine Orenstein also helped me fix many problems, rethink the approach to many chapters, all of which greatly improved the manuscript that I submitted. Oliviero Ponte di Pino, my Italian editor at Garzanti, was enormously helpful in many ways, reading with an Italian eye and doing another, meticulous, level of fact-checking. Together with Corrado Stajano, he saved me from many errors small and large. Judge Piercamillo Davigo very kindly did an extremely helpful lawyer's reading of the book to double-check the thousands of facts in the complex legal proceedings involving Berlusconi and his associates.

CONTENTS

THE SACK OF ROME

INTRODUCTION

In the summer of 1993, Silvio Berlusconi, Italy's richest man and the owner of its largest television and publishing empire, conducted a series of polls to test the possibility of his founding his own party and becoming a candidate for prime minister. One poll found that Berlusconi enjoyed 97 percent name recognition with potential voters, while the actual prime minister, Carlo Azeglio Ciampi, was known to only 51 percent.[1]

The media tycoon who had brought *Dallas*, *Wheel of Fortune* and *Baywatch* to Italy, who had led the Milan soccer team to several championships, whose yachts and villas and beautiful wife were frequently featured in the supermarket tabloids, was of far greater interest than any of the traditional politicians on the market. Another poll conducted among young people showed that Berlusconi was their "most loved," on a long list of names. Arnold Schwarzenegger was second and Jesus Christ third.

The end of the Cold War had wiped out the traditional political parties that had dominated Italy for the previous fifty years. The old ideologies of the twentieth century were waning, and the most influential institution still standing in the rubble of the Berlin Wall was a television media company.

Aware of his opportunity to fill this void, Berlusconi undertook what has to be one of the most extraordinarily innovative election campaigns of our age. All the divisions of Berlusconi's vast empire—from television stations and newspapers to department stores and an insurance and financial services company—were fused almost overnight into an enormous political machine. The ad executives contacted the companies that bought advertising on the Berlusconi channels. The stockbrokers and insurance agents working for Berlusconi's financial services company became campaign workers and set about turning the hundreds of thousands, possibly millions, of financial clients into voters and party supporters. The personnel department of the television advertising company selected more than a hundred of the company's top ad salesmen to be candidates for the parliamentary elections. The candidates took screen tests at the television studios, were given lessons in politics, and were cross-examined to see how they would hold up under the fire of an election campaign. The candidates all were obliged to buy a special kit that included a thirty-five-page booklet and eleven videotapes explaining the party's program as well as lessons on how to speak in public and on TV. The company's media experts, with expertise in testing TV programs, conducted focus groups to hone Berlusconi's message to appeal to the largest possible audience. The party/company set up pay-per-call phone numbers (at about 50 cents a minute) that allowed people to listen to the latest comments of Berlusconi, and earned money for the movement at the same time.

Initially, the work was carried out in secret. Berlusconi vigorously denied that he had any intention of becoming a candidate. The official word was that he was helping found a political movement to promote the values of freedom and democracy through a series of clubs, called Forza Italia! ("Go, Italy!"), the phrase soccer fans chant when cheering on the national team. Much of Berlusconi's fame and popularity was related to his ownership of the soccer club A. C. Milan. Patriotism in Italy was at an all-time low, and almost the only thing capable of eliciting feelings of intense national pride and fervor was the Italian soccer team. To harness those feelings, Berlusconi co-opted the team's slogans and symbols. His "team" was to be the "Blues," the nickname for the players on the Italian team.

Berlusconi and his executives' goal was to create eight thousand Forza Italia clubs, one in almost every decent-sized town in Italy. The number was not arrived at randomly: there are about eight thousand Catholic parishes in Italy. At the end of World War II, after the collapse of Fascism, the Catholic Church with its eight thousand parishes had served as the backbone of the new Christian Democratic Party. But the Church's power, like those of the parties, was on the decline. *"L'azienda della fede"* ("The Faith Business"), as Berlusconi referred to the Church, "is not doing well," he told a corporate audience in the late 1980s, announcing that he intended to buy a series of abandoned monasteries and convents for corporate retreats for his sales force—as if in a kind of symbolic transfer of power. With a Forza Italia club in every parish, the transfer would be complete.[2]

With rumors of Berlusconi's project growing every day, and his figure gaining prominence with each denial of his plans, the terrain was perfectly prepared, as for the launch of a new product.

Then, on January 26, 1994, Berlusconi appeared on the three main private TV networks (which he owns) and announced that he was founding a new political party and running for prime minister.

It looked much like an address from the Oval Office at the White House. Berlusconi was shown in the study of his sumptuous eighteenth-century villa, seated behind a large, commanding desk, with family photographs in the background. He spoke to the nation with a grave and authoritative air. Even though he was only a private citizen and a political novice, it looked as if he were already president. "Berlusconi . . . was the 'virtual-reality' president," says Giuliano Ferrara, one of his chief political strategists and the ghostwriter of the speech. "I understood at that moment that he had changed the form of Italian politics."[3]

Within just two months, Berlusconi was, in fact, prime minister.

ᐳ̇

When I first went to live in Rome in 1980, it was a very different place.

Rome was relatively poor and shabby, with paint peeling from its ocher-brown buildings. Rather than standard Italian, many people spoke regional dialects, a living tie to preunification Italy and its millennial traditional peasant life. When you walked through the neighborhood of Trastevere, its narrow alleyways were filled with women sitting on chairs on the sidewalks so that they could spend their afternoons fanning themselves, chatting and talking to their neighbors—as they still do in poorer cities like Naples or Palermo. Hardly anyone knew English and far fewer people had traveled overseas. People on the left took their vacations in places like Yugoslavia in order to avoid spending money in capitalist countries. Although Italy was growing economically, it had vestiges of a precapitalist culture. I lived for two years without a telephone because it was considered almost impossible to get a phone in less than nine months and it didn't seem worth the trouble. There was a shortage of metal coins and so shopkeepers would give you handfuls of candy instead. By the end of a week, your pockets would bulge with peppermints and gumballs. Stores and restaurants shut down almost entirely in August because people believed in rest and vacation, even though there was a lot of money to be made.

The country was torn apart by political and ideological violence of the left and the right. A day hardly went by in which there was not a Red Brigades killing, kneecapping or kidnapping or a right-wing bombing. There was also a vicious Mafia war going on in Palermo that would ultimately claim thousands of lives. When I moved to Milan, I met people with bodyguards and bulletproof cars, people whose mothers had been kidnapped or whose older brothers had not been heard from for years and were presumed to have entered the netherworld of some terrorist organization. It was already clear that the armed struggle was doomed to fail, that it had lost any wider popular appeal, but, like wounded, cornered animals, the terrorists stepped up their violence as their movement entered its decline and the armed revolution degenerated into a genuine bloodbath.

The terrorism was puzzling since Italy was such a remarkably pleasant place to live—and not only for the rich. The violence came after twenty-five years of economic growth the likes of which modern Italy had never experienced. It was the death rattle of an old order, an age of ideology, precisely on the eve of a consumer boom that would make the idea of radical revolution seem like a barely remembered dream.

I recall visiting a family friend, an old journalist who lived with his wife in a beautiful apartment overlooking Piazza Navona in Rome. Suddenly, at a knock on the door, there was a moment of silence and fear. The journalist's name had been found on the hit list of the Red Brigades. The knock turned out to be that of a friend, a young woman they had wanted to introduce me to. "You were in Lotta Continua [Continuous Struggle] in high school?" the wife asked the young woman, referring to one of a myriad of far-left groups of the time. Lotta Continua, like many of the radical groups of the 1970s, had disbanded a few years earlier, as the revolution began to run out of gas. Many of the young Italians I met were still identified with the political groups they had belonged to in high school or university, the way young Americans might be known by the prestigious colleges they had attended.

It was bracing to live in such an intensely political environment. By the time I reached college, in 1974, the Vietnam War was winding down and American college campuses were largely depoliticized. At the Italian publishing house where I worked, there were frequent strikes to protest this killing or that government act. The strikes ran against the grain of my American notions of efficiency and duty at work, but I appreciated the fact that people cared so passionately and talked so animatedly about politics.

I remember walking into Piazza del Duomo in Milan on Sunday afternoons, where you could generally find crowds of older men collected in expanding circles of political debate—sometimes as many as thirty or forty men crowding around like the pigeons that collected around some choice piece of food on the cathedral steps. They were generally men in their sixties, seventies or eighties—they wore hats and mustaches and suspenders and gray suits, dress of an earlier era—and argued with great animation using the language of a bygone age. There were anarchists and old-style liberals, monarchists and Fascists. I found their body language—

the heated discourse, the animated gestures, the flocklike nature of the crowd pressing forward to watch political debate as they might a prize-fight—more interesting than the debate itself. This brood of old gray men with their hats and suspenders and handlebar mustaches represented the last remnants of an era when city squares filled with people who wanted to talk about politics. For these old men, born long before the age of television, getting out of the house and talking politics was a form of entertainment and sociability.

But there were already signs that this was changing. These were the first years of what was called *il riflusso,* the turning of the tide, a rejection of political commitment. The broken ranks of the revolutionary left were scattering in various directions, some becoming Hare Krishnas or raising chickens on a farm, others going into advertising or business, many slipping into heavy drugs. The parks and streets and public bathrooms of Italian cities in those years were full of syringes, and there were an estimated 200,000 heroin addicts and a thousand deaths by overdose a year.

The same year that I arrived in Italy, 1980, Silvio Berlusconi started Canale 5, the first private national television network. Since there was no TV in my apartment, I didn't notice. Then, one day, the concierge of my building, taking pity on this young foreigner living without either phone or television, insisted on giving me a giant, ancient color television that someone in the building wanted to get rid of. It must have been one of the first color sets sold in Italy, since color TV wasn't available until 1977 and it already had the look of an antique: it was about the size of a refrigerator, took a few minutes to warm up and turned everyone's face either orange or purple.

I didn't pay much attention since Berlusconi's channel simply played back for me the worst aspects of my own American culture—cheesy soap operas and sitcoms, *General Hospital, Love Boat, Dallas, Magnum, P.I.,* reruns of trashy American B movies dubbed in Italian. The original Italian programs invariably involved scantily clad soubrettes and crowds of tackily dressed Italians clapping rhythmically or waving at the camera. But in fact the gaudy colors of the Berlusconi television world, for all its seeming silliness and frivolity, represented a revolution in the black-and-white world of Italian life. In the late 1970s, Italians didn't watch much TV. In fact, RAI (the state TV) didn't even keep track of how many people watched TV and how much time they spent doing so.

Today, old men no longer congregate in Piazza del Duomo. Older Italians stay home more and watch about an average of five hours of television a day. And the more television they watch, the more likely they are to vote for Silvio Berlusconi. A deep change has occurred.

The 1980s—the decade of Reagan and Thatcher—was a turning point in both the United States and Europe. It was the decade in which the post–World War II consensus around the welfare state began to crumble; in which governments looked to privatize and deregulate industries; in which the old manufacturing economy gave way to a postindustrial economy and unionized labor gave way to more flexible and precarious kinds of work, in which the twentieth-century political oppositions of Communism versus capitalist democracy came to an end; in which traditional mass parties atrophied and were replaced by a highly personalized form of politics; in which the culture of solidarity (the New Deal and the Great Society in the U.S., 1968 and the welfare state in Europe) was replaced by a new set of values based on personal success and wealth. The old middle-class virtues of savings and frugality, which had helped bankroll the manufacturing economy, gave way to a consumer economy fueled by a culture of credit card debt and shop-till-you-drop consumption.

Berlusconi, through the introduction of commercial television in Italy, was perhaps the greatest agent of these changes in Italian life. Before the 1980s, virtually all television in Europe was controlled by government. In Italy, Berlusconi broke down the monopoly of the state broadcasting company RAI and created his own virtual monopoly of private television. The old RAI was very much a reflection of the peculiar nature of postwar Italy. The political parties controlled the different channels, and newscasts were literally measured with stopwatches, the minutes and seconds of commentary allocated so that each political party got its say in proportion to its numerical strength in parliament. It was a crude form of pluralism, but pluralism nonetheless.

RAI contained the best and worst elements of Italy's *ancien régime*. On the one hand, there was a good deal of waste, inefficiency and corruption, of political appointments and people on the payroll who contributed little or nothing. Its content was frequently dull but high-minded. Rather than American soap operas and quiz shows, viewers got the pope's Sunday-morning mass and classic Italian cinema. RAI commissioned Roberto Rossellini to do a series of films on the history of science and bankrolled several of Fellini's last films. RAI, in many ways, reflected the culture of Italy's "two churches," the Catholic Church and the Italian Communist Party, which both entertained a certain suspicion of unfettered capitalism and commercial culture and preferred a spirit of solidarity to one of un-bridled competition.

Berlusconi brought about a cultural revolution, introducing American commercial values into this old-fashioned, slow-moving paternalistic world. Before him, Italian TV was technically crude, with newscasters looking down to read their notes rather than reading from a teleprompter and looking at the camera. Berlusconi, a natural salesman, looked to Hollywood for his model and began buying up entire film libraries of movies and TV shows, while adding an Italian accent with original pro-grams such as *Colpo Grosso*, perhaps the world's first nude game show. These programs fit the mood of the times: the Italian middle class, sick of the terrorism and ideological paroxysms of the 1970s, was ready to enjoy a period of prosperity, happy to be awash in the consumer goods being sold on Berlusconi's network.

Soccer—another strategic field that Berlusconi entered and now dominates—has replaced politics as Italians' favorite topic of conversa-tion. The spread of television and the spread of soccer are interrelated. In the old days, RAI televised one soccer game per week, showed only one of the two halves of the match and did so after the match had actually ended, out of a conviction that no one would go to the stadium if games were broadcast live. Berlusconi broke with these conventions, broadcast-ing a number of soccer matches a week as well as numerous talk shows in which armchair soccer coaches discuss Sunday's matches on Sunday night, Monday and into much of the week. (Berlusconi purchased the country's most successful soccer team, A. C. Milan—the source, perhaps even more than his television stations, of much of his fame and popularity.) It is far from coincidental that Berlusconi named his political party Forza Italia. While appeals to revolution and the Fatherland have grown weak, the national soccer team is about the only thing that can arouse powerful nationalist feelings in most Italians, and Berlusconi has very shrewdly channeled those feelings toward his own political aims.

I recall a very strange moment in the summer of 1994, during Berlusconi's first government, which happened to coincide with soccer's World Cup. Berlusconi had just replaced the board of directors and the heads of the three RAI networks—the principal competitor of his own private TV chain—with people close to himself (many of them either current or former Berlusconi employees), but this event—precisely the kind of blatant conflict of interest that Berlusconi had sworn would never happen as he campaigned—passed with almost no public reaction, while Rome was filled with honking cars and jubilant crowds that thronged through the streets until the early hours of night screaming *"Forza Italia! Forza Italia!"* at the top of their lungs and waving Italian flags. It was a brilliant piece of priceless free advertising. One sensed that a terrible new power—mixing entertainment, sports, television and politics—had been born.

Berlusconi helped to move Italy from what Marshall McLuhan termed the Gutenberg Galaxy, the print-based culture of the nineteenth and twentieth centuries, in which politics was about clashing political ideologies, into a world in which personality, celebrity, money and media control are the driving forces. The good thing is that Italians have stopped killing one another over politics. The bad thing is that it's as if there were no more political ideas worth fighting or arguing for.

$\dot{\frown}$

The Berlusconi story is one of the great political adventures of the late twentieth century, an astonishing example of what happens when media, money and politics combine forces in a society with almost no rules.

The election of the richest man and the largest media owner, who is also a defendant in numerous criminal trials, to the highest public office has created a bizarre and anomalous situation and led to a new model of power in the heart of Europe. Imagine if Bill Gates of Microsoft were also the owner of the three largest national TV networks and then became president and took over public television as well. Imagine that he also owned Time Warner, HBO, the *Los Angeles Times,* the New York Yankees, Aetna insurance, Fidelity Investments and Loews theaters, and you begin to get an idea of how large a shadow Silvio Berlusconi casts over Italian life. Imagine also that dozens of members of parliament and most of the key people in government are also current or former employees of the TV-tycoon prime minister, that he has been indicted and convicted in several criminal trials, which his personal lawyers, who also sit in parliament, have legislated or tried to legislate out of existence.

It would be easy but mistaken to dismiss Berlusconi as a uniquely Italian phenomenon, but that his story takes place in Italy is at the same time no accident. Italy has a rather remarkable record in the twentieth century as a laboratory of bad ideas that have then spread to other parts of the world. Fascism was invented in Italy, as was the Mafia, and left-wing terrorism went further in Italy than in any European country. This is not to say that Berlusconi is a Fascist, a Mafioso or a terrorist, but all these phenomena are by-products of a weak democracy with few institutional checks and balances. As a country late to unify and industrialize, Italy is a place where all the strains and problems of modernity are present, but with few of the safeguards that exist in older, more stable nations; ideas get taken to their logical extreme, where they can be seen with particular clarity. The increasingly close relations among big money, politics and television are hugely important everywhere, but in Italy, where a major media business, in the form of Berlusconi, has taken power directly, they have achieved a kind of apotheosis.

While Forza Italia contains vestiges of Italy's past, Berlusconi is also a troubling avant-guard figure, a sort of Citizen Kane on steroids. It is not an accident that the president of Thailand is also the country's richest man and largest media owner, and is interested in acquiring soccer teams. Or that Vladimir Putin, who is a frequent guest at Berlusconi's vacation home in Sardinia, has easily won apparently democratic elections after gaining control over virtually all of Russia's television channels. There are even, in fact, powerful parallels with the Berlusconi phenomenon in the country that likes to refer to itself as the world's oldest continuous democracy, the United States.

The personalization of politics through television, the decline of traditional political parties and the rise of billionaire politicians (Ross Perot, Steve Forbes, Jon Corzine and Mike Bloomberg, to name only a few) who circumvent party organizations by purchasing vast amounts of television time are all very much with us. Moreover, the deregulation and politicization of American broadcasting—starting with the elimination under Reagan of the "fairness doctrine" and public interest requirements, and the recent decisions under Bush to further do away with restrictions of media concentration—all, ironically, follow the Italian model. Information is increasingly in the hands of six or seven international media conglomerates, of which Berlusconi's is one, most of them owned by highly conservative interests who often cooperate with one another. Berlusconi has worked closely with both Leo Kirch of Germany and Rupert Murdoch, using interlocking ownership of media companies to skirt the antitrust legislation of different countries. The much more aggressive, partisan style of Rupert Murdoch's Fox News and Rush Limbaugh is eerily reminiscent of the highly slanted Berlusconi channels.

The affinities between the Italy of Berlusconi and contemporary America are hardly coincidental. Most of Berlusconi's success in his career, from real estate to television to politics, has consisted of importing American models to Europe. "I'm in favor of everything American before even knowing what it is," Berlusconi told the *New York Times* in 2001. "So much so that they used to call me the *amerikano*." He brought Italy the suburban subdivision, *Dallas* and *Dynasty, Survivor* and *Who Wants to Be a Millionaire?;* he brought focus groups, the thirty-second political ad and a "contract with the Italians," based on Newt Gingrich's "Contract with America." More important, like other businessmen-politicians (Ross Perot) and celebrity candidates (Arnold Schwarzenegger and Jesse "the Body" Ventura), he tapped a deep distrust and dislike of politics, which characterizes modern democracy in an age of declining political participation. He helped create a continental model of the politics of antipolitics, the notion, popularized by Ronald Reagan, that "government is not the solution, government is the problem."

While Berlusconi may at first glance appear to be a freakish and uniquely Italian phenomenon, on closer inspection, Italy under Berlusconi may in fact be a not-so-distant mirror, in which many of the same forces at work in our own society can be seen taken to their extreme logical conclusion.

Chapter One

THE MIRACLE WORKER

1. JANUARY 1996: "I KNOW HOW TO MAKE PEOPLE LOVE ME"

I first saw Berlusconi in the flesh in early 1996, at a Forza Italia rally when he was gearing up for a new round of elections, which, as it turned out, he would lose. The atmosphere was electric, more like a concert than a political rally. The crowd was palpably excited as they waited for the star performer to arrive. "SILVIO! SILVIO! SILVIO!," they cried as he began to make his way through the crowd, protected by a phalanx of bodyguards, and the loudspeakers began to play the Forza Italia party anthem, which Berlusconi was said to have helped write. Berlusconi ascended the stage with a Reaganesque "Morning in America" bounce in his step. Only about five foot six, but with a fit, athletic bearing and a robust chest, finely tailored dark, double-breasted suit and a ready smile, Berlusconi had the smooth elegance of a 1950s crooner. Rather than standing behind a podium and reading a speech, he took the microphone and moved around the stage, the better to establish a personal rapport with the audience.

Berlusconi helped to put himself through college working as a nightclub singer on Mediterranean cruise ships, and his skills as an entertainer and irresistible charm figure heavily in his many stories of his miraculous rise, even though crucial details change from one telling to the next.

Addressing the crowd in Rome, Berlusconi spoke for more than an hour without notes, never pausing, never losing his place. Unlike most Italian politicians, who often speak an abstract, and sometimes abstruse, language, he speaks in a clear, concrete manner. "Berlusconi invented a new political language," said Renato Mannheimer, a professor of sociology and one of Italy's leading pollsters. "'A million jobs'—leaving aside for the moment whether it is nonsense or not—is a powerful slogan. Berlusconi expressed himself in concrete images. On the subject of taxes, he said: 'Until July 27, I work for the government, the rest of the year for my family.' Notice that he used the word 'family'—which Italians like—rather than 'I work for myself.' . . . If you ask voters about the slogans of the left, they cannot remember a single one."[1]

On the particular day I happened to attend the Forza Italia rally, Berlusconi's performance was somewhat angrier and more defensive than usual. Prosecutors in Milan were making his life difficult. They had recently discovered a series of Swiss and offshore bank accounts that appeared to show Berlusconi's company funneling millions of dollars to former-Socialist leader Bettino Craxi (at that time, a fugitive of Italian justice in Tunisia)—a charge Berlusconi angrily denied. He railed against the magistrates, the "Communists" and against his many "enemies" who would stop at nothing to destroy him. "My Communist enemies understand the techniques of [Nazi propagandist Joseph] Goebbels, that if you repeat a lie often enough, it becomes the truth," he said. His anti-Communist invective seemed anachronistic—the Italian Communist Party had dissolved five years earlier—and the lies he was denouncing would later be upheld in court.

I was chilled to hear Berlusconi refer with familiarity to Nazi propaganda methods, since the particular technique that he attributed to his "Communist enemies" is one that he uses constantly. Over and over, he hammers away at points that are preposterously untrue—that his "enemies" enjoy a media monopoly and use it ruthlessly against him; that there is no conflict of interest between his private and public roles; that the many criminal investigations of him and his companies have turned up no evidence—and yet amplified and repeated by his newspapers and television stations, they gradually become common misperceptions that one hears coming out of the mouths of ordinary Italians who know few of the underlying facts. Nonetheless, I found myself humming the catchy tune of the Forza Italia anthem as I left the rally.

I met Berlusconi the following day for an interview in his Rome residence just behind Piazza Navona, in the back portion of a baroque palace built in the seventeenth century for the family of Pope Innocent X. Instead of stairs, the way up to the Berlusconi house is a smooth, circular brick ramp that was once used to allow horses and mules to bring provisions straight up to the door. Delicately painted frescoes of cherubs adorn the ceiling of the waiting room.

Berlusconi was dressed informally in blue jogging pants, jogging shoes and a sumptuous blue cashmere sweater. (The color blue plays a large part in the Berlusconi universe. "All the psychologists indicate it as the color that creates a sense of well-being," says Aura Nobolo, press secretary of the Forza Italia group in parliament.) Berlusconi is an assiduous jogger and works hard to stay trim. He was impeccably groomed, thinning hair carefully in place. He hates long or scruffy hair and discourages his company men from wearing beards or mustaches. And although he is a master at working a crowd, he has something of a phobia about germs and quickly washes his hands after pressing the flesh with a group of admirers. "It seems to be typical of tycoons," said Giuliano Ferrara, his former aide. "There is a bit of San Simeon in them all." "Tycoon" is a word Berlusconi uses to describe himself, and he takes obvious delight in his wealth.[2]

Berlusconi made his initial fortune as a real estate developer during the 1960s and 1970s. Although he had no experience in construction, he immediately showed a talent for sales. Berlusconi's greatest assets are a phenomenal level of energy, a great attention to detail and an almost boundless conviction in himself. His deepest beliefs seem to spring from the gospels of American self-help culture such as Dale Carnegie's *How to Win Friends and Influence People,* and Norman Vincent Peale's *The Power*

of Positive Thinking. At a training session for the salesmen of the advertising arm of his company, he told the audience that every morning he
stands in front of the mirror and repeats to himself: "I like myself. I like
myself." He is fond of saying that he carries "the sun in his pocket," and
he instructs his men to project the same sense of total inner confidence.

His success in politics is at least in part dependent on his ability to get
millions of Italians to share his own radiant sense of confidence and opti-
mism. He appears genuinely convinced that there is no problem that cannot be overcome if only he could explain himself to the Italian people.
Berlusconi appears to say whatever is necessary at a given moment to
convince a particular audience, even though some of these statements are
at variance with each other or with factual reality. This, too, is part of the
Berlusconi philosophy. If you want to convince someone, he told his sales
force, make up a quotation and attribute it to some renowned authority:
"So use this method: 'As Bill Paley of CBS says. As Plato said. As Abraham Lincoln said' . . . Who's ever going to go and look it up? . . . People
are incredibly gullible, they love quotations."[3]

In my three-hour interview, I was most deeply struck by his unusual
relationship with factual truth.

One of Berlusconi's most salient characteristics is his ability to convey
an air of total conviction and sincerity even when saying things that appear to have no relation to objective reality. "Berlusconi's psychology is
characterized by two elements," a longtime Mediaset executive who has
worked closely with him told me. "An extraordinary natural vitality and
an immense capacity to convince himself that what he is saying is the
truth. Not only is it the truth, but it is the absolute truth and he is unable
to understand why others are unable to grasp this truth."[4]

For a good part of the interview, I pressed Berlusconi about the
conflict-of-interest problem, with Berlusconi continuing to insist that there
were no conflicts of interest, only a series of vicious attempts to destroy
him against which he has been forced to defend himself. "He simply does
not understand the concept of conflict of interest," the Mediaset executive
explained. "When I mentioned to him that when Harold Macmillan be-

came prime minister of Britain he sold off his interest in his publishing house, Berlusconi's only response was: Why?"

Berlusconi insisted that in fact he had made an enormous personal sacrifice by offering to lead the nation. "Before I entered politics, when I used to appear in public everyone would applaud, now half of the people applaud, and half of them boo," he said. "I have made a radical innovation in the moral and political climate of this country. . . . Other politicians obtained advantages and money out of public life. I have received only disadvantages and I have spent money, a lot of money." How much? I asked. "I can't say exactly. I have spent a small fortune supporting Forza Italia." Ten years later, it would appear to be money well spent. Since Berlusconi's ascent to power, his Mediaset has gone from being dangerously in debt and only marginally profitable to being the most profitable media company in Europe, his personal holdings have tripled in value and he has moved into the top forty in the Forbes 400 list of the world's richest men.

Berlusconi considers himself a utopian idealist and reacts with hurt incomprehension when anyone suggests his motives could be anything other than benevolent. He is lavishly generous with his closest aides, who have displayed iron loyalty toward him—even under the enormous pressures of the bribery investigations. And he would be equally generous toward the entire nation, if it would only let him. "Why do they attack me? Why don't they understand that I am the only person who can fix this country?" he said a few months after our meeting. Because his intentions are only the best, he is convinced that any effort to check or question his power cannot help but be malicious and subversive. He seems deeply convinced that he is a man chosen by destiny to save his nation. [5]

"You don't understand," he said as our talk came to an end, leaning back wearily on the white couch in his living room, as if gathering his strength for one final attempt to make me see the light. "I have achieved everything in life a man can hope for. I have nothing left to gain personally." He suddenly coiled his body forward, turning up his level of intensity several notches, as if to make a final pitch to a recalcitrant client: "I have had this extraordinary, unique experience and I want to make a contribution to the nation. *So creare, so comandare, so farmi amare.* [I know how to create, I know how to lead people, I know how to make people love me.]"[6]

2. IN PRAISE OF FOLLY

I came out of my interview with Berlusconi reeling. The strange monarchic "court" atmosphere surrounding him and the refusal of any contradiction or dialogue brought to mind the words of Berlusconi's best friend, Fedele Confalonieri, who candidly described him as an "enlightened despot . . . a *good* Ceauşescu, but decidedly anomalous as a democratic politician."[7] The notion that the ability to "make people love me" rather than having a convincing program or a demonstrated capacity to govern was the chief qualification for a prime minister suggested a new charismatic model of governance for the TV age. I also found Berlusconi to be psychologically one of the strangest people I had ever met. I had never before interviewed anyone who told so many obvious untruths with such enthusiastic conviction. He said a host of things that were almost childish in their obvious, transparent falsehood—that he has never tried to exert political influence on the media he owns, that his television stations are mostly "left-wing," that his motives for entering politics were entirely selfless and that his political career has, indeed, harmed rather than helped his business, that it would be impossible, even if he wanted to, to pass legislation that would benefit himself—but he said them with such apparent conviction, with such genuine-seeming passion that I actually began to doubt whether two and two still equaled four.

Lying, of course, is common enough among politicians, but most of them recognize the difference between statements given out for public consumption and the strict, factual truth. I had interviewed Giulio Andreotti, seven-time prime minister and the dominant Italian politician before Berlusconi entered the scene, who repeatedly denied that he knew anything about some of his supporters' well-documented ties to the Mafia, but he did so with the tired air of a man who knows he is not telling the strict truth, looking at you as if to say: "I know that you know, that this is not really the case, but public life requires us to maintain certain fictions."

Andreotti would never allow himself the sort of extravagant declarations of his own omnipotence that Berlusconi commonly makes. "If Italy entrusts itself to Berlusconi, it's the country's good fortune," Berlusconi said, referring to himself, as he often does, in the third person. "I am trying hard to suppress my superiority complex," he said at another point.[8]

Yet to categorize Berlusconi simply as a narcissistic megalomaniac is to miss what is most interesting and important about him. In most people, these qualities would be a serious, even fatal, weakness, causing them to seriously misjudge their position and underestimate their opposition, leading to disastrous defeat. But what is exceptional about Berlusconi, it must be admitted, is that he has turned his ability to transform reality into an extraordinary strength, a refusal to be fazed by limits or obstacles, and an incredible capacity to convince others to share his own "delusion." Berlusconi believes that the world revolves around him—the ultimate narcissistic fantasy—but he has bent reality to fit his fantasy, so that much of life in Italy does indeed revolve around him. Does this make him a delusional megalomaniac or the most realistic of men?

Although hardly a man given to self-reflection—and he would never admit to distorting reality—he has himself acknowledged this aspect of his own psychology. He frequently refers to himself as a "visionary," and goes to great lengths to repeat that his favorite book of all time is Erasmus of Rotterdam's *Praise of Folly*. Berlusconi even printed a private edition of *Praise of Folly*, with an introduction by him, to give away as gifts to corporate clients. Even though this may have been largely a public relations gimmick ("Silvio doesn't read much," confided his friend Confalonieri), Berlusconi uses Erasmus to make the point that the most important decisions in life are irrational and that his own bold entrepreneurial style is a kind of lucid folly.[9]

Berlusconi is fond of referring to the various accomplishments of his life as "miracles," and to his own greatest talent as that for accomplishing the impossible. "No one is a bigger dreamer than I am, but I am a practical dreamer because unlike most people, I fulfill my dreams," he has said. Berlusconi's life, in his own view, is a series of miracles that he made happen through a combination of will, courage, extraordinary intuition and a willingness to think on a big scale.[10]

While Berlusconi's accomplishments are not exactly miracles, his ability to do what he has done is, at least in part, due to his ability to filter out contrary information, negative reality, which gives him a distorted sense of reality but exceptional power.

In grappling with Berlusconi's curious relationship with factual truth, it began to dawn on me that what I was encountering was a deep anthropological difference. My obsession with factual accuracy, documentation, objective truth was all part of my baggage as a print journalist, the quaint and naïve and old-fashioned credo of the age of Gutenberg and the Enlightenment, while Berlusconi is a man of a different age, of the age of television and mass media, in which image and perception are all that really matter. Berlusconi is decidedly a creature (and creator) of the postmodern world where it doesn't matter what actually happened, but what people think happened. "Don't you understand," he told one of his closest advisers, "that if something is not on television it doesn't exist! Not a product, a politician or an idea." And because the things we were discussing—his conflicts of interest, the crimes of which he and his associates have been accused (and, in some cases, convicted)—have not been aired on Italian television, they, too, did not exist.[11]

3. MYTHMAKING

Given Berlusconi's penchant for self-mythology, sorting out the facts of Berlusconi's biography is not simple. Much of what we know of Berlusconi's early life comes from him, and from a curious hagiographic literature, some of which reads like a modern-day *Lives of the Saints*. The most famous is *Una Storia Italiana* (An Italian Story), the highly illustrated 125-page campaign biography that Berlusconi sent to virtually all twenty-one million Italian families at a cost estimated somewhere between several tens of millions of dollars and $100 million.[12]

Berlusconi was born in 1936, on the eve of World War II. While Berlusconi describes his early childhood as one of hardship and privation, in fact his father, Luigi, was a bank clerk who ended up as the director of a local Milan bank. The war undoubtedly imposed hardship on the family, as it did on almost all Italian families. During the year and a half of the German occupation of Italy, Berlusconi's father fled to Switzerland to avoid being drafted into the Italian neofascist army that fought alongside Hitler.[13]

Berlusconi's description of his early years in post–World War II Italy has much in common with the more sentimental Italian neorealist films, like Vittorio De Sica's *Miracle in Milan* and *The Bicycle Thief*—except with a happy ending. Berlusconi describes himself as growing up in a bombed-out neighborhood in Milan, where the only place to play was in the yard of the local parish church. His father is described as "severe but affectionate," spending "sleepless nights of work brought home from the office in order to maintain a family in the postwar period." Berlusconi says he and his friends liked to play soccer "if we were lucky enough to find a soccer ball."[14]

Berlusconi's early life is depicted as dominated by family, Church and soccer, father and son going together hand in hand to mass on Sunday mornings, stopping to pick up a dessert for the wonderful Sunday dinner Mamma Rosella was preparing. "Mamma waited for us at home, in the kitchen, where she prepared the Sunday meal, the only one we ate in the dining room with the lace tablecloth and the flowers in the middle." Father and son would then go to the soccer stadium, with young Silvio hunching over "small, small," so he could get into the stadium for free in order to save his family some of its hard-earned money. Berlusconi senior and junior were both devoted fans of A. C. Milan, and "after having talked about my studies and school, we would immediately begin discussing Milan, like the incarnation of our dreams, of our Utopias. 'You'll see, Papa, we'll win. We must win,' as if both of us were heading to the playing field." Berlusconi's acquisition of Milan was seen not as a mere selfish venture on Berlusconi's part but as an act of extreme filial piety, of giving his father the victories he only dreamed of in those hard, meager years of the postwar period.[15]

Mamma Rosella (Rosa) is portrayed, like every good Italian mother, as the reincarnation of the Madonna. We are told that on her seventieth birthday, Silvio gave her a sculpture of the Madonna receiving a flower from a small child. "This is you," Silvio is reported to have said, "and the boy giving you the rose is me."[16]

Berlusconi's account of his days at a boarding school of the Salesian fathers recalls the classics of Italian children's literature from the nineteenth century, with their depictions of severe but well-intentioned teachers, and hardworking young students with a humanizing touch of mischief.

"They were not easy years. We studied a lot, in the afternoon, in the evening after dinner, in the early morning. . . . Dear Father Olmi would start by hammering into our heads Latin and Greek grammar. We were quizzed every day and there was no way out and in the end we really knew those conjugations and declensions. . . . With our classmates there was a perfect understanding and a great humanity that came from our origins. Lower middle-class, sociologists today might say."[17]

The story has a fablelike quality, with its nostalgic "once upon a time" tone, the Cinderella-like atmosphere of these lower-middle-class children working morning, noon and night under the severe eye of the Salesian fathers. The difficulties are then overcome, through the extraordinary harmony among the students and the humanity given by their humble origins. It does not matter that this picture conflicts with reality. The school of the Salesian fathers was and is one of the most important in the city, and Berlusconi's father, the bank employee who went on to become director general of a small bank, was not what one would think of as lower middle-class.

Una Storia Italiana has a dual aim. The first is to manage to make Berlusconi, the country's richest man, seem like a completely typical Italian, or at least an idealized archetype of the Italian everyman—from humble, working-class origins, ready to accept sacrifice, part of a strict but affectionate family, true to his word, devoutly loyal to parents, energetic, enterprising and even slightly mischievous but ultimately obedient to authority, both parents and Church. At the same time, the text is eager to show Berlusconi as exceptional, a superman in the making. "He is enterprising, sometimes hard-headed, but charismatic: in class, he is the leader," *Una Storia Italiana* tells us. "And he shows a decidedly practical sense: he finishes his homework before all the others and then helps his classmates who are slower or less studious. In exchange, a little money. But if the classmate doesn't get at least a 6 [a passing grade], he returns the fee. Already well before the fact, 'the client is reimbursed unless fully satisfied.'"

4. THE FIRST MIRACLES

Berlusconi's stories about his youth and early manhood stress his miraculous ability to overcome any setback, generally through the power of his personal charm, often owing to his sexual prowess. He tells us how when he was playing bass and singing for the nightclub band organized by Confalonieri, he would frequently abandon the stage and dance with the prettiest girls on the floor. Confalonieri, both jealous and annoyed that Berlusconi left his instrument, kicked him out of the band, but had to re-hire him when the owner of the nightclub told him that without Berlusconi the band no longer had the same appeal.

It is difficult to sort out fact and fiction. Berlusconi tells us that he was a "student at the Sorbonne" in Paris for two years; in fact he was never enrolled at the Sorbonne. Berlusconi tells us that he went on a concert tour in Lebanon with Confalonieri; in fact Confalonieri and his band went to Lebanon, but without Berlusconi. For Berlusconi, who is always telling his advertisers that powerful images are more important than facts, the images of the young penniless Italian student at the Sorbonne and a nightclub singer in exotic Lebanon are images too good to give up. As the Italians are fond of saying, *"Se non è vero, è ben trovato."* (If it's not true, it's well said.)[18]

Berlusconi did attend the state University of Milan, where he majored in law and wrote a thesis, appropriately enough on advertising contracts.

(He wrote the thesis in part in order to enter it into a contest being offered by a major Milan advertising company and won a first prize of 2 million lire, $3,200 at that time.) Along with singing in Confalonieri's band, he helped support himself by selling vacuum cleaners and working for a real estate company. He graduated a little late, in 1961, at the age of twenty-five, and seems to have known exactly what he wanted to do: go into real estate and build buildings.[19]

The early 1960s was a period when the building trade in Milan was like the California Gold Rush. Approximately 600,000 people, the equivalent of the population of a large city, moved to Milan during the 1960s, and high-rise apartment buildings grew up around the periphery of the city like a field of mushrooms. After a brief stint working for someone else, Berlusconi quickly decided to strike out on his own, scoped out the land, and planned his own building project, apparently convincing his old boss to become partners with him in the new venture. Berlusconi's father, Luigi, supposedly gave his son all of his pension money as collateral, and the project appears to have been at least somewhat successful. In 1963, after this modest beginning, Berlusconi leapt suddenly and quite unexpectedly into the big time, developing a gigantic apartment complex for four thousand people, the size of a good-sized town, in a rather unpromising location outside of Milan, dominated by industrial and chemical plants, isolated from any shops or other people. That a group of investors would have entrusted a twenty-seven-year-old man with a project of this scale speaks to the boomtown climate of Milan in the early 1960s, but it certainly also speaks to the powers of persuasion of Silvio Berlusconi.[20]

In many ways, Berlusconi's first major deal, even in his own telling of it, set the pattern for his future career. By the time the project got under way, in 1964, the market had begun to slow down and in 1965, with the first 140 apartments completed, it had come to a standstill. Berlusconi did his best to apply his usual powers of persuasion. One of the advertising slogans of the project was "When it's raining in Milan, there's sun in Brugherio!" (Brugherio has the same weather as Milan—foggy, gray and humid—only worse, due to the addition of the fumes from nearby factories and chemical plants.) But it was all for naught. "It's not that we were only selling a little, we were selling nothing," Berlusconi later said. "Can you imagine having started to build a city for four thousand people and being unable to sell even a single apartment? I don't mean ten, I mean one."[21]

Berlusconi's principal investor, Carlo Rasini, the owner of the bank where Berlusconi's father worked, had grown very pessimistic. "There's nothing here: no schools, stores or movie theaters. People are not going to come," he told Berlusconi. The majority of the partners in the venture were in favor of halting construction and trying to rent the apartments that were already built. Berlusconi pleaded for and got two months more time to save the project. He decided to concentrate on trying to persuade some national pension fund to invest in the project. Not knowing people in the Rome political world, Berlusconi turned to Piero Michiara, the president of the advertising company that had given him the prize for his thesis and to whom he had sold an apartment in his first building project. Michiara was able to get the vice president of the acquisition committee of a major pension fund to visit the Brugherio project.

For the arrival of the potential savior of the deal, Berlusconi staged an elaborate production. All his men were out cleaning and straightening and completing as much work as possible to make the place seem relatively finished and presentable. On the day of the visit, he arranged for many of his own relatives to come to the site and pretend to be potential customers interested in buying apartments. The scheme appeared to be working, when "a not-too-bright cousin" ("*una cugina un po' scema*," in Berlusconi's words) of Berlusconi's arrived and began greeting and embracing all of her relations. The vice president's face darkened as it became obvious that he had been conned. "Very strange. Evidently all your clients are not part of a particularly wide circle, since they all know one another!" The vice president then lit a cigarette and tossed the packet in the toilet and said to Berlusconi: "Young man, can you get me another pack?" "Certainly, I'll send out for some right away," Berlusconi responded.

"Tell me the truth," the man said. "Will it take one or two hours to reach the nearest store where they sell cigarettes?"

The visit was a total disaster, but Berlusconi went all-out to repair the situation. "I rushed down to Rome and through some friends got myself introduced to the secretary of the vice president, a very pretty girl. I didn't have to work very hard to start what we might call now a 'friendly' relationship with her, 'a particular friendship.' . . . She took my part and when the vice president next took the train to Milan, she alerted me." Berlusconi flew immediately down to Rome: "I paid my 'penalty' to my informant, which wasn't really a 'penalty,' since it was a very nice relationship."

Berlusconi got up early the next morning and found a seat on the train across from the vice president. When the vice president saw Berlusconi he said: "Now, I have to travel with my enemy!"

> Those words, rather than depressing me, gave me great courage. I put all my "charm" to work, and by the time we reached the Milan train station, we were both at the bar half drunk, with him telling me about how extraordinary the private parts of the women of the Caucasus were, with a thing that starts here and goes to there. The subject of the sexual organs of the women of the Caucasus is not something I had had a chance to study closely, but I had no trouble agreeing with him. We established a friendship based on these common "cultural" elements, so to speak. He became my biggest supporter, my best friend, and I managed it all without having to pay a cent.

Berlusconi liked telling this story as proof that "I have never paid anyone a cent in bribes," and as an illustration that he had succeeded through his own energy, charm and determination, while others relied on their connections in the political world. "There was an internal 'mafia' of Roman officials who handled all the acquisitions," he said.

Of course, Berlusconi's story reveals much else about his way of doing business. His sales tactics are based largely on deception and chicanery, on staging a scene that was purely fraudulent. This vocal champion of the free market was saved from disaster by personal connections obtained through dubious means. He had produced a complex of houses that, by his own admission, had literally no appeal on the "free" market, because they were in a dreary, isolated area where no one wanted to live. He tells us he knew no one in Rome, but suddenly has friends there who can present him to the secretary of the vice president of the pension fund. With characteristic vulgarity, he tells us that he seduced a secretary in order to get an opportunity to be alone with the man who could bail him out of trouble. A pension fund ended up spending millions, perhaps tens of millions, of dollars on apartments it didn't originally want, not because Berlusconi convinced the vice president that they were a good investment, but because he got him drunk and established a "common cultural" bond based on a discussion of the genitalia of women of the Caucasus.[22]

Berlusconi's claim about not paying a cent in bribes is, to say the least, open to question. Investigations of many later Berlusconi ventures, in real estate and elsewhere, show abundant evidence of bribe-paying.

Another aspect of the Brugherio deal is also characteristic of Berlusconi. The project was approved so that the towers of the buildings would be only five stories high—evidently the height that the town felt was appropriate to the site without blocking too much light or creating congestion. Without having permission, Berlusconi's work team rushed ahead and built them up to the eighth floor. Interestingly, Berlusconi hired as the project manager the man who had been in charge of urban planning for the town of Brugherio. In other words, Berlusconi bought the services of the man who was supposed to safeguard the public interest and gave him a piece of the action as well as dramatically increasing the profitability of his project by making the buildings 60 percent higher than he was legally entitled to. Asked about it years later, the urban planner, Edoardo Teruzzi, replied: "Illegal? . . . Let's not exaggerate. It was a misunderstanding and was quickly resolved by our paying 200 million lire [$320,000] and offering to build a nursery school for free."[23]

The Brugherio project made Berlusconi into a major developer and set the stage for his next, even bigger project, known as Milano 2, one of the largest and most ambitious housing developments of the postwar period. As a university student, Berlusconi had said he was going to build "a city with everything from the hospital where you are born to the cemetery" and now he was actually doing it. Built in one of the last green areas in Milan, just a few miles from downtown, on the land of an old aristocratic estate, Milano 2 was an enormous gated community for fourteen thousand people, with housing towers set amid lakes, tennis courts, schools, shops, bike paths and carefully groomed lawns. It was a weird cross between an ideal city of the Italian Renaissance with a sterile, slightly kitschy version of the suburban American subdivision. Built in the early 1970s, when the Italian protest movement was just picking up steam (in Italy the 1960s really started in 1968 and lasted throughout the 1970s), Milano 2 was more than a housing development: it was a cultural statement. In an era when squatters were occupying houses as a political statement, and there was great social pressure for people to disassociate themselves from everything bourgeois, Milano 2 was an oasis of American-style luxury and abundance, a world apart from downtown Milan, where parades of left- and right-wing students fought in the streets and launched Molotov cocktails at each other. Milano 2 was a place where a man could wear a Rolex watch and a woman a fur coat without fear or shame. Of course, Milan's old money still lived in restrained elegance in the palazzi in the streets off Via Manzoni or in old villas outside the city, but Milano 2 offered a life of conspicuous consumption to a new class of upwardly mobile corporate managers, middle- and upper-level executives, stockbrokers and admen. In the left-wing-dominated culture of the time, Milano 2 represented a kind of counter-counter-culture, anticipating the Italian version of yuppie culture of the 1980s and 1990s.

Berlusconi was fully aware of himself as a representative of a counter-counterculture. In 1977, he bought a substantial share of a new conservative newspaper, *Il Giornale,* which was the voice of a part of the Italian bourgeoisie that rebelled against the cultural domination of the left. The paper had been founded a few years earlier when Indro Montanelli, one of

Italy's most famous and distinguished journalists, suddenly announced that he was leaving the *Corriere della Sera*, for which he had written since Mussolini's day in the 1930s, together with about twenty other well-known journalists, because he felt that the *Corriere* was becoming dangerously left-wing. With the principal national newspapers (such as the *Corriere* and Turin's *La Stampa*) increasingly sympathetic to the country's protest movements and flirting with the idea of Italy's Communists entering the government, it was time for an avowedly conservative, staunchly anti-Communist paper with no need to cater to a radical-chic audience. "[Berlusconi] was very courageous," says his good friend Fedele Confalonieri, who became the business manager of *Il Giornale* after Berlusconi became its chief owner. "The so-called 'enlightened bourgeoisie' of Italy and its papers like the *Corriere* and *La Stampa* were all ready to surrender to the Communists and the historic compromise. And *Il Giornale* was the only one that opposed. The unions made it difficult for us to publish. They limited the number of copies we could print, claiming there was a shortage of paper."[24]

Milano 2—for its size and scale and its emblematic nature—made Berlusconi one of the biggest players in Italian real estate. It also gave him something of a national profile. But Milano 2 also contains other characteristics of the Berlusconi style. Political intervention played no small role in making Milano 2 a success. Built in the township of Segrate, near the Linate airport—the smaller of Milan's two principal airports—Milano 2 was seriously handicapped by the deafening noise of jet planes landing and taking off. This allowed Berlusconi to pay far less for the land than he might otherwise have done, but made it initially much more difficult to sell apartments. Berlusconi, who has always complained of knowing no one in the Rome "internal mafia," as he has called it, somehow got politicians at a national level to intervene and change the air routes of the planes at Linate—over the furious and indignant objections of the towns and communities whose tranquillity would be destroyed and which would now bear the brunt of the noise pollution.

He obtained the deviation of the air routes through close connections to members of the right wing of the Christian Democratic Party and a shrewd public relations gimmick. Early in the construction of Milano 2, Berlusconi set about building the San Raffaele hospital and made a point of building the hospital near his development site. As a result, when people from Berlusconi's Edilnord, as his company was then called, went to Rome to lobby for changing the air routes, they could claim that they were acting not to increase the value of their investment, but to ease the suffering of the patients of the San Raffaele hospital. In fact, on a map handed out at one of the meetings at which the air route question was taken up, the entire area of the development bore the letter H—for "hospital"— including the area where Berlusconi's luxury apartments stood. Never mind that the San Raffaele hospital did not yet exist and that, although it sounded like a philanthropic institution, it was a for-profit health clinic, whose direction was handed over to a priest who was later investigated for fraud and for soliciting bribes. The air routes were changed not only over the objections of other nearby towns but against the protests of the citizens of Segrate itself, the town in which Milano 2 was located. Some three thousand Segrate residents signed a petition against the new air routes, at a time when there were only two hundred people living in Berlusconi's development. Moreover, the pilots' union and the Italian airline Alitalia objected to the new routes, because this required them to make take-off and landing maneuvers that they considered dangerous.[25]

Ironically, one of the communities Berlusconi damaged in the air route changes was Brugherio, where he had built his first mega-project. One resident, writing to local authorities to get them to stop the overhead flights, complained of "a genuine bombardment of jet noise from early morning until night over the town of Brugherio."[26]

In order to counter the objections of "noise pollution," Berlusconi's Edilnord trumpeted the findings of an environmental study carried out supposedly by Milan's prestigious Polytechnic University, which concluded that the new air routes represented the "optimal solution" in terms of minimizing environmental damage. It came out several months later that the study was anything but independent: the engineers were commissioned to write the report by Berlusconi's company. In order to avoid expulsion from the university, the professors were forced to apologize publicly and remove the Polytechnic's name from the report.[27]

But Berlusconi prevailed, the new air routes were made permanent and the value of Berlusconi's apartments skyrocketed, going from 130,000 lire a square meter to 280,000 a square meter. With the apartments' value more than doubling, the move gave Berlusconi a windfall that suddenly put him in the category of one of Italy's richest men. Newspapers began referring to him as *"il re del mattone"*—the king of bricks.[28]

5. THE VILLA SAN MARTINO AT ARCORE

The "king of bricks" needed an appropriately regal home, and so while Berlusconi was building Milano 2, he was also busy buying and fixing up a new house for himself. It was the Villa San Martino at Arcore, a grand eighteenth-century villa built on the foundations of a Renaissance-era convent. These princely surroundings—a villa with 145 rooms, vast grounds, a hunting reserve, stables, a rich library with ten thousand antique volumes, an art collection deep in paintings of the Venetian school from Tintoretto to Guardi—provided a suitable showcase for the newest member of Italy's financial aristocracy. The villa became virtually synonymous with Berlusconi; he held company meetings there, and after he entered politics, he used it to entertain heads of state and conduct important policy meetings, turning it into an unofficial presidential villa.

But the true story of his acquisition of Arcore, too, gives off the same powerful stench of deception and conflicts of interest that has attached itself to dealings throughout his political career.

The Villa San Martino, which had been for centuries in the Casati Stampa family, suddenly became available as the result of a lurid tragedy. On August 30, 1970, the *marchese* Camillo Casati Stampa di Soncino, forty-three years old, shot and killed his wife, Anna Fallarino, forty-one, and her lover, Massimo Minorenti, a twenty-five-year-old student. He then killed himself. The scandal, along with filling the Italian newspapers and gossip magazines for months, created a curious inheritance battle. The Casati Stampa estate, including the Villa San Martino, appeared certain to go to their only child, a nineteen-year-old daughter, Annamaria. But the sister of the murdered wife came forward with a curious claim: if by some chance Anna Fallarino had outlived her husband by a few minutes, she would have, however briefly, been the heir to the fortune, and they, as her relations, would be her heirs. The lawyer putting forward this preposterous claim was a thirty-six-year-old attorney based in Rome named Cesare Previti, who would later play an important role in the Berlusconi empire. The claim failed: a technical examination showed that the *marchesa* died almost instantly. But Previti saw no reason for withdrawing from working on such a large estate. Despite having represented her adversary, Previti somehow convinced the teenage *marchesina* to let him act as her attorney.

The young Annamaria, devastated by the tragedy and anxious to get far away from the publicity surrounding her parents' death, moved to Brazil and in 1973 decided to sell the family villa in order to pay the inheritance taxes on her father's estate. She expressly specified that the sale not include "the furniture, the picture collection, the library and the surrounding land." However, because she was young and lived so far away, she also signed a power of attorney, granting broad powers to her legal guardian, a senator and old family friend named Giorgio Bergamasco, and the lawyer and coexecutor for the estate, Previti, to dispose of her property as they saw fit. "The real handling of the Casati Stampa inheritance was virtually in the hands of the coexecutor Previti: the elderly guardian Bergamasco, in fact, limited himself to bureaucratic acts, ratifying with his signature the decisions taken by Previti in his role as lawyer and coexecutor," writes Giovanni Ruggeri, the Italian journalist who did the investigative work to piece together the Arcore story. Some time later, Previti called Annamaria in Brazil and announced that he had found a buyer for the villa: Berlusconi. The price was a shockingly low 500 million lire, which would have been about $850,000 at the time. And contrary to her wishes, Berlusconi also ended up with the library, tapestries, picture collection and the surrounding land. The picture collection contains a Tintoretto and a Tiepolo, both major old masters, as well as a Via Crucis (the stations of the cross), a sequence of fourteen paintings by the Lombard master Bernardino Luini. The value of any one of these works would probably by itself be over $1 million.[29]

Moreover, Berlusconi managed to defer payment for the villa over several years, taking possession of the villa in 1974 but not actually finalizing the sale until 1980. During that time, the young *marchesina* had to continue paying all taxes on the villa while Berlusconi lived there.

What the young *marchesa* did not know was that both Cesare Previti and his father had begun to play an increasingly important role in the nascent Berlusconi empire. In 1977, for example, both Previtis were appointed to the board of directors of a Berlusconi company called Immobiliare Idra (Hydra Real Estate), which was the entity that was acquiring the Villa San Martino at Arcore. Indeed, Berlusconi was fast becoming one of Previti's most important clients, perhaps the most important. Previti thus was guilty of a triple conflict of interest, representing first both sides of the inheritance battle and then both sides in the sale of the Villa San Martino.

But Previti and Berlusconi did not stop at the villa. In 1979, Previti arranged for Berlusconi to acquire another important piece of the Casati Stampa inheritance, a property of 246 hectares (more than 800 acres) of property in the northern Italian township of Cusago. This vast holding, which included a magnificent medieval castle, much of the historic center of the town, about sixty farmhouses and valuable agricultural land, constituted one quarter of the land surface in the entire township, as well as many of its most important buildings. In this case, Berlusconi did not have to lay out any cash whatsoever. The *marchesa* Casati Stampa was given stock in one of Berlusconi's myriad dummy companies, Immobiliare Coriasco. The stock was valued at 1.7 billion lire (just over $2 million dollars), but since the company was not publicly traded and was controlled by Berlusconi, the stock had no market and was of highly questionable value. In fact, when Casati Stampa tried to cash in her stock, she was forced to sell it back to another Berlusconi company (Cantieri Riuniti Milanesi) for 850 million lire, half of its supposed original value. After discovering this swindle, Casati Stampa finally broke off her relations with Previti.

Meanwhile, Berlusconi managed to convince the town council of Cusago to allow much of the parks and agricultural lands he had bought— which were designated as environmentally protected "green" land—to be developed into a substantial condominium development. Land that was bought at 345 lire (about 41 cents) a square meter was then sold for 3 to 4 million lire a square meter, an increase of about 10,000 fold.[30]

In many countries, Previti would have been disbarred for his multiple conflicts of interest in the Casati Stampa inheritance. In Italy, he became Berlusconi's main lawyer. Many rumors and jokes circulated about Previti. One of the most popular: *Previti, se lo conosci, lo eviti*. Previti, if you know him you avoid him, playing on the rhyme between the name Previti and the word "avoid," *eviti*. Even a member of parliament in Berlusconi's own Forza Italia referred to Previti as Berlusconi's "adviser on *illegal* affairs." Previti was later convicted of bribing judges for Berlusconi and other clients.[31]

Chapter Two

THE THIRTEENTH GUEST

1. A KIDNAPPING AT ARCORE

In the early hours of December 7, 1974, after a dinner at the Villa San Martino at Arcore, one of Berlusconi's houseguests was kidnapped as he tried to drive home. The guest, Luigi D'Angerio, an elderly Neapolitan textile dealer who went by the (false) aristocratic title Prince of Saint Agatha, managed to escape when his captors lost control of their car in the fog and crashed into an electrical pole.

When police investigated, Berlusconi told them that there were twelve people present at the dinner the evening of the crime, strangely omitting from his account the name of a thirteenth guest at the table. The thirteenth guest was a man named Vittorio Mangano, a Sicilian who had arrived only a few months before to look after the villa, take care of its stables and act as a chauffeur. Mangano had an extensive criminal record and close ties to the Sicilian Mafia—there was a warrant out for his arrest. The kidnapping turned out to be the work of several Sicilian Mafiosi who were friends of Mangano's, and when police learned about Mangano's presence at Arcore, and about the warrant, they returned to the villa to arrest him and send him back to Palermo, to serve out a jail term for a previous conviction.

In early 1994, when Berlusconi began his first run for prime minister and rumors began to swirl about ties between him and the Mafia, he gave a brief interview to the *Corriere della Sera*, Italy's largest newspaper, to put the matter to rest—one of the few times the media have pressed Berlusconi to address the issue in public. "The only contact I've had with the Mafia was when they tried to kidnap my son, Pier Silvio, who was five years old then. I took my family to Spain, where they stayed for many months. . . . It was the same man whom we fired as soon as we learned that he had tried to kidnap one of my dinner guests."[1]

It sounds simple enough: a wealthy industrialist accidentally hires a man who, unbeknownst to him, turns out to have a criminal record. The man is immediately fired—end of story. Unfortunately, Berlusconi's version is mostly untrue. This was certainly not the only contact between the Mafia and Berlusconi and his inner circle. Mangano was not fired immediately and it is very unlikely that he was hired accidentally.

One thing Berlusconi said does appear to be true: he and his family had in fact received several kidnapping threats after acquiring the villa at Arcore, and Berlusconi took the problem seriously enough to take his family to Spain, where they lived until he was satisfied the danger had passed.

Berlusconi had good reason to worry. In the 1960s, the Italian state adopted the curious strategy in fighting the Mafia of deporting suspected Mafiosi from Sicily and sending them to live in a kind of "internal exile" in Northern Italy. This had the principal effect of exporting the Mafia problem to the North, home by the early 1970s of some 374 Sicilian Mafiosi. Many of them stayed in the North and established a beachhead for the Mafia there, extorting money from businesses, dealing drugs and kidnapping. There were at least seventy-two major kidnappings in the Milan area between 1973 and 1979, the great majority leading either to the payment of large ransoms (the equivalent of several million dollars) or, in several cases, to the death of the hostage.[2] The Mafia strictly forbade kidnapping inside Sicily because the police manhunts and roadblocks were bad for other Mafia business; but in the North, it served as both a lucrative industry and a way of intimidating and gaining access to some of the richest and most powerful people in the country.

In characteristic fashion, Berlusconi dealt with the kidnapping threat informally. He did not notify police that his family had been threatened. Similarly, he did not call the police a year later when someone exploded a bomb at the work site where he was building his corporate offices in Milan. The person whom he called on to deal with these matters was Marcello Dell'Utri, a friend of Berlusconi's from the University of Milan, who was from Palermo. When Berlusconi bought the villa at Arcore, he hired Dell'Utri to come up from Palermo and oversee the refurbishing and running of the property. It was Dell'Utri who hired the gangster Vittorio Mangano to come live at Arcore. Dell'Utri was also one of the thirteen people at the dinner table on the night of the attempted kidnapping.

Dell'Utri occupies a very special place in the inmost layer of Berlusconi's inner circle. Some time after purchasing the villa at Arcore, Berlusconi commissioned an artist to create an elaborate sculptural tomb in marble to hold his earthly remains and those of his family. (The tomb reportedly contains a powerful electrical generator, creating speculation that Berlusconi is planning to have his body preserved there in anticipation of future scientific developments.) A few places were set aside for non–family members, and among the happy few are Confalonieri and Dell'Utri. Dell'Utri went on to become the president of Publitalia, the advertising sales wing of Berlusconi's media empire, which generates most of its cash. Dell'Utri is a devout Catholic and a renowned bibliophile who has spent considerable sums on rare early editions of Saint Thomas More and Erasmus and is a lover of the ancient Greek tragedies. With Dell'Utri in mind, Berlusconi created a replica of an ancient Greek amphitheater for five hundred spectators at his villa in Sardinia. But Dell'Utri has attracted the attention of police, prosecutors and journalists, not because of his cultural refinement, but because of his repeated contact over a period of thirty years with members of the Sicilian Mafia while also acting as Berlusconi's right-hand man. When Berlusconi completed Milano 2, when he acquired the villa at Arcore, when he made the jump from real estate to television and then when he moved into politics, Dell'Utri was by his side, and men such as Vittorio Mangano were at Dell'Utri's side.

At least thirty-seven former Mafia members have given testimony that

Dell'Utri was the Mafia's main contact person in Berlusconi's financial empire and that the Mafia both extorted money from the business as well as invested millions of dollars in Berlusconi's business ventures during its early years. The testimony of former gangsters is always open to question, and Berlusconi and Dell'Utri have dismissed it all as the lies of gangsters eager to obtain benefits from politicized prosecutors anxious to strike at Berlusconi by any means. But well before Berlusconi entered politics, Italian police suspected Berlusconi's company of laundering Mafia money when evidence of Dell'Utri's and Berlusconi's ties to organized crime kept turning up in the course of other investigations.

1980

In 1980, five years after the attempted kidnapping episode, Italian police were tapping Mangano's phone at a Milan hotel in the course of a major investigation into heroin traffic between Italy and the United States. Mangano, investigators had concluded, was one of the Sicilian Mafia's main representatives in Milan, arranging heroin shipments and laundering the enormous profits of the drug trade.

Mangano and Dell'Utri were recorded speaking in a friendly manner, using the informal *tu* rather than the formal mode of address, and mixing phrases of Sicilian dialect with standard Italian in such a way as to give the conversation a further sense of intimacy. There are references to common friends and possible meetings. Then Mangano tells Dell'Utri, "I have a deal to propose to you and I have a horse that's right for you." "Dear Vittorio," Dell'Utri replies, "for a horse, I need dough [*piccioli* in Sicilian] and I don't have any. If you knew what trouble my brother has created for me." (Dell'Utri's twin brother, Alberto, was being prosecuted for his involvement in a fraudulent bankruptcy.) "Have your friend Silvio give you the money," Mangano proposes. Dell'Utri remains firm. "I'm telling you I'm in trouble thanks to my crazy brother, and Silvio *non sura*"—Silvio "doesn't sweat," a Sicilian colloquial expression meaning it was useless to try to squeeze money out of Berlusconi.

When asked about the conversation by investigators, Dell'Utri insisted that it was an innocent conversation about a horse, but in that period, Mangano was not working as a stable hand; he was living in the Duke of York hotel in Milan. From the same hotel room, Mangano had another conversation about horses with another Mafia boss from Palermo. "So what do you want me to do about these horses?" "How are they, Arabian?" "Pure blood. They cost 170 million. You understand what I'm saying?" Mangano's interlocutor this time was Rosario Inzerillo, a member of one of Palermo's main Mafia families, a central figure in the drug investigation, whose clan would later organize the murder of the chief prosecutor of Palermo.

While Dell'Utri might insist—as implausible as it might seem—that he had no idea who Vittorio Mangano was when he hired him to look after Berlusconi's villa and his family in 1974, he certainly could no longer make that claim in 1980, five years after Mangano tried to kidnap one of Berlusconi's houseguests and his criminal record became widely known. "If I adopted a friendly tone in the phone call with Mangano," Dell'Utri later told prosecutors, "it's because at that point I was afraid of him, I was aware of his criminal personality. . . . He would telephone me from time to time—and given his personality—I couldn't reject him."[3]

1993

When prosecutors in Palermo began looking into Dell'Utri and Berlusconi's connections to Cosa Nostra, they found, in Dell'Utri's work diary, a note that Mangano had visited Dell'Utri in November 1993—the very time when Dell'Utri was organizing Berlusconi's first successful campaign to become prime minister. What did they talk about? prosecutors asked Dell'Utri. "Mangano used to come to see me from time to time in Milan usually about personal matters, often related to his health."[4] Even in 1996, after Dell'Utri had been indicted on charges of association with the Mafia and Mangano was back in prison, Dell'Utri was very careful not to disassociate himself publicly from the gangster. "I don't find anything strange in the fact that I socialized in this manner with Signor Mangano. I would see him again even now," he said in a prominent radio interview, repeating in newspaper interviews that he would happily have coffee with Mangano. It would appear that even twenty years after the gangster's employment at Arcore, Dell'Utri still could not say no to Vittorio Mangano.[5]

The implications are incredible: a member of parliament, one of the two or three people closest to the prime minister, goes out of his way to publicly broadcast his enduring sense of loyalty to a convicted heroin trafficker and known Mafioso. Moreover, the Mangano relationship is only the most prominent of a series of contacts with suspected or known Mafia figures over a period of many years.

Having friends in high places is one of the great strengths of the Sicilian Mafia, and it would be difficult to overestimate Dell'Utri's importance in the Berlusconi financial empire and political machine. As one of the creators of Forza Italia and as the Sicilian politician closest to the prime minister, Dell'Utri is, more than anyone, in a position to decide who represents Sicily in the Italian parliament. Forza Italia has a curious habit of picking representatives who share Dell'Utri's unlucky record of embarrassing encounters with organized crime figures.

Perhaps, then, it might be worthwhile to look more closely at how a Sicilian gangster came to be in Berlusconi's employ, as well as some of the rest of the long, troubling history of contacts between his entourage and organized crime.

2. THE HORSE WHISPERER

Who was Vittorio Mangano, and how did he come to work for Silvio Berlusconi? All accounts agree that Dell'Utri and Mangano met in the late 1960s or early 1970s while Dell'Utri was coaching an amateur soccer club in Palermo.

"I met him in Palermo in the 1970s, when I was running the Bacigalupo soccer club," Marcello Dell'Utri said in 2001. "He helped out working with the kids, tracing the lines of the field or acting as line judge during the games. I remembered him when we needed to hire a hand for the villa at Arcore. We made a selection, as we normally did, among people in Brianza [the part of Lombardy in which the villa at Arcore is located], but we didn't find the right person. And so I thought of him. I knew that Mangano worked with livestock, was an expert on horses and raised dogs. This was 1974, and Mangano was certainly not known as a 'man of honor.'"[6]

It all sounds innocent enough—a soccer enthusiast who unfortunately turned out to be a bad apple and just happened to be involved in a check-kiting scheme and a kidnapping. But on reflection, Dell'Utri's explanation is full of holes. It is absurd that at a time when Italian agriculture was being rapidly mechanized and the Italian countryside was full of unemployed or underemployed labor Dell'Utri and Berlusconi would have been unable to find a suitable farmhand in Northern Italy and had to go to the country's southern tip, to Palermo—a city of half a million people and capital of the Mafia—to find someone to run a stable in Lombardy.

Dell'Utri indicates that there was no reason to suppose that Mangano in 1974 was a "man of honor" and implies that the man's only brush with the law was for writing a bad check. (It is curious that Dell'Utri uses the expression "man of honor"—the Mafiosi's own preferred term for a Mafia member.) It strains credulity in the extreme that an experienced Palermitan like Marcello Dell'Utri had no idea before hiring him who Vittorio Mangano really was. In Sicily, the informal information network is highly developed, and it is vitally important to know whom you are dealing with at all times. As a result, Sicilians develop quick instincts for placing people, since either becoming friendly with or getting on the wrong side of a man of honor can have unpredictable and tragic consequences. Mangano had been in and out of jail three times between 1967 and 1974. While it's true that Mafiosi are forbidden from identifying themselves as men of honor to outsiders, it is also important that their reputations precede them as people to be reckoned with. Their power as Mafiosi depends on generating an attitude of respect and fear in others. While in Palermo, Mangano had engaged in an extortion scheme in which he terrorized his potential victims by sending them packages containing the bloody sawed-off heads of dogs.[7]

The terror that the name of Mangano inspired was captured in a series of wiretaps made by Italian police in 1980 recording the calls of a Milan restaurant, La Pergola, which was being harassed with requests for money by a local extortion ring. The restaurant owners went to Arcore to see Mangano and when the extortionists called back, the restaurateur told them they could pick up their money from Vittorio Mangano. The Milanese gangsters, seized with panic, began excusing themselves and insisted that the whole episode had been a terrible misunderstanding. It is a classic example of the Mafia at work, in which a Mafioso's reputation of being the most dangerous person in the area helps him maintain his monopoly on the protection racket.

That Dell'Utri would have had no whiff of this back in Palermo and would have hired such a character to watch over Berlusconi's villa and drive his children to and from school is improbable in the extreme. If Dell'Utri had accidentally hired a dangerous gangster for such a delicate position, putting the entire Berlusconi family at risk, one might expect him to have been fired or demoted for such a colossal blunder; that Dell'Utri was instead elevated to the pinnacle of power in the Berlusconi empire and given a place for all eternity in the Berlusconi family tomb suggests that it was no mistake. The story only begins to make sense when you consider that Berlusconi and Dell'Utri hired Mangano for the same reasons that the owners of the Pergola restaurant went to him: protection. In other words, not because they had no idea who he was, but because they knew exactly who he was.

The key to Mangano's presence at Arcore lies in one of his principal responsibilities: driving Berlusconi's children to and from school.

Although publicly Berlusconi has always insisted that he had no idea who Mangano was before he was hired, privately he told Indro Montanelli, the longtime editor of his newspaper, *Il Giornale*, that he had hired Mangano as a bodyguard. "At the time, I was afraid of kidnapping: who better could protect me than a *mafioso*? He was in the business."[8]

But hiring a Mafioso brought Berlusconi and Dell'Utri into contact with the organization as a whole. In explaining his decision to hire Mangano, Dell'Utri tried to make it appear to be a sudden, almost random choice: "We made a selection, as we normally did, among people in Brianza, but we didn't find the right person. And so I thought of him."[9]

Berlusconi, however, inadvertently contradicted Dell'Utri, making clear that the hiring of Mangano was the result of a complex consultation between Dell'Utri and his friends back in Palermo. "He introduced me to Mr. Mangano as a person he knew, or more precisely through a close friend of his, whom he had known on the soccer fields of the Bacigalupo amateur soccer club."[10] The good friend who helped Dell'Utri run the soccer club was a man named Gaetano Cinà, the owner of a dry cleaner's and a sporting goods store and, according to prosecutors, one of Cosa Nostra's ambassadors in the world of politics and legitimate business.

Vittorio Mangano tried hard to shield Dell'Utri and Berlusconi in his testimony, but his account agrees with Berlusconi's and shows his hiring to have the fruit of intense, high-level consultations:

> I remember that in about 1973 [*sic*; it was 1974] Cinà and Dell'Utri came to see me in Palermo and Cinà explained the reasons for their visit explaining that Dell'Utri was going to propose an interesting job to me in Arcore, where a friend of his had bought a property. . . . Before moving with my family, I went by myself to the offices of Edilnord [Berlusconi's real estate company] at Foro Bonaparte number 24 and met Mssrs. Berlusconi and Dell'Utri.[11]

Both Berlusconi and Mangano agree that Mangano was hired on Gaetano Cinà's recommendation. Notice that in Mangano's description it is Cinà who is mentioned before Dell'Utri and that it is Cinà who speaks first at the meeting, proposing the job to Mangano, as if he were the more authoritative person in Mangano's world. Dell'Utri admits that he originally met Mangano through Cinà, but denied that Cinà had recommended he hire Mangano at Arcore, presumably because it places Cinà in the role of mediator between Dell'Utri and a known Mafioso.

The threat of kidnapping, along with its obvious monetary benefits, was also a way for the Mafia to sink its hooks into people operating at the highest level of industry, real estate and finance. "Undoubtedly, the danger of kidnapping, then very common, brought the industrialists into contact with men of honor, in fact to desire their protection," explains Gaspare Mutolo, a Mafia witness who was a codefendant, close friend and prison mate of Vittorio Mangano's, and whose reliability has been recognized by numerous Italian courts. "Clearly, once having entered into contact with Cosa Nostra, the businessman could no longer stay away, and would have to consent to the various requests that came from the men of honor with whom they were in contact. Of these, undoubtedly, was the reinvestment of capital earned illegally." Mutolo—like many other major Mafia witnesses—insists that the Sicilian Mafia used Dell'Utri to invest its profits in Berlusconi's growing businesses.[12]

According to various Mafia witnesses, it was the Mafia of Catania, Sicily's second-largest city, that originally made the kidnapping threats to Berlusconi, and the Palermo Mafia that intervened on his behalf, sending Mangano to Arcore as a guardian as visible proof that Berlusconi was under their protection. Giuseppe Marchese, the son of a prominent Palermo boss, testified that Catanese Mafiosi had told him when they were in prison together that "in the past their group had had the plan of kidnapping the son of Silvio Berlusconi. But the project didn't go forward because the Palermitans intervened, saying that Berlusconi was a person who 'interested' them. . . . With the expression 'Berlusconi interested them,' he meant that the Palermo Cosa Nostra had a relationship with Berlusconi and that he should not be bothered."[13]

Mangano appears to have felt so at home at Berlusconi's villa that he used Arcore to give safe haven to various fugitives from justice. Dell'Utri—anxious not to be caught by prosecutors in a direct falsehood—did not contradict this: "Many people came to see him. . . . Mangano would sometimes introduce me to various people, saying that they were friends of his, never giving their names. You don't use names when you are meeting people with someone like Mangano."[14]

That Mangano, together with some of these same Mafia friends, would have subsequent involvement in the attempted kidnapping of Berlusconi's dinner guest is not a contradiction of his role as family bodyguard. It is a common practice among Mafiosi to do things from time to time to make the person under their "protection" feel a sense of potential threat, reminding them that they are in the Mafioso's power. Mangano also appears to have faked a break-in at the villa, stealing some paintings and valuable objects and then "recovering" them, in order to demonstrate his value to Berlusconi.

Although Berlusconi stated in his election campaign interview of 1994 that "we fired [him] as soon as we learned that he had tried to kidnap one of my dinner guests," this was clearly not the case. Not only did Berlusconi forget to mention Mangano's presence to police at dinner the night of the attempted kidnapping, but when police returned to arrest Mangano twenty days later, they found him still living at the villa.

In fact, Mangano returned to Arcore after spending a month in prison, and police found him still living there several months later. The decision to leave Berlusconi's employ appears to have been his own as a result of the negative publicity his presence there was generating in the local press.

While paying ransom or protection money seems to have been fairly common among Northern Italian industrialists, hiring a Mafioso as a bodyguard was a more unusual and "proactive" solution to the problem. While it can be seen as a mistake a frightened millionaire might make when threatened with kidnapping, it suggests a willingness to enter into a relationship of active complicity and into a wider set of relationships with the Mafia organization. This notion is reinforced by the fact that these relationships continued rather than ended after Mangano left his position at Arcore.

3. Dell'Utri Takes a Break from Berlusconi

Berlusconi and Dell'Utri have portrayed the Mangano story as an isolated, unlucky episode from their early careers. In fact, though, rather than trying to avoid contacts with the Mafia after his brush with Mangano, Dell'Utri entered into still closer contact. In 1977, after spending four years working for Berlusconi, Dell'Utri spent a curious two-year interlude working for a shady Sicilian financier who operated a large real estate and financial group in Milan until it went bankrupt in 1979 amid evidence of fraud, money laundering and Mafia connections. The financier, Filippo Alberto Rapisarda, admitted to prosecutors that he was a businessman who did not feel he could say no to the Mafia and hired both Marcello Dell'Utri and his twin brother, Alberto, because of their connections to Cosa Nostra. The person who presented Dell'Utri to Rapisarda was the same Gaetano Cinà who had introduced him to Vittorio Mangano.

> Alberto and Marcello Dell'Utri were recommended to me by Gaetano Cinà, whom I had known for many years. . . . In effect, I hired Dell'Utri because it was very difficult to say no to Gaetano Cinà in that he didn't just present himself but a group that reeked of the Mafia, Bontate-Teresi-Filippo Marchese.
>
> Marcello Dell'Utri told me that his acquaintance with all these Mafia people was due to the fact that he had to mediate between people who had made threats and extortion requests to Berlusconi himself. Marcello Dell'Utri later explained that because of these threats, Berlusconi had sent his wife and children abroad for a period of time. Dell'Utri told me that his mediation had served to reduce the money demands of the Mafiosi.[15]

Dell'Utri has admitted that he had indeed told Rapisarda about his friendship with the powerful Mafia bosses and about mediating between Cosa Nostra and Berlusconi, but says he was merely trying to show off. "I was bragging," he told prosecutors in 1996. "Rapisarda was saying he knew important people in the criminal world, and I would say, bragging, 'I know people who are even more important than yours.'" But ordinary employees of the Rapisarda group (not all of them organized crime figures) testified to seeing the same Mafiosi whom Rapisarda mentioned hanging around the offices in Via Chiaravalle in Milan, where Dell'Utri worked and lived.[16]

Dell'Utri acknowledged having dinner in the late 1970s with Antonino Calderone, a Mafioso from Catania whose brother was the head of the city's main Mafia family at the time, and Antonino Grado, who, like Mangano, was a key figure in the Palermo–Milan–New York heroin connection. Dell'Utri initially denied the meeting, but Calderone (who turned state's witness after his brother and much of the rest of their family were murdered by rival Mafiosi) described the place and circumstances of their meeting with such precision that Dell'Utri was forced to acknowledge it, though he insisted that he had no idea who either Calderone or Grado was.

When asked by prosecutors why he happened to find himself at dinner with Mafiosi of the caliber of Antonino Calderone and Nino Grado, Dell'Utri replied: "To tell the truth, as I already explained, precisely because I now understood Mangano's identity, even after his leaving Arcore, I was somewhat frightened of him and when I met him I didn't reject him, I accepted his company. But in the instance recalled by Calderone, I dined with Mangano and his friends without knowing their names. In fact, I don't know either Calderone or the Grado brothers."[17]

Similarly, Dell'Utri was forced to acknowledge having attended a Mafia wedding in London in 1980 by the testimony of a Mafia boss, Franco Di Carlo, who dealt drugs out of London, and whose testimony was corroborated by other members of the wedding party. Again, Dell'Utri insisted that he didn't know either Di Carlo or the groom (another drug dealer), but said he had been in London to see an art exhibition and had tagged along with his friend Gaetano Cinà, a guest at the wedding. This is the same Gaetano Cinà who introduced Dell'Utri to Vittorio Mangano and whom Dell'Utri consulted before hiring Mangano to work at Arcore. The notion of a scholarly businessman who accidentally hires a professional kidnapper to drive his boss's children to school and inadvertently crashes a Mafia wedding might make for good scenes in a Woody Allen movie, but are hard to imagine in real life.

Even if you accept Dell'Utri's minimalist version of these events— that he was reluctantly forced into meetings with Mangano and his friends, whose names he didn't know—it shows a businessman caught in sticky web of relationships with the Mafia he either cannot extricate himself from or does not want to extricate himself from. This pattern, of meeting after meeting, fits with Gaspare Mutolo's testimony that forcing businessmen to accept protection was an effective way of forging relationships with wealthy industrialists.

The Mafiosi whose names keep coming up in these tales of Mangano and Dell'Utri—Stefano Bontate, Salvatore Inzerillo, Mimmo Teresi, Mangano, Di Carlo, Nino Grado—were some of the most important Mafiosi in Palermo in the late 1970s, all of whom figure heavily in the major Mafia and heroin investigations of the time.

"Doesn't it seem strange that major businessmen like Berlusconi and Dell'Utri would be connected to men of honor like Vittorio Mangano?" a French television journalist asked Paolo Borsellino, one of Italy's best and most relentless anti-Mafia prosecutors in 1992, just a few months before Borsellino's assassination.

"Mangano was one of the bridges of the Mafia organization in Northern Italy," said Borsellino, who had investigated Mangano during the late 1970s and had convicted him to a long prison sentence in the 1980s. "At the beginning of the 1970s," Borsellino said, "Cosa Nostra started to become an industry itself . . . in fact, it had a virtual monopoly in the traffic of drugs, and found itself having to manage an enormous mass of money. An enormous amount of capital that needed an outlet. It looked for an outlet in part because part of this money was exported and deposited outside the country which explains the closeness between Cosa Nostra and certain financiers who deal with the movement of capital. It's normal that the owners of these enormous sums of capital would look for instruments to employ this money, both to recycle it and to make money on their money."[18]

It is a fact that the Palermo Mafia in this period succeeded in penetrating very high levels of the Milan financial world. Italian police wiretapped a conversation of a Mafioso threatening Italy's most powerful banker, Enrico Cuccia, although there is no evidence that the Mafia was able to use his bank, Mediobanca, for laundering money. There is no question, however, that it was able to use Michele Sindona's Banca Privata Italiana and Roberto Calvi's Banco Ambrosiano, two of the rising stars of Italian banking in the 1970s, whose risky practices made them welcome large infusions of Mafia money. Both men met violent deaths, quite possibly at the hands of the Mafia. Sindona hired a Mafia killer to murder the poor bank inspector who exposed the true state of his bank and died in prison after drinking a poisoned cup of coffee. Calvi was found hanging from Blackfriars Bridge in London in 1982. His death was initially declared a suicide, but English authorities later performed a second autopsy that ruled he had been strangled and then hung from the bridge so that it looked like a suicide. Already before the second autopsy, numerous Mafia witnesses had ruled out the possibility that Calvi had done himself in. "What fucking suicide? He was strangled by Franco Di Carlo!" Francesco Marino Mannoia told prosecutors in 1991. Calvi had supposedly lost a great deal of money given him by Cosa Nostra. The alleged strangler is the same Franco Di Carlo who sat at the same table with Marcello Dell'Utri at the London wedding of drug dealer Jimmy Fauci.[19]

To Mafiosi such as Antonino Calderone, it had become quite normal to find themselves seated across the dinner table from prominent, respected businessmen. "Dell'Utri's presence didn't particularly surprise me because 'men of honor' were at that point very much used to being in contact with people in high places. Besides 'men of honor' always considered themselves superior to all others, even people with high social standing."[20]

While it's true that the Mafia harassed many important business figures, it was only a small and inglorious minority of those figures who actually did business with them. Generally these were the unscrupulous ones, the overnight millionaires, like Sindona and Calvi, who rose to the top by cutting a lot of corners.

Perhaps the most important part of Rapisarda's testimony is his account of a meeting in 1978 with Mimmo Teresi and Stefano Bontate at which the two men talked about their relations with Berlusconi. "In 1979 I met Stefano Bontate and Mimmo Teresi nearby the offices of Edilnord

[Berlusconi's real estate company] in Piazza Castello [in Milan]. They told me that they were meeting with Marcello Dell'Utri, who had proposed to them that they invest in the television company that Silvio Berlusconi was forming at the time. They both asked me if it was a good idea to go into business with those people. I was very displeased—even though I tried not to show it—because in that period he was supposed to be working for me alone." Rapisarda was particularly upset because in this period, he, like Berlusconi, had started a small private television channel.[21]

Suspicions that the Mafia may have used Berlusconi's Fininvest to re-cycle its money have been reinforced by major gaps in our knowledge about the origins of Berlusconi's fortune. Berlusconi has always main-tained that his early projects were financed with his father's pension money, with loans from the Rasini Bank where his father worked, and through his own hard work. But investigative work done by two enter-prising journalists back in the 1980s, Giovanni Ruggeri and Mario Gua-rino, points to a much more complex and mysterious picture. They discovered that the principal investor and real owner of the Brugherio development was an anonymous Swiss company with a long name, Finanzierunggesellschaft für Residenzen, based in Lugano, capital of the Italian canton of Switzerland. Its legal representative was a tightly but-toned Italian-Swiss attorney named Renzo Rezzonico. Who the investors behind Rezzonico were has never been discovered. When Milano 2 was started, the principal backer was another anonymous Swiss company set up by Rezzonico with an even longer name, Aktiengesellschaft für Immobilienlagen in Residenzzentren.[22]

In 1998, prosecutors in Palermo hired an accountant from the Bank of Italy to try to unravel the complicated origins of Berlusconi's financial empire. The accountant found large amounts of cash of uncertain origin entering Berlusconi's Fininvest during the 1970s, when Berlusconi made his quantum leap into television. In 1977, for example, the capitalization of Berlusconi's Fininvest jumped from 2.5 billion to 10.5 billion lire, with the infusion of 8 billion lire in cash—the equivalent of about $30 million in today's money. The bank investigators were never able to establish where this and other large infusions of cash came from. Prosecutors argue that these cash transactions are instances of the Mafia's recycling its money in legitimate businesses. Because banks are authorized to destroy bank records after a certain period of time, it may never be possible to know for certain what these cash investments in Fininvest represented.[23]

Whatever the truth of Rapisarda's testimony, we know this for certain: in 1979 Dell'Utri returned to work for Berlusconi, after two years of working for a business that was a Mafia front company, to assume a big new job as the head of Publitalia, the advertising wing of Berlusconi's new big business: television.

Chapter Three

TELEVISION (AND MONEY)

"You can do a lot to change people's way of thinking,
their vision of scarcity."
—*Silvio Berlusconi*[1]

1. PET FOOD

To understand the Berlusconi revolution, according to Giulio Malgara, a big Berlusconi supporter and prominent business and advertising figure, you need to know about pet food advertising. "Back in the 1970s, you were not allowed to advertise pet food on RAI. There were all kinds of things you couldn't advertise: you couldn't advertise deodorant because Italians weren't supposed to smell. You couldn't advertise adult diapers because they didn't want people to think about the three million older Italians who pissed on themselves. You couldn't advertise automobiles because the government wanted to protect Fiat against foreign competition." Malgara and I sat on the terrace of his apartment in downtown Milan, where he lives surrounded by museum-quality paintings, attended to by a waiter in a white coat, the rewards of a career that included, as CEO of Quaker Italia, introducing Gatorade and Purina Cat Chow to the Italian market—successes made possible through access to television advertising. "You couldn't advertise pet food because it was somehow considered immoral in a world where children were starving in places like Biafra. Italy had a culture of austerity. 'Rich' was a dirty word; they didn't want to create incentives for consumption—it was something that ran across the political world from the Catholics to the

Communists." The Italian government delayed the introduction of color television—invented in the U.S. in 1954 and widely available by the early 1960s—until 1977, because they didn't want to make Italians go out and buy new TV sets.[2]

In order to reverse the ban on pet food advertising, Malgara had to travel in person for a meeting with Amintore Fanfani, who was in the early 1970s the most powerful politician in the ruling Christian Democratic Party and the most influential at the government-controlled RAI. Malgara finally convinced Fanfani and other Christian Democrats that the sale of pet food, which used unsavory-looking leftovers from the meat-packing process, actually meant that there would be more meat left over for the starving children of Biafra. "We reached a compromise—that lasted for a couple of years—where we were allowed to show still photographs of cats and dogs in our ads, but we were not allowed to show cats and dogs in motion. I'm not making this up."

Owners of many Italian businesses speak about Berlusconi the way former slaves once spoke about Abraham Lincoln. "He liberated advertising in Italy," said Malgara, who is now the president of Malgara Chiari e Forti, a leading Italian food company with 180 million euros ($200 million) a year in business, and the president of UPA, Utenti Pubblicità Associati, the Association of Advertising Users. He is also head of Auditel, the company that provides audience ratings for Italian TV. Along with the moralistic prohibitions that kept products like pet food off the air, the whole structure of Italian television at the time made it almost impossible for all but a few businesses to gain access to television advertising. RAI had a monopoly, gave advertisers very little air time and was extremely expensive. At the time, all broadcasting in Europe was government sponsored, and television was seen as a public service rather than a commercial vehicle, fitting the deep-seated suspicion in both Catholic and Marxist circles of hedonistic commercial culture. Television was run in a way that was almost the direct opposite of market logic. Rather than having salesmen out combing the country for potential advertisers, companies made the pilgrimage to see the powerful Colonel Fiore of SIPRA, RAI's advertising arm, based in Turin, and pleaded to him for the right to advertise. You needed the backing of a major political party, preferably the Christian Democratic Party, and often good standing with the Catholic Church. There is a famous incident, recounted often by Berlusconi, of the maker of the after-dinner liqueur Averna being turned down repeatedly until he placed his soul in the care of a local priest recommended to him by Colonel Fiore. Finally, with access to RAI, Averna became a national brand.

"You needed a lot of money and political clout," Malgara explained. "You didn't have to make payoffs, but in order to get space on TV, you had to buy space in various newspapers, generally party newspapers, all of which followed a political logic rather than a market logic."[3]

2. THE OLD RAI

Italian television, throughout its history, has closely reflected the country's politics. Initially, when it began television broadcasts in 1954, RAI had one channel closely controlled by the Christian Democratic Party. It featured—as it still does today—the pope's mass and benediction in Saint Peter's Square on Sunday mornings, and ended programming at 10:00 P.M., the hour at which the government felt all good Italians should be in bed. In 1963, after the Socialist Party entered the government coalition, a second network with ties close to the Socialists was created. In 1978, after the Italian Communists had entered into an alliance with the Christian Democrats, a third network was created, in which the Communists were the dominant influence.

Italy was typical of Europe at this time in this regard. The state held an absolute monopoly in every major country in Europe, from France, Britain and Holland to Germany, Spain and Greece. Berlusconi was the first to make a significant breach in the wall of state control, and his example had a certain influence in loosening government control in the rest of the continent.

If Italians have failed to react as an outsider might think they should to

Berlusconi's virtually total political control of television, it is in part because Italian television has always been highly subject to political influence. When Filiberto Guala, one of the early directors of RAI, introduced himself to his staff, he announced, "I have come to kick out the pederasts and the Communists." At another point, he announced that "I am simply a modern crusader called to struggle for the holy sepulchre of the public consciousness." After his career at RAI, Guala took holy vows and spent the rest of his days in a Trappist monastery outside of Rome.[4]

In 1962, RAI hired the highly respected journalist Enzo Biagi, then with *La Stampa* of Turin, to direct its main nightly newscast. Biagi fought to have the right to hire journalists entirely on the basis of journalistic merit free of party affiliations, but when he lost the battle, he resigned his position, though he stayed at RAI. Biagi remained a fixture on RAI until 2001, when Berlusconi singled him out for his "criminal use" of television; his popular program was canceled, and other shows were forbidden to invite him as a guest on their talk shows.

RAI was subject to heated power struggles among the major parties, with each pushing to place sympathetic journalists as producers, deputy producers or anchormen of key programs. But even with this and many other obvious defects, RAI's paternalistic approach to broadcasting—with its high-minded sense of public service—also produced some excellent programming. RAI commissioned the great neorealist director Roberto Rossellini to produce a series of films on the history of science and philosophy that included shows on the lives of Socrates and Descartes. The RAI monopoly meant that productions of Shakespeare and Sophocles, film versions of works by Dostoevsky and Gogol and the great Italian novel *I Promessi Sposi*, reached large mass audiences—because there was nothing else to watch. For many years, RAI ran a program called *La TV degli Agricoltori* (The Farmers' TV) which included lots of practical advice and instruction for farmers, with information about things like the proper use of fertilizers and irrigation, offering instruction to a part of the population that was still, in good part, illiterate.

In the 1960s and 1970s, RAI became the country's chief movie producer, financing some of the leading Italian films of its day, from Fellini's *The Clowns*, and *Orchestra Rehearsal* to Ermanno Olmi's *Tree of Wooden Clogs*, the Taviani brothers' *Padre Padrone* and Francesco Rosi's *Christ Stopped at Eboli*.

As the second and third channels got going there was an increasing variety of political views. Programs like *La Forza della Democrazia* (The Force of Democracy; 1977), with the journalist Corrado Stajano, examined the delicate subject of the government's role in a series of right-wing bombings that occurred a few years earlier. The left-wing playwright and comic actor Dario Fo, who later won the Nobel Prize for Literature, returned to RAI in 1977 with a famous play, *Mistero Buffo*, that made fun of the pope and Italy's leading political parties. (Fo had refused to appear on RAI in 1962 after a skit of his was censored.) Highly respected independent journalists in addition to Enzo Biagi, such as Giorgio Bocca, were fixtures on RAI.

By the 1970s, the news was composed, stopwatch in hand, with each party getting its allotted number of minutes and seconds of time according to its strength in parliament. It was a crude system, but it did guarantee a measure of pluralism, though it tended to penalize the smaller parties. Members of the small Radical Party went on a hunger strike to protest the RAI monopoly, and when they were given time to air their views, members of the party appeared in front of the camera with gags in their mouths and produced a program that consisted of twenty-three consecutive minutes of total silence.[5]

By 1974, a number of groups were experimenting with "pirate" radio and television stations in defiance of RAI's monopoly of the public airwaves. Many of them, as it happened, were radical left groups—such as Potere Operaio (Worker Power) and Autonomia Operaia (Worker Autonomy)—who were looking to challenge the hegemony of government-controlled information. "We paved the way for Berlusconi!" Franco Piperno, one of the leaders of Potere Operaio told me when we met several years ago, with an amused sense of irony.[6]

In 1976, the Italian Supreme Court responded to these early challenges by allowing for private broadcasting but specifying that commercial television should operate on a local level, leaving RAI a monopoly on national broadcasting.

Berlusconi's own interest in television began with the construction of Milano 2. In deciding to wire the new development for the new technology of cable television, it occurred to Berlusconi that he might be able to create a kind of private station for the condominium that could be offered as a luxury feature to prospective buyers. But the Supreme Court's decision convinced Berlusconi to create a normal broadcast station rather than something restricted to Milano 2 residents. In 1978, Berlusconi founded something called Telemilano 58. It was at this time one of 434 private television stations that sprouted up almost overnight in Italy.[7]

In this crowded early television market, characterized by hundreds of small stations, only a handful had the capital to launch major ventures. The leading candidates appeared to be three large Milan publishing houses. Rizzoli, the second-largest book and magazine group, had recently acquired the *Corriere della Sera*, the nation's largest newspaper. Mondadori ran the biggest book and magazine group in the country. And Rusconi, which published, in addition to books, mass-market magazines like *Gente* and *Eva 2,000* with a large female audience, created a television station, Italia 1, that successfully targeted women viewers.

While some might have thought that a parvenu builder of suburban condominiums would never have been able to compete against experienced publishers, Berlusconi has always believed that being an outsider has been one of his greatest advantages. The publishers, attached to their origins in the world of books, tried to create programs of cultural value but didn't fully understand either the language of television or the nature of its business.

"They never really believed in it," said Malgara, who as an advertiser and president of the Association of Advertising Users, was familiar with all of the networks. "Television was never their core business. They went into television because they were supposed to, but their core business was the printed word, which, they felt, was a more noble calling, because it was culture, while television was just entertainment.

"Berlusconi grabs this historic moment for the Italian economy and—underestimated by everyone—starts out on his own with an extraordinary idea and the hope that the companies will follow him," Malgara said. "These companies found an incredibly strong anchor in television advertising in order to address the consumer. And Berlusconi—as an entertainer—understood what they wanted."[8]

Berlusconi made a splash in 1977 by hiring away one of RAI's most popular (and most parodied) figures, Mike Buongiorno, a plodding, genial Italian-American everyman with slicked-back hair and a round, doughy face who had presided over a string of quiz shows. To Italian intellectuals, Buongiorno was the symbol of the lowest-common-denominator nature of television: "Mike is the most mediocre and, therefore, the best," one critic wrote. But his simple, unimposing manner gave him a magic touch for selling to Italian housewives the cheeses and prosciuttos that he promoted on air.[9]

"It seems stupid, but it was a fundamental moment," says Magara, "For a housewife in, let's say, Sarzana, in the province of Udine, who lives in the provinces and whose main window onto the world is television, Mike Buongiorno *was* the RAI, and so when Berlusconi made a deal with Mike Buongiorno, people began to think, 'This is important.'"[10]

Not only did he hire Mike Buongiorno, but he made the quiz show host "artistic director" of his nascent TV network, Telemilano. This was typical of the reversal of values that occurred with Berlusconi's TV, which made central things that had been peripheral and peripheral things that had been central. Before Berlusconi, audience, ratings and entertainment had been secondary to RAI's central mission, which was to educate, to produce culture (albeit culture sympathetic to the government). Mike Buongiorno communicated with the silent majority of the country, the less educated provincial parts of the country that were treated with a certain degree of condescension at RAI, whose board of directors consisted of prominent writers and intellectuals. Berlusconi went unabashedly after the lowest common denominator and made the silent majority the protagonist of his television. "Remember that the audience of our listeners, as they say in America, have about an eighth-grade education and were not at the top of their class," he told his sales force in the late 1980s.[11]

While hiring away Mike Buongiorno, Berlusconi also invested millions in flashy new TV studios in the Pirelli skyscraper in downtown Milan. As with everything, from Milano 2 to politics, Berlusconi entered this new market with a splash, paying a premium to make a loud statement and doing it through highly visible symbols. One of the few skyscrapers in Italy, the Pirelli was a symbol of the new against the old that was emblematic of his battle against the RAI monopoly.

Other than Mike Buongiorno's and a handful of other original programs, Berlusconi concentrated on buying up as much American programming as fast as he could borrow money. He bought up entire film libraries at record prices, using a seemingly limitless supply of money.

But perhaps the key to Berlusconi's success in television is that he approached it from the opposite angle to his competitors'. The book publishers thought that the key to television was editorial content; Berlusconi understood that that the lifeblood of television is advertising. Because of the severe limit on advertising on RAI, which made TV advertising too scarce and too expensive for most businesses, Berlusconi understood that there was a vast untapped market of medium-sized companies that could become national brands if they could reach a national television audience. The problem was that some of them didn't know yet that they wanted to advertise on television or on a new, untried channel, and Berlusconi needed to persuade them. As Berlusconi once said about women, "Think of how many women there are out there who would like to go to bed with me, but don't know it. Life is a problem of communication."[12] And so Berlusconi needed to convince this world of potential advertisers that he was their man. He invented a host of clever strategies for reluctant clients to take a chance with him: businesses were told that they didn't have to pay for their advertising unless their sales went up. He made the unusual offer of taking his clients' products in lieu of payment, collecting warehouses full of mineral water, olive oil and liqueurs, motorcycles or cruise ship vacations, some of which could be given as presents to advertising agents at other companies to encourage them to give Publitalia more business. Companies were encouraged to put all of their advertising for certain products on Berlusconi's TV so that they could measure precisely how effective it was. And they encouraged companies to advertise exclusively with Publitalia, to keep business away from their rival private stations. Moreover, while companies like Mondadori and Rizzoli tried to place advertising discreetly into their programming so that it bothered viewers as little as possible, Berlusconi took the opposite approach. Programs were vehicles for selling products, and advertisements should be placed at moments of greatest viewer interest and anticipation to guarantee that they would watch not just the program but the advertisements. "We don't sell space, we sell sales!" was the mantra that Berlusconi repeated.[13]

This was one area in which the Berlusconi myth corresponds pretty closely to reality. There is no question that Berlusconi had a clearer vision of how to make commercial television successful than his rivals and, as a salesman, was at his best. He managed to convey the feeling that he was not just selling a product, but offering a vision of a new, better world, offering a message of empowerment and liberation for small businesses that had been unable to break through into the big time; he offered a kind of utopian vision of infinite growth and infinite prosperity and well-being. Berlusconi is not wrong when he describes himself as a "missionary" of commercial television. And the sales pitch he developed in these years forms the basis of the political speech and his political appeal: a call to arms of the Italian middle class against the asphyxiating oppression of the old political parties, represented by the monopoly of state broadcasting, against the cultural and economic elites that dominated the country and for the promise of liberation and the land of milk and honey.

Berlusconi's television stations helped to make a culture of abundance and excess not only acceptable, but even desirable. "We can do a lot to change the narrow mentality of people, its vision of scarcity."[14]

His talents were not just confined to selling ads. "You had to see him discussing the programming to understand how we were able to take on the RAI," said Fedele Confalonieri. "He was able to predict the audience share each program would receive. He got involved in rewriting the scripts, in the stage sets, in the editing of all the productions. He gave suggestions to writers, directors, to the actors. He invented the formats, the titles of the programs, the sales slogans and promotion campaigns. He was truly the Television Man."[15]

"Berlusconi was very good at fitting the right program with the right product," says Malgara. At every step of the way, Berlusconi started "backward," with the advertiser, and then went for the program. When he hired away Mike Buongiorno, he already had a commitment from several major advertisers to sponsor Buongiorno's new program *Sogni nel Cassetto* (Dreams in the Drawer). (It is interesting that the word "dream," which Berlusconi used in his first big TV success, is also one of the most recurrent in his standard political stump speeches.)[16]

Malgara was present at a lunch at which Berlusconi proposed to several advertisers that they help him acquire the rights to the hit television show *Dallas*. RAI had already aired about a dozen episodes of *Dallas* to great success, but had then dropped the program. "The political world, especially the Christian Democrats, found it a little too daring, because it dealt with things like adultery and divorce. And so Berlusconi told us, 'Help me buy *Dallas*, it's been a hit all over the world, and I will give you favorable placement for your ads.'

"Berlusconi, before anyone, grasped this enormous desire on the part of companies to speak directly to consumers, blew open the system that kept all these companies with all this potential but many of whom were unknown and who didn't have the money or the political clout to advertise on RAI," Malgara said. "He was capable and very courageous. They could have shut him down at any moment."

3. Skirting the Law

But Berlusconi's abilities were only one part of his recipe for success in the television market. Berlusconi also differentiated himself from his competitors in his extreme lack of scruples, a willingness to defy, skirt or break the law and willingness to go to extraordinary lengths to win political protection at the highest levels.

When the Italian Supreme Court legalized private television broadcasting but restricted it to the local level, it did not explain exactly what that meant. In the absence of regulatory legislation, most broadcasters went to considerable lengths to respect the court ruling, applying to themselves antitrust legislation used in the United States, the country with the longest experience of commercial TV. "When we started broadcasting we applied the rules used in the United States, according to which a single network cannot own more than five UHF stations and two VHF stations, for a total of seven," said Edilio Rusconi, who later testified in hearings before the Italian Senate. "The others were independent affiliates that acquired centralized programming." Rusconi tried to establish a network that concentrated on the four largest and most prosperous of Italy's twenty regions (Lazio, Lombardy, Piedmont and Emilia-Romagna). Mondadori initially avoided buying either broadcast towers or local affiliates on the theory that it could provide programming for a series of local TV stations. (Rizzoli decided after only a few months to get out of the television business when faced with its enormous start-up costs.)[17]

Berlusconi, on the other hand, decided that the only way he could compete with RAI and deliver advertisers the sales breakthrough he had promised was to offer them a national market. In seeming defiance of the Italian Supreme Court, he began buying up local stations and broadcast towers as fast as he could. He then came up with the idea of broadcasting the tapes of his programs a few seconds apart so that he could claim that technically he was broadcasting locally, but telling advertisers that he was giving them a national audience. Although it had the same programming, Berlusconi's TV appeared under different names in the North (Canale 5) and in the central and southern regions, where it was called Canale 10.

Berlusconi's national network began full operation in 1981 and immediately gained the upper hand on its competition in terms both of audience share and advertising revenues. His competitors realized that they had no choice but to follow suit and tried furiously to catch up. All three companies went deeper and deeper into debt in the brief scramble for supremacy, but here, too, Berlusconi had a major advantage: he seemed to have an unlimited supply of money.

Mondadori and Rusconi were family businesses that were risking the future of their core businesses—book and magazine publishing—as they strayed deeper into debt. Berlusconi, with much less to lose, went for broke, spending enormous sums of money from a series of state-owned banks. He drove his competitors (and himself) deeper and deeper into debt until they sold out to him. In 1983, he bought out Rusconi's Italia 1; and in 1984, Mondadori, financially exhausted, sold him Rete 4, giving him in effect a monopoly of private television in Italy.

4. POLITICAL CONNECTIONS

Crucial to Berlusconi's ability to defy the Italian Supreme Court and to his seemingly unlimited amounts of money was his friendship with one of the emerging political strongmen of the late 1970s and early 1980s, Bettino Craxi, who became the leader of the Italian Socialist Party in 1976, right at the time that Berlusconi initiated his television ventures. Berlusconi borrowed enormous amounts of money from banks controlled by the Socialist Party, such as the Banca Nazionale del Lavoro.

A Socialist leader and the virulent anti-Communist Berlusconi might seem an odd couple, but Craxi was a different kind of Socialist. Although the Socialists had once been the leading party of the Italian left, Craxi took over a party that had been weakened by the idealistic but woolly-headed direction of their longtime leader Pietro Nenni. The party had moved toward the center by participating in the center-left governments of the 1960s, but also accepted a kind of secondary role to the Italian Communist Party. Craxi felt that Italy needed a strong reformist party of the left, like François Mitterrand's Socialist Party in France, which could preside as the senior partner, together with the Communists, in a left-wing coalition. But the Socialists had only about 9 percent of the vote and the Communists over 30 percent of the vote. To become the largest party of the left, the Socialists set out to attack the Communist Party and in various ways to increase their own power and visibility.

Casting aside the impractical idealism of Nenni, Craxi adopted a highly cynical, arguably ruthless vision of power politics. If he was going to realize his grand political project, he felt he could not afford to be too squeamish about how he accomplished it. Craxi's idea of a non-Communist reformist left had a great deal of appeal. It attracted the support of the U.S. government during the 1980s, and I found myself rooting for Craxi when I first arrived in Italy in 1980. But after a while, I began to get a whiff of the widespread corruption in Socialist-run Milan, Craxi's stronghold. "You have to pay and pay if you want to get anything done here," an architect friend told me. And the signs of the rapid enrichment of the Milanese Socialists were flaunted rather than hidden. This, as it turned out, was part of a conscious strategy on Craxi's part. When Craxi appointed Valerio Bitteto to the board of the national electricity company, ENEL, he told him flatly, "Bring in votes and money."[18] When a director of the Banca Nazionale del Lavoro refused to authorize a large loan that Craxi wanted, he berated the man for daring to think that he, the director, made decisions, when it was Craxi who gave him his job. Corruption had always been a part of Italian life, but there is no question that a quantum leap occurred during the late 1970s and 1980s, when Craxi was making his big bid for power. I remember a high-level manager at a major state-owned company telling me that when the Christian Democrats had a quasi-monopoly of power, their demands for money and patronage were more modest. But with the arrival on the scene of the Craxian Socialists, there was a ferocious competition among the parties to siphon off money to finance their organizations and line their pockets.

This penchant for corruption was combined with a new, arrogant, somewhat authoritarian form of political leadership that was relatively new to post–World War II Italian politics. The Christian Democrats were wily compromisers and artful weavers of improbable alliances; their party was a Babel of clashing constituencies and rival leaders. The Communists had much more centralized leadership, but here too there were different wings of the party, and moderate Social Democrats and pro-Soviet leaders coexisted and debated the party's direction. Craxi felt that a small party could not afford these kinds of differences and ruthlessly defenestrated dissenters. As Indro Montanelli, Italy's leading conservative journalist and someone sympathetic to Craxi's anti-Communism, wrote: "Craxi has a marked—and extremely unfortunate—tendency to view as enemies all those who refuse to become his servants."[19]

As Berlusconi began to emerge as the largest real estate developer in Milan in the late 1970s, he became increasingly close to Craxi. Craxi was often Berlusconi's guest at his fabulous new villa at Arcore. They toasted each other at New Year's, and Craxi was best man at Berlusconi's second wedding.

It would be difficult to overstate the importance of this relationship to Berlusconi's success. During the years between 1980, when Berlusconi founded Canale 5 and began broadcasting nationally, and 1990, when the Italian parliament passed a law recognizing the legitimacy of Berlusconi's three networks, his television empire was operating in a condition of semilegality. "Some people think that unless something is specifically authorized, it should not be done. Others feel that everything that is not specifically forbidden is allowed. Berlusconi is among the latter," said Fedele Confalonieri, his closest and oldest friend and now the man who runs Berlusconi's Mediaset empire in Milan.[20] Unfortunately for Berlusconi, the Italian Supreme Court had specifically stated that private broadcasting was allowed only on a local and not a national level. Most judges in the 1980s interpreted this to mean that Berlusconi's network was illegal. There were constant calls for parliament to bring order to the Far West of Italian broadcasting, with its hundreds of small local stations and handful of emerging national networks. Local magistrates shut down various stations for operating illegally and frequently threatened Berlusconi too. The calls for regulation increased as Berlusconi gobbled up his chief competitors, giving him by 1984 a virtual monopoly of private national television. Then, in October of 1984, magistrates in three cities (including Rome and Turin, two of the largest in the country) ordered Berlusconi's local stations to stop broadcasting nationally and to show only local programming, as stipulated by the Supreme Court. Berlusconi and Fininvest decided to meet the challenge by suspending all programming, leaving viewers in these cities, including Rome, the capital, with a blank screen, giving the impression that the magistrates had in effect blacked out Italian television. Children used to watching the Smurfs, and housewives and pensioners deprived of *Dallas* and *General Hospital,* were outraged, and the home phones of the three magistrates began ringing off the hook.

Bettino Craxi cut short a state visit in London and issued a decree putting Berlusconi's networks back on the air. Craxi even threatened to bring down his government as a way of strong-arming recalcitrant members of the government into converting Craxi's decree into a law that would allow Berlusconi to hold on to his three national networks, pending more comprehensive telecommunications legislation that would finally establish clear norms for the new TV field. "The action of the magistrates is, to say the least, inappropriate at a moment in which the Parliament is rapidly examining and elaborating the new law on private broadcasting," Craxi's brother-in-law Paolo Pillitteri said at the time.[21]

The country had already been waiting eight years since the Italian Supreme Court opened the way, on a limited basis, to private broadcasting and would wait another six years for the legislation that was supposedly rapidly making its way through parliament. In fact, Craxi's Socialists would block every attempt at writing legislation during these years at Berlusconi's urging. Berlusconi understood that the longer his ownership of three national networks lasted, the harder and harder it would be to take them away from him. With the state broadcasting system its only real competitor, Italian TV rapidly evolved into a kind of "duopoly," the three major public networks and Berlusconi's three networks, which divided between them more than 90 percent of the audience and with Berlusconi's channels taking 60 percent of the advertising since RAI had strict limits on the amount of advertising it could run. It was like a license to print money.

At the time, in the United States, Berlusconi's model and the home of free-market capitalism, one was not allowed to own more than one national network and could not, at the same time, own any newspapers. When Spain allowed private television, no individual was allowed to own more than 25 percent of one national network. But in Italy, the more time parliament fiddled with a law, the more Berlusconi's virtual monopoly of private TV would come to seem a permanent part of the Italian landscape.

5. THE P2 MASONIC LODGE

Craxi and the Socialists were not the only powers that Berlusconi turned to as he looked to solidify his growing empire. On January 26, 1978, Berlusconi became member number 1816 of a secret Masonic lodge known as Propaganda 2, or P2. This secret P2 Masonic Lodge was founded by a strange and sinister character named Licio Gelli, who was a fervent Fascist during his youth, who had volunteered to fight with the Fascists in Spain, and who remained Fascist after the collapse of Fascism in 1943 and fought alongside the Nazis against the Allies and the Italian partisans during the last phase of World War II. He appears to have saved his skin by informing on his own comrades in the final months or weeks of the war. Along with a number of Nazi war criminals, he went to Argentina and became close to the Argentine strongman Juan Perón and returned to Italy and ran a mattress factory near Arezzo in Tuscany. Gelli, like many right-wing Italians, was alarmed at the leftward lurch the country had taken during the 1970s. Strikes were epidemic, and militant unions were extracting generous concessions from industry and the Italian Communist Party's vote total reached 34 percent, nearly surpassing that of the Christian Democrats. There were various attempted right-wing coup d'états planned, and bombs planted in hopes of provoking an authoritarian response; at the same time, left-wing terrorism grew and became increasingly violent. The Catholics and the Communists entered into a strange political partnership known as the "historic compromise," whereby the Christian Democrats continued to govern but with the external support of the Communists. The partnership was meant to stave off the risk of a right-wing coup as well as create a united front against left-wing terrorism; the Catholic–Communist alliance—anathema to Italian conservatives—greatly expanded and strengthened Italy's welfare state and social safety net. Although the historic compromise ended up benefiting the Christian Democrats more than the Communists politically, to many Italian conservatives it appeared to be the first step in a surrender to the hated Communists.[22]

Gelli's P2 Lodge appears to have been formed as part of an effort to reverse this leftward trend. He assembled an extraordinary collection of powerful figures, more than a dozen generals in the army and air force, the heads of military intelligence and foreign espionage, three ministers of the government, the commander of the Treasury Police, leading figures in the Carabinieri (the military police), the presidents of several leading Italian banks, leading figures in industry and the world of information, including Berlusconi and Angelo Rizzoli, who, at the time, owned the Rizzoli book and magazine group, the nation's leading newspaper, the *Corriere della Sera,* and, for a time, one of the new private TV networks. Many have described the P2 Lodge as a vast right-wing conspiracy and Gelli as a kind of evil puppeteer, pulling the strings behind the scenes of the country's political and economic life. Others have suggested that the P2 was little more than a somewhat unsavory mutual enrichment society, a huge networking operation that people joined in hopes of promotion, career advancement and lucrative connections. The reality appears to have been somewhere in between, with strong elements of both. Berlusconi, who initially lied about his enrollment in the P2 Lodge, once said that the "P2 assembled the best people in the country."[23] It is certainly true that it assembled many of the most powerful. But it could be argued that it assembled the worst of Italy's governing class: Italian generals, colonels and admirals who thought nothing of betraying their oath to serve the Italian state, swearing allegiance to the dubious enterprise of a notorious neofascist; high-level officials in the secret services who passed on classified information and secret personal dossiers that allowed Gelli to blackmail and intimidate people; presidents of state-owned banks who gave away public money in risky loans to fellow Lodge brothers who fit into some occult scheme or other. Gelli, for example, personally brokered a huge 8 billion lire ($30 million in current dollars) under-the-table payment made by the Banco Ambrosiano to Craxi and his Socialist party. As the financial condition of the Ambrosiano deteriorated, its president, Roberto Calvi, increasingly became putty in Gelli's hands, making more and more financially reckless moves in order to buy the political protection he hoped would stave off his bank's increasingly likely failure. At Gelli's instigation, the Ambrosiano purchased a large share of the Rizzoli–*Corriere della Sera* group, and Rizzoli and his general manager Bruno Tassan Din became P2 Lodge members. It is not an exaggeration to say that through the Ambrosiano, Gelli became a kind of secret de facto owner of the *Corriere* who exercised an important influence on the paper's direction. Rizzoli moved the paper decisively from center-left to center-right and picked an editor, Franco Di Bella, who was also a member of the P2 Masonic Lodge. The newspaper, among other things, ran a long, favorable interview with Gelli conducted by a journalist, Maurizio Costanzo, who was also a P2 Lodge brother (and ended up the host of Berlusconi's principal evening talk show), the interview that introduced this shadowy figure to the broader public for the first time. The Lodge's more sinister activities were uncovered in 1981 in the course of a Mafia investigation. Prosecutors were investigating the disappearance of Michele Sindona, the failed, fraudulent Sicilian banker who had faked his own kidnapping to release himself from the arms of American justice and had himself spirited back to Italy with the aid of Italian-American and Sicilian Mafiosi. In Italy, Sindona tried to blackmail his political friends to whom he had previously made illegal financial contributions in order to get them to bail out his failed bank. Sindona's network of protection consisted of a troubling mix of Sicilian Mafiosi and members of the P2 Lodge; by following one of the people who left one of Sindona's fake kidnapping demands, investigators were led to Gelli's secret files in Arezzo and Castiglion Fibocchi. There, investigators found a list of the P2 Lodge members, including Berlusconi.

Although Berlusconi may have been sympathetic to Gelli's desire to move the country toward the right, he probably joined principally out of simple economic self-interest and not out of some grand political design. There is little question that he did derive clear benefits from his membership. During the time of his membership, he was able to take huge loans on extremely favorable terms from banks whose directors were also P2 members. One parliamentary inquiry wrote that Berlusconi and other Lodge brothers "found support and financing way beyond their credit worthiness." An internal report of the Monte dei Paschi bank in Siena, one of the most generous lenders to Berlusconi, wrote that the "position of risk toward the Berlusconi group has exceptional dimensions and characteristics." The report noted that Berlusconi had enjoyed "preferential treatment," including lower than usual interest rates to be paid back over much longer than usual periods of time.[24]

Berlusconi was also a beneficiary of the P2's new hold over the *Corriere della Sera*. Just three months after joining the P2, Berlusconi became a prominent commentator on economic affairs for the *Corriere,* preaching a gospel of free-market economics, "less Karl Marx ... and more Adam Smith." It was certainly odd that the principal owner of one newspaper, the conservative *Il Giornale,* should be a columnist for one of its main competitors, but the years of the P2 were full of such anomalies.

Among the documents found during the investigation (captured at an airport in Gelli's daughter's suitcase) was his so-called "Plan for Democratic Renewal," which was his blueprint for reorganizing Italian politics. It indicated the politicians and parties that should be favored (Craxi and the Italian Socialist Party, conservative Christian Democrats, Giulio Andreotti and Arnaldo Forlani), all of whom ended up being the dominant political figures of the 1980s and among Berlusconi's political benefactors. Also on the list was a Socialist politician, Enrico Manca, whom Bettino Craxi would later make president of RAI during the 1980s, when RAI adopted a much more cooperative and less competitive attitude toward Berlusconi's Fininvest—and during which time Berlusconi's networks took away about half of RAI's market share.

Interestingly, a key part of Gelli's plan for "democratic renewal" involved taking control of the press. "We must make up a list of at least two elements for each daily newspaper, so that none of them knows of the others' existence. . . . To the journalists acquired will be given the task of 'sympathizing' with the political leaders mentioned above. At a later time, we must: a.) acquire magazines that do battle politically; b.) coordinate the local press through a centralized agency; c.) coordinate many cable television stations together with the agency for the local press; d.) dissolve RAI-TV in the name of freedom of broadcasting." Gelli's plan also included other elements that later became central parts of Berlusconi's political platform, such as creating a "presidential republic" that would give much more power to the executive branch, and placing the Italian judiciary under political control in order to limit the autonomy of the magistrature. Many Italian observers have noticed the considerable resemblances between Gelli's plans and many of Berlusconi's future actions (in particular the sponsorship of private television over public television) as proof that Berlusconi's political career has been little more than the enactment of Gelli's occult blueprint. Certainly, given Gelli's plan to reorganize Italian media, favoring private over public television, one can understand his interest in having Berlusconi as a member, but Berlusconi's interest in the P2 Lodge was probably primarily political protection and access to unlimited cheap credit.[25]

Still, the P2 episode greatly contradicts Berlusconi's claims of being a self-made man who succeeded entirely through his own talent despite opposition from the political world. Berlusconi sought undue advantages from a sleazy clique of public officials who thought little of violating their sworn duties in order to distribute public resources to other members of their confraternity as part of a plan for a rather undemocratic form of national renewal. The large number of prominent people in the P2 suggests that it was not an isolated phenomenon. If the principal disease of Italian political life is favoring the private clan over the public good, the P2 is one of its ultimate expressions. Still, its membership of approximately one thousand suggests that it was a relatively small minority, collecting the dregs of the Italian governing class—public officials with little faith in democracy resorting to private cabals; businessmen seeking personal gain at all cost; and managers of state enterprises prepared to mismanage the public resources for their own professional advancement—all under the banner of a sinister neofascist with a vague but troubling plan.

Many of those caught up in the scandal paid a considerable price for it. The *Corriere della Sera*, for example, was wrested away from Angelo Rizzoli, and its P2 editor, Franco Di Bella, was forced to resign. Berlusconi survived with little damage, playing down his involvement with a series of mendacious statements. He insisted that he had not really been a member, that he'd filled out an application at the insistence of a friend but never paid his dues. He joked about the absurdity that the "king of bricks" and builder of cities was listed as an "apprentice mason." He insisted that he had applied for membership shortly before the scandal broke in 1981. In fact, the parliamentary inquest into the scandal demonstrated clearly that Berlusconi had signed up and paid dues in 1978.

Berlusconi's ability to handle the potentially disastrous publicity from the P2 scandal is instructive for his later political career. When two enterprising investigative journalists, Giovanni Ruggeri and Mario Guarino, documented the mysterious origins of Berlusconi's fortune—the anonymous Swiss companies—as well as his involvement with the P2, Berlusconi took them to court before the book they were writing had even appeared. Rather than sue the book's publisher, Berlusconi took the rather innovative strategy of suing virtually any newspaper or magazine that tried to review the book or interview its authors. When the popular newspaper *La Notte* published a long interview with Ruggeri and Guarino, Berlusconi immediately threatened suit. Berlusconi personally called the editor, Pietro Giorgianni, telling him, "Writing about that book, you have risked my good will . . . I will reduce you to poverty." To which Giorgianni replied: "You can't, I'm already poor." Interestingly, in typical fashion, Berlusconi later hired Giorgianni to help run one of his cable TV networks and withdrew the lawsuit against him. Although Berlusconi is considered hot-tempered, he rarely lets personal feelings get in the way of his objective, in this case, silencing a potentially dangerous adversary, which he accomplished by threatening him with poverty and, eventually, giving him wealth.[26]

According to Guarino and Ruggeri, Berlusconi managed to have the publication of their book delayed by several months and even explored the possibility of buying the publishing house. They claim that a functionary of Fininvest, Sergio Roncucci, came to them and, "showing off a check book told us: 'We'll buy your book sight unseen. You can write the amount. . . .' He also mentioned the possibility of a position for us at the magazine *Sorrisi e Canzoni TV* [Smiles and Songs TV]."[27]

The book came out in the spring of 1987. Two editions were printed, each of which sold out in a matter of days, leading the authors to suspect that Fininvest had bought up most of the copies to keep them out of circulation. Despite the book's rapid sales, the publisher chose not to reprint. The authors suspect that the publisher's behavior may have been influenced by a favorable publicity arrangement involving Fininvest and the publisher.

"That's all garbage," says Fedele Confalonieri, Berlusconi's best friend and the president of Mediaset, Berlusconi's company. "We never sued the authors of that book, because we thought so little of it. It's nothing."[28]

But Berlusconi made good on his threats to sue virtually any newspaper or magazine that dared to talk about the book. These lawsuits were eventually thrown out, and Berlusconi was ordered by the courts to pay the defendants' legal fees. In a countersuit filed by Ruggeri and Guarino, Berlusconi was himself found to have lied in discussing his involvement with the P2 Lodge. In 1990, a court in Verona found that Berlusconi's sworn testimony "did not correspond to the truth," but Berlusconi avoided a conviction for perjury due to an amnesty passed that year—the first of many such pieces of good fortune in his career.

Chapter Four

❧

PROFESSIONE: AMICIZIA (PROFESSION: FRIENDSHIP)

1. "IT'S . . . IMPORTANT TO . . . LIKE YOURSELF, LIKE YOURSELF, LIKE YOURSELF"[1]

W hen we came out of our meetings with Berlusconi we really believed that we could sell the Cathedral of Milan or the Tower of Pisa," said Fabrizio, a salesman with Publitalia, the advertising wing of Berlusconi's TV empire, run by Marcello Dell'Utri. "Very little that Berlusconi has said or done in politics has surprised me, because so much of Berlusconi the politician was already in his management style and in the speeches he gave to the sales force." (Although Fabrizio expressed admiration for his company, he preferred that I not use his real name.)[2]

The way that Berlusconi ran his company was as much of a cultural revolution in the Italy of the 1980s as the programming on his TV stations. "The model of the Italian corporation at that time was extremely hierarchical; you were supposed to genuflect before a statue of the mother of the director general as you entered the office each morning like in the Fantozzi movies," Fabrizio said, referring to a series of popular Italian films of that period. Instead, Dell'Utri told his salesmen that they should not hesitate to call him directly if they needed his help to close a deal, without informing their immediate superior. Salesmen received incentives and bonuses, and advanced and made money more quickly than in most Italian companies. And although Berlusconi was an exalted figure, there was a lot of personal contact between the rank and file and their leader. "We would go to Milan once a month for meetings with Berlusconi himself where he would speak directly to the sales force. They organized courses and training sessions with leading people in all sorts of fields, sociology and politics—very innovative, unheard of in Italy at the time—that really created a kind of group spirit."

By contrast, the offices of SIPRA—the RAI advertising division—at that time seemed more like a sleepy government ministry; the clients were supposed to line up and wait. "They didn't go out and get clients, they just handed them a list of their prices," Fabrizio said. "We, on the other hand, did everything to win and keep our clients. We were supposed to do whatever we needed to make them our friends. We were supposed to know and remember the birthdates of our clients and their families, send flowers and gifts." Whenever a new Disney movie was about to come out, the company would organize a screening before the official opening, and invite all its clients and their families. Berlusconi hammered away at the sales force, encapsulating his message in a series of slogans he repeated like mantras: *Professione: amicizia* (Profession: friendship); *Il cuore oltre l'ostacolo* (Your heart beyond the obstacle); *Il sole in tasca* (The sun in your pocket).

Even after Berlusconi was a major national and international figure, he never forgot his sales force, speaking at training sessions and attending annual company retreats that were generally held in luxurious resort hotels in places like Saint-Tropez and Monte Carlo. "I remember once toward the end of one of these dinners, when we'd all had quite a bit to drink, I suddenly called out a Milan soccer chant—even though I'm not a Milan fan—'*Chi non sta con la Juve, salta!*' [Those who aren't with Juve, jump!] in which the fans are supposed to shout and then jump. Berlusconi heard it and leapt up onto the table—a table with white linen and glasses in a fancy hotel—and takes a table napkin and begins leading a cheer. '*Chi non sta con la Juve, salta!*' And the whole room begins to jump! Later, during that same retreat, some of us were drinking and singing late into the night and Berlusconi heard us up in his room and came downstairs and took the microphone and led the singing. That was very much the spirit of the company in those years."

Some have described Berlusconi as the greatest salesman in Europe, and transcripts of the talks that Berlusconi gave to his TV ad sales team give us an idea of the secret to his success. At different times, they resemble the rallies of a military leader, a politician, an athletic coach, but most of all they resemble the inspirational talks of an American self-help guru: "It's extremely important to be able to look at yourself in the morning and like yourself, like yourself, like yourself, like yourself. If you don't like yourself, you start the day off wrong, you're not sure of yourself and therefore you don't work well and can't do your best."[3]

The place to start, in Berlusconi's view, was with simple, elemental things like personal hygiene and physical fitness. "The first thing is the importance of being in shape, of feeling at ease," Berlusconi said. Berlusconi was a devotee of jogging at a time when physical exercise was as un-Italian as putting ketchup on spaghetti.[4]

Berlusconi's company salesmen were strongly discouraged from smoking, wearing beards or mustaches or having long or scruffy hair, and were told to keep their breath fresh, watch out for dandruff, and never, ever, to allow their palms to be sweaty. (I noticed that Fabrizio strictly observed the company canon.) "If you look bad, you won't sell anything," Berlusconi said. "Your physical appearance is a necessity. Why be surprised by all the talk of sweaty hands? There is nothing more unpleasant than receiving another person's bodily fluids when they shake your hand. The outcome of a contract—and therefore the life of the company—depends on a handshake, on the image that we present to clients, who are the real bosses."[5]

Being in shape, looking good, feeling well, liking yourself are keys to a radiant self-confidence. "You must have the sun in your pocket," he told his salesmen. "We must have a warm heart and the sun in our pockets. Because we must give this sun to others, it must always be there ready at hand, so that we can offer it, with a smile, to the person we have in front of us. Not only to our clients, but to all those around us, our officemates, our loved ones; remember this, when we go home the sun must enter with us, our loved ones expect it, they live waiting for it. . . . When we enter a room people must see and feel a positive, true presence. . . . With a smile, a gesture, a word, we must give to others what we have inside. . . . Along with the sun in our pocket for others, we must have one for ourselves as well, our own personal sun. Only this way can we have self-esteem, can we be satisfied and happy. Therefore, 'the sun in your pocket' always."[6]

One Publitalia executive, Enzo Ghigo, told a story about accompanying Berlusconi from the airport when Berlusconi asked him what kind of tree was lining the road at a certain point along their route. Ghigo didn't know but said he would find out and then telephoned Berlusconi's office with the answer. "Well, about four months later, when I saw Berlusconi with a group of people, he took me aside and said, 'Thanks for the information you gave me.' With all the commitments and problems he has, to remember me and those trees—it was one of those messages and attitudes from which you can really learn something. After something like that you realize the effect that remembering the birthday of your clients and their families can have. That's the key: the profession of friendship, based on lots of small gestures. You have no idea how many flowers I have brought to secretaries, how many invitations to La Scala [the Milan opera house], to the movies, to the theater. All things that don't cost anything—the company pays—but which are useful. The Doctor repeated to us, not once, but a hundred times: be nice to everyone."[7]

Along with exhibiting kindness, the perfect salesman must know how to play on the chords of human vanity and credulity. When driving home a point, Berlusconi told them, make up an anecdote or a quotation and attribute it to some famous person. "People are totally gullible, they drink up quotations!"[8] Berlusconi told the salesmen. "When I started to do television and no one believed me, I would attribute my own ideas to this or that American figure," he said in one of his company talks. "This way, the people listening to me looked at me . . . and thought: 'Well, if the Americans say so.'"[9] One of Berlusconi's favorites was an anecdote he made up about an encounter with William Paley, founder of CBS. In the apocryphal story, Paley, sitting in his office amid the skyscrapers of Manhattan, asked Berlusconi to tell him what time it was, based on the position of the sun. "'That's what a real TV station does: you should be able to turn on your TV and tell what time it is based on what program is on.' If I had told them it was my idea, they would have said: 'Who does this guy think he is?' Instead, they took it in with their mouths agape."[10]

The Paley story illustrates another sacred principle of Berlusconi's sales decalogue: always use images and stories instead of abstract concepts or ideas. "Every time you see your clients, speak to them in images rather than concepts," he said. "Logic is convincing but is easily forgotten, while the image strikes and remains in the memory. . . . That's why I talk to you in images: 'the sun in your pocket,' 'the heart beyond the obstacle.' When you tell someone that forty-six percent of Italians don't read newspapers, you offer them a statistic, important but cold. It has a much greater effect to tell them forty-six percent of Italians have never seen a newspaper advertisement. This is a fact that, once it's entered the client's head, isn't going to leave it."[11]

Still, the essential goal must always be "profession: friendship," getting along with the client, putting him at ease, making him feel that you are on his side. "Be concave with the convex, convex with the concave," he repeated again and again in an elegant reformulation of the famous nostrum "The customer is always right." The nastier and more unpleasant the client, Berlusconi said, the more kind and agreeable the salesman should be. One of Berlusconi's most memorable sales talks was about *il cliente stronzo*—"the asshole client" (literally the "shit client"). The talk is like the Sermon on the Mount of salesmanship, in which instead of the meek inheriting the earth, the worst clients become the best.

These are the clients that we must conquer at all costs, the clients we must absolutely not let slip through our hands, they are the clients we must absolutely reach above all others. Because when they wake up in the morning and look in the mirror, what do they see? An asshole. Day after day, every morning, the same horrible image. . . . And so the gentlemen who belong to this category are in a foul mood from the moment they wake up and stay in a foul mood for the whole day. . . . Because they are assholes, everyone treats them like assholes, since that's in fact what they are. . . . But this is where you enter the picture, with all your art and your cunning. Since everyone treats the asshole like an asshole, if someone comes along and treats him differently, he will be grateful, in fact extremely grateful, and will be less of an asshole. And so we have rendered a service to humanity. . . . Therefore we must win over these clients because they will become our most sincere friends, our most valuable clients, because they will always be grateful to us.[12]

2. "[Craxi's] the One Who Is Supposed to Do the Law for Us About Television"[13]

During the 1980s, you could say that Berlusconi's most important single client and, consequently, his best friend was Bettino Craxi, head of the Italian Socialist Party. Craxi was Berlusconi's guest almost every weekend at the villa at Arcore, as well as at his vacation villas in Portofino on the Italian Riviera and on the Emerald Coast of Sardinia. Later Craxi would be godfather to Berlusconi's children and best man at his second wedding.

In 1977, the year that Berlusconi officially became a media baron—buying an ownership share in the conservative newspaper *Il Giornale* and expanding his local TV channel Telemilano—he gave what is thought to be his first major press interview. On the subject of politics, he spoke favorably about the right wing of the Christian Democratic Party and the new conservative trend in the Socialist Party of Bettino Craxi. When asked how he intended to support these groups, he replied, "Certainly not by paying bribes"—a strangely defensive reply, since no one had mentioned anything about bribery—"but by placing my mass media at their disposal. First of all, Telemilano which I am reorganizing and which will become a meeting place for politicians who demonstrate that they have not lost contact with the world of economics, culture and public opinion."[14]

"Our news will be like the world that sees in people like Craxi, Forlani and in Andreotti the acceptance of freedom," Fedele Confalonieri announced, discussing the treatment of current affairs on the Berlusconi channels.[15] The choice of names on Confalonieri's part was hardly casual: these three men, Bettino Craxi, Arnaldo Forlani and Giulio Andreotti (a Socialist and two Christian Democrats), were the pillars of the political system that governed Italy from the end of the 1970s until the Berlusconi era that began in 1994. Based on an alliance between the Socialists and conservative Christian Democrats, it was known as the CAF, named after Craxi, Andreotti and Forlani. Of course, the freedom of private television from all regulation was part of the freedom that Confalonieri had in mind.

In its first years, private television in Italy did not have regular nightly newscasts but did run talk shows and information programs. In the summer of 1982, Berlusconi's TV network (now renamed Canale 5) broadcast live the congress of the Socialist Democratic Party, which had come out strongly in favor of private television and Berlusconi. Perhaps not coincidentally, the party's secretary and vice secretary were also fellow lodge brothers in Licio Gelli's P2 Masonic Lodge.

The political influence of Berlusconi's channels grew throughout the 1980s, in part because of the severe restrictions placed on the RAI. Political discussions on public television were carefully organized, somewhat dull and static *tribune politiche* (political debates) carefully monitored for equal time by the parliament. Perhaps more important, the state channels were not allowed to run any political advertising, leaving the entire lucrative and influential market of political advertising to Berlusconi. "The two Berlusconi networks [they expanded to three in 1984] became the principal means of communication for candidates and parties," write the authors Ruggeri and Guarino, in their early history of Berlusconi's television empire. "Hundreds of advertisements appeared on Canale 5 and Italia 1 and the handling of the cost of those ads became an important lever of pressure that Berlusconi could exercise vis-à-vis the government parties and their leaders. Obviously, the presence of Craxi and the Italian Socialist Party is dominant on the Berlusconi networks, thanks to which Craxi became prime minister [in 1983]." While this may be overstating things, a combination of Craxi's more aggressive leadership and greater visibility helped his party jump from 8 to 11.4 points in the 1983 elections, after which he became prime minister and one of the two or three most dominant figures of the governments of the 1980s.[16] Offering ads at well below market price may have been a means of indirectly financing the campaigns of friendly parties.

This support was not enough for Craxi, who was highly sensitive to criticism and expected unqualified support from all of Berlusconi's media holdings. While it was easier for Berlusconi to offer this on his TV stations, where he was absolute lord and master, it was harder with *Il Giornale,* the conservative Milan newspaper of which Berlusconi was a major shareholder but which was dominated by its editor and founder, Indro Montanelli, whom some believe to have been the greatest Italian journalist of the twentieth century. A youthful Fascist turned anti-Fascist, Montanelli began working for the *Corriere della Sera* in the 1930s and remained one of its most prestigious journalists until 1974, when he felt the newspaper began veering dangerously toward the left. Although traditionally a pillar of the Northern Italian bourgeoisie, in the 1970s the *Corriere* had begun to look with some sympathy on the so-called "historic compromise," the alliance between the Christian Democrats and the Italian Communist Party, and the possibility of the Communists' participating in the national government—something Montanelli regarded as anathema. Northern industrialists and the newspapers they owned were, in Montanelli's view, caving in to the increasingly aggressive demands of Communist labor unions amid an atmosphere of growing left-wing violence. Although the *Corriere* represented a wide range of views in its pages, Montanelli felt that the times called for a clear anti-Communist stance and an avowedly conservative paper. He led an exodus with about twenty prominent journalists from the *Corriere* and formed *Il Giornale,* making off with what Montanelli liked to call the *Corriere's* "family silver." In addition to many leading Italian journalists, *Il Giornale* also published a number of prominent foreign authors, such as Jean-François Revel and Raymond Aron, the playwright Eugene Ionesco, and the novelists Tom Wolfe and Anthony Burgess. Along with its militant anti-Communism, *Il Giornale* was an intelligent, lively and sophisticated paper. Although it had a clear political position, Montanelli was too honest and too much of a journalist not to cover, often with brutal candor, the warts and blemishes of the political parties his newspaper supported. "Hold your nose and vote Christian Democrat," Montanelli told his readers in 1976, when it looked as if the Italian Communist Party might overtake the Christian Democrats.

Although it was originally founded as a "cooperative" owned by the journalists who wrote the paper, *Il Giornale* quickly ran into financial difficulties, and in 1977 Berlusconi acquired a 12 percent share of the ownership, which he increased to 37.5 percent in 1979. Then, in 1987, with the newspaper still badly in debt, the journalists gave Berlusconi an absolute majority.

In 1977, Montanelli was "kneecapped" (shot in the legs) by the Red Brigades, and Berlusconi rushed to his hospital bed in tears. When Berlusconi's father died in 1989, Berlusconi told Montanelli that he now considered him his father. "He was very sincere and moving, although I'm sure he said the same thing to about ten different people."

Because their relationship began when Berlusconi was a young and little-known real estate developer and Montanelli was nearly twice his age and the country's most famous journalist, the journalist was in the dominant position, even as Berlusconi gradually acquired a larger and larger share of the newspaper. Although Berlusconi had hoped to be able to place "my mass media" at the disposal of his political allies, with Montanelli this proved difficult. While they shared a generic anti-Communism, Montanelli did not break with the *Corriere* and found his own newspaper in order to do Berlusconi's bidding, and his undiplomatic candor and poisonous wit created numerous problems for Berlusconi.

While Montanelli shared many of Bettino Craxi's political positions, he offered his readers a withering description of Craxi's arrogant and authoritarian personality. "Craxi has a notable—and most unfortunate—tendency to consider as enemies all those who are not prepared to act as his servants. To be fair, there are more than a few politicians with this same vice, but many of them at least manage to hide it. Craxi is among those who show it off to a point where he appears to be creating a cult of personality. Not that this necessarily displeases many of us Italians, quite the contrary. But when it comes to thugs [*guappi*], after Mussolini we have become more demanding: we can smell those who are made of cardboard right away."[17]

In the summer of 1983, after Craxi became prime minister—a position he would hold for the next four years—he began complaining vociferously to his friend Silvio about Montanelli and *Il Giornale*. The Treasury Police recorded some of these conversations because in that period Berlusconi was under investigation on suspicions of laundering Mafia money—a case that would eventually be dropped due to lack of evidence. Craxi was furious because *Il Giornale* had published a negative report on a cabinet meeting and run a photograph not of Craxi but of the leader of a small rival party. "It is a hostile newspaper . . . and naturally we will draw all the necessary consequences," Craxi fumed. "Along with its editor in chief repeatedly insulting me, it continues to maintain a hostile attitude—period—and we will take note of this and draw the necessary consequences."

Berlusconi tried to calm Craxi and promised to get tough with Montanelli: "I'll bang my fists on the table" and "cut off his funds," "I am going to show my claws . . . I'll tell him to fuck himself, Christ."[18]

Berlusconi then called the offices of *Il Giornale* and, after learning that Montanelli was away on vacation, chose to speak to the deputy editor, Gian Galeazzo Biazzi. He may have been relieved, because for all his bluster about banging his "fists on the table" and telling Montanelli to go "fuck himself," Berlusconi, who loves to be loved, has never been fond of direct confrontation. He handled the matter according to his own canon of good salesmanship, by being "concave with the convex and convex with the concave," promising toughness to Craxi but avoiding a fight with Montanelli, working quietly behind the scenes, trying to influence the direction of *Il Giornale* by secretly establishing a private relationship with the deputy editor. At that point, he might well have lost a showdown with Montanelli, who counted for much more on the national scene than Berlusconi. On reaching Biazzi, after describing Craxi's furious rage, Berlusconi was very plain about what was at stake: "He's the one who is supposed to do the law for us about television. . . . He also did me a particular favor, which I will tell you about when I see you. . . . We have this friend [Craxi], I've done everything I could to help him with his election campaign, and then to ruin the friendship because of, all things, *Il Giornale*."[19]

All things considered, Berlusconi appears to have had limited success in influencing *Il Giornale*. Montanelli liked to brag that Berlusconi was "the owner but not the boss" of the paper and that he didn't let him stick his nose into the paper's business. Montanelli told friends that Berlusconi begged Montanelli to at least spare Craxi in the Saturday paper, since the Socialist leader was almost always his houseguest at Arcore during the weekends. "So after that I made a point of attacking Craxi in my Saturday column," Montanelli said.

But it is not entirely true that Berlusconi had no influence on editorial policy at *Il Giornale*. Montanelli briefly resigned from the paper when Berlusconi managed to water down a long exposé on the P2 Masonic Lodge, which could have been embarrassing for former members like him. Berlusconi managed to kill an interview with the captain of the Milan soccer team who was quoted as saying that Berlusconi was more useful on the sidelines as a fan than as the team's owner. It is also quite possible, as the wiretapped conversation between Berlusconi and the deputy editor shows, that Berlusconi may have been able to influence coverage in the paper more than Montanelli knew by going behind his back.

A daily newspaper is a large, complex organism, publishing hundreds of pages of copy each week, more than any single person can effectively edit and control. By the 1980s, Montanelli, while still vigorous, was in his seventies and delegated much of the day-to-day operation of the newspaper to his deputy editors, with whom Berlusconi seems to have gone out of his way to cultivate close personal relations. While Montanelli and the newspaper published many pieces that may have annoyed Berlusconi and Craxi, the paper also ran a number of pieces that played nicely into their hands. For example, *Il Giornale* backed Craxi's campaign for a "more just justice," an attempt to hold Italian magistrates criminally responsible for judicial errors, as well as to limit the powers of the Italian judiciary. Since Craxi was greatly expanding the party's efforts to collect bribes to finance his party, he appears to have been moving proactively to try to prevent the kind of political-corruption investigations that would later emerge, in the early 1990s, known as Operation Clean Hands. Craxi, for example, brought charges against a magistrate, Carlo Palermo, who had tried to prosecute a member of Craxi's entourage involved in an arms-trafficking case who was later revealed to be one of Craxi's principal "bag men" in collecting under-the-table funds for the party. *Il Giornale* also adopted a strangely critical attitude toward the anti-Mafia pool of Palermo—a group one might have expected a conservative paper with a strong appreciation of law and order to have looked on with particular favor. The paper also conducted a long series of tough investigative pieces about the corruption and stealing of earthquake relief funds in Irpinia, an area in Southern Italy. The principal target of the pieces was Ciriaco De Mita, the Christian Democratic boss of Irpinia, the politician who most energetically tried to break up Berlusconi's TV monopoly in the 1980s and early 1990s and one of Bettino Craxi's main opponents.[20]

3. The Girls from *Drive In*

The profession of friendship was frequently an arduous one, occupying Berlusconi's evenings, nights and weekends as well as his working days. We get a glimpse of this from a wiretapped phone call between Berlusconi and Marcello Dell'Utri on New Year's Eve, 1986. They spoke in order to exchange greetings and to commiserate about their respective New Year's plans. Dell'Utri was preparing to go to a dinner at the home of a major advertising client—"2.6 billion lire for us in 1986 and hopefully more in 1987"—while Berlusconi was toasting with Craxi, who was in another foul mood. [21]

BERLUSCONI: The New Year is off to a bad start!

DELL'UTRI: Why?

BERLUSCONI: Because two girls from *Drive In* [a Fininvest TV show]
    were supposed to come and they stood us up! And Craxi is out
    of his mind with anger!

DELL'UTRI: What do you care about *Drive In*?

BERLUSCONI: What do I care? It means we're not going to fuck! If the
    year starts like this, it means we won't fuck anymore!

DELL'UTRI: Okay, but let him go fuck somewhere else![22]

Craxi, in many ways, fit the classic definition of the *cliente stronzo*: arrogant and imperious, endlessly and unreasonably demanding, irascible and
prone to fits of rage, but, at the same time, fiercely loyal and prepared to
stop at nothing for his friend Berlusconi.

Sex and corruption were hardly new to Italian political life, but the os-
tentation of the *dolce vita* among Italian politics was something new.
While there was a fair degree of corruption among the Christian Democrats and a couple of sex scandals, the national leaders such as Alcide De
Gasperi, Aldo Moro and Giulio Andreotti were gray, austere-looking
men, with a priestly bearing who appeared to live modestly and whose
public appearances tended to be limited to attending mass at their local
church. The Italian Communists were required to give one-third of their
salary back to the party, and the party deputies generally lived in small,
book-lined apartments. Even if some of them flouted convention by living with rather than marrying their female comrades, they tended toward
stable long-term relationships and regarded leading a disorderly personal
life as another manifestation of bourgeois decadence. The Craxian
Socialists—like the "Greed is good" followers of Ronald Reagan—were
an anthropologically new breed, who wanted to do away with all
hypocrisy about money, power and other matters.

Craxi brought a new cold-eyed realism to Italian government. He
dared to eliminate automatic cost-of-living increases for workers in order
to combat inflation. He challenged the ambiguous foreign policy of the

Communists, who hovered between NATO and the USSR, and pushed for an unabashedly pro-Western, pro-American foreign policy. But somewhere along the way, he and his party lost track of many of the ideals that may have originally animated them. "At the beginning of the 1980s, with the triumph of Reaganism and the failure of social democracy, Craxi's old ideals collapsed and were replaced by the new values of success, extreme competitiveness and a passion for money," explained a former close friend and Socialist, Carlo Ripa di Meana.[23]

On a personal level, the Socialists seemed to go out of their way to show that they had money and knew how to spend it. While moving toward the right politically, the Socialists wanted to distinguish themselves as culturally to the left, supporting divorce and abortion rights and showing that at least in terms of personal and sexual mores they had not abandoned their allegiance to the revolutions of the late 1960s. Claudio Martelli, Craxi's deputy—a man with movie-star good looks and spectacularly grand homes in Rome—was briefly detained at an airport security check with marijuana on his person, proving that he was a politician of a new breed, combining the libertine habits of his generation with the arrogance of power typical of Craxism: presumably, it never occurred to him that the right-hand man of Bettino Craxi would have to worry about airport searches or complying with drug laws. And who could blame him? The episode passed without repercussions, and he went on to become minister of justice and deputy prime minister.

There was Gianni De Michelis, who, even when he was a government minister, had no qualms about appearing regularly in the popular press, dancing the night away in the capital's hottest discothèques—awkwardly gyrating his obese frame and swinging his long, permanently greasy hair amid a harem of starlets or pretty young things. He was unembarrassed to give interviews about his sex life. "I like to be seduced," he said.

Then there was Craxi himself, nicknamed Bokassa (after the corrupt African dictator), who lived between Milan, his villa in Tunisia, and apartments in New York and Barcelona he bought with bribe money, and who held court in the Hotel Raphael in Rome, where he took over an entire floor for more than ten years, without, apparently, ever paying a lira in rent. It was also an open secret that Craxi kept a mistress in Rome, the former actress Anja Pieroni, for whom he bought an apartment, furs and a job as the head of local TV station, which he kept afloat with 100 million lire a month (about $100,000) in party funds and by strong-arming friendly businesses to give money to the station in the form of advertising.[24]

Berlusconi, unlike some of his Socialist Party friends, did not have a reputation as a party animal. He had grandiose villas and a private jet and helicopter and entertained lavishly, but he preferred to do so at home rather than attend other people's parties. He was famous for working twelve- or sixteen-hour days. His closest friends, like Fedele Confalonieri and Marcello Dell'Utri, were also his closest colleagues, and dinners at Arcore were often work meetings that continued after dinner. He rarely drank to excess, never smoked, tried to jog regularly and watched his weight. He did, however, develop a large reputation as a ladies' man, something he did little to discourage. He referred to his sexual conquests in his public speeches, and on arriving late to business meetings, even with strangers, he would excuse himself by saying he had been delayed by an amorous dalliance.

Sex has anything but a trivial place in Berlusconi's life, in the image of himself he has constructed, in the popular culture he created in Italy and in his political appeal to voters. On the one hand, Berlusconi is a traditional Italian macho, the kind of guy who can be found bragging about his sexual prowess at the local bar in most towns across Italy. On the other, there is something new and subversive about Berlusconi's attitudes toward sex, pushing and overstepping boundaries. He has introduced sex into whole new areas of public life—television, sales meetings, press conferences and encounters with world leaders.

"Silvio, even from the time we were in short pants, was the good-looking kid in the neighborhood who knocked out the girls," Fedele Confalonieri said.[25] All of Berlusconi's stories about his youth, and not only his youth, invariably turn to his sexual adventures and conquests. His way of breaking the ice with foreign leaders has been to tell them about some woman from their country whose favors he has enjoyed. Seduction is part of his strategy as a salesman. "As a young man, I used to think, How many women would like to go to bed with me but don't know it. Life is a question of communication."[26]

In his personal life, Berlusconi has managed to play the roles of Latin lover and devoted family man simultaneously. He married Carla Dell'Oglio in 1965 and with her produced two children, Pier Silvio and Marina, who currently help run his business empire. But in 1980 he fell violently in love with a beautiful young actress, Miriam Bartolini, who went by the stage name Veronica Lario. Berlusconi first saw her at the Manzoni theater in Milan, a theater that Berlusconi bought as a favor to the Craxian Socialists of Milan. Veronica was acting in a play called *The Magnificent Cuckold*, whose dramatic climax occurred when the beautiful young actress removed her blouse, revealing her famously voluptuous nude figure. "There was no thunder or rain, but I was struck by lightning," Berlusconi later said. When Veronica returned to her dressing room after the show, the owner of the Manzoni theater was there waiting for her. While still married to and living with his wife, Berlusconi set Veronica and her mother up in an apartment near his office. In 1984, Veronica gave birth to a child, Barbara. Although he kept things quiet, Berlusconi acknowledged the child and her mother and indeed had her baptized in his name. The godfather was Bettino Craxi. Thus, for a period of about six years, Berlusconi led a double life, with two women and two families. Then, in 1986, he divorced Carla. He and Veronica had two more children out of wedlock, Eleonora in 1986, and Luigi in 1988. In 1990, he finally married Veronica at a very small private wedding. The witnesses were Bettino Craxi and his wife, Fedele Confalonieri and Gianni Letta, another top Fininvest executive.

Berlusconi is characterized by a combination of classic gallantry and misogyny in his relations with women. He urged his salesmen to give flowers to their secretaries and to all female employees on "women's day." As prime minister, he wrote and recorded an album of love songs and gave a copy to all the women who worked in the prime minister's palace.

At one point he told an audience of clients, "I have the good fortune of being attracted to stupid women. Don't laugh, let me explain. . . . There is an undeniable reality: often men prefer women who are less intelligent than they are. You women have everything: extraordinary talent, a superior sensibility, lasting beauty and charm. You have everything. If you also have greater intelligence, you make our life impossible."[27]

At the same time, Berlusconi is by all reports a model son, who always invites his elderly mother to the dinners at Arcore no matter how important the other guests. He also has the reputation of treating the women who work under him extremely well. "Berlusconi has an enormous respect for the people who work with him and for him," his devoted long-time secretary, Marinella Brambilla, has said. "He has a sense of humor. He has enthusiasm and an interior force that he transmits to all the people he meets. . . . He is capable of astounding you by remembering some date related to a highly personal family or professional event, sending you a note, giving you a little present, making an unexpected phone call." Berlusconi is a generous employer who enjoys giving raises without being asked. "Marinella, you just got richer!" he will suddenly tell his secretary.[28]

Berlusconi, like many Latin men, seems to have two groupings for women: the Madonna and the whore. His television stations play nicely into these two deeply ingrained categories. Part of Berlusconi's success in taking away the audience from RAI was the heavy emphasis on sex in his programming. In the course of the 1980s, Italy went from a country where *Dallas* was too risqué for Italian audiences to one in which sex and nudity (almost always female) were commonplace even on prime-time TV. For the men, it was the classic formula of "sex sells" abundantly on view on the Berlusconi networks. This was captured on one of the wiretaps recording conversations between Berlusconi and Marcello Dell'Utri. "Let the tits be tits! Make sure the tits get plenty of makeup!" Berlusconi told Dell'Utri.[29]

The archetypal Berlusconi program was *Colpo Grosso* (Big Hit), perhaps the world's first nude game show, featuring a male and female contestant who would be forced to gradually remove their clothes. The rules at the game were inane and incomprehensible, but what mattered was that, invariably, at the end of each game, the two were reduced to their underwear, the man in his briefs, the woman topless. The program was so successful it was exported to various other countries—anticipating a form of reality TV and spreading a new form of Italian culture, so to speak, around the world.

At the same time, there was a softer, gauzier sexuality for the shows with women audiences, based on Berlusconi's assumption that women want to dream about romance. In one of his training sessions he made modifications in an advertising trailer with women specifically in mind. "This part of the promo is for a feminine audience and so we need beautiful, intense images that make them dream. What you have shown here does the opposite. . . . Look at the background behind that kiss: a squalid house, a run-down wall and what furniture in that room! I don't want to see these things . . . I want a beautiful sequence of kisses and close-ups of the faces of the characters."[30]

Berlusconi helped to create an imaginary world in which there was no poverty, no squalid houses, a world of wealth, beautiful houses and beautiful men and women. "Beauty is the logical and natural objective toward which everyone is naturally drawn," he said.[31]

But Arcore is fundamentally a male domain. Veronica and her children were placed in their own villa nearby, leaving Berlusconi's showcase to himself and his guests. One of the greatest pleasures of sex was being able to talk about it with friends. The dinner meetings at Arcore were always lightened up with ribald stories and references to the boss's prodigious sex life. "When we would have our evening meetings at Arcore, which might go on to midnight or one in the morning, Berlusconi would bid us good night, saying something like 'Lucky you who can go off to sleep, I have much, much left to do!'" said his former corporate attorney Vittorio Dotti. Part of the cult of personality that developed around Berlusconi was based on the notion that even in the sexual realm Berlusconi was a miracle worker. After a dinner celebrating his soccer team's international championship victory, Berlusconi, after bidding good night to his guests at the gates of his villa, clapped his wife Veronica on the rear end and said, loud enough to be overheard by the departing revelers, *"Adesso, vedrai come scopa il campione del mondo!"* "Now you'll see how the champion of the world fucks!"[32]

And yet the sex in Berlusconi's world appears to be as much or more about the men as about the women, as one of the principal pleasures of sex consists in talking with your male friends about it. One of Berlusconi's favorite jokes is the story of an Italian truck driver, Mario, who is shipwrecked on a desert island with German supermodel Claudia Schiffer. After a while, Schiffer gives in to Mario's advances and then falls head over heels in love with him. After achieving his great conquest, Mario gradually becomes impatient and bored with the German beauty and finds himself missing his best friend back in Italy. At a certain point, he asks Claudia Schiffer if she minds wearing pants. She obliges. He asks her if she minds painting a mustache on her face and she agrees. Finally, he asks her if she minds his calling her Domenico, the name of his best friend. When she agrees, Mario then says. "Domenico, you're not going to believe it, I'm fucking Claudia Schiffer!"[33]

Berlusconi was a bit this way about Veronica as well; he was known to show off photographs of her that left few mysteries about her centerfold figure. When Indro Montanelli first encountered Veronica at Berlusconi's villa at Portofino (on the Italian Riviera), she was sunbathing in the nude on the rocks, reading a philosophy book. "Don't worry," Montanelli said, "you're not showing me anything I haven't already seen in the photographs your husband showed me."[34]

In the male inner circle, there is fierce loyalty toward Berlusconi. Fedele Confalonieri speaks about him as a genius, the Mozart of Italian business and a beautiful person who has created jobs and a good life for tens of thousands of people, while giving entertainment and prosperity to millions of others. "He's our guiding star," Cesare Previti has said. "Berlusconi is extraordinary not only for what he's done but what he's allowed others to do," said Marcello Dell'Utri. "The world is full of ordinary people like me," said Confalonieri several years ago. "Generally, those kind of people stand and watch life from high up in the balcony.

I have had the good fortune of knowing a man who took me up into the front row with him. And from there, I have had a chance to see a world of important people like Craxi, Agnelli, Montanelli . . ."[35]

Berlusconi has fused his business and private life almost totally. His oldest childhood friend, Confalonieri, is president of Mediaset. Two of his closest friends from the Salesian boarding school that he attended as a child are, respectively, a senator with Forza Italia and an undersecretary of education. He turned his tennis instructor into a television ad salesman. He has used cousins, aunts and uncles in numerous business affairs, usually as the titular owners of some of the complex holding companies and shell businesses that have helped hide the real ownership of Mediaset. Berlusconi always brings his friends with him on vacation.

Some are more cynical about the bonds of loyalty within Berlusconi's world. "The thing you need to understand about Berlusconi," a Milanese businessman told me, "is that he has made all of the people around him rich. I don't just mean well-off, I mean *really, really* rich." Indeed, prosecutors investigating Berlusconi's company finances were surprised to find enormous personal gifts, beyond bonuses and raises, of millions of dollars to Confalonieri, Dell'Utri and others.[36]

"Berlusconi is one of the coldest people I've ever met. He does nothing that is not strictly calculated," said one high-level executive who worked with him for several years. "These friendships are based on blackmail. The people in his inner circle are the ones who know where all the skeletons in the closet are hidden."

Others believe that the loyalty toward Berlusconi is very real. "I have spent time with Berlusconi's secretary, Marinella, and I have no doubt that if she knew a bullet were heading toward Berlusconi she would put herself in front of it," a fellow journalist told me. "Not many people can count on that kind of loyalty."

$\dot{\sim}$

While Berlusconi set about making new friends, he did not forget about his old ones, or rather, they did not forget about him. Just after midnight on November 29, 1986, just a month before the New Year's Eve in which

Berlusconi and Bettino Craxi were stood up by "the girls from *Drive In*," Berlusconi placed an anxious call to the home of Marcello Dell'Utri. Someone had exploded a bomb at the gates of the Fininvest corporate offices in Milan. "It's Mangano," Berlusconi speculated. He said that he and Fedele Confalonieri were "scared to death" leaving the office and urged Dell'Utri to find out who might have set the bomb. "It's important!"

Dell'Utri immediately set up a meeting with his friend Gaetano Cinà, the dry cleaner from Palermo who introduced Dell'Utri to Mangano and who helped him get his job with Filippo Alberto Rapisarda. The day after the bomb in Via Rovani, Cinà reassured Dell'Utri that Mangano was still in prison and that Berlusconi had nothing to worry about. Dell'Utri then called Berlusconi to pass on the good news. "Tanino [nickname for Gaetano] told me that this [possibility] can be excluded, categorically excluded."[37]

After Mangano became the focus of several major criminal investigations in the 1980s and began to spend most of his time in prison, Dell'Utri and Berlusconi heard less frequently from their old stable hand. But Dell'Utri continued to see a great deal of his friend Gaetano Cinà. Various Mafia witnesses have testified that Cinà was delegated by Cosa Nostra to take over the role as go-between for the Mafia and Berlusconi's businesses after Mangano was rearrested in 1980. Mangano, they say, had proved too unpredictable in his behavior, and after his conviction for heroin trafficking, he was on trial or in jail for much of the rest of his life, making him poorly suited to the role of "ambassador" to what was becoming one of the biggest businesses in Italy. Cinà was much better suited to the task. Although his name kept cropping up in police wiretaps, he did not have a criminal record and was by all appearances a respectable small businessman, owner of a dry cleaning shop and a sporting goods store in Palermo, and he was in regular contact with Dell'Utri.

Dell'Utri has defended himself against accusations of collusion with the Mafia by saying of Cinà that he "never had any sensation that he might be close to Mafia circles" and he was simply a very good old friend. Cinà had helped Dell'Utri run the soccer club he managed in Palermo and Cinà's son was an aspiring professional soccer player who was a member of Dell'Utri's team. But the idea that Dell'Utri would have had no idea that Cinà had any connection to the Mafia is patently absurd. It was Cinà who introduced Dell'Utri to Vittorio Mangano, Cinà who introduced him to Filippo Alberto Rapisarda, the mob-connected businessman, and it was Cinà who took him to the London wedding of convicted drug trafficker Jimmy Fauci. Given all the gangsters whom Cinà introduced him to, one might think that Dell'Utri would have begun to wonder about who Gaetano Cinà was.

That Dell'Utri understood very well that Cinà was closely connected to the Mafia is demonstrated clearly by the episode of the bomb that exploded outside of the Fininvest offices in November of 1986. Why would Dell'Utri go to see someone he never suspected of being "close to Mafia circles" to find out whether the Mafia had planted a bomb near Berlusconi's office?

In fact, another thing that the wiretapped conversations and the bomb episode make very clear is that Berlusconi also knows very well who Gaetano Cinà (referred to without any introduction by his nickname "Tanino") is, and he finds it natural that Dell'Utri should go see Cinà to find out who might be planting bombs outside his office.

Although his businesses were in Palermo, Cinà appears to have spent a lot of time in Milan and went with Dell'Utri (and perhaps Berlusconi) to the soccer stadium to watch Berlusconi's soccer team, A. C. Milan, play. Cinà also appears to have visited the Fininvest offices in Milan and to have participated in a company meeting that included Berlusconi. For the owner of a dry cleaning shop and a sporting goods store in Palermo, Cinà moved in pretty high circles.

Berlusconi's rise to the top, rather than moving him away from the frightening world of Vittorio Mangano, exposed him to new risks and made him vulnerable in new ways. In establishing his national television network, Berlusconi bought up local television stations and set up broadcast towers in Sicily as in other parts of Italy. It is axiomatic among those who have done business in Sicily that it would be impossible to put up and operate television towers in Sicily without paying *il pizzo* (protection money) to Cosa Nostra. (Mafia witnesses have testified that the conduits for these payments were first Mangano and then Gaetano Cinà.)

What the wiretapped conversations make clear is that Berlusconi turns to Dell'Utri when he has a problem he suspects is Mafia-related. He expects and encourages Dell'Utri to use his contacts in this world to help him resolve a problem. Thus Dell'Utri's connections to organized crime are not a liability but an asset, part of Dell'Utri's function in Berlusconi's world, the source of part of his power.

Police captured another flurry of phone calls around Christmastime in 1986, less than a month after the bomb exploded in Via Rovani, that show another curious aspect of this strange web of friendship. They regard a series of *cassate siciliane* (Sicilian cakes) that Cinà has had specially baked for Berlusconi, Dell'Utri, Fedele Confalonieri and Alberto Dell'Utri, Marcello's twin brother, who also works for Berlusconi. The cake for Berlusconi was so large—about twelve kilos (more than twenty-five pounds)— that Cinà had to have a carpenter make a special wooden box to ship it from Palermo to Milan. Cinà went to a great deal of trouble to have a bison, the symbol of Berlusconi's company, depicted in icing atop the cake. Cinà phoned on Christmas day to make sure that Berlusconi's giant *cassata* had arrived safely and that its monumental size was appreciated.

Certainly all these lavish, ceremonial gifts and such extreme familiarity are more reflective of a person whom prosecutors have termed an "ambassador of Cosa Nostra in Northern Italy" than a typical Palermo dry cleaner. The magnificent *cassate*—with the symbol of Canale 5 on them— seem like a kind of feudal tribute to Berlusconi, a recognition of his exalted position in the world. At the same time, the cake's excessive size and extravagance is also an assertion of power that calls attention to the importance of its giver as well.

The wiretaps show Cinà speaking to Dell'Utri in favor of a couple of corrupt politicians with known ties to the Mafia, in one case discussing the man's legal defense in a criminal investigation—apparently part of his role within Cosa Nostra. "[Boss of bosses Salvatore "Totò"] Riina was interested in the contacts with Dell'Utri for two reasons," said Calogero Ganci, a Mafia witness who was part of the boss of bosses inner circle. "First because he was part of a group that could generate wealth in Sicily and that always interests Cosa Nostra. In the second place, because

Dell'Utri was Berlusconi's man and Berlusconi was close to [Bettino] Craxi at the time. Riina was always very interested in acquiring contacts with important politicians. I remember that in 1987 Riina gave the order to vote for the Italian Socialist Party, and the order was followed in rock-solid fashion." Craxi, at the time one of the two or three most powerful politicians in Italy, began pushing penal reform in 1987 that greatly favored criminal defendants over prosecutors. The Socialists increased their vote total in Sicily during the 1987 elections.[38]

4. FEAR FACTOR

The Christmas cakes of 1986 did not, however, signal eternal peace between Berlusconi and the Mafia. Less than two years later, in February of 1988, Berlusconi revealed to a friend in a telephone call that was recorded by police that he had once again received kidnapping threats against his children.

BERLUSCONI: I'm in bad shape and have all kinds of problems. One particularly bad one, for which I have to send my kids out of the country. They're leaving the country now, because they're practicing extortion . . . in a very ugly way. . . . It's something that's happened to me other times, ten years ago . . . they've turned up again. You know, they've told me that if I don't do something before a certain date, they will send me my son's head and display his body in Piazza del Duomo . . . and so those aren't very nice things to hear and so I'm going to send them to America.

RENATO DALLA VALLE [FRIEND]: When is the deadline these criminals have given you?

BERLUSCONI: In six days.[39]

According to Mafia witnesses, Totò Riina orchestrated these threats, obtaining Berlusconi's private number at Arcore through Gaetano Cinà. He arranged to have the threatening calls placed from Catania to create a kind of "good cop–bad cop" dynamic, with the Catanese Mafia playing the role of villain so that the Palermo Mafia could again play the role of Berlusconi's protector. While Berlusconi was certainly a victim in this situation, it shows once again that he was deeply enmeshed in a long-standing relationship of threats and blackmail with Cosa Nostra that had by this point been going on for fifteen years. For whatever reason, Berlusconi did not feel he could pick up the phone and call the police even now that he was one of the richest men in the country and the close, close friend of Bettino Craxi, who had just finished a four-year term as prime minister and remained one of the most powerful men in Italy. The ability to get to Berlusconi and genuinely frighten him at repeated intervals is a recurring leitmotif in his life. Berlusconi refused to tell judges in Palermo what it was the potential killers wanted him to do or whether he in fact did it.

At about that time, in 1988, Berlusconi increased his presence in Sicily by acquiring the national department store chain Standa. Subsequently, some of his stores in Catania, Sicily, were firebombed, causing significant property damage. Apparently, Berlusconi wanted to have Standa expand into the food business, and in Catania the supermarkets were in the hands of one of the local Mafia families. In 1992, Dell'Utri traveled to Catania thirty-two times, up from four trips the previous year. Standa decided to get out of the food business and the arsonous fires stopped.[40]

Chapter Five

THE *PAX TELEVISIVA* AND THE EXPANSION OF FININVEST

1. TAKEOVERS

The friendship/alliance between Berlusconi and Craxi worked in an increasingly synergistic fashion during the 1980s. In 1986, the Ministry of the Post Office and Telecommunications authorized (indeed, required) the Fininvest channels to broadcast news each day. Later that year, Craxi appointed one of his Socialist faithful, Enrico Manca—whose name had turned up in the membership lists of the secret P2 Masonic Lodge—president of RAI. Manca was also a client of Cesare Previti, Berlusconi's lawyer, and Previti reportedly hosted a meeting between Berlusconi and Manca that led to what has been termed the *pax televisiva,* a kind of truce between RAI and Fininvest. As an editorialist for the *Corriere della Sera* commented at the time: "It is not surprising that the term *pax televisiva* was coined by the socialists and then repeated by Enrico Manca. Normally, however, the side that sues for peace knows it can no longer win the war, and even though the new socialist president of RAI presents himself as an ardent supporter of public TV, it is clear that he has been put in his current job also to prevent the defeat of the private networks."[1]

How the "television peace" worked is clear from a couple of episodes from this period. When the director general of RAI, Sergio Zavoli, convinced a popular TV personality to turn down an offer from Fininvest and remain with the state network, Craxi had him summoned to the prime minister's office for a dressing-down, made him wait outside and then re-fused to see him as a form of humiliation. At another point, the Socialists fought hard to lower the limit of advertising that RAI could collect, leav-ing Berlusconi's Fininvest with a larger share of the pie. In the years of Craxi's mandate as prime minister (1983 to 1987) and the *pax televisiva*, Fininvest's audience share grew from about 34 percent to nearly 45 per-cent.[2]

In 1998, when called to testify in the bribery trial of Cesare Previti, Manca revealed that Berlusconi's lawyer had opened and managed a Swiss bank account for Manca that contained 1.2 billion lire—(more than twice what Berlusconi paid for the villa at Arcore). What was the president of RAI doing with a private Swiss bank account managed by the lawyer for Fininvest, his biggest competitor? Manca insisted that Previti had not given him money but simply helped him move money he had gained from an inheritance and the sale from a house to Switzerland. (This would have made Manca guilty merely of tax evasion—a crime whose statute of lim-itations had run out.) But it is rather striking that Manca's financial good fortune and the opening of the account date from 1986, the year that Manca became president of RAI and became a person of great value to Berlusconi. (It's also interesting how so many public officials who have been called on to testify in Previti's trials seem to have enjoyed similarly sudden and undocumented financial windfalls: a winning streak at the roulette wheel, a lucky pick on the stock market, an unexpected inheri-tance, undeclared earnings from house sales.)[3]

At the same time, Craxi began using Berlusconi as a kind of corporate battering ram to fight takeover battles against financial interests that Craxi considered hostile to him. In 1985, for example, Craxi called on Berlu-sconi and asked him to help organize a takeover bid for the food company SME, which manufactured, among other things, the pasta brand Buitoni. At the time, SME belonged to the Italian state and was being sold off to try to reduce the government debt and begin a process of privatization.

But Craxi was alarmed because the state-owned company IRI had agreed to sell SME to the financier Carlo DeBenedetti, whom Craxi regarded as an enemy. DeBenedetti, who had been the head of the Olivetti typewriter and computer company, although a wealthy capitalist and hardly a radical, was perceived as being too sympathetic to the Italian left. Moreover, the deal had been negotiated by the economist Romano Prodi (future prime minister and opponent of Berlusconi), who was associated with the left wing of the Christian Democratic Party, the wing of the party that was more open to negotiation with the Italian Communists, and regarded both Craxi and Berlusconi with suspicion.

Prodi and DeBenedetti had agreed to a sale price of 500 billion lire (about $260 million at the time)—considered a fair market price by various independent audits. Berlusconi, although having no interest in entering the food business, helped organize a consortium, including two Italian food companies, that suddenly came up with an offer of 600 billion lire. Craxi, Berlusconi later testified, "was insistent that . . . I try to come up with an offer . . . and I have to say I didn't really mind because I had some unfinished business with Mr. DeBenedetti." DeBenedetti insisted that his deal, signed and approved, was complete, but the Berlusconi consortium insisted that the higher offer obliged the state to halt the sale in the name of the public good. The matter ended up in court. The sale of SME was blocked, and having taken too much heat, DeBenedetti moved on to other projects. Having achieved their objective—preventing DeBenedetti from acquiring SME—Berlusconi and his group withdrew from the field.[4]

Berlusconi played a similar role in a considerably more important takeover battle, one in which he had more to gain. In 1986, Carlo DeBenedetti had acquired an important ownership share of the Mondadori publishing group, which was then and continues to be the largest publishing conglomerate in Italy. Along with being the biggest publisher of books, Mondadori publishes a raft of popular magazines, including *Panorama,* the country's largest-selling newsmagazine. Berlusconi also held a share of Mondadori—8 percent to DeBenedetti's 16 percent—while two branches of the Mondadori family owned just over 50 percent. In 1987, Mario

Formenton, the CEO of Mondadori and husband of Cristina Mondadori (who owned 25 percent of the company) died suddenly, and a battle for control of the company ensued. In 1988, DeBenedetti entered into an agreement to acquire the shares of the Formenton-Mondadori family, giving him effective control of the company. A price was stipulated and the agreement signed, but the shares and the money were not to change hands until December 30, 1989.

In April of that year, DeBenedetti also acquired a majority stake in the *L'Espresso-Repubblica* group, which publishes *La Repubblica,* the country's second-largest newspaper, and *L'Espresso,* the second-largest weekly magazine—both with a clear left-of-center identity. As the head of this mega-Mondadori, DeBenedetti was overwhelmingly the master of Italy's printed press. In economic terms, he was now on a par with Berlusconi, and the political clout of his media holdings was arguably greater. There were no antitrust laws in Italy at the time, so nothing prevented DeBenedetti from owning the two largest newsmagazines, but the creation of a media colossus in the hands of an "enemy" businessman with left-of-center friendships was terrifying to Craxi and others in the Italian government, as well as to Berlusconi. In early December 1989, less than a month before the sale to DeBenedetti would have been irrevocably completed, Berlusconi held a press conference announcing that the Formenton-Mondadori family had changed their minds and agreed to change sides and sell the same shares to him instead.

A legal battle ensued in which DeBenedetti appeared to have the upper hand. The sales agreement was clear, and it stipulated that should there be any disagreements between the parties of the sale, they should be resolved through an arbitration board. The board ruled in DeBenedetti's favor.

But in 1991, the Court of Appeals in Rome overturned DeBenedetti's seemingly solid sales agreement. A second court case awarded Mondadori to DeBenedetti, but in the third and final round in 1992, Berlusconi prevailed, winning control of the Mondadori empire.

More than ten years later, an Italian court found that some of the judges who played key roles in both the SME takeover battle and the Mondadori case were paid substantial bribes by Berlusconi's lawyer, Cesare Previti. The court ruled that Previti, using money from Berlusconi's Fininvest, kept a series of important judges on his payroll. The final ruling in the Mondadori case appears to have actually been written by Berlusconi's own legal team. Many years later, a search warrant produced an early draft of the ruling in the office of one of Berlusconi's lawyers, entire passages of which had been incorporated word for word into the final ruling. At the time, the Mondadori case appeared to be political in nature. Clearly, Craxi and other powerful figures in the government orbit did not want such an important media company falling into the hands of someone considered to be on the left. But even in the era of Craxi, the notion that judicial rulings in cases of national interest could be bought and sold was hard to imagine. The Rome court, in fact, went so far in Berlusconi's favor that it not only gave him Mondadori but also awarded him control of the *L'Espresso-Repubblica* group, which DeBenedetti had acquired in a consensual agreement independently of the Mondadori affair.

If this had gone through, it would have created the most extraordinary concentration of media in Europe: Berlusconi would have owned almost all of private television, the largest book publishing firm, two major daily newspapers (including the second-largest) and the largest magazine publishing group, including the two biggest weekly newsmagazines. Moreover, in the case of *La Repubblica* and *L'Espresso*, it would have essentially meant their death. Just as *Il Giornale* had been conceived as a conservative newspaper, both *L'Espresso* and *La Repubblica* had been created in order to offer a left-of-center alternative to the centrist and conservative press. In the hands of Berlusconi and Craxi, they would have been essentially killed off and/or turned into something entirely unrecognizable. This concentration of power worried even conservatives in the Christian Democratic Party, and an emissary of Giulio Andreotti, the gray eminence of the party, was dispatched in order to straighten things out. With no legal authority whatsoever, but the full backing of the powers that be, Andreotti's man persuaded Berlusconi to hand *L'Espresso* and

La Repubblica back to DeBenedetti, restoring some semblance of balance to the country's media market. Nonetheless, it was a huge victory for Berlusconi, who got to keep Mondadori; as a result, Italy's biggest TV owner was now also the biggest book publisher and the biggest magazine publisher, making him overwhelmingly the country's biggest media baron.

2. AU REVOIR, PARIS

The patronage of Craxi, vice president of the Socialist International, was instrumental in allowing Berlusconi's Fininvest empire to expand into France and Spain.

The 1980s were the era of privatization, not just in the United States and Italy. In France, as in Italy, a Socialist president, François Mitterrand, undertook a partial privatization of television. At the time, there were four national networks in France, three public ones and one private pay-per-view channel, Canal+, which was created by a trusted friend of Mitterrand, his former chief of staff, André Rousselet. At the time, Mitterrand was concerned that the Gaullists would win the next elections and privatize two of the three public networks, giving them to business interests close to the French right, in particular to Robert Hersant, owner of *Le Figaro* and about one-third of the French press.

Mitterrand decided to head off the Gaullists' privatization plan by creating two new private stations, La Cinq (Five) and La Six (Six). With two new private networks, the market would be saturated, and rather than clamor for the privatization of the public network, the existing networks would probably resist the introduction of new rivals. The government assigned 60 percent of La Cinq to a consortium of French businesses, including the movie company Gaumont, with its rich library of French films. The remaining 40 percent was up for grabs and represented Berlusconi's big chance to break into the French market.

There was considerable resistance to the idea of a Berlusconi network in France. Critics began referring to it as the "spaghetti" network, and

Jacques Lang, Mitterrand's minister of culture, said that "Berlusconi is the Trojan Horse for American subculture."

On April 13, 1985, Berlusconi was able to obtain a secret meeting with President Mitterrand at the Elyseé Palace. "The private meeting with President Mitterrand was very important," he later said in one of his speeches to advertisers. "We remained alone for more than an hour, and our conversation lasted longer than the time allotted. But I couldn't tell what impression I had made, whether he liked me or not and to what degree. . . . As we parted, Mitterrand surprised me. Instead of showing me to the door, he accompanied me along the hallway along the courtyard of the Elyseé. At that moment, I had a stroke of genius. . . . On my way in, I had passed a room with a beautiful grand piano. And as we came upon that room, I slipped past the President and then sat down at the piano and played *'Au Revoir, Paris.'* The Chief of Protocol had a moment of dismay, Mitterrand's secretary turned pale, but the President approached the piano with a faint smile. I had struck the right chord. I had hit the target. . . . After a minute, I stopped singing, but the President asked me to continue; he liked the way I sang. Afterward, we said good-bye. Since I knew he had planned an official visit to Milan, I invited him to my villa. *'Au revoir à Milan, au revoir,'* he replied."[5] They saw each other at the end of June at Arcore, and again in Rome under the auspices of Craxi.

Whether through the charm of his singing or the influence of Craxi, Mitterrand allowed Berlusconi to acquire 40 percent of La Cinq and gave the new channel serious competitive advantages over the public channels. It had a higher ceiling for the amount of advertising they could show and lower requirements for the amount of original broadcasts and French-made films and shows. While other channels had to wait three years after a film had finished showing in movie theaters, La Cinq could show films two years after their release.

Berlusconi set about conquering France much as he had Italy. He showered famous French actors and showgirls with flowers and gifts and put his private plane at their disposal. He gave a dinner to which he invited a group of advertising executives and Jacques Séguéla, Mitterrand's com-

munications adviser. When Séguéla and his wife opened their dinner nap-
kins they found wildly extravagant gold watches inside—worth thousands
or even tens of thousands of dollars each. They were briefly perplexed: to
keep them would seem like accepting a bribe, but to refuse them would
seem an insult. Séguéla kept the watches and went to work for Berlusconi.[6]

But Berlusconi's French adventure showed that in a highly competitive
market without sufficient political backing, he was extremely vulnerable.
In March 1986, the French right won in national elections, meaning
the government began a complex period of "cohabitation" between the
Socialist president Mitterrand and the Gaullist prime minister Jacques
Chirac. The new prime minister set about reorganizing the TV industry.
He privatized the first and largest state channel. Although more of a free
marketer, Chirac also passed an antitrust law that limited any single person from owning more than 25 percent of a single network. As part of the
reorganization, Berlusconi would have to sell 15 percent of his share, and
a new French ownership group brought in. There were two leading con-
tenders. One was the ownership group of the daily newspaper *Le Monde*,
close to the Socialists of Mitterrand; the other was Robert Hersant, an
older man with a controversial past as a Nazi sympathizer and anti-Semite
during the German occupation of France during World War II.

But if he was hoping to win the sympathies of France's new prime
minister, Chirac, it proved a mistake. As a nationalist, Chirac regarded
him as an Italian interloper and his brand of crass, commercial TV unbe-
coming of French grandeur. He referred to Berlusconi as a "minestrone
salesman." Although one of only six networks, La Cinq was unable to
draw more than 10 percent of the French audience. Berlusconi blamed his
French partners who wouldn't follow his advice and made a mess of
things. They in turn maintained that Berlusconi's Italian-made programming wasn't suited to French tastes. "One of the problems is that we
didn't have a French audience," said Amanda Lear, a French entertainer
who was one of the stars of La Cinq. "All the programs were shot in Italy
and then the applause and the laughter added afterwards, giving them an
artificial, manufactured quality."[7]

Whatever the reasons, the network's losses and debts mounted. Moreover, even though political connections mattered plenty in France, the state was still the state, and even well-connected companies were expected to respect the law. When La Cinq violated the ceiling on advertising—something that Fininvest did routinely in Italy, with little tangible consequence—it was hit with a serious fine: more than $10 million. Its bank accounts were frozen when it failed to pay its rent. In new elections in 1988, the Socialists won and returned to power, after which Berlusconi found himself in another difficult situation. He had tried to please the right by making the right-wing Hersant his partner; now he tried to reduce Hersant's role in La Cinq, replacing him with another shareholder close to the Socialists, but to no avail. Berlusconi's constant changes of sides resulted in his being regarded with distrust by both camps. By 1990, La Cinq's losses had reached 600 billion lire (about $500 million) and Hersant decided to sell out. Two years later, La Cinq was closed and Berlusconi had to absorb his losses and move on.

If Berlusconi's La Cinq adventure was a failure, it left its mark on French television: the nudity and scantily clad women on the Berlusconi channel soon became a staple of other channels. Mitterrand's former communications adviser Jacques Séguéla said that he thought that among the reasons the French president gave the green light to Berlusconi was because he, too, liked showgirls and wanted to break the excessive seriousness and intellectualism of French television. If this was his goal, in this he succeeded.[8]

3. TELECINCO—THREE BLIND MICE

Although Berlusconi was forced to concede defeat in France, he was more successful in Spain, perhaps because his political patron there, Socialist prime minister Felipe González, remained in power for much longer than Mitterrand's Socialists in France.

In 1989, Spain, among the last of European countries, agreed to open up its broadcasting system to private television. It granted licenses to two private networks; one of them, thanks to Bettino Craxi's good offices with the Spanish Socialists, was awarded to Berlusconi.

With its history of restricted media under dictatorship, Spain was a market ripe for the taking. The Spanish newspaper business was still in its infancy, and could give television little competition. Only 8 percent of Spaniards bought a daily newspaper, as opposed to 30 percent of British adults, while 87 percent watched television each day and some two-thirds reported forming their political views from television.[9]

As in France, Spain adopted laws to limit the ownership share of foreign investors in television to 25 percent of a single channel. But having learned from his French experience, Berlusconi was careful not to let this get in his way. Shrewdly, he teamed up with a thirty-four-year-old blind man who headed a Spanish national charity for the blind. He then ousted another Spanish partner who was fighting Fininvest's control over Telecinco and inserted Leo Kirch, a German media mogul who had much in common with Berlusconi in terms of his politics, coziness with his country's conservative leaders, tolerance for high debt and risky ventures, and willingness to skirt or flout the law.

Gradually, Berlusconi would form alliances across Europe with two conservative-minded media tycoons, Leo Kirch, who was close to Christian Democratic leader Helmut Kohl, and Rupert Murdoch, the Australian press baron who took American citizenship in order to buy the *New York Post* and Twentieth Century–Fox and start his own Fox network. The three became partners in various ventures, bought shares in one another's companies and appeared to juggle ownership so as to circumvent antitrust laws.

In Spain, prosecutors would eventually discover that some of Berlusconi's partners in Telecinco were dummy investors and that Fininvest actually controlled 90 percent of the network's shares. Berlusconi was able to impose his own management of the station, which quickly turned into a dubbed Spanish version of his own Fininvest stations in Italy. With its usual mix of sex, violence and quiz shows, Telecinco quickly became the most watched station in Spain, which, after some forty years of sexual and political repression under right-wing dictator Francisco Franco, was ready to relax and have fun. Berlusconi's nude game show *Colpo Grosso* hit Spanish TV screens under the title *¡Uf, Qué Calor!* (Wow! What Heat!). Some complained about *"la tele porno-erótica"* and others called the show "commercialized sex at its most cynical, degrading and embarrassing." Nonetheless, Telecinco helped start a "sleaze war." Spanish state TV began its own weekly striptease and began broadcasting X-rated movies.[10]

With a friendly government in power, the investigation into Fininvest's violation of Spain's antitrust legislation remained stalled for years. And in the meantime, Berlusconi was able to reproduce an empire in Spain that resembled his one in Italy to a good degree: he established a major advertising company, a film company and one of the largest book publishing companies, creating strength across the entire media field.

·
~

Berlusconi's mixed record in Europe, which seemed to depend more on the presence or absence of strong political backing, raises an interesting question: how good a businessman is Berlusconi? In Italy, he succeeded in a television market where he had to compete for only a few years and then enjoyed a virtual monopoly position with his only rival, RAI, limited in the amount of advertising it could run and operated by someone who was appointed by his political godfather and who may have also been on the Berlusconi payroll. His big real estate bonanza, Milano 2, was successful in part because the government changed the flight patterns of the Milan airport. Milano 3, his next big real estate project, was not a great success. He sold the national department store and supermarket chain Standa in the late nineties after ten years of fairly lackluster economic performance.

"I would say he has a rather mixed record," said a highly respected business executive who worked at a high level in Fininvest for a number of years. "Berlusconi is an excellent salesman, but not a very good manager. He has courage, enormous physical stamina and capacity for work and great confidence. He has a deep conviction that luck is on his side. When we were debating whether to do this or that, he would say *'A me, le*

cose vanno bene. Facciamolo!' [Things tend to work for me. Let's do it!]"
But sometimes they didn't. At a certain point, he became infatuated with
Giancarlo Paretti, the Italian entrepreneur who briefly took over and ran
the Hollywood studio MGM. "Berlusconi gave him a loan of more than
$100 million, and for a while, it looked like we might lose most or all of it.
At a certain point, Berlusconi said to me: 'It's lucky this isn't a publicly
traded company or they might fire me!' If you look at his record, you
would say, Real estate, so-so; after Milano 2, it went badly. Standa, the department store, didn't go very well. In soccer, he lost money. With *Il Giornale*, he lost money. With Mondadori he inherited a strong business that
continued to go well. Basically, if you removed television, the balance
sheet didn't look good at all. Berlusconi was good at looking at the big
picture, but he had no real interest in execution. He wanted things done
and didn't care what it cost. I found we were paying absurd prices for
things like the office space we rented."[11]

But Berlusconi could afford this attitude because the flow of television
advertising dollars meant that all losses could be absorbed. A quasi-
monopoly of private television in which other competitors are kept out
and the state television is not allowed to compete fully is like a license to
print money. Perhaps he was right not to worry about the small things that
other businessmen worried about—profit and loss, keeping expenses
down, reducing bank debt—when ultimately the battle for the future of
his empire was going to be determined in the political arena. A number of
things that Berlusconi did that lost money—like owning *Il Giornale*, the
department store Standa, which was in virtually every Italian town (its
corporate slogan was "The Home of the Italians"), and the soccer team
A. C. Milan—had a symbolic value that cannot easily be measured in dollars. What Berlusconi was doing that other Italian businessmen were not
particularly concerned with was creating an image of himself in the
national consciousness. Berlusconi had his marketing department run
monthly opinion polls about Italy's leading businessmen, Gianni Agnelli
of Fiat, Carlo DeBenedetti of Olivetti, Leopoldo Pirelli of the Pirelli
tire company and himself. The index that seemed to matter most to him

was the answer to the question about who was the most *simpatico,* the best liked.

The best example of Berlusconi's making what would appear to be a financially bad move for symbolic advantage was his decision to buy A. C. Milan, the soccer team he rooted for during his youth but which had fallen on hard times during the 1970s and early 1980s, owned by a string of businessmen who ended up in bankruptcy, under indictment and/or as fugitives from justice overseas. As with everything, Berlusconi entered the soccer market with a huge splash, a tidal wave of publicity provided by his own television networks and big promises. "In my business activities, I'm used to being number one, and I'm so used to it that if I should end up number two in soccer, I would take it very badly," he said on taking over the Milan team. As he had when he entered television, Berlusconi went on a spending spree, buying the top players from other, poorer teams, handing out record-setting contracts, turning the soccer market upside down. After assembling his team of all-stars, he presented them to a stadium of expectant fans, arranging to have the players descend on the stadium in three large helicopters that arrived to blaring music of Wagner's *Die Walküre*. On the strength of these hopes and a massive television advertising campaign, Milan sold 65,000 season tickets.[12]

As Indro Montanelli noted at the time, "Fans of the red-and-black are jubilant. They are convinced that Berlusconi will transform Milan into a championship team in a heartbeat—and they may be right. There's only one danger: that the new president of Milan also wants to be the general manager, the coach, the team masseur, the captain and the center forward. Which might even be a good thing—as long as he gets to be the referee as well."[13]

Success did not come immediately, and Berlusconi fought with the team's coach, Nils Liedholm, who bristled at Berlusconi's attempts to handle the team. Berlusconi fired the coach and defended his prerogatives. "Given my abilities to evaluate and decide, not to mention my intelligence, which have produced results that are obvious to everyone, I don't think it's scandalous for me to speak up. . . . Often, you win with imagination."[14]

Whether through imagination or by paying stratospheric prices for the best players, Milan won the national championship in 1988, European championships in 1989 and 1990, when it also won an intercontinental cup.

What Berlusconi certainly understood is that soccer and television could be mixed together into an explosive synergy. While owning a soccer team might not be lucrative, televising soccer certainly was and is so popular it became a genuine cultural force. As we've seen in the old days, RAI televised one soccer game per week, showed only one of the two halves of the match and did so only after the match had actually ended. Berlusconi broadcast several soccer matches a week as well as numerous sports talk-show programs. The result was a national soccer boom: the stadiums (at least of the big, well-publicized teams) were full, and so were the airwaves.

As television became the prime source of revenue for soccer, Berlusconi's team was in a position of advantage with respect to all others. In soccer, as in everything else, Berlusconi's presence in the field had the effect of transforming the industry. His desire to buy up the best players from around the world set off a bidding war among all the Italian teams, many of whom did not have Berlusconi's deep pockets. The promise of seemingly unlimited television revenue from broadcasting games made teams giddy in their offers. Most of the teams went deep into debt and did not have a television empire to compensate for their losses.

Along with the Sunday matches, Berlusconi and RAI began running sports talk shows in which armchair soccer coaches discussed Sunday's matches on Sunday night, Monday and into the week. In the late 1980s, with the decline of the Soviet Union and the end of the Cold War, soccer seemed to replace politics as the prime topic of conversation in Italy. It is now almost impossible to get into a cab or a shop in Italy and not hear the chatter of radio shows in which every aspect of the game is analyzed and discussed in detail.

A. C. Milan was already one of a handful of soccer teams with a national following, and it increased exponentially as the team became national champions and represented Italy in international competition.

Milan fan clubs sprouted up all over Italy and were part of Berlusconi's capillary presence through the country. As Milan began to win, Berlusconi's private monthly polls registered huge gains in his popularity ratings. When Berlusconi went around the country, people responded to him in a way they had never done before. "Silvio, you're God, you're the Messiah," one fan called to him, as he proudly recounted.

"The most beautiful compliments in my life I've received from soccer fans," Berlusconi told an audience of advertising clients in 1989. "In Como, right after Milan won the championship in 1988, a fan saw my car, ran up to it and screamed: 'Silvioooo, Silviooo, you're a gorgeous piece of ass!' It was the greatest compliment of my life. . . . Another one, a big, strapping guy over six feet said to me, 'Silvio, I love you.' Seeing my look of surprise, he added. 'I love you, but I'm not a faggot!'" Another fan who made a great impression on Berlusconi was one who yelled: "Silvio, if you want we'll vote for whatever party you tell us. We'll give eight million votes to the party you want. To be able to give them to you personally would be the best!" Berlusconi says he was so struck by this that he got out of his limousine and said to the man, "My friend, as a matter of fact, I'm thinking of founding a party of my own."[15]

Mussolini had first discovered the political potential of soccer, building nearly three thousand soccer stadiums in the 1920s and virtually imposing it as Italy's national sport. Italy went on to two World Cup victories and an Olympic gold medal in Berlin in 1936, demonstrating the superiority of Fascism and stirring national feeling in Italy. (In addition, Bologna, Il Duce's home team, won four national championships between 1936 and 1941.) Berlusconi almost certainly didn't get into soccer with politics in mind, but at a certain point, he realized that through soccer he had stirred up emotions that had political weight. "When I went to Rome, in the ministries, the ushers and doormen rushed to greet me. They would stop elevators in order not to keep me waiting. Traffic cops would block traffic. . . . When I went to the stadium with Craxi and Forlani, people wanted only my autograph. They would surround me, trying to pull me away from the politicians; I tried to remain as near to them as possible so that they did not feel left out. And as I signed my name, I would tell the fans under my breath, 'Go and ask Forlani for an autograph, go and ask Craxi.' And they would respond: 'Who gives a shit about Craxi? about Forlani?' "[16]

Berlusconi realized that he had touched a nerve, the nerve of anti-politics, which was growing throughout the 1980s, and realized that he—the symbol of something different, a completely different kind of culture, the world of television, of sports and entertainment, of entrepreneurship and economic success—was a powerful lightning rod for that sentiment.

$\stackrel{.}{\frown}$

In some ways, it may seem strange that Berlusconi—one of the principal beneficiaries of Italy's old political system—should become a powerful symbol of anger and protest against that system. After all, he was at the stadium with Bettino Craxi and Arnaldo Forlani, the politicians to whom he owed much of his good fortune.

But in Berlusconi's mind, the very fact that he needed the protection of these politicians, men who, in his view, could probably never have run a TV station or a soccer team, was in itself a galling injustice. If the Communists and a handful of Catholic moralists within the Christian Democratic Party were not always trying to interfere with his business—threatening to expropriate one or two of his networks—he would not have needed to spend all his time worrying about Craxi's sex life and foul moods.

After all, he had started out trying to create television under impossible conditions with a state monopoly of broadcasting that left him in a precarious position, operating semilegally, knowing that the judges or politicians could pull the plug on him at any moment. He had beaten and outsmarted more established competitors—Rizzoli, Rusconi and Mondadori—and still people wanted to take it all away from him. Throughout the 1980s, he lived with the sword of Damocles hanging over him, as the parliament talked and talked about a new communications law that would finally regulate television. It left him vulnerable and prey to the blackmail of every two-bit politician who might threaten to propose an antitrust law if they didn't like the way they were being treated in one of his newspapers, magazines or TV shows. "These politicians hold a pistol to our heads with this law they are supposed to give us," Berlusconi said at the time, referring to the communications antitrust law that had been under discussion between 1977 and 1990.[17]

When asked about it, executives in the Berlusconi group would acknowledge that in no other country could a private citizen control three national networks, but the real anomaly, they would explain, was RAI, a state system with two networks. In Britain, the BBC had only two channels; in France, the state had privatized one of its three government channels in order to make room for private competition. But Italy seemed to be going in the opposite direction in the mid-seventies, the government adding a third state channel in order to give it to the Communists in 1976 instead of getting out of the way and leaving the field to the market. With such a powerful adversary, Berlusconi argued, he was almost physiologically required to match RAI channel for channel. His own Fininvest empire was simply the mirror image of RAI. And the same Communists who were always clamoring for antitrust legislation recoiled in horror at the idea of privatizing one or two of the RAI networks to create a truly diversified, competitive television marketplace. While there was some truth to Berlusconi's argument, it omitted a number of inconvenient facts: even if the state networks in France, Britain and Germany had only two channels, they still occupied close to half the market, as in Italy, and yet the remaining private market was still able to maintain more than one healthy competitor.

But Berlusconi was not far from the truth when he said that he needed his political friends, because in Italy a businessman was always at the mercy of an interfering and parasitical state. The million laws, rules and regulations of the Italian state—applied unevenly and often according to a business's political connections—meant that Italian entrepreneurs were constantly having to fend off or bribe politicians and bureaucrats to be able to function. When Berlusconi traveled around Italy talking, he spoke, businessman to businessmen, as a victim of this predatory system. "They tried to stop me in every way with attacks of all kinds," he said in a 1989 speech. "They were always against me because they were against a television that spread a market economy, that spread the idea of freedom."[18]

Even with his seemingly impregnable position—with three TV networks, the Mondadori publishing empire, *Il Giornale,* a championship soccer team, the Standa department store chain and vast real estate holdings, Berlusconi was right that he could not feel secure. In 1987, Craxi's government fell after four years and, in 1988, one of Berlusconi's most dreaded adversaries, Ciriaco De Mita, leader of the "left wing" of the Christian Democratic Party, became prime minister. "Berlusconi is an adventurer and will meet the same end as all adventurers," De Mita proclaimed.[19] The *pax televisiva* was over. De Mita appointed a new head of RAI, Biagio Agnes, who declared war. Berlusconi told his audience of businessmen-advertisers that Agnes had said, "Berlusconi must die," quoting him in Roman dialect to emphasize the idea of the ignorant, parasitical government in Rome—a bogeyman in the eyes of the Italian entrepreneur. "I tremble at the thought that a man like De Mita held in his hands the destiny of Azienda Italia [Italy, Inc.]." (Berlusconi was already beginning to refer to Italy as a badly managed company.)

Just as Ronald Reagan developed what became his standard stump speech while traveling around the United States making speeches for General Electric, so Berlusconi hammered out the essential features of his basic political message during his frequent talks to advertisers. It had a lot in common with Reagan's: a call to liberate businessmen from the dead hand of the state, combined with a strong, emotional anti-Communism. Years before the emergence of the entrepreneur-businessman in the form of figures such as Ross Perot and Steve Forbes in the United States, Berlusconi was already creating a similar persona for himself, as champion of the beleaguered Italian businessman in the face of the corrupt Italian state. "The only ones who have helped us in these years have been you entrepreneurs, here as elsewhere. The political system has sucked our lifeblood, has absorbed ninety percent of our energies, because we have had to stave off, to try to modify five different proposed laws, each of which would have annihilated us."[20]

In 1990, Berlusconi had to fend off another attempt at antitrust legislation. After thirteen years of private broadcasting, without any regulation or legislation, after Berlusconi had solidified his control over 60 percent of the television advertising revenue and gained control of Mondadori, momentum had built in the Italian parliament for a law establishing once and for all clear rules and limits in the broadcasting field. The principal task of drawing up the law was assigned to the minister of communications, Oscar Mammi, a representative of the Republican Party, a small but respected minor party that had generally been part of the government coalition but had a reputation for seriousness and moral rectitude. For a time, it appeared likely that the new law would require Berlusconi to sell one or two of his three networks, but when the minister presented his final draft, the law established that no one individual could own more than three national networks, which just happened to be the number Berlusconi owned. In short, the law was little more than a photocopy of the current "duopoly" between RAI and Berlusconi.

To preserve the appearance of fairness, the law seemed to require one small sacrifice of Berlusconi: it ruled that one could not own a national television network and also own a national daily newspaper. This would mean that Berlusconi would have to give up his interest in Montanelli's *Il Giornale*. In practice, Berlusconi simply got around the measure by handing over his shares in the newspaper to his brother Paolo—a scandalous mockery of the spirit of the law that went entirely unchallenged. In reality, this particular provision was not a sacrifice but another extraordinary gift to Berlusconi; it meant that his principal rivals, the big publishing empires that owned the daily papers *Corriere della Sera*, *La Repubblica* and *La Stampa*, and the financial newspaper *Il Sole 24 Ore*, were banned from entering the television field. Although the law made it illegal for newspaper publishers to own TV stations, it placed no restrictions on the publishers of weekly and monthly magazines, allowing Berlusconi to keep the Mondadori publishing group.

That the law, after working its way through the Italian parliament, should have ended up so closely matching Berlusconi's interests turned out not to be an accident. Prosecutors would later discover that Mammi's legislative aide, the young Davide Giacalone, who actually drafted the law, received 600 million lire (about $500,000 at the time) from Fininvest, something prosecutors considered a bribe and that Fininvest insisted was a consulting fee. Moreover, Giacalone had also received 10 billion lire (about $8 million) under-the-table payment—allegedly 9 billion for his party and 1 billion for himself—from a man who prosecutors believed was operating on Fininvest's behalf. (The case was taken away from the prosecutors in Milan and never brought to trial. Jurisdiction was granted to Rome, in whose Palace of Justice Cesare Previti had many, many friends, including some on his payroll.)[21]

And this was in all likelihood only a fraction of the money that changed hands around the Mammi law. In 1991, Fininvest asked a small investment firm in Milan to engage in a complex set of transactions involving the buying and reselling of 91 billion Italian treasury notes (the equivalent at the time of about $70 million). First one set of treasury notes was purchased and then, passing through five different banks in the Republic of San Marino, was turned back into cash, presumably to hide the money's origin. Fininvest then had the entire sum delivered in cash—trucked in special armored cars from San Marino to Milano 2—which it used to buy a brand-new set of treasury notes. While these sorts of transactions are usually conducted on computer screens or kept in bank vaults, Fininvest wanted to take physical possession of all 91 million in treasury notes. Collecting that quantity of printed treasury notes is difficult and highly unusual, and the money manager, Giovanni Manzo, asked the treasurer of Fininvest, Mario Moranzoni, the reason for this strange and costly operation. "Politicians cost a lot. . . . The Mammi law is under discussion," the manager said he was told.[22] The law had actually been passed at that point, but the next two years were spent working out the details of its enactment and beating back attempts to amend it in ways that might have been unfavorable to Berlusconi.

In that same year, 1991, an overseas bank account belonging to Fininvest sent 21 billion lire (over $12 million at the time) to a secret account belonging to Bettino Craxi. It turned out that more than the agreed sum had been sent and Craxi returned 5 billion. Politicians in the Italy of the late 1980s and early 1990s certainly did cost a lot.

Berlusconi was almost certainly one of the principal beneficiaries of Italy's old political system—it is hard to think of anyone who benefited more—but the enormous costs exacted and the constant threats and political blackmail he endured convinced him that he was one of its principal victims. Thus it was that he could tell his advertisers with a straight face that "the political system has sucked our lifeblood, has absorbed ninety percent of our energies."[23]

Chapter Six

OPERATION CLEAN
HANDS AND THE ENTRY
INTO POLITICS

1. Weeping in the Shower

During the spring and summer of 1993, Silvio Berlusconi's world appeared on the brink of collapse. The political parties that had acted as his friends and protectors had been hammered by indictment after indictment on charges of political corruption and were on the point of extinction. Bettino Craxi, with eleven indictments to his name, had resigned as secretary of the Socialist Party and was greeted by menacing jeers when he appeared in public. In early June, police arrested Davide Giacalone, the legislative aide who had drafted the Mammi law, after discovering that, of the millions of dollars in under-the-table party financing and "consultant's fee," he had personally pocketed $500,000 from Berlusconi's Fininvest.

Later that same month, police arrested a Fininvest executive, Aldo Brancher, on charges of having given 300 million lire (about $250,000) in bribes in order to convince the minister of health to place a larger-than-expected share of anti-AIDS public health advertisements on the Fininvest networks. Prosecutors were holding Brancher in San Vittore prison, pressing him to tell them who at Fininvest had authorized the bribes. Unable to visit Brancher in prison, Berlusconi and Confalonieri got in their car one summer evening and drove around the prison walls. "Confalonieri and I circled the prison," Berlusconi later said. "We wanted to communicate with him." Presumably, Berlusconi and Confalonieri were sending Brancher telepathic messages to hang tough.[1]

With the parties of the center and the right in total disarray, polls were showing a victory of the left as virtually inevitable. Some were talking about taking away one or two of Berlusconi's networks, which could spell his ruin. Fininvest was nearly $4 billion in debt and had delayed paying the suppliers of its department store chain in order to keep up with its interest payments. An unfavorable modification in the communications law could push Fininvest into the red, cause the banks to call in their loans and, potentially, bring about Berlusconi's ruin.

Berlusconi considered the possibility of getting involved in politics to stave off a victory of the left, but the idea met with stiff resistance among his closest friends and advisers, throwing him into a rare moment of self-doubt and despair. "I'm exhausted, on the point of a nervous breakdown," he said at the time. "Confalonieri and [Gianni] Letta tell me that it's madness to enter politics and that they will destroy me. That they will do anything, poring through documents, say that I'm a *mafioso*. . . . What can I do? Sometimes I even find myself weeping in the shower."[2]

But in what can be described only as a strategic and organizational stroke of brilliance, Berlusconi managed to turn what was perhaps the greatest crisis of his career into his greatest triumph—short-circuiting all his potential problems by taking direct control of the political system.

2. THE DECADENCE OF THE ANCIEN RÉGIME

Berlusconi's entry into politics and lightning success is comprehensible only within the context of the crisis that destroyed the political parties that had governed Italy between 1946 and 1993. The short-term cause of the crisis was the corruption investigation known as Operation Clean Hands, but its roots go much deeper, and are found in the changing geopolitical landscape of the time.

Operation Clean Hands began modestly enough. On February 17,

1992, an obscure but powerful local official of the Socialist Party, Mario Chiesa, head of an august Milan charity for the elderly, was arrested trying to flush a $6,000 bribe down the toilet. As it turned out, this was just an average day at the office for Chiesa, who had socked away some $10 million in Swiss bank accounts. Chiesa had found a way to profit from virtually every transaction and, like a character in Gogol's *Dead Souls,* was even making money off every dead body he sent to the cemetery.[3]

Scandals of this kind—some much bigger—had surfaced from time to time in Italy at previous moments, but always seemed to stop before reaching the highest levels of responsibility. In the past, the government always found a way to sandbag investigations without paying a significant political price. For example, in 1987 prosecutors arrested the head of the Milan subway system, a prominent Socialist, for soliciting bribes, but Bettino Craxi put him up for election to the Senate in a safe district in order to give him parliamentary immunity. This meant that prosecutors could continue their investigation only if parliament voted to waive the senator's immunity, which, despite ample evidence of wrongdoing, it refused to do.

But in 1992, the political class was unable to stop Operation Clean Hands in the way it had cut off other investigations just a few years earlier. The collapse of the Soviet Union and the end of the Cold War had changed the political dynamic in Italy. Italy's governing parties—the Christian Democrats, Socialists and their satellite parties—were, paradoxically, the victims of their own success. They were united by a common commitment to the Atlantic alliance and an opposition to Communism. The late 1980s and early 1990s represented the ultimate triumph and vindication of their political vision. The Soviet Union under Mikhail Gorbachev admitted that its system had failed and tried to institute economic and political reforms. The Berlin Wall came down in 1989, and the regimes of Eastern Europe collapsed almost overnight. In Italy, the government's main adversary, the Italian Communist Party, was lacerated by internal debate and split in two: a majority of reformists voted to renounce Marxism-Leninism and change the party's name to the Democratic Party of the Left, while a sizable minority decided to hold fast to the Communist tradition.

But the end of the Cold War wound up being more costly to the parties on the winning side. Anti-Communism was the glue that had held the government majority together and without it, the ruling coalition suddenly lost much of its reason for being. "Hold your nose and vote Christian Democrat," Indro Montanelli had advised the readers of *Il Giornale* in the mid-1970s, when the choice had seemed to come down between an adventure in Euro-Communism and the safe and familiar but corrupt government parties. By the early 1990s, however, the economic unification of Europe had replaced the Cold War at the top of the political agenda, and Italians were much more worried about competing with German and Japanese cars and a flood of low-priced products from East Asia than they were about holding off an invasion of Soviet tanks. Italians had put up with one of the most corrupt and inefficient governments in Europe on the grounds that it was preferable to Communism. Now Italians could stop holding their noses, and they didn't like what they smelled.

The governing parties, feeling a false sense of omnipotence, ignored numerous alarm bells and signs of public discontent with a system that more and more Italians began to regard with contempt. Even as the Cold War threat diminished, the politicians' demands for bribes grew in size and scope, becoming like a second layer of taxes in an already overtaxed country, and a genuine drag on the economy. In the early 1990s, there were a growing number of scandals that were like tremors presaging the earthquake to come. There was the "golden prisons" case, involving government officials skimming money on prison supplies. There was the "golden bedpans" case, which revealed a nasty world of no-show patronage jobs and people paying party officials for even the lowliest hospital jobs. There was a curious story in the Rome papers about a woman who, in an argument with her politician paramour, threw a suitcase of lira notes out the window and shouted: "That's what I think of you and your bribe money!" In the course of this *grande bouffe,* the crime rate in Italy had risen to record highs—mostly concentrated in Southern Italy, where the

Mafia seemed to reign unchecked and often in happy collusion with the government parties.

In keeping with the sense of a country careening out of control, Francesco Cossiga, Italy's president of the Republic, normally a quiet, dignified figurehead position, appeared to have gone mad, telephoning call-in radio shows at odd hours, making weird rambling speeches, threatening to resign one moment, to dissolve parliament the next, to have the leading magistrates in the country arrested (something he had no power to do) and then going on television vowing to take a "pickax" to the country's political system. But the wilder and more mercurial his behavior, the more popular he became, appearing a bit like King Lear, who began to speak the truth as he descended into madness. "In any normal country, they would have kicked me out by now. Does this seem like a normal country to you?" Cossiga himself said at one point.

People began to speak with great frequency and disgust about Italy's system as a "partyocracy," in which political parties invaded almost every corner of the Italian economy. In the 1970s and the 1980s, Italy had tried to spend its way out of every social problem, buying up failing businesses, propping up troubled industries, sponsoring public works in distressed areas. The Italian state sold cookies and pasta, owned supermarkets and insurance companies, controlled 75 percent of the banking system, ran the national airline, the electrical and telephone systems, and produced steel, oil, natural gas and chemicals. Italy's hypertrophic state had meant that by the early 1990s, Italy's national debt was actually greater than its gross national product—twice that of any major country in Europe. As a result, 10 percent of the government's expenditures went just to servicing the national debt. Italy's deficit was more than twice the ceiling required for it to participate in the single currency, the euro, that was scheduled to begin soon. Italy was borrowing and spending itself out of its place in the new unified Europe.

Growing public dissatisfaction began to manifest itself in the sudden proliferation of new political parties. As Italy prepared for elections in 1992, some 207 different political movements applied to get on the ballot.

There were ecological parties, hunters' parties, antihunting parties, car owners' parties, pensioners' parties, regional parties, antiregional parties, and even something called the Party of Love—founded by two porn stars. The politics of antipolitics was in the air.

On a more serious note, a group of reformist Christian Democrats in Sicily protesting political collusion with the Mafia began to draw support in the South with a new party called La Rete ("The Network"). But the most important and emblematic of the new movements was the Lombard League (later called the Northern League), which advocated political autonomy and even independence for Northern Italy. At first blush, the Lombard League, which took its name from a military alliance of Northern Italian states during the Middle Ages, seemed a weird, anachronistic throwback: its party symbol was a medieval knight holding aloft a sword, and it fought for seemingly lost or marginal causes like having dozens of tiny local dialects used on street signs and limiting Southern Italians' access to public jobs. But in the early 1990s, the Lombard League began to strike a deep chord by attacking Italy's corrupt and parasitical central government. *"Roma, Ladrona"* ("Rome, the Big Thief") was one of its favorite slogans. Rather than simply express nostalgia for a largely fictional medieval Northern Italian unity, the Lombard League turned into a modern tax-revolt movement, the first to call into question Italy's large and expensive modern welfare state. During the 1970s and 1980s, state spending had come to occupy 52 percent of the GDP, and in Southern Italy—which depended on public works projects, economic subsidies, disability pensions and welfare benefits—government spending made up some 70 percent of the local economy. The rebellion of the wealthy North against the bureaucracy in Rome and the assisted economy of the South very much resembled the Proposition 13 tax revolt in California in 1978, which was a harbinger of the Reagan revolution against the American welfare state in the 1980s. The Northern League appealed to a new and dynamic part of the population, the small and medium-sized businesses in Northern Italy that had become one of the motors of the Italian economy. Most of these businesses were family-owned, and many were operated by people who were not highly educated but were extremely hardworking, people who had gone to work straight out of high school and had never stopped. These were people who had managed to succeed despite the inefficiency and corruption of the Italian state, but who saw their hard-won prosperity threatened by government regulation and taxes.

These businesses on the whole got poor services and infrastructure in exchange for high taxes and much political interference. For example, in 1991, the Socialists and Christian Democrats were fighting over who would get to appoint the head of the national phone company, while no one was worrying much over how to make the phone system work. An incredible 47 percent of all phone calls in Italy were either cut off in the middle or never got through, and it took an average of thirty-three days to have a phone installed. Italy was paying three dollars a minute to call the United States; as a result, Italy was second to last in Europe, after Greece, in the number of phones per inhabitant.

How could Italian businesses compete under these conditions? There was a sense throughout the country that all the system's deficiencies were coming to a head and could no longer be sustained. "The contradictions of Italy are becoming increasingly evident," the governor of the Bank of Italy at the time, Carlo Azeglio Ciampi, warned. "Companies that compete successfully throughout the world must coexist with an inefficient state and with sectors of the economy protected from competition."

3. Heads Will Roll

When Operation Clean Hands began in early 1992, it was like starting a fire in a parched landscape waiting to burn. In April, just two months after the arrest of Mario Chiesa, Italy held national elections that made it clear how much the political wind had changed. The big winner was the Lombard League, which went from 0.7 percent to nearly 10 percent nationally, almost all of its support from Northern Italy. In some places, like Milan, it became the largest single party. The traditional parties, from Christian Democrats and Socialists to the ex-Communists, all suffered major setbacks. The five parties of the government majority actually received less than 50 percent for the first time and had to scramble to cobble together a government. They had been put on notice that voters wanted change, and this meant that when Operation Clean Hands started, the parties could not afford to stop it.

It is significant that the scandal broke in Milan, which had been the stronghold of Craxism and was now the base of the Lombard League. "The investigation became unstoppable because of the great ability of the judges . . . but also because of the rise of the League and the general distrust of people in the parties," one of the confessed bribe-takers said during the summer of 1992. "'Throw them in jail,' is the cry of the crowd. And this undoubtedly helped the judges. . . . I don't know whether they could have succeeded in something like this four years ago." Popular support reached across the ideological spectrum. There were candlelight vigils outside of prosecutors' offices, and the walls of Italian cities were suddenly filled with pro–Clean Hands graffiti. The Milan magistrate who had started the investigation, Antonio Di Pietro, became a national hero overnight. Graffiti writers scrawled *"Grazie Di Pietro!"* (Thanks Di Pietro) and *"Fateci sognare, Di Pietro"* (Let us dream, Di Pietro) across walls throughout Milan. Di Pietro T-shirts became collectors' items.[4]

In the past, Italian businessmen had refused to talk about the bribes they paid; now they were lining up in front of prosecutors' offices asking to be heard. The prosecutors, moving gradually up the chain of responsibility, uncovered a system of bribery that was so pervasive, so rapacious and so scientific in its application that it was shocking to even the most cynical Italian observers. In the Milan subway, for example, the percentages being skimmed by politicians had crept up from 0.5 percent of all contracts to 3 to 4 percent on most new construction, and sometimes reached as high as 13.5 percent. The division of spoils was calculated down to the decimal point: 37.5 percent for the Socialist Party, 18.75 to both the Christian Democrats and the Communists, 17 percent to the tiny (but very greedy) Socialist Democratic Party and 8 percent to the Repub-

lican Party, another member of the government coalition. Milan became
known as Tangentopoli, "Bribe City," a term that became synonymous
for the corruption investigation throughout Italy.

According to one Italian economist, bribes were siphoning off about
10 trillion lire (about $8 billion) a year, which went quite a ways toward
accounting for the national debt of $140 billion.[5]

As prosecutors moved from businessmen and local officials to party
treasurers, members of parliament and top party officials, the Italian parliament did not dare intervene. When the government tried to pass a
decree granting a kind of political amnesty for crimes of political corruption, crowds surrounded the Milan Palace of Justice in a scene that was
reminiscent of Moscow in 1991 when the public crowded around the parliament in order to protest a government coup. In an indecorous but in-
dicative moment, a deputy for the Lombard League swung a noose from
within the halls of parliament.

Berlusconi's attitude toward the investigation was initially ambivalent.
He, too, considered himself a victim of the incessant demands of the political parties and identified himself with a productive, competitive Northern Italy that had succeeded despite and not because of the government.
His newspaper, *Il Giornale*, and its editor, Indro Montanelli, gave full and
enthusiastic support to the investigation. But at the same time, Berlusconi
understood that an investigation whose epicenter was Milan, dominated
by Bettino Craxi and the Socialist Party, presented, if nothing else, the
risk of losing the support of his principal benefactor.

In fact, on Febrary 21, 1992, just four days after the arrest of Mario
Chiesa, Federico Orlando, who was then the deputy editor of *Il Giornale*,
received an unexpected visit from Paolo Berlusconi (who was supposed to
have taken over from his brother Silvio as the owner and publisher of the
paper because of the Mammi law) and one of the top Socialist leaders of
Milan, Ugo Finetti. "Finetti was carrying a folder of articles of our Milan
coverage, marked up with a pea-green highlighter. He handed them to me
so that I could give them to our journalists. 'The magistrates,' he said,
'start their cases with articles like these . . .' Paolo Berlusconi intervened

and said, 'We have to work with city and the regional government, so we have to maintain good relations with the institutions.'"[6]

In the early days of the scandal, Craxi's son Vittorio, known as Bobo, phoned some of the journalists who were covering it for *Il Giornale* and issued an umistakable threat: "After the elections of April 5, there's going to be a shake-up, and heads are going to roll at *Il Giornale*. . . . Before talking to your boss, you should stop busting our balls." Federico Orlando also received an angry call from Fedele Confalonieri because *Il Giornale* had published a photograph of Mario Chiesa and Craxi together. "Is this an attempt to sabotage Berlusconi?" Confalonieri asked Orlando. "If we have to make an enemy out of Craxi in order to keep *Il Giornale*, then we're better off giving up *Il Giornale*."[7]

Montanelli, learning of the various attempts at interference, wrote a note to his journalists that included biting references to Bobo Craxi. "While remembering that we should not react to the intemperate behavior of others, especially that of politicians, and should simply tell the truth, all the truth, without prejudice or animosity toward anyone, I authorize you to tell that aforementioned gentleman [Bobo Craxi], that, if the occasion arises, the only head likely to fall after April 5, is his own. And you can tell him, on my behalf, that I don't consider it a great loss."[8]

Montanelli went to see Berlusconi and told him that if his brother turned up again at the newspaper's editorial offices with a politician in tow, he would throw them both out on the street. Berlusconi replied by asking Montanelli not to alienate the Socialists at a moment in which they were working out the details of applying the Mammi law and assigning the television frequencies: "In fifteen days, I hope my plan for the frequencies will be taken care of. In the meantime, see if you can treat the Chiesa case as a purely criminal matter, without emphasizing his political ties."[9]

4. "It's Mangano"

The first to intuit the possibility that Berlusconi and Fininvest might need to enter politics directly was Marcello Dell'Utri, the former administrator of Berlusconi's villa at Arcore and the head of his advertising company, Publitalia.

In June of 1992, when the full extent of Tangentopoli was only just emerging, Dell'Utri hired Ezio Cartotto, a Christian Democrat politician from Milan whom Dell'Utri had already used to give lessons in the care and feeding of politicians to the sales force of Publitalia, to explore the possibility of Fininvest's entrance into politics. "In May or June of 1992, I was contacted by Marcello Dell'Utri because he wanted to involve me in a project he was keen on," Cartotto later said. "In particular, Dell'Utri felt that, with the collapse of its usual political friends, the Fininvest group should 'enter politics' in order to avoid a victory of the left, which could pose serious difficulties for the Berlusconi group. . . . Berlusconi, extremely worried about losing his television licenses, commissioned a study from me on the Italian political crisis."[10]

Dell'Utri gave Cartotto an office in the Publitalia headquarters but urged the politician to keep a low profile, making clear that this was top secret. "Dr. Dell'Utri decided to assign me the task of creating an accelerated 'course' to transform the leadership of Publitalia into a new political leadership."[11] As a result, Cartotto accompanied Dell'Utri to Publitalia's annual sales conference in September 1992, where Berlusconi made it clear that he did not intend to stand by and watch the left come to power without a serious fight: "The friends who have helped us have less and less clout, and our enemies count more and more. We must prepare ourselves for any situation in order to combat them."

Shortly afterward, Cartotto began traveling around Italy to sound out moderate and conservative forces in Italy who expressed the desire to support a new centrist party. But the existence of the group that worked on the eighth floor of Publitalia's office remained top secret. "Dell'Utri made it clear that this project encountered a lot of resistance within the Berlusconi group itself, and using a metaphor, he said we must operate as if 'under military orders,' prepare plans, shut them in a drawer, and bring them out if necessary."[12]

The fact that Dell'Utri, friend of Vittorio Mangano and other notorious Mafiosi, was perhaps the biggest promoter of Berlusconi's entrance into politics at Fininvest aroused the suspicion of prosecutors in Sicily, some of whom have hypothesized that Cosa Nostra itself was pushing Berlusconi to enter politics. This may be fanciful; it is more likely that Dell'Utri, like Berlusconi himself, saw the danger that the changes under way in Italy represented for the Fininvest group. But it is true that the "hawks" in the Fininvest group, Dell'Utri and Cesare Previti, who favored Berlusconi's entrance into politics, were those same members of Berlusconi's circle who were later accused and convicted of extremely serious crimes.

Events gradually but steadily began to force Berlusconi's hand as he considered Dell'Utri's emergency plan. As Italy tried to find a solution to its political crisis, many on both left and right became convinced that the only solution was a radical restructuring of the country's electoral system. A reform-minded Christian Democrat, Mario Segni, proposed a national referendum that would abolish Italy's proportional election system and replace it with a majoritarian winner-takes-all system. The proportional system, Segni and his supporters believed, encouraged the endless bargaining, negotiation and division-of-the-spoils behavior within a government majority. Governments were always held hostage by small parties and forced to sacrifice principle and clear programs in exchange for granting this or that favor to each of its coalition mates. The majoritarian system would, it was hoped, produce two major voting blocs (as in England or the United States), each with its own candidate for prime minister, who would then have a clear mandate and a stable government and reduce the Machiavellian maneuvering and revolving-door governments that had plagued Italian political life. Berlusconi was opposed to the referendum, understanding that it would be the death knell to the old party system and would usher in a world of dangerous uncertainty.

"To make that system work, you need a really strong leader, of which there are none here in Italy—except, that is, for me," Berlusconi told a group of his executives. But the referendum was put forward, and 83 percent of voters voted in favor of a new electoral system. More than 60 percent of eligible voters showed up at the polls—a high level of participation for a referendum. So, just a year after the national elections of 1992, there was little left for the new parliament to do but prepare its own demise: to write a new election law and then hold new elections. This lame-duck parliament, with about one-third of its members under indictment, was particularly weak and unable to protect itself. The Italian magistrature, long the weakest of the three branches of government, was in the ascendant. When the parliament voted to deny the Milan prosecutors the right to continue investigations into Bettino Craxi, public reaction was so scathing that parliament abolished its own immunity, giving prosecutors the green light. Angry crowds pelted Craxi with coins when he appeared in public, and before long he fled the country to avoid prosecution.

The same month, Giulio Andreotti, another longtime supporter of Berlusconi, was indicted on charges of collusion with the Mafia. Between that, the corruption scandal and the referendum, the Christian Democratic Party decided to dissolve.

On the eve of Easter 1993, Berlusconi unburdened himself to Federico Orlando, the deputy director of *Il Giornale*: "I passed a Christmas in anxiety over the [television] frequencies that kept not being assigned, now I find myself with Andreotti and Vizzini [Prime Minister Giulio Andreotti and Carlo Vizzini, minister of communications, responsible for assigning TV frequencies] paralyzed. I have to spend Easter in anguish. I am a psychophysical disaster: I have lost [the French TV station] La Cinq and have lost the possibility of the English market because I didn't have the physical energy, psychological serenity and the necessary mental clarity."[13]

That same April, Craxi, understanding that his own days in power were numbered, came to see Berlusconi to encourage him to get directly involved in politics. According to Cartotto, who attended the metting, Craxi paced the room like a hunted animal as he talked. "We must find a label, a new name, a symbol that can unite the voters who used to vote for the old five-party coalition," Craxi told Berlusconi. "You have people all over the Italian peninsula, you can reach that part of the electorate that is disoriented, confused, but also determined not to be governed by the Communists, and save what can be saved." Then Craxi sat down and began drawing a series of concentric circles on a piece of paper. "This is an electoral college. It will have about 110,000 people in it, about 80,000 to 85,000 with the right to vote. Of these only about 60,000 to 65,000 will actually vote. With the weapon you have with your television stations, by hammering away with propaganda in favor of this or that candidate, all you need is to bring together 25,000 to 30,000 people in order to have a high probability of reversing the projections. It will happen because of the surprise factor, because of the TV factor and because of the desire of many non-Communist voters not to be governed by the Communists."

Craxi then got up to go. After showing him out, Berlusconi said, "Good, now I know what to do."[14]

But even though Berlusconi began to warm up to the idea of some form of political involvement during the spring of 1993, the idea encountered stiff opposition from some of the most influential people in his inner circle. Most outspoken against the project was Confalonieri, who was president of Fininvest and Berlusconi's oldest and closest friend. Gianni Letta, the number-two man at Fininvest, a smooth political operator, and, along with Confalonieri, one of Berlusconi's most respected counselors, was also against it. "Confalonieri in particular insisted that it was bad for both the company and for the country if a company with such a powerful presence in mass media were to become directly involved in politics, given that it would be able to directly influence the free choice of voters," Cartotto later said.[15]

Then, as the summer progressed, prosecutors turned their attention to Fininvest. There were the arrests of Giacalone and Brancher in May and June. Prosecutors had a confession from the chief aide to the former minister of health about Fininvest's paying to get the government to place advertising on the Berlusconi networks: "Brancher came to me on behalf of Fininvest in order to guarantee that Fininvest would get a larger share of the advertising in the anti-AIDS campaign. When this in fact happened, he returned in order to give me a significant show of gratitude paying 300 million lire [$250,000] in two installments."[16]

The week after this confession, police inspectors showed up at the offices of Fininvest in downtown Milan and at Milano 2, spending hours hunting down documents. They were investigating Fedele Confalonieri for illegal financing of Craxi's Socialist Party and for falsifying receipts. These events caused Berlusconi and Confalonieri to make their evening ride around Milan's San Vittore prison to communicate telepathically with Brancher, who was under pressure, Berlusconi believed, to implicate him in the bribery scandal. It was perhaps Berlusconi's darkest hour.

Concerned about the future, Berlusconi commissioned a political scientist in Milan, Giuliano Urbani, to prepare a report on the political consequences of the new electoral law. Urbani came back with alarming news: if elections were held immediately, the left, dominated by the ex-Communists, would win a landslide victory, obtaining more than 400 seats in parliament out of 630 (65 percent) with only 35 percent of the vote. The reason was the total disarray of the center-right forces. Three or four splinter movements had emerged from the ruins of the Christian Democratic Party, and were already fighting with one another. The Lombard League was growing in power, but as the antiparty par excellence, had no ties to any other party. Polls were showing a surprising revival of the neofascist party, the Movimento Sociale Italiano, which, like the ex-Communists, was trying to reposition itself in the post–Cold War world and had renamed itself the National Alliance (Alleanza Nazionale, AN). But they, even more than the Lombard League, were political pariahs, isolated from the mainstream parties.

The prospect of a massive victory of the left served as a kind of wake-up call for Berlusconi, warning of a potential catastrophe for Fininvest. The ex-Communists had always opposed him and the expansion of private television. Aware of the same polls and flush with the prospect of victory, they were already talking about revising the Mammi law and forcing Berlusconi to give up one or two of his TV networks. The culture commission in parliament was discussing banning a form of on-air sponsorships, called "telepromotions" in Italy, in which hosts plug products in the middle of their shows. The European Community had passed a norm outlawing such telepromotions, indicating that advertising should be kept distinct from programming, and Italy was now moving in line with the other European countries. But from the dawn of Canale 5, with Mike Buongiorno and the hosts of Fininvest's other game shows, quiz shows and talk shows had been working their magic on Italian housewives by oohing and aahing over the salamis and cheeses of Fininvest's advertisers. This brought in about 400 billion lire (about $350 million) a year. Losing this income would potentially ruin Fininvest's delicate financial equilibrium. Fininvest, although it generated a lot of cash, was barely profitable and owed 4 trillion lire (just under $2.6 billion) to banks. "If they take away 400 billion in telepromotions," Berlusconi told his troops in a meeting that summer, "we move from profit to loss, and the banks will no longer give us credit. We are like a trapeze artist: they don't have to shoot us, a little shove would be enough to make us fall."[17] Already that summer, Fininvest had delayed paying the suppliers of its department chain Standa in order to make the interest payments on its loans.

Berlusconi was acutely aware of the disaster that had befallen Raul Gardini, another of the major robber barons of the 1980s in Italy. When prosecutors in Milan found out about the megabribes Gardini had paid to gain control of Italy's chemical industry, banks refused to grant Gardini further credit. Unable to make further payments, faced with imminent failure and possible jail time, Gardini shot himself.

But Berlusconi correctly saw opportunity as well as danger in Urbani's study. The analysis made clear that the new electoral law rewarded broad coalitions and punished fragmentation and small parties. The Communists would win not because they had a majority but because they were more united than the parties of the center and the right. So it was obvious that the center-right simply needed to form a broader coalition. What was needed was a figure or a banner that could unite the heterogeneous forces of the right and center into a winning coalition. Urbani's analysis was consistent with Craxi's: Craxi had told Berlusconi that he needed "a label, a new name, a symbol that can unite the voters who used to vote for the old five-party coalition." The center and the right represented a majority of the country but lacked direction. There was plenty of demand, but a poor supply. No one on the political scene was giving the public what it wanted. Essentially, it was a question of marketing and sales. Politics had moved into a realm that Berlusconi understood very well and onto terrain where Berlusconi felt, with some justice, that he was unbeatable.

Initially, Berlusconi explored the less risky route of putting his marketing muscle behind another candidate capable of representing the center-right. The most likely candidate was Mario Segni, the ex–Christian Democrat who had promoted the referendum. A member of the old system who remained unscathed by scandal and was committed to reform, he seemed in a perfect position to inherit the mantle of the centrist parties. But Segni had little of the Machiavellian political genius of his Christian Democrat forebears. When Berlusconi explained that it was necessary to form alliances with the former Fascists and the separatist Lombard League, Segni recoiled with horror at the idea of teaming up with people who until that moment had been considered beyond the pale. Segni stood on principle but failed to grasp what Berlusconi had understood: within the new winner-take-all system brought about by Segni himself, victory depended on making common cause with diverse groups, even if it meant unsavory alliances and ideological incoherence. Segni would insist on running alone with his own electoral list, and as a result became a marginal figure in Italian politics. Thus he squandered the enormous popularity he had created through the referendum: as one popular saying put it, he was like the man who won the lottery but misplaced the ticket.

The other candidate whom Berlusconi tried to persuade to accept his support was Mino Martinazzoli, who formed the largest of the new Catholic parties that were cobbled together out of the wreckage of the old Christian Democratic Party. Martinazzoli, a Catholic politician of the old school, spoke a completely different language from that of Berlusconi, the TV showman and marketing whiz. "Politics isn't like selling soap," Martinazzoli told Berlusconi, "it's about ideas, values and programs."[18] But Martinazzoli was living in the past: politics had quite a bit in common with selling soap. When the Christian Democratic Party came into being after World War II, it was enough to have the backing of the Catholic Church.

Voters followed religious and ideological lines, and few if any Christian Democrat prime ministers were charismatic men. But in the post–Cold War world, television and personality and marketing mattered. Berlusconi was dismayed that the professional politicians of Italy's ossified system failed to grasp what to him was obvious.

While trying to decide whether to enter politics, Berlusconi provided himself with ample proof that he knew far better than the professional politicians how to move public opinion. The battle he and Fininvest waged to stave off the elimination of telepromotions made it clear that Fininvest had much more vigor than the political parties contending for the public's attention. For several weeks straight, the stars of Fininvest's favorite programs, from newscasts to entertainment shows, seemed to talk of nothing else, spoke warmly of the value of on-air sponsorship and warned that this abridgment of free speech was only a small taste of what one could expect from a future dominated by the former Communists. There were reports and hints of lost jobs, canceled programs and lost income likely to result from the law. Berlusconi himself appeared for a long interview on the program of Mike Buongiorno, Mr. Telepromotion himself, an appearance that, ironically, was not interrupted by advertising of any kind. Maurizio Costanzo, whose nighttime program was and remains Italy's premier political talk show, dedicated an entire program to telepromotions called *Vietato Vietare* (Forbidden to Forbid), at the end of which he urged his viewers to "bury the Ministry of Communications in faxes and telegrams."[19] Obedient viewers fired off thousands of faxes and telegrams, and plans to eliminate telepromotions were dropped.

The campaign was in a sense a muscular demonstration of the potential of the Fininvest networks as a political tool. It was in many ways a trial run for Berlusconi's election campaign.

Berlusconi spent much of the summer and fall of 1993 watching all the political talk shows on the twenty or thirty TV sets at his villa at Arcore. The figures he saw seemed mostly dull, gray party hacks, creatures of an era when organization rather than media appeal was what mattered. Used to speaking to other politicians rather than communicating on television, they made long-winded, sometimes incomprehensible speeches. Frequently Berlusconi would say: "Look, there's no one. No one." Fedele Confalonieri later recounted: "And he was right. The political class that survived Tangentopoli might be more honest—we'll see—but it was made up of second- and third-choice people, the bench players of the First Republic. Berlusconi's superiority complex got ahold of him."[20] Berlusconi was intimately convinced (and events proved him correct) that he was a much more formidable politician than all the others trying to give direction to Italian politics. What he saw was the opportunity of a lifetime: about 50 percent of the Italian electorate was up for grabs, and was being contended for by a group of mediocrities. Berlusconi's sense of his own superiority was bolstered by the private monthly polls measuring his own personal popularity. As we've seen, he had 97 percent name recognition, while the sitting prime minister was known to barely 50 percent of the population. Another poll he commissioned told him that 78 percent of the population looked favorably on the idea of "a new liberal-democratic political formation composed of people who were new to politics." (A third poll showed him as better known and more popular among Italian schoolchildren than Jesus Christ.) The political market in Italy had all the characteristics of the different businesses he had entered during his career: there was a wide-open market just waiting to be conquered. "An opportunity like this comes along only once in a lifetime," Confalonieri said in a 1994 interview. "It happened to Berlusconi as it happened to Napoleon: he saw there was a void and in three months he took Italy. . . . What is Berlusconi? A genius of marketing. Fininvest was built by filling voids. There was no green, suburban area in Milan? Here's Milano 2! No one is collecting advertising among small and medium companies? Let's start Publitalia! There's no private TV? I'll create Canale 5. No shopping malls? And so on, right up to Forza Italia."[21]

Gradually, seeing Berlusconi's determination, Confalonieri came to accept Berlusconi's decision—perhaps helped along by the fact of his own indictment and that of other Fininvest people. "If Berlusconi hadn't entered politics, we would have ended up sleeping under a bridge, on trial for Mafia ties," Confalonieri later admitted.

Berlusconi's first formal act was, characteristically, to register the trademark on the party name, Forza Italia (Go, Italy!), the slogan that Italian soccer fans chant when cheering on the national team. It was cheerful and apolitical; it lifted the spirits without indicating a clear political direction that might attract some but alienate others. It was the perfect label—the sort Craxi had sought in vain—to unite the disparate voters of the center-right.

$\dot{\frown}$

As Berlusconi began to prepare this new political movement (it was still far from clear whether he himself would be a candidate), he began to ratchet up the pressure on the media he owned to turn them from a constellation of independent or semi-independent news organizations into a well-oiled campaign war machine responding to a single commander—himself.

His biggest challenge in this regard was, once again, Montanelli's *Il Giornale*. Although now over eighty, Montanelli remained extremely vital, in top journalistic form and—self-confessed "anarcho-conservative" that he was—as hard to control as ever. There had been a kind of low-grade feud going on between the two for years and Berlusconi had taken to trying to starve Montanelli into line by making few funds available to modernize, computerize the paper, hire new journalists or increase salaries. Montanelli began to perceive the belt-tightening as a means of making him more cooperative. On the possibility of Berlusconi's entering politics, Montanelli was decidedly negative. "They will tear you apart if you enter politics," he told Berlusconi. "They will tear me apart if I don't enter politics," Berlusconi replied.[22]

In theory, Berlusconi should have had no say at all in the running of *Il Giornale* at this point; the Mammi law had supposedly forced him to sell it to his brother, Paolo. Montanelli and his deputy editor, Federico Orlando, were enthusiastic fans of the Milan prosecutors directing Operation Clean Hands. They applauded at the political demise of Craxi, Andreotti and the old guard. They supported the referendum of Mario Segni and were rooting openly for Segni to be the leader of a new centrist formation. But when Fininvest came under investigation and Berlusconi grew increasingly inclined to enter politics, he expected Montanelli's backing. When the editor of the center-left newspaper *La Repubblica*, Eugenio Scalfari, attacked Berlusconi's "trash television" and urged an investigation into the obscure origins of Berlusconi's fortune, Montanelli refused to respond directly, forcing Berlusconi to write a long, angry reply in the pages of *Il Giornale*. Montanelli responded by writing a note to Berlusconi saying that while Berlusconi was a business genius, he should leave the journalism to Montanelli. In a rage, Berlusconi telephoned deputy editor Orlando: "I have used my business genius for years, spending millions of dollars, so that he could write what he wanted in *Il Giornale*. Now he should spend some of his polemical genius against Scalfari and others so as to be useful to me."[23]

"*Il Giornale* never reacts," Berlusconi said in another tirade with Orlando. "*La Repubblica* called it 'chilling' that a poll revealed that I was better known and better loved among schoolchildren than Jesus Christ. But you didn't reply explaining why that might be, about the values that I defend that bring about this popularity. We must attack [Carlo] De-Benedetti, [Gianni] Agnelli, Scalfari, [Cesare] Romiti, [Carlo] Caracciolo [all either owners or editors of major newspapers], the way they attack me. Maurizio Costanzo [Fininvest talk-show host] said to me the other day: 'These people are not used to being attacked, if we attack them they will crawl into a shell.'"[24]

When Montanelli and Orlando failed to comply adequately, Berlusconi began to issue not-so-vague warnings. "My dear editor, I am bitterly disappointed by your lack of commitment toward me. And you should know that when I fall out of love, I fall out of love for good. I am not asking that you defend me, which Indro [Montanelli] evidently finds distasteful, but at least attack my enemies, as they do with me."[25]

To mobilize support for his new movement, Berlusconi began going over Montanelli's head by directly commissioning articles by prominent contributors to *Il Giornale* to press his agenda and attack his perceived enemies. Giuliano Urbani, distinguished professor of Italy's leading business school, Bocconi in Milan, and political counselor to Berlusconi, was enlisted to write a polemical piece against Carlo DeBenedetti, Berlusconi's rival suitor for Mondadori and owner of *La Repubblica*. Antonio Martino, a well-known conservative economist who trained under Milton Friedman at the University of Chicago, was induced to write a front-page attack against Eugenio Scalfari, editor of *La Repubblica*. Both men had much to lose by saying no to Berlusconi and much to gain by saying yes: they were already consultants to Fininvest (and, one may presume, generously compensated) and both would go on to become ministers in future Berlusconi governments. "Martino explained to me that Silvio Berlusconi asked him to write a front-page editorial against DeBenedetti," Orlando noted in a diary entry. "The professor was obviously embarrassed about the situation: he has been contributing to *Il Giornale*, working closely with me, but at the same time is a consultant of Fininvest. He asked me to help him out of this mess." They came up with a solution that at least placed a fig leaf over Martino's questionable conduct. "He will write the piece but hand it in to me rather than to Berlusconi's office as Berlusconi asked him to do."[26]

At the same time, Berlusconi was trying to find a diplomatic way of pushing Montanelli aside and placing someone prepared to fight Berlusconi's battles in charge of the political coverage of the paper. In late July, Berlusconi sent Urbani to propose this idea. "The owner is furious because he needs *Il Giornale*. If he can't have it the nice way, because of the opposition of the Old Man [Montanelli], he will find another way. He needs it to fight his battle. You don't bite and he needs the front page to shout, to do battle." Berlusconi proposed putting Vittorio Feltri, editor of a newspaper close to the Lombard League called *L'Indipendente*, in charge of the front page. Urbani supposedly told Orlando he considered the possible marriage of Montanelli and Feltri an unlikely one. "I told [Berlusconi] that he who thinks doesn't go along with him who shouts."[27] Feltri had certainly mastered the art of shouting, and having run various papers with different ideological stripes, had shown the necessary editorial "flexibility" needed to run a Berlusconi newspaper. As editor of

L'Indipendente, he had applauded the corruption investigation and written that the indictment of Bettino Craxi had given him an "almost erotic pleasure"; now he was prepared to place himself at the service of Craxi's best friend and to attack the same prosecutors.[28]

In a meeting in early August, Berlusconi proposed the Feltri solution to Montanelli, who, predictably, rejected it.

That August, when every self-respecting Italian was on vacation and entire factories were closed for the better part of the month, Berlusconi decided to remain at Arcore and invent Forza Italia. He and the advertising men from Publitalia began working up all the apparatus of a political movement, including flags, gadgets and bumper stickers. Berlusconi even wrote a party hymn. "With a hymn like this, we'll conquer Italy!" he said.[29]

Marcello Dell'Utri became campaign manager, and sent out twenty-six of his most trusted Publitalia executives to scour the country to begin identifying six hundred potential candidates, most of them from the world of business, many of them directly or indirectly connected to some part of the Fininvest empire. The nucleus of men that Berlusconi and Dell'Utri had formed to prepare for a possible political project were activated and began tapping into the various arms of the Fininvest corporate group to transform a vast commercial network into a political one.

When the editorial meetings began again in September, the tone was different. There were new, unknown people present, and the gatherings had clearly taken on the feeling of campaign strategy sessions rather than business or editorial meetings. "Today, we must talk about politics," Berlusconi began a meeting on September 25, 1993. "And the first thing we need to talk about politics and do politics is we must feel like a team. Every editor or director, with his autonomy, must play the same music. We must avoid disagreements among ourselves, one newscast against the other, one network against the other. . . . We must warn the public of the red peril that exists. . . . We must give birth to a liberal-democratic movement of the center, which allies itself with the Lombard League in order to have the largest number of deputies in parliament."[30]

Then he returned to his principal theme: a single message for all Berlusconi media. "We must sing in chorus on the themes that interest us. . . . You must understand, you top editors, that we must respond to those firing against us with a concentrated attack of all our means against them. If those who attack us unjustly . . . were assaulted simultaneously by all the various media of our group, the aggression would end there."[31]

That Berlusconi was serious about this new militarization of Fininvest was plainly evident from some of the new faces in the room. Vittorio Sgarbi, an art historian turned professional talk-show guest, who had earned a popular following by insulting and humiliating people on television, was given a TV show that went on the air for twenty minutes each day on Berlusconi's principal network, Canale 5. If Berlusconi wanted a combative journalism that "shouted," he got it with Sgarbi, whose program consisted of a bizarre twenty-minute rant in which he often literally shouted, the veins in his neck bulging as if about to burst, inveighing against Berlusconi's enemies: prosecutors who dared to investigate Berlusconi were accused of dark conspiracies, even murder. Sgarbi used such astonishingly violent language and wild, undocumented accusations that he generated dozens of slander suits, some of which led to convictions, and he was eventually taken off the air, but his work had been done.

The nightly news on Italia 1, one of Berlusconi's three networks, was assigned to Paolo Liguori, another professional polemicist, who had sharpened his tongue in the service of an extremist far-left group during the 1970s and had served various ideological causes since then—a right-wing Catholic magazine, and Montanelli's secular *Il Giornale*—the one constant being a sarcastic, vitriolic tone and contempt for his enemies of the moment. Berlusconi wanted attack journalism and he was calling out the Dobermans.

After Berlusconi dispatched Dell'Utri's Publitalia executives across the country to identify candidates, he announced, "As for me, I won't be directly involved as a candidate, I will present myself as a businessman who looks with concern on the future of the country."[32] But those who were directly involved in the secret political project had little doubt that Berlusconi was preparing to run. He already had a warehouse full of campaign kits, bumper stickers, videocassettes and audiocassettes of the party anthem he had written. "He has already passed over my dead body," Fedele Confalonieri said to Federico Orlando at the end of the September editorial meeting.[33]

Dell'Utri, Cartotto and those in charge of the political operation were already busy converting the many arms of the Fininvest commercial network, with its approximately thirty thousand employees, advertising agencies, real estate offices, supermarkets and department stores, life insurance salesmen and stockbrokers, into a vast political machine. Advertising clients were recruited; department store and supermarket suppliers were enlisted. The same means that were used to sell products to tens of millions of Italians were marshaled for the new cause. Angelo Codignoni, who had worked on Berlusconi's French TV network, La Cinq, was recruited to create Forza Italia clubs throughout Italy. "The goal was to create at least 7,000 to 8,000 clubs," Codignoni said. "Why 8,000? The experience of the Catholic Church was the model. In Italy there are about 8,000 parishes. I thought, somewhat in a competitive spirit, I have to start a club wherever there is a church."[34]

One of the pillars of this vast national network were the salesmen of Programma Italia (later called Mediolanum), which had thousands of representatives peddling life insurance, annuities and mutual funds. "Dell'Utri's admen were considered the 'aristocracy' of Fininvest: they dealt with high-level corporate executives to sell television advertising and most had become quite rich in the process," Codignoni said. "But Programma Italia instead had a client base of hundreds of thousands if not millions of small investors. Its target was much lower than the big institutional investors that Publitalia dealt with. But in compensation, they gave us a very concrete, capillary presence on the entire territory, the possibility of reaching millions of savers to whom we could talk about investment programs and about our new political idea. It was, believe me, a real force and a formidable means of penetration."[35]

As he was creating what was probably the largest and certainly most expensive campaign organization in Italy, Berlusconi continued to deny that he intended to enter politics but was rather creating a "research association . . . in order to identify the candidates who were closest to the liberal-democratic idea." (The term "liberal" in Europe means almost the opposite of what it means in the U.S.: it refers to free, unregulated markets rather than support for government intervention to promote a progressive social agenda.) But Berlusconi was shrewdly exploring and forming new political alliances. In November of 1993, he let slip (almost certainly with much premeditation) that if he lived in Rome he would vote for the postfascist candidate for mayor, Gianfranco Fini—a remark that caused a small overnight scandal. Although Fini had taken some steps to distance his party from its neofascist roots, and changed its name to the National Alliance, it was still walled off in a political ghetto, considered disreputable by mainstream politicians. Berlusconi understood that in the current political vacuum, Fini's party stood to gain between 10 and 15 percent of the conservative vote and needed to be brought in under the big tent that Berlusconi was busy creating. Berlusconi's surprising expression of support, far from being a misstep, was a calculated first move to bring the National Alliance in from political quarantine and make it respectable.

When asked, that same day, about his own political plans, Berlusconi was coy, if not flat-out deceptive. "I'm a publisher. My TV networks and my newspapers are free spaces inserted in society where everyone—I repeat—everyone, even those who think differently from how I do—has had and will continue to have the right to speak. I don't use my media to conduct battles against this or that person or to destroy my adversaries. Impartiality is my rule. And on the basis of this, it's obvious that I can't become a political figure. I can't. But I have to say, a lot of people have asked me . . . ordinary people, fellow businessmen, politicians."[36]

In his editorial meetings, Berlusconi continued to say and do the exact opposite, insisting that all his newspapers must attack, attack, attack. And as Berlusconi prepared to announce his own candidacy, the obstinate independence of Indro Montanelli and *Il Giornale* became more and more galling to him. It was inconceivable that his own newspaper, for which he had absorbed millions of dollars of losses, would not support him. Having it sing out of tune with the chorus that Berlusconi had assembled could weaken his message and confuse his potential voters. Although it had only a few hundred thousand readers, *Il Giornale* was extremely influential, an opinion maker that had been a beacon to a generation of conservative voters. At the same time, firing Montanelli for political disobedience might blow up in Berlusconi's face and cause him more harm than good. Berlusconi liked to brag that he had never laid anyone off during his business career—part of the image as paternalistic entrepreneur he was busy cultivating—and taking out the country's most famous journalist seemed a bad place to start. Finding a way to force him to resign was far preferable.

The campaign to force out Montanelli established the pattern of how Berlusconi would use his media after entering politics: it would begin with apparently random scattered potshots that might seem like purely personal initiatives (from which Berlusconi could distance himself if needed). Then, after a skirmish began, the heavy artillery of the Berlusconi media would be called in to deliver what Berlusconi had been calling for in his editorial meetings: *fuoco concentrato,* or "concentrated fire." It was symphonic in its orchestration, involving the coordination of seemingly unconnected instruments.

It began with one of the newly hired Dobermans, Vittorio Sgarbi, who dedicated his daily rant on Berlusconi's main channel, Canale 5, for three successive broadcasts (December 4 to December 6) to attacking Montanelli, calling him a Fascist, talking about his having volunteered to fight in the Italian invasion of Ethiopia (nearly sixty years before) and reading from his youthful journalism. Montanelli's early adherence to Fascism (shared by most people of his generation) was no secret and had never bothered Berlusconi in the fifteen years he had been an owner of *Il Giornale,* so why was it suddenly an issue? The answer was close at hand. "Yesterday, Montanelli fell in love with Mussolini, today he's in love with Segni."[37] Montanelli's unpardonable sin was pushing for Mario Segni to lead the moderate voting bloc rather than Berlusconi. The disingenuousness of the attack was breathtaking: the fact that Berlusconi was busy negotiating with real neofascists who had been praising Mussolini and practicing the Roman salute in the 1990s and not the 1930s did not concern Sgarbi. What mattered was throwing dirt on Montanelli.

Shortly thereafter, Emilio Fede, the anchorman of the nightly newscast on Rete 4, another of Berlusconi's three channels, raised his voice and joined the chorus. In an interview in *Corriere della Sera* of Milan, Fede criticized Montanelli for his lack of loyalty to Berlusconi and called for him to resign. "Montanelli should be grateful to Berlusconi for the rest of his life," Fede said. "There is a limit to freedom. If I were his publisher, although I wouldn't kick him in the shins, I would relieve him of his post since this is one of the prerogatives of the publishers." Up to this point, Berlusconi liked to brag about the independence and impartiality of his media. Now Fede was offering a new standard of journalistic excellence, in which integrity and "coherence" were defined by the degree of loyalty a journalist showed to his publisher. He was thus substituting a rare and all-too-infrequent quality in Italian journalism—real independence and editorial integrity—with an ethical value—faithfulness—that struck a deep chord in the Italian national psyche. (Fede, whose name literally means "faith," has made loyalty to his boss the trademark of his journalism, weeping when Berlusconi won and threatening to leave the country if he lost.) In a second interview a few days later, Fede continued the polemic, claiming that supporting Berlusconi politically was Montanelli's obligation after having taken his money for twenty years and that if Montanelli wanted to support Mario Segni he should get Segni to pay the debts of *Il Giornale*.[38]

Montanelli replied with characteristic sarcasm and humor: "I would never fire Fede because I never would have hired him."[39] Before Montanelli joined RAI, Fede had been forced to leave because of a serious gambling problem: he was found to have frequented illegal gambling parlors and was suspected of padding his large and poorly documented expense account in order to cover his mounting debts. Berlusconi saved

Fede's career and paid him generously enough to cover his losses at the casino, and Fede, in exchange, offered Berlusconi complete, even slavish loyalty. (There is a curious pattern of Berlusconi's hiring people with serious vices, or personal and monetary problems, that make them vulnerable to transformation into journalistic or political soldiers of fortune. Maurizio Costanzo, the host of Canale 5's most important talk show, was hired after he had been disgraced by having been a member of the secret P2 Masonic Lodge. The popular talk-show host Vittorio Sgarbi, who also joined in on the Montanelli kill, had been convicted of fraud and caught red-handed trying to remove precious rare books from a famous British art library and has a wild, disorderly and extravagant personal life that requires an extremely generous cash flow to maintain.)

In the days following Fede's and Sgarbi's attacks, there were news reports that Berlusconi was already negotiating a contract with Montanelli's successor, Vittorio Feltri—a story that rings true, as Berlusconi had already proposed hiring Feltri (another "shouting journalist") to take over the front page of *Il Giornale*. There were reports that Berlusconi was planning on closing most of *Il Giornale*'s foreign bureau to put the screws on Montanelli and his journalists to toe the party line. Then there was another prominent interview of Fede calling for Montanelli's resignation.

Montanelli pointed out, "Berlusconi didn't hire me as editor, I hired him as owner." At the same time, he began exploring the possibility of leaving *Il Giornale* and starting another newspaper.[40]

At three in the afternoon on January 6, 1994 (just twenty days before Berlusconi's official entrance into politics), Fede sent out a press release announcing that on that evening's newscast he would call for Montanelli's resignation. Delivering an ultimatum in the course of a nightly newscast on one of Berlusconi's channels gave the anti-Montanelli campaign the company imprimatur. If Berlusconi disagreed with Fede's extraordinary action he had three and a half hours to call him off. He did not.

Fede's attack was long and detailed: "Today, I found it objectionable the way in which Montanelli laid out the front page, dedicated mostly to the party of Mario Segni, while Berlusconi—who, aside from being our publisher, is at the center of attention—was relegated, almost hidden on the second page of the paper. . . . And so I say, when someone chooses an editorial line that differs from that of his publisher, he should, out of coherence, resign. . . . Montanelli is one of the fathers of Italian journalism and he is certainly the father of *Il Giornale,* but he is not its owner. . . . There is a relationship of trust that must exist between editor and publisher and when that trust is missing, one must draw the necessary consequences. I had the courage to resign from RAI. . . . I know it's not easy to resign, but sometimes coherence requires it."[41]

Sgarbi followed Fede's broadcast with another attack from his own TV program on Berlusconi's Canale 5, saying "Montanelli's refusal to resign is pure cowardice."[42]

Il Giornale did not respond right away to the attack, but two days later, it published a short, sarcastic note: "Thursday evening, in a surprise announcement, Emilio Fede declared, 'Now I want to speak about journalism.' Well, I guess there's a first time for everything. . . ." Then in a longer editorial about another subject, Montanelli added a brief reply to those who urged him to counterattack. "Perhaps I have disappointed many readers who expected some attack from me in reply to the extravagant remarks of a TV talking head who has called for my resignation from *Il Giornale.* I'm sorry. But, as Chateaubriand said, contempt should be used with frugality in a world where so many deserve it."[43]

These attacks set the scene for the denouement—Berlusconi's sudden and unexpected arrival at the offices of *Il Giornale* two days after Fede's broadcast, asking to speak to the assembled journalists and editors of the paper. On his arrival, Berlusconi said he had "come to renew my affection, faith and admiration for Montanelli and the journalists" and to disassociate himself from the attack of Emilio Fede. "That incident has been distorted and misinterpreted. I am not behind Fede's views. I have come to reestablish the truth." But quickly enough, Berlusconi made it clear that he wanted to renew his efforts to force *Il Giornale* to support him and become "a combative newspaper."[44] He engaged in a little old-fashioned blackmail, promising new financing for the newspaper if it would do as he wished and issuing threats if it failed to do so. "I think that if *Il Giornale* shows signs of wanting to fight this battle and to fight it with a strategy and tactics equal to those of our adversaries, there should be no lack of support for the paper. I think you have to come to understand . . . there are some battles you can fight with a fencing blade but you can't fight with a fencing blade when your opponent is using a machine gun." The alternative model he proposed was *L'Indipendente*'s Vittorio Feltri, Montanelli's designated successor, who had turned a dull and moderate (but independent) paper into the loud, angry voice of the Lombard League. Failure to comply would lead to cuts or closure. "We can't invest in a newspaper that loses money," Berlusconi said. "If it were to regain its position . . . we would certainly commit ourselves more."[45]

With this single act, Berlusconi had made a mockery of the Mammì law, which had required him to sell *Il Giornale,* as well as his claims of never interfering in the editorial affairs of his media holdings. Humiliated by this violation of his newsroom and seeing that his position had become impossible, Montanelli resigned. "[Berlusconi] promised conspicuous benefits to the staff if they adapted themselves to his tastes and rebelled against mine. I have no choice: either accept becoming Berlusconi's megaphone or resign."[46]

After Montanelli's departure, Berlusconi vigorously denied that he had anything to do with it. "I am not behind Emilio Fede. I am no longer even the publisher of *Il Giornale*. I didn't fire Montanelli, it was he who left to start another newspaper."[47] Berlusconi expressed disappointment at Montanelli's departure, saying that he had expected Montanelli to write front-page editorials for *Il Giornale* for eternity, saying that he, Berlusconi, had purchased a special fax machine so that Montanelli could continue to send in his pieces from paradise after he died. And so one of the last obstacles to Berlusconi's campaign had been removed, and all of Berlusconi's media guns were pointed in the same direction, ready for battle.

Chapter Seven

BERLUSCONI ENTERS THE PLAYING FIELD

1. THE VIDEOTAPE

Berlusconi's entrance onto the political scene was unlike anything that had ever before occurred in Italian politics. It began, appropriately enough, with a videotape, sent in the late afternoon of January 26, 1994, to all the networks, in time to air on the evening news but allowing hardly any time for journalistic preparation. At 5:30 in the evening, Berlusconi appeared on the screen of Emilio Fede's network, Rete 4, and addressed the nation from the study of his villa, with photographs of his family in the background. The pose was clearly modeled on American presidential addresses from the Oval Office.

The tone was of someone addressing the nation in a time of emergency, projecting a calm determination to save the country from imminent threat:

Italy is the country I love. Here, I have my roots, my hopes and my horizons. Here, I learned from my father and from life, my profession as an entrepreneur. Here I learned my passion for freedom.

I have decided to enter the playing field and to take up public affairs because I don't want to live in a country that is not free, governed by immature political forces and by men who are bound hand and foot to a past that was both a political and economic failure.[1]

Most of the speech was retransmitted by the other networks, and it had a huge impact. It was the grand finale of a buildup that was brilliantly modeled on successful commercial-product launches. He already had the country waiting to see what he would do next.

By the previous month, December of 1993, when it was clear that there would be elections in a few months, there were already Forza Italia clubs in every major town in Italy, with a total of some 200,000 members. Rumors were circulating—correctly, as it would turn out—that candidates had already been selected for districts across Italy and were taking screen tests and TV training sessions to prepare for the race. And yet in the months leading up to his official announcement, Berlusconi continued to vigorously deny that he intended to enter politics. "I have always said no and this will be the twentieth time that I repeat it," he said in an interview in one of his own newsmagazines, *Epoca*. "Those who say otherwise just want to pit me against the current protagonists of the political world. And so they will pretend not to read this latest denial, and I'll have to repeat it a twenty-first time and who knows how many other times."[2]

Berlusconi cited, as his reasons for staying out of the political fray, the inevitable conflicts of interest that would arise out of a double role as candidate and media owner. "I would not want to involve my media. It would be in complete contradiction with my principles and unfair to the other candidates."[3]

The frequent denials together with the evident signs of a growing party increased speculation and talk and allowed Berlusconi to dominate the political scene without having to lay out any political program or answer tough political questions. Meanwhile, the ground was continuing to be laid, in terms of both organization and image. At Christmastime, Emilio Fede's Rete 4 filmed a Yuletide special at Berlusconi's spectacular villa at Arcore, decked out with a magnificent display of holiday lights.

Berlusconi's speech moved between dark but unspecific warnings of the danger of being governed by former Communists and the prospect of a "new Italian miracle" that he offered.

The parties of the left pretend they have changed. They claim they've become liberal-democrats. But it's not true. The men are the same, their mentality, their culture, their convictions and their behavior are the same. They don't believe in the market, they don't believe in private enterprise, they don't believe in the individual. They don't believe that the world can get better through a free relationship between different people. They've not changed. Listen to them talk, look at the television shows, paid for by the State, read their newspapers. They don't believe in anything anymore. They want to turn the country into a noisy square where everyone shouts, accuses one another, condemns one another.

For this reason, we are obliged to oppose them. Because we believe in the individual, the family, in business, in competition, in development, in efficiency, in the free market and in solidarity, the child of justice and of freedom.

The speech had been carefully crafted to hit a few important notes, to awaken the strong vein of anti-Communism that had played such an important role in Italian life since World War II but which had become increasingly attenuated in the previous ten years as Communism faded from the international scene and the already moderate Italian Communists adopted more and more centrist and even conservative positions. The invocation of Communists set to take over the country seemed to many strangely anachronistic. The Italian Communist Party had broken up three years earlier and the leaders of the left were tripping over themselves to outdo one another in expressions of moderation and political realism—and now made pilgrimages to Washington, Wall Street and London to demonstrate their bona fides to the lords of the global market economy. Rather than identifying with French Socialists or German Social Democrats, they were trying to refashion themselves in the spirit of the centrism of the new American president, Bill Clinton. There were certainly legitimate reasons not to vote for the ex-Communists, but fear for Italy's democratic freedoms was not one of them.

But fear of the Communist bogeyman tapped powerful emotions in a country where, after World War II, the Catholic Church had excommunicated any believers who voted for the left. Berlusconi also touched a number of carefully market-tested positive chords as well. He characterized Forza Italia as "liberal-democratic," a term that garnered a highly positive response in his advance polling.

His message was intentionally short on specifics, following his own often repeated advice to advertisers to create a simple, clear message and repeat it again and again. He made liberal use of a series of key words that carried with them extremely positive associations: "free" or "freedom" (mentioned fourteen times in nine minutes), "Italy" or "Italian" (thirteen times), "new" (eight times), "hope" (three times), "dream" (twice), and "trust" (twice), culminating in a kind of rhetorical flourish, with three of his favorite words joined together in the phrase "new Italian miracle."

He made heavy use of the language of soccer, not only in the name of his party, but in announcing his candidacy by saying that he had decided to *"scendere in campo"*—enter the playing field.

> If I have decided to enter the playing field with a new movement, and if I ask you, all of you, to enter the playing field, too—now, right away, before it's too late—it's because I have a dream, with my eyes wide open, of a free society of women and men where there is no fear, where, instead of class hatred and social envy, there is generosity, dedication, solidarity, love of work, tolerance and respect for life.
>
> The movement I propose to you is called, not by chance, Forza Italia. What we want to create is a free organization of women and men of a totally new kind: not the latest party or the latest faction created in order to divide people but a force that is born with the opposite objective: that of uniting, of finally giving Italy a majority and a government that is capable of meeting the deepest needs of ordinary people.[4]

Like Ross Perot, he emphasized his difference from other, traditional politicians, presenting himself as a practical-minded businessman and concerned citizen who had nothing in common with the "professional politicians" who had brought the country to near-ruin.

At the same time, he gave voters what he had said he wanted to give them in his TV shows: to make people dream.

> I tell you it is possible to put an end to this politics of incomprehensible chatter, of stupid polemics. . . . I tell you that it is possible to fulfill together a great dream: of a more just Italy, more generous toward those in need, more prosperous and serene, more modern and efficient, a protagonist in Europe and in the world.
>
> I tell you that together we can, we must, create for ourselves and our children a new Italian miracle.[5]

For all his talk about concreteness, he had not made a single specific proposal or mentioned a single policy he favored, and he refused to move from the plane of vague generalities: work, market, freedom, individual, prosperity, solidarity and generosity. Nor did he explain how he intended to conjugate the values of "solidarity" and "generosity toward those in need"—the usual province of the Catholics and the Communists—with the values of the market, freedom and the individual, which seemed to indicate a preference for laissez-faire economics which might require cutting back Italy's generous welfare state.

But Berlusconi understood that form mattered much more than content. Berlusconi had scored a major coup by "entering the playing field" in a totally new way. Italian politicians held party conventions, gave rallies and public speeches, held press conferences. They invariably wanted to present themselves surrounded by supporters and like-minded allies. No one in Italian politics had ever founded a political party using videotape, appearing alone to directly address the nation of television watchers. In doing so, he placed himself above the fray, above the other political parties, who had to hustle for television coverage, who had to appear with others at rallies, who had to lower themselves by answering questions at press conferences. Berlusconi, instead, alone, spoke directly to nearly all

58 million Italians in their living rooms, like the Wizard of Oz. Refusing the mediation of political parties or of the press, Berlusconi was simply following the methods of television advertising. (Perot had done the same thing by buying unprecedented amounts of TV time in order to leapfrog over the mainstream media.)

Of course, Berlusconi was in a unique position to make this strategy work: he owned three of the six largest television networks, which could be counted on to run most or all of his nine-and-a-half-minute infomercial. In fact, Emilio Fede ran the entire videotape as soon as it arrived in his office, at 5:30 P.M., apparently without even watching it first, and would show the tape again in its entirety on the nightly news on prime time just two hours later. This "scoop" made the speech a national event, which the other networks felt obliged to cover. Paolo Liguori, one of the new Dobermans of the Fininvest empire, followed suit and showed the tape in its entirety on the evening news of Berlusconi's other openly partisan network, Italia 1. Berlusconi's third and largest network, Canale 5, whose nightly news program liked to present itself as strictly nonpartisan, ran "only" three minutes and forty-seven seconds of the speech—an eternity nonetheless in the age of the eight-second sound bite. On the public networks, the left-wing third network ran only a minute of Berlusconi's speech, RAI 2 a little over two minutes, while the most-watched network ran a little under two minutes of the speech, but then dedicated an hour-long special program that evening to discussing Berlusconi's decision. Berlusconi himself did not appear on the program, although parts of the speech were repeated, and a series of other politicians were brought in to comment on Berlusconi's entry into "the playing field." Among the chief guests were Berlusconi's chief opponent, Achille Occhetto, head of the Democratic Party of the Left, and Gianfranco Fini, one of Berlusconi's chief allies, the head of the postfascist party, which had recently renamed itself National Alliance. In some ways, this set the tone for the election, in which Berlusconi appeared as the protagonist and his political rivals appeared in the role of spectators commenting on his performances; he led and they followed and he even dominated events in which he was personally absent. "The head of the Democratic Party of the Left made a mistake, he never should have gone on that program," Sandro Curzi, a prominent left-wing journalist said at the time. "Berlusconi obliges all of us to follow him, to do what he wants. He decides everything. He doesn't accept interviews. He sends videocassettes. We should all be very worried."[6]

2. The Devil and Holy Water

Equally new was the strange set of alliances that Berlusconi proceeded to form. He had the arduous task of bringing together two political movements that loathed each other, the Northern League (Lega), which was pushing for the autonomy, even secession, of Northern Italy, and the post-fascist National Alliance (NA), whose zeal for Italian patriotism and a strong state was an echo from its Mussolinian past. "We'll never enter the government with those fascist swine! Never!" Umberto Bossi, leader of the Lega, declared with his characteristic hyperbole, mockingly referring to the members of the National Alliance as the "grandchildren of *Il Duce*."[7] Conversely, the National Alliance regarded the Lombard League, with its constant attacks on Italy and its loose talk about secession, as little more than treasonous. Combining the two was, as the Italians put it, like putting together "the devil and holy water." But both parties were outsiders, appealing to the desire to break with the traditional parties, and Berlusconi came up with an ingenious solution to bring them together without actually bringing them together: make two separate alliances, one with the Lega in Northern Italy and the other in Rome and the South with the National Alliance, since the Lega had virtually no following outside the North and the National Alliance did best in the conservative South of Italy. The Alliance had begun to expand its base by appealing to state employees and defending the privileges and prerogatives of Italy's vast government bureaucracy, which was the greatest source of wealth in Southern Italy. Getting the two parties into the same government and ironing out their differences would be postponed until after the elections. The different names of the two alliances—Casa delle Libertà (House of

Liberties) in the North and Lista del Buongoverno (Good Government List) in the South, underlined their differences. This made for complete incoherence and schizophrenia on the one hand—attacking the state bureaucracy in one part of the country and defending it in the other—but it was a great marketing tactic that allowed Berlusconi's coalition to appeal to the widest possible public. It was a classic example of the strategy Berlusconi preached to his salesmen: "Be concave with the convex, and convex with the concave." When asked about the strange bedfellows with whom he now found himself, Berlusconi replied: "There are lots of marriages of convenience that work better than love matches."[8]

To gain the allegiance of Bossi, the leader of the Northern League, Berlusconi offered extremely favorable terms: the Lega would get 70 percent of the seats that the House of Liberties won in the North. Characteristically, the deal worked out much better for Berlusconi than for his partners, for this odd set of alliances placed Berlusconi at the center as the essential linchpin that held everything together. Both the Lega and the National Alliance by themselves seemed a bit frightening to the Italian middle class. Bossi was a firebrand and a demagogue; his colorful and foul-mouthed rants captured the antigovernment mood of Northern Italy, but most Italians were not ready to trust him to lead a country he had threatened to break into pieces. The National Alliance had done much to distance itself from its Fascist roots and its leader, Gianfranco Fini, appeared to be the soul of moderation, but most Italians could not overlook the fact that only a few years before, many of AN's leaders were fervent neofascists, wearing the Fascist black shirt and giving the Roman salute. Even in 1994, Fini himself had said in a newspaper interview that he still considered Mussolini "the greatest statesman of the twentieth century." Berlusconi was the guarantor of the alliance, the one who would make sure that both the Lega and the National Alliance would complete their transformation from fringe opposition parties to responsible parties of government.

Perhaps Berlusconi's greatest triumph in the 1994 election was in capturing and channeling the energy and antigovernment mood that the

Lega had stirred up in Northern Italy. Although some followers of the Lega described Berlusconi as "Craxi with a toupee" (*"Craxi col parrucchino"*), Berlusconi was extremely able in presenting himself, not as Bettino Craxi's best friend, but as something new, the businessman-politician, representative of the industrious Northern Italy, sick of the parasitic old political class and ready to replace the "politics of chatter" with the "culture of doing." He would cut red tape and Byzantine regulations, reduce taxes, get the government off business's back and release the immense productive energies of the country. After all, hadn't he done the same thing in his own business, creating private TV out of nothing, opening up a whole new advertising market for smaller businesses that then grew into big national companies? He was able to use his long-standing battles with the state TV, RAI, as a symbol of the healthy, private Northern Italian business culture against the parasite government in Rome. Whereas before he had associated RAI with the corrupt old political parties in Rome, now he described it as a nest of Communists trying to impose a statist vision on the rest of the country. And as president of the soccer club A. C. Milan (written in Milanese dialect, *Milan,* rather than *Milano,* as it would be in standard Italian), he was the head of a beloved Northern Italian institution and had turned it back into a championship club. He loved using soccer metaphors in talking about politics, referring to himself as both a center forward and the coach who designed the team's plays. Although Forza Italia's official program was radically conservative—tax cuts for business that would have required massive reductions in highly popular government services—soccer gave Berlusconi a populist aura that cut across class lines. In a debate with Luigi Spaventa, a professional economist who was Berlusconi's opponent for a parliamentary seat in Rome, rather than having to answer questions about his economic program, Berlusconi could simply cut short the discussion by saying: "How many Intercontinental Cups have you won? Before trying to compete with me, try, at least, winning a couple of national championships!"[9] The remark had the air of unassailable truth—however irrelevant it might be to Berlusconi's fitness to govern. Thus, while Spaventa and others on the left went to pains to explain how Berlusconi's program would damage ordinary working people, Berlusconi, the billionaire, shrewdly managed to switch class roles, making opponents like Spaventa appear like an effete university professor and himself appear like a doer and a winner, a person that the average workingman and soccer fan could relate to and admire.

This was a classic move of the antipolitician. A few years later, when former professional wrestler Jesse "The Body" Ventura was elected governor of Minnesota, he responded to a question about how he would deal with the complexities of the state budget by saying: "I've jumped out of airplanes in a parachute, that's a lot harder than fixing a state budget." (As it turned out, maybe not.)

The leaders of the Lega naïvely thought that they would be the principal beneficiaries of the alliance with Berlusconi, since, after all, they would get 70 percent of the seats in parliament won by the coalition in the North. Berlusconi allegedly told them that "the Lega will provide the votes and I'll supply the TV." "If Berlusconi doesn't want the Communists to eat up his TV stations, let him come with us!" Bossi said. Roberto Maroni, the number-two figure in the Lega, said at the time, "On the right, Bossi will beat Berlusconi three to one, because the Lega, unlike Forza Italia, is a popular force."[10] But in fact Berlusconi managed to steal a lot of the Lega's thunder, the antigovernment anger of the North, while at the same time greatly expanding its appeal. Bossi, with his rumpled raincoat and his loud, often foulmouthed rhetoric, looked and sounded like a rabble-rouser and a street brawler. Bossi was known for his obscene tough-guy slogan *"La Lega ce l'ha duro!"* (The Lega has got it hard!). Berlusconi in his impeccable double-breasted blue blazer and his glittering, twenty-four-karat smile was a far more reassuring figure, the soul of respectability. He could appeal to the shopkeeper or small business owner who was furious about rigid labor laws and high taxes, but also to the shopkeeper's elderly mother who was at home watching Berlusconi's quiz shows and soap operas.

Berlusconi understood instinctively that after the end of the Cold War, the ideological appeals on which the old parties based their strength no longer worked. In the past, urban working-class Italians tended to vote al-most as a bloc for the Italian Communist Party or other parties of the left, while devout Catholics, especially in rural areas, and especially in Southern Italy, tended to vote for the Christian Democrats. The 1994 elections showed clearly that this was no longer the case. Voters were mo-bile, unhinged from their traditional ideological moorings and prepared to change positions. In a postideological age, personality, charisma, celebrity, language and image would count for much more.

The left had a series of perfectly sensible programs, proposals to re-duce bureaucracy and red tape, a financial platform that was a model of responsibility, meant to reduce inflation and trim Italy's huge budget deficit so as to allow Italy to participate in the economic unification of Eu-rope and join the single currency, the euro. It was, in fact, a fairly conser-vative program and virtually obligatory if Italy wanted to stay within the parameters of the Maastricht Treaty and not drop out of the unified Eu-rope, but there was little to inspire voters. The old Communist Party had held out the prospect of utopia, a worker's paradise. Their heirs were of-fering sound but dull technocratic measures meant to guarantee long-term prosperity, but which, in the short term, involved austerity measures that would have warmed the heart of a central banker or an official at the International Monetary Fund, but were unlikely to bring a crowd to its feet. They insisted it was a time for realism and responsibility, dismissing the need to make an emotional appeal to voters. They did nothing to make people dream.

Berlusconi, on the other hand, promised to create "a million new jobs," to reduce the number of taxes from two hundred to only ten, to reduce the overall tax burden of the country from 50 percent to only 30 percent—without cutting services, pensions and health benefits or funds for educa-tion. A lot of Berlusconi's campaign was pure demagoguery. Italy was facing a difficult situation thanks to the profligacy of the old governing class: the national debt was about 120 percent of the gross domestic prod-uct and the deficit was 7 percent and needed to be reduced to 3 percent for Italy to participate fully in the economic unification of Europe—a goal that a vast majority of Italians supported enthusiastically. The notion that Italy could cut its taxes by 40 percent, reduce its deficit and avoid cutting essential services was pure fantasy (and ten years after Berlusconi's entrance into politics, Italy has not come close to accomplishing any of these measures).

Berlusconi was also masterly in his use of polling as a political weapon. He owned his own private polling company, Diakron, which he insisted at the time was financially independent of him, but which would invariably come up with surprising results that were extremely favorable to Berlusconi. As all pollsters know, the way in which questions are framed affects the answers they elicit: Diakron came up with curiosities like the fact that schoolchildren preferred Berlusconi to Jesus Christ. Using polls that indicated that many voters were well disposed toward him, Berlusconi would suddenly make announcements like, "One out of three Italians is ready to vote for me." "Now at this point, Berlusconi's support was at maybe 10 percent, but by announcing that he was at 36 percent, people would be attracted to a candidate who appeared to have so much support, and Berlusconi would get a sudden jump in the polls," Renato Mannheimer explained. "In this way, appearance became reality. Of course, those of us who conduct polls are not supposed to lie, but politicians can do it."[11]

Berlusconi's campaign made constant, obsessive use of focus groups and market research to test out the response to his slogans and proposals, something that the traditional political parties in Italy regarded with disdain. "I remember when the antiparty attitudes began to surface in the polling data, I talked to a lot of political leaders who would tell me: 'It's not true, they've always voted for us, they'll continue to vote for us,'" Mannheimer recalled. "I remember Bettino Craxi telling me, 'I'm an old socialist, I'll never use these new instruments. If I want to know what people are thinking, all I have to do is talk to my chauffeur.' The leaders of the old parties, on the left and the right, didn't understand the elements of novelty in the political market."

"There's a radical difference between our campaign and that of the left," Gianni Pilo, Berlusconi's chief pollster said. "They impose a program on the heads of the country. We interrogate people in order to find out what they have in mind. . . . We then move to the focus group, the technique used in the U.S. that allowed James Carville, the consultant to Bill Clinton, to beat George Bush." Berlusconi and Pilo spent millions on almost daily polls and for months Berlusconi spoke virtually every day with his pollster to gauge the ebb and flow of Italian public opinion. Pilo's main finding was that ideological and religious affiliations of Italian voters were much weaker than in the past and that voters' principal aspiration was to make money and get ahead.[12]

Berlusconi understood that voters were more interested in personality than in programs, and that what he needed to do was to sell himself and the lifestyle he represented. His own story as self-made man and billionaire soccer club owner was more convincing and appealing than the explanations by economists of the left of the short-term sacrifices and long-term benefits involved in Italy's joining Europe's single currency.

The center-left refused to state who their prime minister would be should they win, so they were a coalition without a clear leader. The campaign was conducted largely by Achille Occhetto, the secretary of the Democratic Party of the Left, the largest party in the center-left alliance. The ex-Communists agreed to accept a centrist without a Communist past as prime minister but didn't want to alienate their left-wing base by making this compromise before the election. In the old system, parties competed with other parties, not with people, but the left failed to understand that in the television era, things had changed. In a somewhat desperate attempt to "personalize" his campaign, and give it some life and sex appeal, Occhetto allowed himself to be photographed passionately kissing his wife; but the act looked awkward and forced, like a transparent effort by an old-school politician to pander to the new realities. Al Gore, another candidate desperate to inject life and sex appeal into his pale and bloodless public image, did almost the exact same thing at the Democratic Convention in 2000, giving an extremely long and rather embarrassing French kiss to his wife Tipper on prime-time television.

3. THE CORPORATION AS CAMPAIGN WAR MACHINE

Berlusconi also introduced a series of other novelties to Italian campaigning, using the money, technology and know-how of his media empire. An executive from Programma Italia, Berlusconi's investment company, wired all the several thousand Forza Italia clubs for satellite transmission so that Berlusconi could address the club members live and in real time. During campaign events, huge video screens were placed in piazzas throughout Italy. "Imagine you are in a place like Catanzaro [a city in Calabria, in Southern Italy], and in the middle of a rally with all the local candidates, the president of the local Forza Italia club, and then suddenly, at a certain point, on the video screen from Arcore, Silvio Berlusconi himself materializes," says Angelo Codignoni, one of the many Fininvest executives drafted to help organize the campaign. "You can imagine the drama, the effect it made in the provinces."[13]

The Berlusconi campaign took ideas from the business world and applied them to the political forum. The campaign set up pay-as-you-go phone numbers so that Berlusconi supporters would pay several dollars a phone call to listen to Berlusconi or some of the stars from Berlusconi's TV empire like Emilio Fede or Mike Buongiorno while making a financial contribution to the campaign. Another money-making campaign strategy was to put Forza Italia coupons in the Berlusconi magazine *Sorrisi e Canzoni TV* (Smiles and Songs TV), an extremely popular magazine of light entertainment. Readers were encouraged to cut out the coupon and send 100,000 lire (a little less than $100) to the nascent Forza Italia movement. Berlusconi's executives-turned-campaign-workers were strong believers in these money-making devices, not just as a way of financing the campaign but as a way of creating a political movement. "If people participate financially, they believe in it more," said Mario Valducci, one of the many Fininvest men working on the campaign.[14]

Even the candidates for Forza Italia were obliged to pay. Potential candidates who were interested in running for office were encouraged to pay 5 million lire (about $4,000 at the time) to take a screen test and a training session at Arcore. Along with the fee, they paid for their own transportation and hotel, but they did get a dinner at Arcore attended by Berlusconi. All candidates for Forza Italia were required to spend a million lire (about $800 at the time) to buy a candidate's kit, like a salesman's kit—a briefcase with a candidate's manual on how to communicate with voters; Forza Italia pins, buttons and bumper stickers; little Forza Italia flags and a video with the election program of Forza Italia. There were also tapes with the Forza Italia hymn, in both regular and karaoke versions. The hymn was supposedly written by Berlusconi himself. ("With a hymn like this, we can't lose!" he is supposed to have exulted.)

To Forza Italia's candidates, Berlusconi dispensed much the same advice he had been handing out to his television advertising force.

> Pay attention to your breath, stay a certain distance from the people you are speaking to.... Keep a handkerchief in your pocket to dry your hands from time to time.... If you use a public toilet and it's dirty, clean it, otherwise, those who come after you will think you dirtied it....
>
> In your contact with people, you must always try to create an atmosphere of sympathy. Remember that for everyone there is a music that is particularly welcome: their first name and last name. So continue to repeat the first and last name of the people you meet because this will be seen as a sign of attention and will make them trust you.... You must always pay people sincere compliments, like, What a beautiful smile you have, What a beautiful tie.... Give the Italian flag to couples who are getting married, send a note to congratulate people on their fiftieth wedding anniversaries, give the constitution to kids who are turning eighteen....[15]

> Remember, repetition always helps. Always repeat the same speech. The public that watches you on television has more or less a seventh-grade education and probably didn't finish at the top of the class. The most they know is: I like this, I don't like that.[16]

Although many people made fun of the candidate's kit, and the corporate model of candidate as detergent salesman, these did reinforce the impression that if nothing else Berlusconi represented something genuinely new on the political scene. The technological razzle-dazzle of the satellite hookups and the pay-as-you-go phone calls, the ability to create a political party out of nothing in a few short months, gave the impression that Berlusconi could apply his entrepreneurial flair to politics and turn it into something different.

Berlusconi and his acolytes from Fininvest were convinced that their being political novices from another world was their great advantage. "We are the innovators because we are starting from scratch," said Gianni Pilo, Berlusconi's chief pollster in 1994. "The big railway companies thought only in terms of railroads and so when the automobile came along, they didn't get it. None of the people in the movie business saw the potential of television. Those already working inside a market are not able to see real, radical innovation. Politicians in Italy are unable to change their mentality. They look at us like Martians because we are Martians—we come from another world, the trenches of the business world. They will understand only after the vote, when it will be too late for them."[17]

Added to this difference of mentality, Berlusconi's money and television stations also gave him a series of huge advantages. Although the Italian parliament passed a law that banned political advertising on television during the final four weeks of the campaign, there was a month between Berlusconi's entrance into politics and the time when the ban went into effect in which Forza Italia carpet-bombed the country with TV ads. Because the state TV was forbidden from taking political advertisements, Berlusconi's opponents were in the difficult position of having to either advertise on his networks or forgo TV advertisements altogether. In fact, the center-left coalition relied almost exclusively on billboard advertisements in an age in which more than 70 percent of Italians got virtually all their news from television.

Was it a mistake for the left not to advertise on TV? Probably not, since it's not clear how effective advertising on Berlusconi's networks would have been. As all advertising executives understand, the impact of an ad is greatly affected by the context in which it appears. Berlusconi had been telling potential advertisers that at Fininvest he had created a programming environment—with soap operas and TV dramas showing glamorous and opulent lifestyles—that was extremely favorable for selling their products. Since Berlusconi's image was inextricably linked to Fininvest, and the devoted fans of his TV programs (about 45 percent of the Italian public) had a higher regard for Berlusconi than did the population at large, Forza Italia's ads were playing before an extremely receptive audience. Conversely, an ad for a rival party, particularly one under constant attack from Berlusconi, might have little impact in an environment dominated by their chief adversary. Appearing on Berlusconi's networks, they might have appeared diminished, like guests of the great impresario, while Berlusconi would emerge enlarged, like the magnanimous host who allowed even his political enemies to appear on his TV networks.

Moreover, after Berlusconi had "militarized" his media during the previous summer, insisting that all his newspapers, magazines and television stations "sing in chorus," the Fininvest networks had taken political partisanship to a whole new level. Less than a week after Berlusconi's "enter the playing field" speech, Ambra Angiolini, the teenage heartthrob of one of Fininvest's most popular programs declared in the middle of a skit, "God is rooting for Forza Italia, while the Devil, we know, is rooting for [the left]."[18]

Berlusconi's network Rete 4, directed by the ever-faithful Emilio Fede, canceled its usual programming on Sunday afternoon, February 6, and broadcast the entirety of a Berlusconi speech for the better part of an hour, from the rousing applause with which he was greeted to the rousing applause at his speech's conclusion. "Never before, even the days when [Christian Democratic leader Arnaldo] Forlani was the boss of RAI 1 and [Bettino] Craxi was the boss of RAI 2 had anything of the kind happened: never had the regular programming of a television network been interrupted to broadcast live, in its entirety, the speech of a political leader," wrote political journalist Gianni Statera.[19] Fede defended himself, insisting that he would have done the same for any number of political figures of the left or the right, but of course he never did.

Berlusconi alternately denied and defended the political slant of his networks, insisting that he and his party were "the most excluded and badly treated on television." It was typical of what would become one of the trademarks of his political career: attacking on the points on which he was weakest, accusing others of the things of which he himself was guilty. He insisted that RAI was in the hands of the Communists and that RAI was engaging in "a shameless campaign for the progressives."[20]

A close analysis of the 1994 campaign shows that there was some degree of center-left bias at RAI, but it was considerably less one-sided than the Berlusconi networks. Far from being a nest of Communists, RAI had been divided up by the main political parties, with the preponderance of influence going to the parties of government. RAI 1 was filled with journalists who owed their jobs to the Christian Democrats, RAI 2 with people handpicked by Bettino Craxi and his associates. Only RAI 3 had a clear left-wing orientation. It's true that with Operation Clean Hands and the fall of the old parties, RAI had responded to the shifting political winds and moved somewhat toward the left. It's true that a number of its journalists who had a clear left-of-center orientation (Michele Santoro, Mario Deaglio) were given a lot of air time, but it's also true that their programs were extraordinarily successful. They had intuited the dissatisfaction with the old parties and were rewarded with large audiences in the wake of Operation Clean Hands. Their presence on the air had ample professional and commercial, as well as political, justification. The nightly news programs, if tilting slightly toward the left, were careful to give space to all sides and performed very few of the political stunts that Emilio Fede and Paolo Liguori engaged in on a regular basis on the Rete 4 and Italia 1.

Despite directly controlling about 40 percent of the Italian press, Berlusconi continued insisting that the Communists "could count on ninety percent of Italian journalists." He even insisted that he was penalized by his own television networks. "On my own networks, there is a kind of 'boss' complex, and, so far, they give more space to my adversaries than to me," he declared during the 1994 campaign. The official monitoring of the main six TV stations demonstrates the exact opposite. Emilio Fede's Rete 4 dedicated 68 percent of its coverage to Berlusconi and Forza Italia, and a full 77 percent to the center-right coalition. The little coverage dedicated to the center-left was mostly disparaging. Italia 1, another of Berlusconi's networks, dedicated 53 percent of its coverage to Forza Italia, even though it was only one of several parties contending for votes, while Canale 5, the most balanced of the Berlusconi networks, reserved 30 percent of its time for Forza Italia and 56 percent for the center-right. The RAI networks, in fact, dedicated slightly more space to the center-right coalition than the center-left (37.4 percent versus 40.5 percent).[21]

A qualitative view shows that the state networks did treat the center-left more favorably than Berlusconi's center-right. In one study by the University of Rome, RAI broadcasts made favorable comments about the center-left 11 percent of the time, while only 5.6 percent of comments were favorable about the center-right and 5.3 percent for a smaller coalition of the center. Fourteen percent of comments about the center-right were unfavorable, compared to 11 percent of the comments about the left and 10.5 percent about the center. But opinion and bias were much more present on the Berlusconi networks: 37.5 percent of the reportage about Forza Italia had a clearly favorable tone, while 41.2 of the references to the left were clearly negative. An analysis of the three major daily newspapers—supposedly all hostile to Berlusconi—shows a much more balanced picture with a slight but significant advantage for Berlusconi: 14.4 percent of comments favorable to the left, 17.1 percent favorable to the center and the largest percentage, 23.2 percent, favorable to Berlusconi's center-right coalition. So much for 90 percent of the press being in the hands of the Communists.[22]

4. A Minor Inconvenience: The Corruption Investigation

There was, however, one way in which Berlusconi was at a serious disadvantage with respect to his principal competitors. The Milan prosecutors of Operation Clean Hands already had a few investigations open against Fininvest executives as well as several others that would eventually lead them in the same direction.

In November 1993, two months before Berlusconi entered politics, Bettino Craxi, tired of taking the blame for so much political corruption, filed a memorandum in which he made it very clear that all the major "national and international companies" in Italy, including Fininvest, which he mentioned specifically by name, had paid the political parties and many of their leaders. A few days later, without naming names, Francesco Saverio Borelli, the chief prosecutor of Milan said: "Those who want to run for office should look inside themselves. If they are clean, let them go ahead. But if they have skeletons in their closets . . . open the closet and then step aside. Step aside, I say, before we arrive."[23]

This represented something of a problem for Berlusconi, who was running as a candidate who had nothing to do with the old system of corruption, which he deplored on the campaign trail. "Enough of the old politics, we want a politics that is different, new and clean! We are the Italy that saves against the Italy that steals. We are the Italy of decent people against the Italy of the old parties."[24]

While the Milan prosecutor's office had refrained from taking any actions that might affect the elections in 1992, Borelli said that this time the office would not put its investigations on hold for the election campaign. Two years after the beginning of Tangentopoli, the Italian political class had been put on notice. Thousands had been arrested and politicians could no longer claim that political corruption was a widely accepted practice. The prosecutors, Borelli said, were not interested in affecting the outcome of the elections, and since candidates shouldn't have anything to hide, Operation Clean Hands should not have any influence at all.

The members of the anticorruption pool of Milan had become national heroes, and they were actively courted by different political parties to run for office. They decided, however, to resist the temptation so that their work would not be interpreted as an attempt to pave the way for any particular parties.

Berlusconi's company was already under investigation; his entrance into politics guaranteed that any further efforts to pursue cases that led to Fininvest would be seen as "political."

On February 1, 1994, prosecutors in Milan arrested the president and chief executives of one of Milan's chief savings banks, Cariplo, on charges of taking bribes from real estate developers who were looking to sell buildings and apartments. The under-the-table payments were said to have been passed on by the bank to various political parties, in particular the Christian Democratic Party, of which the bank president was a prominent member. (The bank president was eventually acquitted, although the existence of the payments was confirmed.) Since the investigation led into the heart of the Milan real estate industry, it is hardly surprising that it soon led to the doorstep of the Fininvest of Berlusconi, the "king of bricks." One executive testified that he had taken about 1 billion lire (approximately $613,000) from Paolo Berlusconi for agreeing to buy three real estate properties. On February 12, prosecutors issued a warrant for Berlusconi's younger brother, who, after avoiding arrest for two days, acknowledged making the payoffs.[25] Even though his brother had admitted paying substantial bribes, Berlusconi immediately denounced the prosecution as a political plot by left-wing judges against him, sounding a theme he would repeat obsessively during the next twelve years anytime anyone tried to prosecute members of his inner circle, no matter how solid the evidence against them. Berlusconi's claim was not easy to support at this point, since a number of former Communists had also been prosecuted by the Milan judges. In fact, on the day of Paolo Berlusconi's arrest, a high-level official of the Democratic Party of the Left was also indicted, prompting speculation that the scandal might lead to the party secretary, Berlusconi's main adversary.

In March 1994, just a few weeks before the election, prosecutors in both Milan and Turin discovered evidence that Marcello Dell'Utri and his company Publitalia had systematically falsified company payment receipts in order to divert large sums of cash that he either kept for himself or used to make cash payoffs to others. Dell'Utri would eventually be convicted of the charges. Berlusconi denounced the indictment as an "ignoble political maneuver."[26]

Berlusconi had to some degree prepared for such an eventuality by convincing a prominent critic of Operation Clean Hands, Tiziana Parenti, to run as a candidate with Forza Italia. Parenti was herself a magistrate who had worked for a brief time on the corruption investigation but claimed that her colleagues were going easy on Communist defendants. Her fellow prosecutors had decided that the evidence in a case she had investigated on a particular left-wing official was too thin to go to trial; an appeals court agreed with them. But even a marginal figure in Operation Clean Hands who was willing to lend a little anticorruption luster to Forza Italia while simultaneously attacking her colleagues as Communist tools was a very welcome addition to the team. This allowed Berlusconi both to appear to support the anticorruption investigation, and to be able to argue, should it be necessary, that some of the magistrates were politically motivated.

Parenti succumbed to a Berlusconi charm offensive straight out of his "Profession: Friendship" sales talks. "Berlusconi is an exquisite person, hospitable, gallant and amusing," she said at the time. "I remember the first time I met him at dinner, although we had never met before, he recalled a number of things about me, he complimented me right away, almost as soon as we met."[27] Parenti was introduced at the congress of Forza Italia as the future minister of justice—quite a heady leap for an obscure and not particularly distinguished magistrate who was most famous for a prosecution she had failed to make.

Of course, a magistrate running for office by attacking prosecutors who had refused offers of political office that she had accepted is something of a contradiction in terms, but Parenti's charges that the Milan prosecutors had played political favorites seemed to be supported by some objective facts: more Craxian Socialists and Christian Democrats had been prosecuted than Communists.

This did not, however, necessarily mean that the magistrates singled out the conservative parties and spared the ex-Communists of the Democratic Party of the Left (Partito Democratico della Sinistra, PDS). On the whole, political parties were hit by the corruption scandal to the degree that they held the purse strings of government. The Socialists ran Milan and it was inevitable that they would be the hardest hit by the Milan prosecutors, together with their principal allies, the Christian Democrats. In many city agencies, there was an established formula: 5 percent of the value of a contract would be kicked back, with 80 percent of the money split between the Socialists and Christian Democrats and the remaining 20 percent divided among the other parties.

The Communists also participated in many of these schemes, particularly in cities where they were part of the governing majority. But the Communists were excluded from the national government and thus were cut out of many of the biggest deals. In Milan, where the ex-Communists helped run parts of city government, the party was virtually decapitated. Less than two weeks after arresting Paolo Berlusconi, the supposedly "red robes" of Milan issued 102 indictments for bribes within the Milan subway system. Of these, six were for extremely prominent members of the Democratic Party of the Left, including the Milan party secretary, two city council members and the number-two executive of the Milan subway system. They didn't indict the top political leaders of the party, but prosecutors insisted that they never had sufficient evidence to do so. It was not entirely for lack of effort. The Milan prosecutors held Primo Greganti, a party official who collected millions in payoffs, in prison for months—longer than almost any other defendant—insisting that he must have acted with the knowledge of higher-ups. But while most others gave in and confessed, Greganti held out and allowed himself to be convicted without seeking to implicate others.

A leading prosecutor from Venice, Carlo Nordio, much beloved of Berlusconi and the Italian right, insisted that the Communist leaders had gotten off easy and tried to bring cases against the leading politicians of the center-left. He had to drop the cases because of lack of evidence.[28]

If the Milan prosecutors had been making cases on political grounds, they would have gone after one of Berlusconi's main political allies, the right-wing party, the National Alliance. But it was almost entirely spared by the corruption scandal because, before 1994, the neofascists were virtually excluded from the seats of power.

In fact, the National Alliance made a great show of support for the Milan judges in its early years, before its destiny was linked so closely with Berlusconi's. Two of the four core members of the anticorruption pool in Milan were law-and-order conservatives, considered, rightly or wrongly, to be "right-wing." Antonio Di Pietro, the motor of Operation Clean Hands, was an idol of the National Alliance at this time, and the party also tried to recruit Piercamillo Davigo, another central figure in the pool, to be minister of justice. Davigo refused, fearing that it would give a political coloring to his and his colleagues' work. If half of the pool was "right-wing," was it really credible that the investigation was a tool of the left?

Berlusconi shrewdly adopted a double policy toward the corruption probe. The great majority of the time, he continued to praise Operation Clean Hands. "We are all more free," he said. At the same time, some of his surrogates began attacking the prosecutors. Vittorio Sgarbi, the attack dog of Canale 5, dedicated two entire programs of his daily show to the unjust arrest of Paolo Berlusconi. Each broadcast began and ended with a photomontage of Chief Prosecutor Borelli dressed up as a woman accompanied by the sound of chickens clucking. With Berlusconi in politics, a new, savage kind of journalism—entertaining, vicious and wildly partisan—was taking shape.

But part of Berlusconi's genius in announcing his candidacy only two months before the vote was that it gave the Italian public and the press a very short time to examine his record and investigate his involvement in the system of corruption that had just collapsed. In his public appearances, Berlusconi made repeated statements that he had received no benefits from Bettino Craxi and had lived far from the world of political corruption. "Accusing me of corruption is like arresting Mother Teresa because a little girl under her care stole an apple," Berlusconi said at one point, referring to the bribes paid by his companies.[29] Of course, Paolo Berlusconi and Marcello Dell'Utri were as much little orphan girls as Silvio Berlusconi was Mother Teresa, but in the end Tangentopoli ended up not being a major issue in the 1994 campaign.

Rather than asking themselves how Berlusconi had amassed his vast fortune in such a short time, many voters more or less took for granted that Berlusconi had done the kinds of things most other businessmen had done, but they did not necessarily see this as a problem. Since many voters assumed that most politicians were corrupt, they felt that a rich businessman might be less inclined to milk the system than a professional politician. "He's too rich to steal," many voters said at the time.

Rather than seeming to be a product of the old system, Berlusconi was particularly able at portraying himself as a fresh alternative to the tired old faces of Italian politics. Speaking about the two top leaders of the Democratic Party of the Left, he said: "Both of them have only been party functionaries. Imagine me and them being questioned by an ordinary citizen: what have you done in your life? I can talk about making buildings, newspapers, television stations, the second-biggest corporation in Italy. And they? They can only say that they were Communists and picketed in front of factories."[30]

Italians, voters and journalists alike, paid remarkably little attention to the problem of the conflicts of interest represented by such a major economic figure, particularly in the delicate area of the media, combining so much public and private power. Berlusconi insisted that he would resolve the problem shortly after the elections, and no one made a big issue out of it. Neither the other political parties nor the press thought, for example, to force Berlusconi to promise to sell his company if he should become prime minister. It would not have been unreasonable to ask Berlusconi to choose between being the biggest figure in public life or the dominant figure in private media. But the idea of "conflict of interest" was a new and alien concept to Italy, where insider trading had only been recently made a crime. After all, wasn't it simply smart business to use all the knowledge at one's disposal to try to make money?

5. THE RETURN OF THE REPRESSED: THE MAFIA PROBLEM

Another specter hung over Berlusconi's campaign: the accusation of Mafia ties. When he was contemplating entering politics, he later said, his closest advisers warned him against it, predicting that his opponents would destroy him by tying him to the Italian mob.

Sure enough, a few newspapers and magazines began looking into the strange story of Vittorio Mangano, the stable hand at Arcore who had been convicted of heroin trafficking, and the curious career of Marcello Dell'Utri, who was now Berlusconi's campaign manager. After all, Mangano had been tried and convicted in numerous cases, including the maxi-trial of Palermo, the largest Mafia trial in history and some of the wiretaps and police reports involving Dell'Utri had made it into the public record.

Unbeknownst to the public, Vittorio Mangano, out of prison again, paid a visit to Dell'Utri at the end of November 1993, just as Dell'Utri was preparing Berlusconi's much-rumored but yet-to-be-announced election campaign. Although he was both campaign manager and the president of Publitalia, one of Berlusconi's most important companies, Dell'Utri somehow made room in his schedule for the old Mafioso. Years later, when prosecutors asked about the visit, Dell'Utri replied: "Mangano used to come see me from time to time about personal matters, often related to his health."[31]

Was Cosa Nostra, having lost its traditional political protectors in the Christian Democratic Party, anxious to make contacts with the new protagonists of Italian politics?

"We will vote for Berlusconi," Giuseppe Piromalli, one of the heads of the Calabrian Mafia known as the 'Ndrangheta, announced publicly in open court in the middle of the election campaign. It's hard to know whether this was the fruit of contact between organized-crime figures and people within the Berlusconi campaign, or whether the gangsters were operating on the tried-and-true axiom that "the enemy of my enemy is my friend." Some of the same prosecutors who were making life close to impossible for the Mafia might decide to take a look at Marcello Dell'Utri and Berlusconi's friends in Sicily. Forza Italia, especially in Southern Italy, had begun to criticize the magistrates who had "gone too far" in pursuing corruption and the Mafia. One of the effects of Tangentopoli was to shut down many public works projects in order to make sure that they were not indirectly controlled by organized crime. The call to get construction sites working again was a popular one in the South, even though most of these projects had proven to be colossal wastes of money, disasters for the environment and boons to organized-crime groups.

The 1994 campaign was full of strange signs and portents. Vittorio Sgarbi, TV star and attack dog, presented himself as a center-right candidate for Calabria, even though he had no connection to the region, and went around fulminating against the crimes and misdemeanors of the arrogant Mafia prosecutors. This was music to the ears of men like the Calabrian boss Piromalli, whose organizations were in pieces. (The fact that the Mafia crackdown had succeeded in lowering the murder rate in Italy by nearly 50 percent by putting thousands of gangsters in jail was not discussed.) There were growing suspicions that in Southern Italy, Forza Italia had recycled a lot of candidates from the old political parties, some of them with friends in organized crime. As the vote approached, a prosecutor from Calabria sent police agents to the Forza Italia headquarters. More immediately threatening for Berlusconi were rumors that prosecutors in Sicily were reopening old investigations into Marcello Dell'Utri. Privately, Berlusconi began to grumble that Dell'Utri might cost him the election.

Berlusconi was able to avert a public relations disaster, but it took a little help from the Italian press. About two weeks before the election, a journalist for *La Stampa* of Turin published a front-page article, presented as a major scoop, claiming that the president of the parliament's anti-Mafia commission, the former Communist Luciano Violante, had allegedly told him that Dell'Utri was under investigation by prosecutors in Sicily. There was an immediate furor. For the president of a bipartisan commission of parliament to leak confidential information to damage a political opponent was perceived to be a grave abuse of office. There was little new in the substance of the story: newspapers had already printed rumors about possible investigations of Dell'Utri. It was the alleged source that made it a scoop. The conversation took place at the coffee bar of parliament, where the journalist buttonholed the parliamentarian. Violante, normally tight-lipped with journalists, insisted that it was the journalist, Augusto Minzolini, who expounded his theories about the Dell'Utri case and then put them in Violante's mouth. "I listened and I don't think I even said yes or no," Violante said. "I might have said, 'Maybe so.'" It has never been clearly established what happened—and the newspaper later apologized for the story. But the way the story was written and publicized—the headline was "The Secrets of Violante: What I Know About Dell'Utri"—made Violante look bad and played perfectly into the hands of Berlusconi, who immediately held a press conference calling for Violante's resignation. That evening the newscasts of Berlusconi's networks denounced the uncovering of a plot against Berlusconi and mounted a drumbeat of calls for Violante's resignation.[32]

The story, based on an off-the-record remark that may or may not have been made in the course of an informal conversation, completely reversed the situation in Berlusconi's favor. The Dell'Utri case suddenly turned, overnight, into the Violante case. No one bothered to discuss whether the future prime minister and his campaign manager did or did not have worrisome relations with the Sicilian Mafia; they were too preoccupied with whether Violante should or should not resign as president of the anti-Mafia commission. Fearing that he was becoming a distraction, Violante resigned.

The Violante case had the effect of inoculating Berlusconi and Dell'Utri against Mafia accusations. Politicians on the left, who might well have extremely legitimate reasons to call for investigations to get to the bottom of Dell'Utri's liaisons, have remained almost entirely silent for twelve years, even after significant amounts of new evidence were unearthed by prosecutors. They have been afraid to raise the issue publicly for fear it will turn into another Violante case.

Not long after the Violante episode, the journalist who published the "scoop," Minzolini, was approached about going to work for Berlusconi's Mediaset television networks, and, for a time, was given a lucrative consulting TV contract as well as a weekly column in Berlusconi's newsweekly magazine *Panorama*, while continuing to hold down his job at *La*

Stampa. It is hard to say whether Minzolini was rewarded for his services to the cause, but certainly by giving Minzolini a second income, the Berlusconi people were coopting one of the country's more influential political journalists. Minzolini's colleagues at the paper noted that he was suddenly driving a fancy car. In a country with a more independent press, *La Stampa* would never have allowed one of its own journalists to earn a second salary from one of the principal subjects he would need to cover in his work. Perhaps not coincidentally, Minzolini went on to write extensively about Berlusconi and was the journalist to whom he granted two relatively rare longer one-on-one interviews, including one in which the journalist accompanied Berlusconi to his vacation home in the Bahamas. The pieces are notable for their lack of Minzolini's usual distinctive biting sarcasm. *Non si sputa sul piatto da cui si mangia*—you don't spit on the plate you eat from, as a popular Italian saying puts it.

On March 25, just two days after Violante's resignation, Mike Buongiorno, the pudding-faced host of *Wheel of Fortune* on Berlusconi's main TV channel, decided to inform his faithful viewers about the upcoming election. "Good, good, and now the moment has come for me to talk to you about our president, our great sponsor, the man all Italy is talking about!" He went on to sing the praises of Berlusconi.[33]

On the night of March 28, 1994, Berlusconi's coalition won the elections, besting the center-left alliance by 46.3 percent to 34.3 percent (various parties of the center accounted for the rest). Berlusconi's Forza Italia narrowly became the country's largest party, with 21 percent of the vote, compared to 20.3 for the Democratic Party of the Left. On Berlusconi's Rete 4 that evening, Emilio Fede wept with joy. "Silvio Berlusconi has won his battle, with great courage, alone with everyone against him. I must tell you now," Fede said, visibly tearing up, "he telephoned me, and told me, as one friend to another, 'Let's hope to get down to work for the good of Italy.' What can I tell you, since I have been here, he has always allowed me to work in complete liberty." He paused as if unable to go on, a tear falling from his eye.[34]

Italy had entered the Berlusconi era.

Chapter Eight

BERLUSCONI IN POWER

1. WHY BERLUSCONI WON

As the dust settled, politicians, political scientists and ordinary citizens began to ask themselves: how had a political novice been able to take over one of the largest countries in Europe in just two months? Many foreign observers, who were familiar with Berlusconi's checkered past, asked themselves how a country seemingly sick of corruption and anxious for reform could elect a man who was tied so closely to the leading figures of the old system, his companies under investigation for handing out bribes and suspected of ties to organized crime?

Berlusconi won, in part, for fairly conventional political reasons. He filled the void left by the parties of the center and the right—the Christian Democrats and the Socialists—who had, together with their smaller allies, represented a majority for the previous forty-five years. He had understood better than his adversaries the nature of the new winner-take-all electoral system and built the widest possible alliance. He produced a clearer and more appealing message and communicated it more effectively than his adversaries. He had successfully (if disingenuously) appealed to the desire for change, offering himself as something new—the businessman in politics—managing to tap into and channel the Northern protest vote, the anger against the state, the desire for lower taxes and less regulation. At the same time, he represented a reassuring continuity, sweeping the old Christian Democratic stronghold in the South, which would resist the very changes his Northern supporters wanted.

To some degree, Berlusconi's electorate resembled that of the old Christian Democratic Party: the less educated segments of the population concentrated in smaller towns and rural areas. "It is not true that Berlusconi won because he interpreted elements of novelty," said Piergiorgio Corbetta, a scholar of Italian electoral politics at the University of Bologna. "His electorate represents many elements of an older Italy, less educated, more rural, with the classic traits of 'amoral familism,' distrust of others, distrust of institutions, lack of connection to the state."

But there were elements of genuine novelty in the Berlusconi phenomenon. At least in 1994, Berlusconi did slightly better among younger voters, especially those who grew up watching his TV stations and who read less. He did better among entrepreneurs and small-business owners, who were the most dynamic part of the Italian economy. (The center-left, however, did better among high-level business executives.) He also did surprisingly well among working-class voters, which represented something of a breakthrough. In the past, the working class voted along ideological lines, voting with great consistency for the Italian Communist Party. One of the novelties of the 1994 vote is that these abiding ideological loyalties that had dominated Italy for fifty years—both toward the Catholic Church and toward the Communist Party—had largely passed away.

On close inspection, the social scientists found that Berlusconi voters— whether shopkeepers or housewives, North or South—had a common denominator: an unusual degree of loyalty to an entirely different institution, Berlusconi's TV networks. In fact, voters were distinguished to an astonishing degree by the television networks and programs they watched. "In other words, the world of show business and television distinguishes the electorate more than the divisions of class," Roberto Cartocci, a professor of political science at the University of Bologna, wrote.

"Put another way, the two coalitions are separated not so much by the traditional division of labor and capital but rather by the competition between RAI and Mediaset. It is hard not to read into this fact a peculiarity of 'post-modern' politics in which loyalties with the immaterial world of the media are stronger than the traditional divisions of class that marked the modern era."[1]

Most Italian voters were rather skeptical of the media. Among the nearly 80 percent of the population who didn't vote for Forza Italia, only 8.3 percent expressed a "great deal of trust" in Berlusconi's TV channels and only slightly more (11.7 percent) in RAI. But among Forza Italia voters, 26.2 percent showed great trust in the Fininvest networks, more than in almost any institution in the country, including Italy itself, which only 17.9 percent of Forza Italia voters said they trusted a lot.

But many observers warn against an overly simplistic reading of this data. "Berlusconi didn't win because he controlled three TV stations during the campaign," said Giuliano Ferrara, who served as one of Berlusconi's speechwriters, advisers and ministers in Berlusconi's first government. "But TV did matter in the sense that Berlusconi changed and shaped the values of the Italians over a period of nearly twenty years."

A number of social scientists not tied to either political campaign agree with this assessment. Renato Mannheimer insists that television was more important in forming a deep consumer "brand loyalty" to Berlusconi over the course of nearly a generation than through the short-term effects of controlling political speech during the election campaign. "Despite its image of novelty, Forza Italia's origins reach back much further in time," Mannheimer wrote after the 1994 elections. "It constituted an effective marketing vehicle for placing on the political and electoral market a product, namely Berlusconi, whose reputation had been constructed over a long time and whose 'cultural model' had been promoted for many years through the Fininvest networks. . . . The availability of television undoubtedly mattered—not the mere fact of owning TV stations, which probably would not have guaranteed, by itself, success—but as a channel for forming and reinforcing the 'cultural model' that was rewarded by the vote."[2]

Berlusconi may be unique in the history of modern politics in having to some degree created his own electorate. He helped create a culture built around the idea of success, personal wealth and material well-being, and that culture made his political career possible. At the same time, he himself seemed to fulfill the very dreams that his television stations were promoting: he was a larger-than-life overnight billionaire, who seemed to have walked off the set of *Dallas*—an Italian version of J. R. Ewing. "I incarnate the Italian dream," Berlusconi told me.

Berlusconi started his first national channel in 1980, and by 1987, the number of minutes Italians spent watching TV had risen dramatically to almost three hours a day (178 minutes), with children, pensioners and housewives watching the most.

Berlusconi did much better among women than men (53.4 percent against 46.6 percent) and did best of all among one particular category: housewives. The more television they watched, the more likely they were to vote for Forza Italia. This does not mean that they were necessarily convinced by the pro-Berlusconi coverage on his channels. In fact, his voters were often those who expressed the least interest in politics. But years of watching Fininvest programs made them favorably disposed toward Berlusconi and the attitudes he represented.

It was natural that Berlusconi, as a leading conservative candidate, would have tapped into the electorate of the Christian Democratic Party. But whether they chose Berlusconi or another of the center-right candidates, such as Mario Segni, the former Christian Democratic reformer who headed up a centrist coalition, depended on television habits. A study of female former Christian Democratic voters showed that an astonishing 75 percent of those who watched four or more hours of TV a day cast their ballot for Berlusconi, while only 40 percent of those who watched two hours or less did so.[3]

The siren song of the billionaire candidate was particularly persuasive among voters who had only a grade-school education and those who said they had not read a book in the past year; 65.7 percent of those with only a fifth-grade education voted for Berlusconi while his support dropped to 35.9 percent among Christian Democratic voters with a high school or college education. These unskilled and generally poorer segments of Italian society were unlikely to be beneficiaries of the "liberal revolution" that Berlusconi, modeling himself on Reagan and Thatcher, was promising. But these voters acknowledged having little interest in politics and had formed an extremely positive image of Berlusconi from watching the soap operas and listening every night to Emilio Fede, whose audience was prevalently older, female and less educated.

Even if the principal effect of Berlusconi's TV was in creating a general cultural-political disposition that was favorable to him, his unusual access to television during the campaign cannot be dismissed as an unimportant contributing factor. Berlusconi's campaign is simply inconceivable without his television networks. Being able to immediately reach half the households in Italy whenever he wanted is something no other candidate enjoyed. It's true that RAI's coverage partially compensated for Berlusconi's dominance on the Fininvest channels, but even if you look at both RAI and Fininvest coverage together, Berlusconi, by a wide margin, received more coverage than any single candidate. On all six national networks taken together, Berlusconi talked for an incredible 1,286 minutes in about six weeks, while his center-left rival, Achille Occhetto, received only 395 minutes of air time. Moreover, Berlusconi's principal allies, Umberto Bossi of the Northern League and Gianfranco Fini of the postfascist National Alliance, received almost as much time as Occhetto, so only one person of the center-left coalition was even among the top five candidates seen on TV. The centrist parties were more penalized than either left or right. Mario Segni, who might have represented a dangerous competitor to Berlusconi, received less than a fourth of the air time, speaking for a total of 317 minutes.[4]

2. THE LOOK OF THE NEW

The parliament that was elected and the government that it expressed were indeed something new. Nearly 700 of the 930 members of the two houses of parliament had no legislative experience. The age of the average Italian member of parliament dropped by nearly twenty years. There was something refreshing about the change, although many in the new political class were more than a little rough around the edges. The number-two man in the Northern League, Roberto Maroni, the new minister of the interior, played in an amateur rock band, frequently didn't bother to shave and often wore sunglasses indoors in an adolescent attempt to look like the Blues Brothers. Another Lega leader who was now joining the national leadership class was drinking beer in the middle of the afternoon in his office when I had interviewed him a few years earlier. There were more than a few newly elected deputies whose first political experience had been using their fists against left-wing demonstrators as members of neofascist bands.

By contrast, the typical new Forza Italia parliamentarian was clean-shaven and well-groomed, like the sales force of Berlusconi's Publitalia. Indeed, fifty deputies elected to parliament on Berlusconi's original Forza Italia list in 1994 were in fact Publitalia employees. Dozens of others worked for other Berlusconi companies or owed their livelihood to him in one way or another, working as lawyers, consultants, television stars, advertising clients, journalists or expert commentators holding contracts as contributors to his vast galaxy of newspapers, magazines and TV stations. The number-two man in Fininvest, Gianni Letta, although under indictment for bribery, was made Berlusconi's chief of staff. Joining the ranks of the new governing class were Berlusconi's childhood friends from the boarding school run by the Salesian fathers and his next-door neighbor at Arcore. Two of the stars of his TV networks, Giuliano Ferrara and Vittorio Sgarbi, assumed prominent roles. Ferrara, at least, had the decency to give up his reported million-dollar-a-year position as talk-show host to take on the position of Berlusconi's official spokesman. Sgarbi continued to take his generous salary from Berlusconi along with his parliamentary pay, and fulminated against Berlusconi's enemies each day on TV; he claimed that as an independent candidate elected in Berlusconi's coalition but not a member of Forza Italia, there was no conflict of interest. Berlusconi's tax lawyer, Giulio Tremonti, became minister of finance. His main corporate lawyer, Vittorio Dotti, would become the Senate leader of Forza Italia, and work on tax breaks for some of the companies he continued to represent.

In the euphoria that followed its initial victory Forza Italia enjoyed a huge bounce in the polls and in the European elections in early June jumped from 21 to 31 percent.

3. Blind Trust

As the Berlusconi government dug in and got down to work, it began to be apparent how complicated life could be for a prime minister who owned the nation's second-largest business (which, during his time in power, would become its largest business) while also now running the public economy; who owned the nation's largest media group while also running the state broadcasting system; who owned a company, many of whose executives were under criminal investigation, while in charge of the criminal justice system.

Berlusconi at first promised that he would sell off his Fininvest media empire, but took no steps in that direction. To resolve his conflict-of-interest problem, he personally selected three "wise men" to study the problem. Not surprisingly, the three men came up with a solution that required no changes in the property structure or management of Fininvest. Berlusconi talked grandly about putting his company in "blind trust"—an American term that he used like a mantra, as if its mere repetition would have the magical effect of making the conflict of interest disappear. But Berlusconi failed to explain how a trust could be blind if he and everyone else in Italy knew that the company still belonged to him.

Berlusconi made a great show of stepping out of the room when his cabinet discussed measures that directly affected his business, but they somehow always seemed to arrive at positions that seemed to favor his interests. The minister of finance, Giulio Tremonti, authored a law that gave his former client Berlusconi's companies a tax write-off of 250 billion lire (about $150 million at the time). The law was supposedly designed to encourage new investment but Berlusconi's Fininvest simply shifted assets from one Berlusconi company to another. When the write-off was challenged, the minister insisted that it was perfectly consistent with his law.[5]

Berlusconi stated unequivocally after the election that he would entirely separate himself from any decisions affecting RAI, which was, after all, his chief competitor. "I will not even move a potted plant at RAI," he said. But as a man of the media, Berlusconi found the temptation to remake RAI irresistible. "It is certainly anomalous that, in a democratic system like Italy's, the public broadcasting system should be against the government."[6] In other words, RAI should support the government rather than act as a partial counterweight to Berlusconi's own TV stations.

Alessandra Mussolini, granddaughter of the Fascist dictator and a new member of parliament, went so far as to suggest that in light of the election results the editors of all the major newspapers should resign because their opinions were out of harmony with the will of the electorate. Francesco Storace, another leader of the National Alliance, suggested setting up a government authority that would approve top editors.

Taking over the daily newspapers proved elusive, but the government had much more luck with RAI, since it was under its indirect control. The occupation of RAI literally began on the evening of the election victory. When the *Corriere della Sera* asked Maurizio Gasparri, newly elected post-fascist deputy and future minister of communications, what the happiest moment of his life was, he replied with complete candor: "The evening of March 28, 1994, when I entered the studios of RAI and, for the first time, they looked at me the way you look at a winner."[7] The well-established tradition of serving whoever was in power might have made changing the board of directors at RAI entirely unnecessary. As the prominent journalist Enzo Biagi, with forty years of experience at RAI, observed: "At RAI, power doesn't need to ask, many offer spontaneously."[8]

But Berlusconi was not going to take any chances and wanted to be able to choose a new board of directors at RAI. Technically speaking, the board of directors was appointed by the presidents of the Senate and the lower house of parliament.

Berlusconi solemnly swore he had nothing to do with this unedifying spectacle, but Fabrizio Del Noce, a former RAI journalist who was now a member of parliament for Forza Italia, could not keep himself from bragging that he and Berlusconi had gotten their way. "If I showed you the note I wrote for the 'Big Boss,' you'd see that we got four out of the five names we wanted," he told a journalist for *La Stampa*.[9]

Berlusconi employees Carlo Rossella, deputy editor of the newsweekly *Panorama*, and Clemente Mimun of Canale 5 were placed in charge of the newscasts for RAI 1 and RAI 2. Now five out of the six national networks were headed by Berlusconi employees.

This obvious political interference in a delicate area that Berlusconi had promised to avoid did not particularly scandalize Italian public opinion. Political control at RAI was nothing new; the governing parties had always done it, and the left had played the game whenever possible. What they failed to understand was that because of Berlusconi's iron control of private television, the new occupation of RAI was something different. On top of this, the new Italian right was much hungrier and more aggressive than past governments. The Christian Democrats, whatever their many faults, were great compromisers. (It was their strength and their downfall: they compromised with the political opposition but also with the Mafia.) For the new majority, this was part of the world of tawdry deal-making the country needed to get away from. The postfascists and the Northern League, having been excluded from the old division of spoils, were eager to get their share of power and influence, and Berlusconi was clearly convinced that bringing the press to heel was a key to being able to govern. But the takeover of the RAI, in an area Berlusconi had specifically promised he would stay out of, helped poison relations with the political opposition, who quickly gave up the idea that this was a government with which one could deal.

The RAI battle had shown the aggressive tone of the new Italian right, its take-no-prisoners attitude toward the opposition, its tendency to refer to critics as "enemies," its quickness to resort to invective and insult, to shout down opponents in debate as well as a readiness to cross over ethical and institutional boundaries with great impunity. But this was actually part of its appeal to many Italians. "These people may be kind of crude—they are the kind of people who put their hand on their secretary's rear end—but they are the ones who will change Italy!" I recall Fernando Adornato, a formerly left-wing journalist who had found favor and fortune in joining the Berlusconi movement, telling me in that period. "They are not necessarily people you would enjoy spending an evening with, but they are going to smash this rotten old system in a way the left never could! By comparison, the people on the left are the real conservatives."[10]

This quickly proved to be an illusion. Almost immediately upon taking power, the Berlusconi government announced plans for amnesties for tax evasion and illegal building. This was a common strategy of the Christian Democrats and had played its part in the gradual degeneration of the old system. It sent a signal that there was no point for honest citizens to obey the law, since eventually violators would go unpunished and save a lot of money in the bargain. To pay taxes or follow building codes became, in effect, a foolish waste of time and money: in the end, citizens spent far less by paying the amnesty fines. The amnesty for illegal building was particularly poorly conceived: it was up to citizens to estimate the amount they owed. Town governments had one year to challenge their claims and perform their own alternative assessments. Mayors and town governments protested that they did not have the resources to process all of these cases in such a short time, and so people were more or less left to pay what they wanted.

The government also made a priority of starting up more public works projects. This seemed the exact opposite of the Thatcherite "more market, less state" approach that Berlusconi had promised. Public works as a means of creating employment had been the centerpiece of Christian Democratic rule (with ample help from the Communist left) and it had mostly proved a disaster. It had produced much waste and little growth, while serving as a principal source of political corruption and, in the South, a bonanza for organized crime. Included in the government's plans was a kind of amnesty that would allow construction firms that were caught paying bribes to compete for public contracts. This ran completely counter to the reforms that began after Tangentopoli. In the wake of Operation Clean Hands, the cost of numerous important public works projects had dropped by nearly half. For example, costs in building new track for the Milan subway had fallen from 300 to 350 billion lire per kilometer to 150 to 200 billion per kilometer, while the cost of refurbishing one of the Milan airports had gone from 5 trillion lire ($3.5 billion) to under 2 trillion. To open the system back up to the same old firms was an invitation to return to the past.[11]

On the front of administrative reform, the new government missed a historic opportunity for change. The interim government of Carlo Azeglio Ciampi had passed a decree that would have, for the first time in modern memory, allowed the Italian government to actually fire public employees for failure to do their jobs. A public employee in Italy practically had to be caught in the act of murder to lose his job. Being absent from work for weeks or months at a time wasn't enough. The impunity of Italian public employees helped to explain the long lines and the attitude of arrogant indifference that greeted many citizens in Italian public offices and helped to explain the anger and alienation many Italians felt vis-à-vis the state. Making it possible to fire employees—albeit with many legal protections for the workers—seemed to promise a new era of accountability that responded to calls for change on the left and right.

But, strangely, when the Berlusconi government came to power, the decree was allowed to lapse without being converted into law. The reason was simple. The National Alliance gained many of its votes from public employees and the party had campaigned against the decree. The postfascists were indeed moving toward the center, but in order to expand their appeal, both they and Forza Italia were simply taking over many of the patronage networks of the old Christian Democracy. So much for the liberal revolution.

Foreign investors were evidently not convinced by the Berlusconi government, and began withdrawing money from Italy, a total of 27,200 trillion lire (about $17 billion) in the summer and fall of 1994. The stock market fell by about 25 percent. Instead of gaining 1 million jobs, the Italian economy lost more than 200,000.

4. CONFLICT OF JUSTICE

The issue that became the consuming focus of the Berlusconi government was that of keeping the Italian magistrature from pursuing its various investigations into his company's dealings.

To anyone with any knowledge of Italian affairs, it should have been perfectly obvious that a political corruption investigation centered in Milan, the stronghold of Bettino Craxi, would inevitably have involved the city's biggest company, Fininvest, and the businessman who was closest to Craxi, Berlusconi.

Craxi himself, in a memorandum he filed with the court in November 1993, two months before Berlusconi entered the playing field, was extremely plain about the involvement of Fininvest in the system of bribes and illegal party financing. "All the major business groups should tell the truth about the practices followed since time immemorial and quit trying to play blind, deaf and dumb as some of them now do. I am referring to all the major national and international companies, who directly and indirectly financed the political parties and personally helped individual leaders, from Fiat to Olivetti, from Montedison to Fininvest."[12]

Magistrates in Turin and Milan had arrested top executives at Fiat, and the Fiat management had finally decided to cooperate with the investigations. Olivetti's president, Carlo DeBenedetti, Berlusconi's great nemesis in the battle for Mondadori, the supposedly left-of-center publisher, was not spared prosecution. He admitted paying out bribes for government contracts, was arrested and spent a night in prison. The top executives of Montedison (then called Enimont) had been put on trial in late 1993 and early 1994, and a number of them admitted their roles in paying off all the parties, including members of the Democratic Party of the Left. Having prosecuted three of the four groups mentioned by Craxi, were magistrates supposed to ignore the fourth?

Berlusconi certainly realized this. "I am forced to enter politics, otherwise they will put me in prison," he told the journalists Indro Montanelli and Enzo Biagi.[13]

That the prosecutors did not intend to favor any one party is evident in the fact that one of the magistrates of the anticorruption pool, Gherardo Colombo, who was always identified as politically to the left, proposed a "political solution" to Tangentopoli already back in 1992. Because illegal financing and bribe taking was a vast, systemic problem, Colombo argued, it made no sense to prosecute tens of thousands of people and put them in prison. The solution, he suggested at a legal conference, was an amnesty for all those involved in the system on three conditions: that they give a full testimony about their role, return the money they had pocketed and withdraw from political life. The other magistrates of Operation Clean Hands agreed with Colombo's proposal, but it was rejected as too permissive. Most Italians at the time were still too angry about the levels of corruption and wanted punishment for the perpetrators.

So the prosecutors in Milan and elsewhere had no choice but to continue with their work. This put them, inevitably, on a collision course with Berlusconi. Despite his claim of having been singled out because he had entered politics, there were already a number of investigations into Fininvest under way before Berlusconi entered politics, and prosecutors would have to have made an exception of Berlusconi and not pursued these cases in order to avoid investigating Berlusconi. Prosecutors had first found evidence of bribes paid by Paolo Berlusconi in 1992, and his name came up again when they were looking into corruption at the pension fund of the Cariplo bank. Prosecutors were already investigating both Fedele Confalonieri and Gianni Letta, numbers two and three at Fininvest, for suspected bribes for the assigning of TV frequencies at the time of the Mammi law. They had already arrested another Fininvest executive, Aldo Brancher, for allegedly paying off public officials to get advertising for the Berlusconi networks.

In the course of 1994, all of these cases moved forward and new avenues of investigation opened up. The web of corruption in Italy seemed to be a never-ending tangle; the more the prosecutors pulled the thread, the more it continued to unravel. They had begun to find traces of many millions of dollars that Craxi had socked away in foreign bank accounts; it was only natural to want to learn where Craxi had gotten the money, requiring subpoenas, search warrants and foreign bank searches. It was obvious that any attempt to pursue this and the other cases, let alone pursue the overall investigation into political corruption in Milan, was going to mean a constant political crisis: either the Italian criminal justice system was going to have to be stopped, at least in Milan, or the prime minister and his inner circle were going to wind up in the defendants' dock.

As Berlusconi prepared to confront the justice system, he proposed making his own personal lawyer, Cesare Previti, minister of justice, which would have meant placing a man later convicted of bribing judges in charge of his future prosecutors. At the time, Previti, although elected to parliament, was a relative unknown. His role in helping Berlusconi buy the villa at Arcore at the expense of his teenage client was unknown, and no evidence of his bribing judges had yet surfaced. But his reputation as a courthouse fixer had already become a subject of political gossip. Cristina Matranga, a newly elected deputy of Forza Italia, disparagingly referred to Previti as "Berlusconi's adviser for illegal affairs."[14]

Oscar Luigi Scalfaro, the president of the Republic, flatly refused to accept him as minister of justice. Instead, Berlusconi made Previti minister of defense, so that he had under his control a branch of the secret services and the Carabinieri, Italy's military police, who perform many of the country's most important criminal investigations. Berlusconi appointed an old defense lawyer, Alfredo Biondi (who, significantly, had represented defendants in Tangentopoli), as minister of justice. But as events would later show, Previti intervened frequently in the internal affairs of the Justice Ministry, so much so that he quickly gained the nickname there as "the real Minister of Justice."

Another part of Berlusconi's strategy for dealing with Operation Clean Hands was to try to hire away some of the members of the anticorruption pool. Far from being the nest of Communists as Berlusconi would describe it, two of the four core members were law-and-order conservatives who were considered to be politically on the right. In fact, the postfascist National Alliance tried to offer Piercamillo Davigo, one of the key figures in the pool, the position as minister of justice.

Precisely to avoid having his work assume a political coloring, Davigo declined the exploratory offer, saying that it would be inappropriate "for a referee to put on the jersey of one of the contending teams and enter the playing field."[15]

But the idea of bringing in an important member of the pool had great appeal. Not only would it help give the government some anticorruption glamour, but by removing the conservative members of the pool, it would make it easier to brand those who remained behind as "red robes." Berlusconi decided to use his own personal charm to try to turn the man who, if he remained in the pool, would be his most dangerous adversary into one of his government's greatest assets: Antonio Di Pietro, virtually the only person in Italy who enjoyed greater popularity and name recognition than Berlusconi himself.

On May 4, the Milan prosecutors asked to be able to arrest Marcello Dell'Utri and two of his associates. Prosecutors had been investigating Dell'Utri for inflating Publitalia receipts in order to divert cash either for personal use or for undisclosed cash payments; now they discovered evidence that a number of payees were mere shell companies that didn't seem to provide any services at all. Prosecutors insisted that a period of two months' incarceration was necessary to avoid the possibility of the destruction of evidence.

Three days later, Berlusconi picked up the phone while he was in the office of the president of the Republic, Scalfaro, and asked Di Pietro to become his minister of the interior. An offer coming from the president of the Republic's office was not something to be rejected on the phone, and so Di Pietro agreed to meet Berlusconi in Rome the next day. His colleagues in the anticorruption pool argued strongly against the move. Accepting a job from a potential defendant, whose brother and top executives Di Pietro was already prosecuting, would, if nothing else, have the appearance of impropriety and would seriously compromise the office's investigations.

Di Pietro went to the meeting in Rome, which to his surprise was at the private home of Cesare Previti. He also found a crowd of newspaper reporters waiting outside for him. Obviously, the Berlusconi team had advertised the offer to Di Pietro to the press. Di Pietro refused the offer and returned to his investigations.

Accepting Berlusconi's offer at that time would have been particularly inappropriate. Only a few days earlier, Di Pietro had stumbled upon a vast new area of political corruption, which would end up leading to Berlusconi himself. On April 26, 1994, a young agent of the Treasury Police reported that his immediate superior had tried to give him 2.5 million lire (about $1,550 at the time), saying: "The people at Edilnord [Berlusconi's real estate company, which was then operated by his brother Paolo] want to give us a present." The young agent brought the incident to the attention of the Milan prosecutor's office. When Di Pietro got wind of it, he immediately took over the investigation. "We certainly could not have foreseen, Piercamillo [Davigo] and I, that in several weeks the investigation would lead us directly to Berlusconi, the head of the government that we had both been asked to join," Di Pietro later said. "Even more impossible to predict was that this investigation, which emerged entirely by chance, would soon be presented as a plot of 'red robes.' Two robes that were so red that Berlusconi and the National Alliance both wanted them as ministers."[16]

A police search of the house of the suspected tax police agent turned up 47.5 million lire in cash, which, together with the 2.5 million given to the young brigadier, made a round 50 million (about $31,000). Investigators then began looking into all the companies whose books the corrupt official had inspected recently: along with Edilnord was Telepiù, the pay-TV network that Berlusconi had started. One of the few sacrifices that the Mammi law had imposed on Berlusconi was that he sell 90 percent of his stake in Telepiù; but many suspected that Berlusconi had merely transferred nominal ownership of most of the company to friends. If this were the case, it could explain why the company might have been paying tax inspectors not to look too closely at the company's books.

As Di Pietro and Davigo probed bribery among the tax police, in the coming months they would end up with more than 600 defendants, about

130 agents of the tax police and more than 500 business people, including some of the country's leading businesses—Fiat, the Falk steel company, leading fashion designers from Armani and Versace to Gianfranco Ferrè and Krizia. It was hard to say that Fininvest was singled out for exceptional treatment, but different companies reacted in different ways. "There were companies that chose a low profile, pled guilty in exchange for a reduced sentence and those who denied everything and screamed about being the victims of a conspiracy," Davigo later said.[17]

Despite the pressing affairs of state, the growing number of arrests did not go unnoticed by Berlusconi, who kept in close touch in this period with the Fininvest employee named Massimo Maria Berruti, who was following the investigation for the company. Twenty years earlier, as a young tax inspector, Berruti had presented himself at the offices of Berlusconi's real estate company Edilnord for an audit; Berlusconi misrepresented himself as a mere "consultant" to the company rather than the owner. But Berruti found Edilnord's books in perfect order and wound up on the Berlusconi payroll shortly thereafter. On the evening of June 8, Berruti visited Berlusconi at the prime minister's palace. Two tax inspectors would later admit that Berruti had promised them that they would be generously rewarded if they kept the name of Berlusconi's companies out of their depositions when they were questioned during the investigation.

At the time, the Milan prosecutors did not know about Berruti's meeting with Berlusconi, but by early July they had reason to believe that bribes to tax inspectors had been authorized by Paolo Berlusconi and by Salvatore Sciascia, who was the chief financial officer of Fininvest, whose boss at the time of the payoffs was not Paolo but Silvio Berlusconi.

As rumors circulated about the possible arrest of the prime minister's brother on July 13, the Berlusconi government suddenly announced a special decree that would make it illegal for the judiciary to issue arrest warrants for a whole series of white-collar crimes, including virtually all forms of political corruption and financial fraud. It would make it impossible, for example, to arrest or extradite some eighty defendants of Tangentopoli who had fled overseas. The decree also made it illegal to publish information about ongoing investigations—threatening journalists with prison sentences. All defendants arrested for crimes of corruption were released from jail.[18]

The decree was announced on the evening that the entire Italian population was glued to their TV sets watching Italy beat Bulgaria in the World Cup soccer tournament being held in New York. That evening the streets of Rome were filled with wildly celebratory soccer fans honking horns, running through the streets and leaning out of car windows wrapped in the Italian flag and yelling, *"Forza, Italia! Forza, Italia!"*

Italy didn't go on to win the World Cup, and in the sober light of its defeat, most Italians were disconcerted to see more than 2,700 criminal defendants walk out of prison, including some of the most notorious cases from Tangentopoli, ex-ministers and party apparatchiks who had been caught with millions socked away in Swiss bank accounts. Also leaving prison were some forty-nine of the tax inspectors arrested during the Treasury Police probe.

The members of the anticorruption pool were outraged by the decree and decided they needed to do something extreme. On the evening of July 14, four members of the pool held a press conference at which Antonio Di Pietro announced their resignations.

By taking on the Milan magistrates, Berlusconi was pitting himself against a media star even brighter than himself. Since the corruption investigation started in early 1992, Di Pietro had become a national hero. His dramatic resignation and the images of some of the most notorious defendants of the corruption scandal walking out of prison caused a national uproar. The government measure quickly acquired the nickname *il decreto salvaladri,* "the save-the-thieves decree."

Almost overnight, Berlusconi's principal government allies, the neofascists and the Northern League, turned against the decree they had accepted only days before. Roberto Maroni, minister of the interior from the Northern League, said that he had been deceived: "They tricked me, they gave me a different text to read from the one I ended up signing.

[Alfredo] Biondi [minister of justice] assured me that the bribe-takers wouldn't be let out of prison."[19]

Berlusconi threatened to bring down the government and force new elections if his decree was not accepted. He insisted that the problem was one of miscommunication created by a hostile press corps. He mounted a media counteroffensive. On one evening in late July, all three Fininvest stations featured lengthy interviews with Berlusconi, the shortest of which lasted seven minutes. One of them, on Emilio Fede's Rete 4, occupied a full twenty-two minutes of the nightly newscast.

In a not-so-subtle effort at subliminal advertising, Rete 4 changed its scheduled programming and exchanged a Fred Astaire movie with a comedy called *A Prisoner Awaiting Trial*, satirizing the abuse of pretrial detention.[20]

In his very different style, Vittorio Sgarbi took a much harsher line. "Di Pietro, Colombo, Davigo and the others are murderers,"[21] he said, referring to people who committed suicide in the course of the corruption investigation. (The people he mentioned were either not defendants of the Milan prosecutors or not in prison when they took their lives, making it difficult to blame their deaths on pretrial detention.) At another point, Sgarbi went further: "Death to Di Pietro, who brings death. . . . The prosecutors of Operation Clean Hands should be arrested, they are a band of criminals with a license to kill, aiming at the subversion of our democratic order."[22]

But the media blitz failed. Opinion polls showed Berlusconi's approval rate plummeting, and he was forced to back down. He agreed to bring the question before parliament and fashion a bill that addressed the problem of pretrial detention without hamstringing the corruption cases.

How could Berlusconi—the master of mass media—have so badly misjudged public opinion?

As it turned out, Berlusconi's chief pollster, Gianni Pilo, then also a member of parliament for Forza Italia, had conducted a series of market tests to sound out possible reactions to the decree. But the results showed the dangers of government-by-polling: the survey asked people whether they thought defendants should have a trial before they were sent to prison but did not ask how they would feel if politicians who had admitted taking bribes were suddenly released.

After the decree was dropped, more tax inspectors confessed to having taken bribes from various Berlusconi companies. On July 22, the Milan prosecutor's office issued a new series of arrest warrants, including those for two Fininvest executives, Salvatore Sciascia, the chief financial officer, and Gianmarco Rizzi, another former tax inspector who wound up on the Berlusconi payroll. Both men did not report to the police and while they were still at large, Berlusconi held a dinner at Arcore where Previti and Gianni Letta (two members of his cabinet who were also Fininvest executives) met with the defense lawyers of two defendants in the bribery case. Was the prime minister using the occasion to work out a common defense strategy with the lawyers of employees who might be in a position to implicate him before they turned themselves into police? Or was it, as Berlusconi insisted, nothing more than an innocent dinner among friends? "Even if we were to accept that rather improbable explanation," the Milan daily paper *Corriere della Sera* commented, "that is just the problem: no one can tell where the family business ends and where the business of state begins."

This grotesque spectacle of the prime minister / CEO and his cabinet ministers / employees meeting with the defense attorneys of his fugitive-from-justice / employees looked like a textbook illustration of the dangers of the conflict-of-interest problem. "Either we establish a blind trust right away or all that will remain of this government are smoking ruins," commented Giuliano Ferrara, the government's official spokesman.[23]

Andrea Monti, the editor of *Panorama*, Berlusconi's own newsweekly magazine, broke a long period of awkward silence by criticizing the prime minister. "In the first two months [Berlusconi] appears to have misunderstood something [Margaret] Thatcher told him: 'Immediately do three good things that people will remember.' By attacking the RAI and the magistrates he has taken on two problems he should have avoided like the plague. Now, to recover his lost credibility he should cut all ties between the government and Fininvest and work on the problems that people elected him to address: the economy, unemployment and administrative and market reforms."

5. PRIME MINISTER AS CRIMINAL DEFENDANT

Concentrating on the nation's business is difficult when the company you've built, your close friends and family are at risk of going to jail and you yourself might become a criminal defendant. Berlusconi had dismissed the evidence of bribery by saying that any money that his brother and employees had paid out had been done so under absolute necessity, extorted by a Treasury Police force that was little more than a criminal enterprise. Angry at being depicted as a gangster and seeing large, powerful corporations disavowing all responsibility in the system of corruption, one of the defendants, Colonel Angelo Tanca, asked to see Piercamillo Davigo in early August. He insisted that many businesses offered bribes without being solicited. As an example, he cited the case of Fininvest executives who invited him for a drink and gave him money. He then revealed that on June 10, just two months earlier, a retired colleague of his, Alberto Corrado, came to see him and told him that if, when questioned, he said nothing about the Mondadori audit the company would show its gratitude.

Corrado confessed that he had been asked to try to silence potential witnesses against Fininvest by Massimo Maria Berruti, the former Treasury Police inspector who worked for Berlusconi. ("Tell Tanca that his conduct will receive adequate recognition from Mondadori," and that talking about the payoffs would "damage Berlusconi and Forza Italia.") Prosecutors ordered Berruti's arrest and, on November 8, found in one of his business agendas an official pass from Palazzo Chigi, the prime minister's office, dated June 8. Berruti's phone records showed that immediately afterward, while still a few blocks from Palazzo Chigi, Berruti called Alberto Corrado's house in Milan and then met with him shortly after returning to Milan the next day. The call to Corrado seemed to provide powerful confirmation to the tax inspectors' story that Berruti had used

Corrado to buy their silence. Moreover, the fact that Berruti had visited Berlusconi only minutes before calling Corrado seemed to offer proof that Berlusconi was directly involved—giving Berruti the green light to move ahead with the plan.[24] Phone records showed that Berruti and Berlusconi had spoken some sixty times, sometimes even after midnight, in the weeks in which the bribery case was heating up—a surprising amount of contact between a sitting prime minister and a mid-level executive of a company that Berlusconi was supposedly no longer involved in.

If the two men, as circumstantial evidence strongly suggests, discussed Berruti's efforts to keep the Treasury Police investigation from touching Fininvest, then Berlusconi would be guilty of suborning perjury as a sitting prime minister, not merely being accused, as Berlusconi has always insisted, of bribes that were committed years earlier when bribe-giving was the norm in Italian business.

Having reconstructed both the bribes by various Berlusconi companies to the Treasury Police and the efforts to cover them up, prosecutors prepared to take the ultimate step of questioning Berlusconi and listing him as a suspect. (In fact, Italian law requires that prosecutors formally notify potential defendants that they are under investigation.)

On November 21, 1994, while Berlusconi was holding an international summit in Naples on organized crime with the leaders of the G8 such as François Mitterrand and Bill Clinton, the *Corriere della Sera* published the news that Berlusconi had been sent a request to be interrogated by the Milan prosecutors. The news of the judicial action, at a moment when he was at the center of international attention, was confirmation to Berlusconi that the case against him was timed to cause him maximum political embarrassment. The timing of the indictment was poorly handled but there is little evidence of the plot that Berlusconi has often denounced. The prosecutors felt that it was improper to wait a substantial period of time once the indictment had been decided. After all, the prime minister of a country is always involved in important business. They waited until they thought the Naples summit was over, but Berlusconi remained a day longer than they expected.

For years, Berlusconi has used the scoop by the *Corriere* as evidence of a plot of the Milan prosecutor's office in what he has described as a judicial coup d'état. The Milan prosecutors were almost certainly not the source of the leak for the *Corriere*'s front-page story—the scoop caused the office nothing but trouble and embarrassment. The reality is that journalists had been camped out in front of the Milan prosecutor's office for more than two years. The major papers had sources throughout the Palace of Justice, including clerks and police agents who sometimes alerted them to unusual movements among the people working on Operation Clean Hands. There is also the possibility that the Berlusconi camp leaked or helped confirm the story. Berlusconi was read the first part of the subpoena over the phone the day before the story ran. The published version mentioned only the first couple of counts on which Berlusconi was being investigated. Reporters, if they had gotten wind of the subpoena, almost certainly would have called for confirmation. It would be far more like Berlusconi to move proactively, preferring to let the story come out prematurely so that he could go on the counteroffensive, as he immediately did.[25]

Perhaps the Milan prosecutors would have been wise to have waited a few more days, depriving Berlusconi of useful ammunition to use against them, but their failure to do so demonstrates a lack of political savvy on their part, not their excessive politicization. Besides, any action on their part at any time against the prime minister would have been interpreted as a political attack.

Berlusconi blamed his indictment for the fall of his first government. In reality, it was only the beginning of the final act. Equally important was a general strike in which more than a million people descended on Rome to protest the government's financial plan requiring painful cuts for workers. But the decisive move that brought the government down was the abandonment of the government coalition on the part of one of its two largest partners, Umberto Bossi and the Northern League. Bossi quickly began to realize that his deal with Berlusconi was much more to the latter's advantage than to his own. With Berlusconi as prime minister and dominating the media, Forza Italia continued to gain strength at the expense of the

Lega. Bossi began to complain of Berlusconi's using his TV networks to "brainwash the Italian people." In the European elections held in June of 1994 (just two months after Berlusconi's election), Forza Italia jumped ten points in the polls, almost exclusively at the expense of his own coalition allies, principally the Northern League. Rather than following through on promises made to the League of granting more autonomy to Italy's regions, Berlusconi seemed to be looking out for himself. "Instead of governing, Berlusconi is trying to keep his friends, relatives and employees out of jail," Bossi said back in July at the time of the "save the thieves decree."[26]

During the next months Bossi began referring to Berlusconi as Berluskaiser and comparing him to the Argentine strongman Juan Perón. "Do you really think that a man who owns 140 companies can act in the public interest? When he starts crying, it's time to laugh: it means things are going well and he hasn't yet found the combination to the safe. . . . Every so often, I have to grab Berluscosa [literally: Berlusc-something] by the wrist and say, 'Stop right there!' because he's about to put his hands in the cash register. He keeps trying and trying: with RAI, with the magistrates, with the amnesty for his real estate buddies, with the copyright law for Mondadori, pension reform. . . ."[27]

In mid-December, Bossi made a formal break with Berlusconi, withdrew his support from the government and agreed to form a new government with the various parties of the opposition. Berlusconi attempted to stave off the defection by trying to convince a substantial number of the representatives of the League in parliament to disobey Bossi and remain allied with Forza Italia. Bossi began to declaim that Berlusconi was "buying" his followers with promises of money and future positions.

"They are offering 25 million lire [about $15,000] a month for the rest of the legislature in exchange for betraying Bossi!" a senator of the League announced publicly. "Here in the Senate there are blank checks circulating!"[28] These allegations were never proven, but the discovery of billions of dollars in offshore Fininvest accounts, false receipts and accounting fraud meant to generate large amounts of cash, and the existence of millions of dollars at the personal disposition of Berlusconi have done little to dampen suspicions. But even without bribes, Berlusconi's ability to legally dispense money and favors—consulting contracts, lawyers' fees, book contracts, newspaper and magazine columns, television air time—has put him in an extraordinary position to win the allegiance of members of other parties, while at the same time to enforce iron discipline within his own party's ranks.

Bossi, once roundly praised on the Berlusconi networks, now felt the effects of the "concentrated fire" of a full-out media assault in which he was regularly denounced as "Judas," a "traitor," a "madman," and "a sell-out to the Communists!" According to one former Forza Italia deputy, his colleagues in parliament who came from the ranks of Fininvest were up-front about using the power of television to intimidate their former coalition mates. "Our television networks can destroy the League, and it's time for the members of the parliament in the League to realize this. . . . If they make our government fall we'll have early elections and they can forget about their seats in parliament!"[29] In fact, Bossi virtually disappeared from the Fininvest networks and the two state channels run by former Berlusconi employees, while minor personalities with the Northern League who dissented from Bossi and agreed to follow Berlusconi were briefly turned into household names.[30]

Bossi held on to enough of his deputies to bring the government down and form a new one, thus putting an end to the brief and inglorious seven and a half months of the first Berlusconi administration. There was much premature celebration among the forces of the center-left that the "little dictator," as Bossi called him, had been brought down.

The jubilation over the fall of Berlusconi was premature. One who was opposed to the abrupt end of the Berlusconi government, despite being strongly opposed to Berlusconi, was Indro Montanelli, the founder of *Il Giornale,* who after unsuccessfully trying to launch another daily newspaper had returned to his old place at the *Corriere della Sera.* "Berlusconi is one of those diseases that you must cure with a vaccine. And to recover from Berlusconi the people need a strong dose of Berlusconi. They must see him in power."[31]

Chapter Nine

BERLUSCONI OUT OF POWER— COUNTERPUNCHING

1. Buoyant in Defeat

Many men would have been deflated by such a disastrous first experience of government and of political defeat. Indeed, Berlusconi liked to repeat that the quality of his life had deteriorated greatly as a result of entering politics. "Before, whenever I went anywhere everyone would applaud," he told me in late 1995, "now only half of them applaud and half of them boo." He had much less free time, less time for family and for his beloved soccer team. Politics had even put a cramp in his sex life, he admitted with characteristic candor. "After a life as a sinner, I've had to learn to live in total transparency, surrounded by bodyguards. I have no more secrets and can't even eat in a restaurant."[1]

But a first taste of political power seemed to have left him with an appetite for more. Even as his government was beginning to fall in about his ears in late 1994, Berlusconi's expressions of self-regard multiplied. "Looking around, I don't see any better government than my own. I have a superiority complex I have trouble restraining," he said in July, after losing the battle of the "save the thieves decree." ("I have nerves of steel and the patience of a saint," he said a couple of weeks later.) "I have the intention of governing for a long time in order to change Italy profoundly. In fact, I'm convinced that I'm the only one who can." His tendency to refer to himself in the third person as a figure belonging to history became more accentuated. "The recovery of Italy is called Forza Italia. In point of fact, it's called Silvio Berlusconi," he said just two days after being subpoenaed by the prosecutors in Milan in the Treasury Police bribery case. "Who would I be if I couldn't be Berlusconi?" he asked in that same period. "The son of Berlusconi," he replied.[2]

As prime minister, Berlusconi felt he was finally on the planetary stage suited to his own greatness and, having sized up his fellow world leaders, he found none that quite measured up to himself. "Berlusconi built an empire—find me someone else in Europe who has done the things that Berlusconi has done."[3] He had found that the informal style that had served him well in business worked well in world diplomacy: he told reporters that he had warmed up François Mitterrand with conversation about aphrodisiacs, and at the G8 summit in Naples, he remarked on the beauty of the evening by saying that it was a great night for making babies under the stars. The *Corriere della Sera* reported that at one point he had told a joke to Bill Clinton about a man who had a mark on his penis, in obvious reference to rumors about the anatomy of the American president that had emerged during his sexual harassment litigation.[4]

No longer being prime minister, but only one of six hundred members of the lower house of parliament, presented some challenges to Berlusconi. Forced to take his seat like an ordinary deputy, Berlusconi was assigned a seat toward the front of the semicircle, where party leaders generally sat; but this presented a serious problem. It meant that the television cameras would frequently film him from above, revealing his growing baldness and his short, five-foot-six frame. Berlusconi, who was used to being filmed, even on the state networks, according to the strict rules set down by his own image consultants—from below and to the left, with a special filter added to hide the wrinkles of age—demanded a change in seating. "Furious negotiations began . . . so that our Boss was able to obtain one of the desks highest up in the semicircle, so that the truth of his baldness would be hidden to the Italian people and to create the illusion of greater stature," wrote Michele Caccavale, author of a disenchanted memoir of his experience in the first Berlusconi legislature with Forza Italia.[5]

But in many ways, being out of power and working to get back in was more congenial to Berlusconi than governing. It spared him the complexities and difficulties of governing, the hard choices and compromises, which he never much liked. Being out of power allowed him to do what he did best, which was to present himself as an outsider pitted against the political system, conducting a kind of permanent election campaign. Between 1994 and 2001, Berlusconi worked relentlessly to return to power, losing a national election in 1996, but recovering to build a much greater success in 2001 than his original one in 1994. In the meantime, he secured the future of his company, which passed from being the second largest in Italy to being the largest and went from a position of perilous debt into being possibly the most profitable media company in Europe.

Indeed, Berlusconi is generally at his best when he is down. In power, his sense of omnipotence gets the better of him; he immediately oversteps his bounds and makes continual mistakes of arrogance like the occupation of RAI and the "save-the-thieves decree." But out of power, he is brilliant at playing the victim and attacking his enemies. Although the disappointing results of his first government were evident, he quickly shifted the blame to others. *"Non mi hanno fatto lavorare"* (They didn't let me work) became his plaintive refrain. It was the fault of Bossi's "stab in the back," behind-the-scenes plotting by the Communists, the "red robes" in the Milan prosecutors' office.

Berlusconi's comeback, however, was also possible only through extraordinary determination, shrewdness and stamina, as well as a ruthlessness and willingness to take risks that surpassed anything attempted during his days as entrepreneur.

2. BACK TO THE WALL

If the euphoria of national office was not incentive enough, the need to defend himself from prosecution and avoid the breakup of his TV monopoly—

the same things that had drawn him into politics—were more present than ever. Berlusconi was always at his best with his back to the wall.

Having seen the effects of one man's controlling five of the six national networks, various Italian groups collected signatures to hold a national referendum that would have made it illegal for anyone to own more than one national TV network. A second referendum would have limited advertising during TV movies to the beginning, middle and end of the film. Fortunately for Berlusconi, the four television referenda were on the ballot with eight other measures, from one regulating store hours to another regarding the treatment of Mafia defendants. Rather than facing a clear yes or no, voters needed to make sense of a complicated series of choices.

In any event, many Italians were confused about what the referenda were designed to accomplish, and Italians who relied on commercial television for their news had a close-to-impossible time figuring it out. From early in the year, the Fininvest networks started a massive campaign against the TV referenda, sending some of their biggest stars out on the campaign trail and running frequent ads on their networks, despite prohibitions against campaign advertising. Weepy game-show hosts waved good-bye to their viewers, suggesting that they might soon be off the air. Before broadcasting films, the Fininvest networks warned viewers that they would no longer be able to see movies on TV if the referendum succeeded. Fininvest even ran animated cartoons singing the praises of commercial television. Some of the ads offered a completely distorted picture of the effect of the vote, saying that they would put an end to commercial television and remove movies from the airwaves. One prominent spot contained the following message: "In order not to return to the State monopoly of television, to continue to see great movies on TV for free, in order not to damage Italian cinema, because free competition is the best way to guarantee you the best programs without paying subscription fees. If you don't want to lose your TV, vote no." The underfinanced sponsors of the television referenda were hopelessly overmatched and put virtually no ads on television. RAI could not broadcast political advertising.

The toothless and understaffed government authority that had been set up to try to guarantee pluralism and fairness in Italy's lopsided television market called for equal time for the proponents of the referenda, but to no avail. The ombudsman for telecommunications judged some of Fininvest's antireferendum ads to be plainly misleading, and called for them to be taken off the air and for compensatory ads for the other side. Fininvest tied the matter up in court, and although the courts ultimately agreed with the authority, by then it was too late. The no's had already won the referendum with 57 percent of the vote. Berlusconi declared the referendum "the judgment of God," but in many ways the campaign was a perfect illustration of the need for the referendum. A political subject with near-total control of television was in a powerful position to influence the outcome of a democratic vote, particularly when voters were choosing not between parties that they more or less knew but on complex questions whose consequences they didn't understand well. If Italian voters had been told that the effect of the vote would not have been to eliminate commercial television, but to have increased choice by creating three major private companies instead of one, would they have voted differently?

Above all, the victory showed there was plenty of life left in the Berlusconi political-media machine.

3. *Drôle de Guerre:* A Funny Kind of War

After Berlusconi stepped down as prime minister in December 1994, he was not really out of power. The parliament with which he had been elected remained in place; the only difference was that the Northern League now supported a center-left coalition. Because the new government had only a slender majority, it tried to govern by winning over some of Berlusconi's center-right bloc, picking ministers, for example, that were agreeable to both left and right. The new prime minister, Lamberto Dini, was, in fact, a rib taken from the Berlusconi government (his minister of the treasury), and Dini chose a number of people for his cabinet who were meant to win favor with Forza Italia.

Michele Caccavale, who wrote a disillusioned memoir about his experience in the first Berlusconi parliament called *Il Grande Inganno* (The Big Trick or Big Fraud) said: "We had to be both 'for' and 'against,' pretending to be in fierce opposition together with our coalition allies while careful to keep the government on its feet."[6]

Berlusconi was in a perfect position to play a double game. He could criticize the government, take no blame for its actions and still get it to do a great deal of what he wanted. In public, he denounced the Dini government as illegitimately usurping the will of the people and called for new elections immediately, while in fact working behind the scenes to keep the government alive and to get it to pass legislation that was highly profitable to his own companies.

Caccavalle tells the story of a bill designed to reform the pension system. In the committee where the bill's contents were being discussed, Caccavalle objected to certain provisions of the legislation. "Immediately, I get a telephone call from Arcore, it's Berlusconi himself who tells me: 'Yell, scream, do what you want in the committee; in fact it's good to give the impression we're not going along with the government. But remember that on the floor that bill must be approved just the way it is.' It was an order—end of phone call."

Later, party leaders (who were also Fininvest lawyers) explained the desire for the law they were publicly criticizing. Originally, reformers of the pension system had wanted to impose some controls over the way in which pension funds bought and sold real estate, in order to avoid sweetheart deals and under-the-table payments that had been an important source of corruption, as well as a major source of income for Berlusconi's Edilnord. (Readers will recall that Paolo Berlusconi had been arrested for bribing pension fund executives in exchange for buying Edilnord properties.) The final version left pension funds free to buy real estate as before and it passed with the tacit support of Forza Italia, which abstained from voting.[7]

When I met Berlusconi in late 1995, he insisted that it was impossible for him to pass any legislation that favored his own interests: "There are so many controls and, besides, I am only one of about a thousand members of parliament." In a more candid moment, Berlusconi once said of his parliamentarian delegation, "I'm like Prince Charming: they were pumpkins and I turned them into parliamentarians." With even greater candor, Claudio Scajola, who was the secretary of Forza Italia, made clear what the main criterion would be for a Forza Italia deputy: loyalty. "It doesn't matter if we have Nobel Prize winners for candidates, what matters to me is that they will vote for a law of which they know nothing."[8]

Berlusconi was also able to get a favorite magistrate of his placed in the delicate position of minister of justice. An irascible elderly Sicilian magistrate named Filippo Mancuso, the new minister seemed consumed with a single obsession: the anticorruption pool of Milan, which he considered a threat to democratic order in Italy. Other pressing problems, such as the Mafia in Southern Italy, the length and slow speed of trials, and widespread corruption (including within the judiciary) did not seem to exist for Mancuso. He sent wave after wave of inspectors to Milan, widely considered one of Italy's more efficient and better-run judicial offices, even though none of the inspectors seemed able to find evidence of the judicial misconduct that the minister insisted was rife. It was then revealed that Mancuso had held a series of secret, unofficial meetings with Berlusconi in Mancuso's private residence of Rome. The leader of the political opposition and a criminal defendant seemed to enjoy privileged access to the minister of justice who was busy investigating Berlusconi's accusers. Mancuso's apparent monomania had so thoroughly discredited him that eventually the parliament removed him through a nonconfidence vote. Mancuso became a senator for Forza Italia in the next legislature. Meanwhile, he had kept up the pressure on the magistrates who were bothering Berlusconi. "Protected politically by the Berlusconians," Michele Caccavale wrote, "Mancuso is trying to carry out what the Berlusconi government didn't manage to do: disassemble the anticorruption pool of Milan, paralyze the most active and efficient prosecutor's offices [Milan and Palermo] in order to stop the investigations that are a problem for Berlusconi."[9]

4. THE PLOT TO DESTROY ANTONIO DI PIETRO

Stopping Operation Clean Hands had become increasingly imperative. The investigations that had led to Berlusconi's indictment in late 1994 had been only the beginning. As the prosecutors in Milan moved ahead, they were to find much, much more: hundreds of millions of dollars in secret, unreported offshore bank accounts; payoffs to politicians; payoffs to sitting judges; millions of dollars in cash at Berlusconi's personal disposal, unaccounted for; lenient court sentences regarding Berlusconi's companies; expensive jewelry and lavish gifts for the wives of judges; and witnesses who seemed to have been paid to perjure themselves.

In fairness, counterrevolution to these investigations, when it came, was not entirely Berlusconi's doing. It was also the work of a whole chunk of the Italian governing class that had been devastated by the corruption investigation and was determined to fight back. Already, in 1994, the tax inspectors who had been caught taking bribes (from Fininvest and others) drafted a complaint seeking to have their case transferred to the nearby city of Brescia on the grounds that the Milan prosecutors had a particular animus against them. The transfer took an important avenue of investigation away from the Milan anticorruption investigation and opened the way for similar claims. A long line of defendants would make the pilgrimage to Brescia to accuse their accusers of almost everything under the sun.

Italian law requires that an investigation be opened when any evidence is brought to prosecutors' attention, making it very easy to place someone under "criminal investigation." But there is a certain latitude in interpreting the obligation to investigate, and the accusers of Operation Clean Hands found a receptive audience in a couple of Brescia prosecutors who seemed prepared to make cases out of almost every wild accusation and anonymous letter. Thus, over the next several years, the Brescia prosecutors would initiate fifty different criminal proceedings against the Milan prosecutors, and fifty more against Antonio Di Pietro in particular. None would result in a single conviction or even an official sanction or job transfer. All but one would be thrown out before reaching trial, in some cases drawing sharp criticism from higher courts regarding the poverty of the evidence and the prosecutors' one-sided approach.

But amplified by the Berlusconi media, the cases were extremely useful in creating the appearance of moral equivalence between Berlusconi and his accusers—they were after all both defendants in criminal cases, weren't they? There would be hundreds of similar examples over the next ten years. Bogus mini-scandals that bubbled up, popped and were forgotten but created a kind of credibility to the main theme of what became known as the *Così Fan Tutte* defense: "They all do it."

The efficacy of Berlusconi's efforts can be seen in his systematic attempts to destroy the reputation of Antonio Di Pietro, the man who had become the public symbol of Operation Clean Hands. In November of 1994, just before Berlusconi's first indictment, his minister of justice, Alfredo Biondi, ordered an internal investigation of the Milan prosecutor's office, sending a group of ministerial inspectors to look into allegations of improprieties on the part of the anticorruption pool: many of the allegations came from Berlusconi himself, and members of his inner circle for things such as the "unusual vehemence and decisiveness" of the investigations into Fininvest as well as the anticorruption pool's alleged failure to investigate corruption in the ranks of the Democratic Party of the Left.[10] The inspectors reported that they found no evidence of wrongdoing but later said they were ordered to keep up the investigation. "From the ministry we received pressure to keep the investigation going in order keep the tension high until Berlusconi's deposition," one of the two inspectors later said.[11]

But as the official inspection was foundering, the Berlusconi camp stumbled on something infinitely better. In fact it was the Holy Grail that corrupt politicians had been seeking for the past two years: damaging information about Antonio Di Pietro that would force him to abandon the Clean Hands investigation. In November of 1994, the Berlusconi people stumbled on a live witness who was prepared to testify that Di Pietro had taken money from him. Giancarlo Gorrini, the head of a Milan insurance company, said he had given Di Pietro an interest-free loan of 100 million lire (about $80,000) as well as a stolen Mercedes that had been returned by police to the insurance company. The loan was arranged by a friend of Di Pietro's who worked for Gorrini, and while Di Pietro says he thought it was a loan between friends, the money came from Gorrini's company. Gorrini, who in fact ended up in the grip of the corruption investigation, may have felt it might come in handy to have a friend in the local prosecutor's office. The loan did not have the desired effect: his company went bankrupt, and Gorrini was later prosecuted for fraud.

Gorrini decided to hold the ace up his sleeve until its value suddenly increased in November 1994, when the Milan prosecutors subpoenaed Berlusconi in the Treasury Police bribery case. Gorrini paid a call on Paolo Berlusconi, the prime minister's brother, and laid out his evidence implicating Di Pietro. Paolo Berlusconi sent him to speak with Cesare Previti, then minister of defense. Previti sent Gorrini over to the Ministry of Justice, where an investigation into Di Pietro was immediately begun. Previti, although minister of defense, was in constant touch with the office of internal investigations. Afterward, Previti picked up the phone and placed a call to Di Pietro himself, telling him about Gorrini's visit, as if to give him a friendly heads-up, saying that the evidence against him was just garbage dug up to trap him. But the ministerial inspectors arrived and interrogated Di Pietro about his relations with Gorrini and the 100-million-lire interest-free loan. Although it was clear that Di Pietro had not been influenced by the loan, it was also poor ethical judgment for a magistrate to have taken a large interest-free loan, even from a friend. He decided to resign rather than face humiliating charges of corruption. Interestingly, the investigation was never properly registered in the ministry records— a serious departure from normal procedure—and all knowledge of it was kept strictly secret. Equally unusual was the role of Previti, the minister of defense, conferring directly with the investigators working on the case. The investigation into Di Pietro was dropped immediately after his resignation.

Di Pietro then made a great strategic error: he said nothing about the reasons for his resignation. Thus, the whole operation, which had the appearance of a well-organized blackmail scheme, had the double benefit of both neutralizing Di Pietro, the motor of Operation Clean Hands, and silencing him. Since Di Pietro refused to explain his reasons for resigning, Berlusconi claimed publicly that Di Pietro had done so because he was not in favor of the investigation into Fininvest, in which Di Pietro had, in fact, played a leading part. At the time of Di Pietro's resignation, 71 percent of the Italian population said it would like to have Di Pietro for prime minister, against only 29 percent for Berlusconi. Separating Di Pietro from the anticorruption pool allowed Berlusconi to pursue a strategy of divide and conquer. Berlusconi was thus able to say that Di Pietro, the national hero, was on his side and not with the "Communist magistrates" in Milan, who were, he said, always plotting against him. The Berlusconi camp then began to actively court Di Pietro, offering official positions to the same man on whom they had been digging up dirt. Di Pietro eventually refused, but this brief flirtation seemed to give the impression that Berlusconi and Italy's champion of clean government were allied against the *"toghe rosse"* (red robes) of the Milan prosecutor's office.

Having left the magistrature, Di Pietro was at a crossroads, uncertain about what to do next. All the major political forces wanted to recruit him, the country's most popular public figure. Some within Forza Italia wanted Di Pietro to join their party and replace Berlusconi in order to transform it from a "company party" entirely at the mercy of Berlusconi into a more normal political force. Berlusconi was personally terrified that Di Pietro would create his own party and replace Forza Italia as the main party of the center-right. As usual, he decided to try to neutralize his adversary by co-opting him.

Di Pietro agreed to meet privately with Berlusconi in early 1995 at his villa at Arcore, and Berlusconi offered him a position as minister of the interior in a future Berlusconi government. Although Di Pietro had established before the meeting that the topic of Berlusconi's legal problems was to remain off-limits, Berlusconi promptly raised the subject, looking to use Di Pietro to discredit the prosecutors in Milan. Afterward, Berlusconi told the press that Di Pietro had admitted that he had agreed with his former colleagues on the indictment of Berlusconi. Di Pietro initially denied having met with Berlusconi, but was then forced to acknowledge that the meeting had taken place, eroding his credibility.

At this same time, an anonymous hand saw fit to send a dossier outlining Gorrini's charges to the prosecutor's office in Brescia. The Brescia magistrates opened a criminal investigation into the charges, making them public for the first time. In this same period, Gorrini was seeking help from Berlusconi, through his brother Paolo, for a financial bailout for his bankrupt company, whose main creditor, a major Italian bank, had blocked all further funds. Moreover, Gorrini had changed his story since his initial deposition, making it considerably more damaging to Di Pietro and, consequently, more valuable to those interested in discrediting the former hero of Operation Clean Hands. Gorrini was now prepared to say that he had not simply given Di Pietro a friendly loan, but that Di Pietro had actively extorted it from him, using his position as prosecutor—the threat of future prosecutions and the promise to protect him—to get the money. If true, the new charges would elevate Di Pietro's behavior, which before had seemed merely unprofessional and ethically obtuse, to the level of genuine criminal conduct.

After receiving the dossier with Gorrini's charges, the Brescia prosecutors had bugged his phone and thus were able to hear him discussing with various people how he intended to "sell" his story. To his girlfriend, Gorrini complained about the ingratitude of Paolo Berlusconi, who hadn't even given him "a couple of bottles of champagne at Christmas" even though Gorrini's charges had helped lead to Di Pietro's resignation just a few weeks earlier. But now Gorrini said he expected Paolo Berlusconi to "fight for a deal with the Banca Popolare di Novara"—Gorrini's principal creditor. If not, "I will tell the truth, drag Paolo into it, Dinacci [the chief inspector of the Ministry of Justice] and the minister." The following day, Gorrini was overheard speaking to his attorney, who warned him against committing perjury: "You must tell the truth." Gorrini responded: "Mario, by now, I've climbed on a certain horse. . . . Today I've climbed on the winning horse. . . . If I'm to have any hope of saving it, or reaching an agreement, I don't think I'll have it again. It seems foolish not to sell it to these sharks."[12]

But Gorrini's story failed to hold up under scrutiny. His tale of extortion was directly contradicted by the employee who had actually handled the loan to Di Pietro, who testified that it had been offered freely as a gesture of friendship. The loan dated from 1989, long before Operation Clean Hands began; and if Di Pietro had taken the money in exchange for using his influence on Gorrini's behalf, he had certainly reneged on that promise. Not only had the Milan office prosecuted him, but Gorrini admitted that he was particularly angry with Di Pietro because the prosecutor had arrested the real estate magnate Salvatore Ligresti, just at the point that Ligresti was about to acquire a company belonging to Gorrini. The arrest killed the deal and was one of the factors that forced Gorrini into bankruptcy. The fact that Gorrini was wiretapped discussing how to "sell" his story in order to get help from the Berlusconi clan did not help his credibility. But the Brescia prosecutors pushed their case against Di Pietro for months until it was dismissed for lack of evidence.

Still, Di Pietro's image had been brought down to earth and sullied. Fifty-two percent of the Italian people said they were convinced that Di Pietro had done nothing wrong, only 9 percent were convinced that he had, while the rest wanted more evidence. The magistrate, while somewhat weakened, still enjoyed massive public support. Di Pietro had said that unlike Berlusconi, he would not run for office as long as he was under indictment, and with the end of the Gorrini affair close at hand, Di Pietro loomed as a major factor in Italian politics. The new government of Lamberto Dini would prove to be only a temporary solution, and Italy would hold elections in early 1996. Polls showed that Di Pietro's support could tip the balance.[13]

5. THE PLOT TO DESTROY DI PIETRO, PART II

When Berlusconi repeated on national TV his claim that Di Pietro was opposed to the first indictment against him in November 1994, Di Pietro finally repudiated the charge, publishing an article called "Le Frottole di

Berlusconi" (The Tall Tales of Berlusconi) in the left-of-center paper *La Repubblica*. Di Pietro gave a fiery speech at a prominent conference insisting that he would fight any amnesty for crimes of political corruption. Di Pietro was clearly contemplating entering the political fray—and not on Berlusconi's side.

As a result, Berlusconi picked up the phone and called a man named Antonio D'Adamo, telling him, "Your friend has gone out of his mind. . . . Prepare yourself. We are in your hands." And so began a second plot to destroy Di Pietro. D'Adamo was a close friend of Di Pietro's, the former boss of Di Pietro's wife and a former employee of Berlusconi who had gone on to start his own construction and real estate development company. Like Gorrini, D'Adamo had a company in bankruptcy, crippled with debt, and a series of banks unwilling to extend him any more credit. D'Adamo had tried to use his close ties to Di Pietro to gain Berlusconi's help with his financial troubles by offering to act as a kind of ambassador to the ex-magistrate. D'Adamo first promised he could bring Di Pietro into the Forza Italia camp, and now that that had failed, D'Adamo offered to help get Di Pietro out of the picture.[14]

D'Adamo claimed that in the early stages of Tangentopoli, Di Pietro had told him to go for financial help to a mysterious banker who operated between Switzerland and Rome, a man named Pierfrancesco Pacini Battaglia. "You'll find the door wide open," Di Pietro allegedly told him. Pacini Battaglia then proceeded to buy for 9 billion lire (about $5.6 million) a company belonging to D'Adamo, who then bought it back nine months later for half that amount, making a profit of 4.5 billion lire (about $2.8 million). The profit from the deal, D'Adamo said, was destined for Di Pietro in exchange for lenient treatment for Pacini Battaglia during Tangentopoli.[15]

In September of 1995, D'Adamo agreed to prepare a dossier outlining these charges for Berlusconi and Cesare Previti. As Previti later testified: "On a visit to Arcore, I met D'Adamo, who was also waiting to see Dr. Berlusconi." D'Adamo told Previti about his evidence against Di Pietro, Previti suggested that he put it in writing and helped him draft a memorandum. "When it was written, Dr. Berlusconi arrived and advised against taking initiatives of that kind." But D'Adamo supposedly "insisted in handing them the memorandum . . . for some future eventuality."[16] Previti's account of the creation of this anti–Di Pietro dossier is quite fantastic, apparently designed to shield both himself and Berlusconi. He makes it seem a total accident that he happened to be there at the same time as D'Adamo. Previti would also have us believe that D'Adamo then confessed these dark secrets to a person he met by chance in a waiting room and that Previti helped D'Adamo draft the incriminating document in the time they both happened to be waiting for Berlusconi. By testifying that Berlusconi had nothing to do with the preparation of the Di Pietro dossier and was reluctant to accept it, he appears eager to shield his boss from possible blackmail charges. Berlusconi's innocent lack of involvement is difficult to believe in light of the fact that he secretly taped his meeting with D'Adamo in which he pushed D'Adamo to repeat his charges against Di Pietro, a tape he would later pull out of the drawer and try to use as evidence against Di Pietro. (Berlusconi insisted that the tape had been made "by chance" by one of his security men and without his knowledge, as if a Berlusconi employee would tape his boss conducting a top-secret meeting without his knowledge.)

That D'Adamo was not pursuing this matter out of a disinterested desire to establish the truth became clear from a series of wiretapped phone conversations that showed that he was working hard to sell his story for the highest possible price. Since his name had been mentioned in some of the anonymous dossiers sent to Brescia, the prosecutors in Brescia had placed D'Adamo's phone under surveillance. At one point, D'Adamo's daughter asks about his latest meeting with Berlusconi. "Papa, were you able to help him?" "Certainly, Patrizia, and he will be able to help me."[17] At this point, D'Adamo's construction and real estate company was in bankruptcy, with some 40 billion ($25 million) in debt. The banks refused him any more money to use as operating capital and the company's work had come to a standstill. Berlusconi orchestrated a complete financial bailout. One of the Fininvest companies, Edilnord, bought property from

D'Adamo's company to the tune of 14 billion lire (about \$8.7 million), providing an immediate advance of 3 billion lire, which convinced the Bank of Rome to concede another 5 billion in credit. Fininvest's financial company, Mediolanum, provided D'Adamo with another 2 billion in financing. Thanks to Berlusconi's personal intercession, another one of D'Adamo's creditors, Comit, finally relented and gave D'Adamo an infusion of 12 billion lire. Berlusconi personally interceded with the government of Libyan dictator Muammar Gadhafi in aid of a large construction project that D'Adamo had begun in Libya, which had been halted. Using his status as a former and future prime minister, Berlusconi helped convince Libya to unblock the major real estate development and even invest money in it.

D'Adamo's charges would eventually dissolve under investigative scrutiny. (Pacini Battaglia said he paid no bribe to Di Pietro and explained the transaction as simply a bad business deal on his part: the company went from bad to worse during the months that he owned it and he decided to get rid of it at a loss.) Prosecutors would later search high and low for secret Swiss bank accounts and come up empty.

But in the fall of 1995, when Berlusconi and Previti first gathered D'Adamo's testimony, they presumably believed that Di Pietro, Italy's most famous prosecutor, was guilty of massive corruption. But what did the former and future prime minister and his former minister do with this evidence of serious criminal wrongdoing? Surely, a statesman committed to the rule of law would have informed authorities so that the charges could be investigated. No, Berlusconi and Previti would hold it in their drawer waiting for the right moment, while making vague allusions about the skeletons in Di Pietro's closet.

6. A TUNISIAN LAWYER

Berlusconi and Previti may have figured they would eventually need the D'Adamo material because their own legal situation was becoming increasingly difficult. Investigating the offshore treasure of Bettino Craxi, the magistrates in Milan had uncovered traces of what turned out to be a whole network of secret offshore accounts of the Fininvest empire. They found a payment of some 21 billion lire to Craxi from an account called All Iberian. Berlusconi insisted this account did not belong to Fininvest, but in 1995, the Milan magistrates located a London lawyer who helped manage the secret accounts for Fininvest, and they requested numerous cartons of documents from Britain. The documents revealed, and the lawyer confirmed, that Fininvest had what were called "very discreet" offshore accounts through which literally billions of dollars moved.

With these accounts, Fininvest had bought stakes in the department stores Standa and Rinascente in order to get around the oversight of the Consob, Italy's equivalent of the Securities and Exchange Commission. The "very discreet" accounts had been used to get around the antitrust laws of Spain and Germany in buying up television stations there as well as getting around the Mammi law in Italy by appearing to sell, but maintaining control over, the pay-TV network Telepiù. Along with all this, one of the very discreet accounts, All Iberian, had passed 21 billion lire (about $18 million in 1991) into an account belonging to Bettino Craxi. Craxi's own former aides confirmed his control of the account. Since Berlusconi had promised to abandon politics if it should ever be proven that he had given a lira to Craxi, the new evidence presented a serious problem.

When stuck with public relations disasters of this magnitude, having a major media empire at your disposal comes in handy. Suddenly, Canale 5, Berlusconi's largest and most respected network, broadcast an exclusive interview with a mysterious Tunisian lawyer in Paris who claimed that the money belonged to him and not to Craxi. This story was shown at trial to have no substance whatsoever, and the Tunisian attorney, Tarak Ben Ammar, refused to come to Italy to testify under oath, but part of the genius of the Berlusconi media machine is always to supply an alternate story— no matter how flimsy—that at least provides a small element of doubt, something for Berlusconi's supporters, reluctant to think ill of their charismatic leader, to hang on to.[18]

It is significant that the interview appeared on Canale 5, and was handled directly by its anchorman, Enrico Mentana. The episode demonstrates the extraordinary division of labor among the Berlusconi media. Unlike Emilio Fede's Rete 4 and Paolo Liguori's newscasts on Italia 1, Mentana's nightly newscasts had much more journalistic credibility. The tone was more neutral: stories damaging to Berlusconi were avoided, and his adversaries were at least not exposed to ridicule. Mentana liked to don the robes of a high priest of journalistic neutrality, advertising the fact that he did not vote. Berlusconi liked to brag that his biggest newscast was more-or-less left-wing. This is patently false: it still gave much more space to Berlusconi and Forza Italia, but considerably less than the two other Berlusconi networks. But because of its lack of obvious partisanship, Mentana's TG5 was by far the most authoritative and popular among the Berlusconi news programs. Precisely for this reason, the interview with the mysterious Tunisian lawyer claiming to be the recipient of the money destined for Bettino Craxi had far more impact appearing on Canale 5 than on the other, highly tendentious Berlusconi networks. It performed a critical service in helping to muddy the waters when the financial relations between Berlusconi and Craxi were becoming clear. Needless to say, there was no journalistic follow-up on Canale 5's part to find out whether the content of its interview was true or not.

When the case came to trial, Berlusconi was in fact convicted of illegally giving money to Craxi. But, in the meantime, months and years went by, people became distracted and everything was appealed and thrown into doubt again. Berlusconi was able to draw the case out for long enough to benefit from the incredible generosity of the Italian legal system. Before the conviction could be confirmed on appeal, Berlusconi was "absolved" on the grounds that the statute of limitations had expired. Italy is virtually the only country in the world in which the statute-of-limitations clock is not stopped once legal proceedings have begun. In most countries, prosecutors are required to bring charges within a certain period of time from the commission of the crime, but if a person has been charged with the crime within the proper period of time, the defendant cannot avoid judgment by drawing proceedings out for many years. In

Italy, this is not the case. Moreover, defendants have two levels of appeals, so that technically a person is not legally guilty until a conviction has been confirmed at the third level of judgment. The fact that the statute of limitations continues to run means that in the case of a whole host of crimes, in particular the crime of corruption, Berlusconi and his associates have been convicted at the trial level, only to run out the clock by drawing out proceedings for years and years. This allows them to say that Berlusconi has never been convicted of anything.

7. *TOGHE SPORCHE*, DIRTY ROBES

An even bigger threat to Berlusconi emerged during the summer of 1995 in the form of an attractive blonde socialite named Stefania Ariosto, who asked to speak to the anticorruption magistrates of Milan. Ariosto was the girlfriend of Vittorio Dotti, who was the longtime corporate lawyer of the Fininvest group in Milan and also the head of Forza Italia's group in the Senate. Ariosto, who had an elegant shop that sold art and expensive antiques in Milan, also had a serious gambling problem and had come to the attention of police because she was being pressed by loan sharks to pay off her gambling debts. After providing testimony about loan-sharking, Ariosto hinted that she had things to say about more important matters. Eventually, she agreed to talk to prosecutors. Ariosto testified that during the 1980s, she had been on close terms with Cesare Previti and had seen a parade of powerful judges and prosecutors move through Previti's home in Rome, frequently celebrating Fininvest's legal victories. In many instances, she had heard them talking about bribing judges and buying sentences. "In particular, [Previti] told me that he had many magistrates on his payroll and that he was in a position to buy the third branch of government as well as the 'fourth estate,' in the sense that he also paid many journalists. He also added that he paid many women. Many times, Previti would brag, in the presence of other people, not just myself, that the 'war of Segrate' [the takeover battle fought for the Mondadori publishing empire with Carlo DeBenedetti] had not been won by Dotti [the official lawyer on the case] but by himself, buying the judges. I heard him say that often, as a point of pride."[19]

Ariosto claimed to have even witnessed scenes of judges actually walking off with envelopes stuffed with cash, in particular Renato Squillante, one of the most powerful judges at the Rome Palace of Justice, in charge of reviewing all investigations initiated by prosecutors.

After hearing her initial testimony, judges in Milan granted her a police escort, as much because she had been threatened by loan sharks as because of her explosive testimony about Previti. Ariosto then went off on vacation with her companion Vittorio Dotti, the other big Fininvest attorney, sailing off the coast of Sardinia with police escort in tow. While sailing, Dotti received a phone call from Silvio Berlusconi asking him why Stefania Ariosto had a police escort. "Is it true that she is testifying against our group?" Dotti tried to reassure Berlusconi that the escort was due to threats from loan sharks.[20]

The call from Berlusconi is revelatory, a textbook example of why a criminal defendant should not be in politics. The granting of a police escort is supposed to be strictly secret. That Berlusconi found out about it within little more than twenty-four hours demonstrates that he has an extraordinarily efficient intelligence network and that he has no difficulty using the machine of state to help him protect himself against any attempt to investigate him. Equally revealing is the content of the conversation. Why would Berlusconi think that Ariosto would be in a position to testify against Fininvest particularly, unless she had been in a position to witness some of the skeletons in the company closet that Berlusconi always insisted did not exist?

Prosecutors were initially reluctant to believe Ariosto. Even hardened corruption investigators found it hard to believe that the buying and selling of court sentences was so common or that it would take place practically out in the open in Roman living rooms where sitting judges mingled with lawyers who had cases before them. But when the magistrates in Milan placed these people under surveillance, they found immediate confirmation of much of Ariosto's tale. The judges and lawyers in question were all in close contact, talking about leaving and picking up envelopes and using special foreign cell phones that were supposed to be immune to wiretapping.

Just before Christmas, Ariosto received a gift package containing a dead rabbit whose guts had been cut open. Ariosto's testimony was supposed to be top secret, but evidently it was not.

Just a few days later, as midnight approached on New Year's Eve, Judge Squillante successively called the phones of Silvio Berlusconi, Paolo Berlusconi, Gianni Letta (the number-two man at Fininvest) and Cesare Previti to wish them happy New Year.

In January of 1996, Squillante and the members of his circle accidentally found a police electronic bug that had been placed in an ashtray of a bar they liked to hang out in. They were in a state of panic; their conversations made it clear that they had much to hide. A typical example was a conversation recorded between Judge Squillante and Attilio Pacifico, an associate of Previti's who (by Previti's own admission) brought enormous sums of cash into and out of Italy for him.

PACIFICO: I've got all the official documents.

SQUILLANTE: Of all the secret funds? [Literally *fondi neri,* "black funds"]

PACIFICO: Let's stay united and not make any mistakes and we'll get through this. . . . In Monte Carlo, it's all under control.

SQUILLANTE: Did you pay them?

PACIFICO: Don't name any names!

Police followed Squillante as he traveled to Switzerland with one of his sons and emptied one of his secret bank accounts. Then they heard him discussing his fears of being caught with another Rome magistrate, who tried to reassure him, "Look, the only thing that can come out is . . . a billion lire [about $800,000]." (In point of fact, Squillante's interlocutor was naïve: his Swiss bank accounts contained several million dollars.) Squillante replied that he would say that he had made the money speculating on the stock market, in which case his only crime would be massive, system-

atic tax evasion. In the course of the same conversation, Squillante revealed that he had contacted Silvio Berlusconi through his brother Paolo
about some information regarding a case that interested them.[21]

When Squillante was arrested in March of 1996, about a month before
national elections, the Berlusconi camp mounted a ferocious counterattack. Rather than asking explanations of Cesare Previti, Berlusconi was
furious with Vittorio Dotti and put heavy pressure on him to repudiate
Ariosto, insisting that she was lying. The stakes for Dotti were extremely
high: not only did he owe a seat in the Senate and a leadership role in
Forza Italia to Berlusconi, Fininvest business accounted for nearly three-
quarters of his legal office's business. "I told Berlusconi I couldn't do
that. I was in no position to say whether Stefania was lying because I
wasn't there," he now says.[22] Dotti had, however, told prosecutors that
Ariosto had spoken of the episodes of corruption she had witnessed before approaching prosecutors. Despite pressure from Berlusconi, he refused to retract his earlier testimony. He then got to experience what it's
like to move from friend to enemy in the Berlusconi world. The same media that had once built his reputation as a top legal mind and national
statesman now portrayed him as a weak-willed coward under the influence of a hysterical pathological liar. Ariosto became the subject of cover
stories in the Berlusconi press and daily attacks on the television programs of Fede, Sgarbi and Paolo Liguori, in which she was described as a
"courtesan" and an "adventuress," a police stool pigeon prepared to say
anything to save herself from her gambling debts.[23]

By contrast, Renato Squillante was portrayed as an outstanding jurist
who had led a simple life of public service but had fallen into the grip of a
police state run amok. "He lives in a rented apartment," said Luciano De
Crescenzo, one of Squillante's many celebrity friends. "No boats, no luxury, never the shadow of the life of someone who takes bribes. . . . Judicial
errors are the order of the day." Squillante in fact owned, among other
things, a large, luxurious yacht worth hundreds of thousands of dollars.

Ariosto, furious at the attacks against her, pulled out a series of photographs (published by *L'Espresso*, the newsmagazine partly owned by

Berlusconi's archenemy Carlo DeBenedetti) that showed many of the same magistrates she had denounced together with Previti and other members of the Berlusconi court. A number had traveled, many at Cesare Previti's expense, to participate in the celebrations in the United States when Bettino Craxi was made "man of the year" by a prominent Italian-American organization. The photographs, which were given wide publicity, provided a grotesque picture of an important piece of the Italian judiciary at the beck and call of leading political figures.

The attacks against Ariosto continued relentlessly. No aspect of her private life was off-limits. "She's a mytho-maniac, she claims to have had three babies who died, and it's not true at all," said Domenico Contestabile, a parliamentarian for Forza Italia and former Berlusconi defense lawyer. In fact, Ariosto had had three children who died of cystic fibrosis. She sued Contestabile and won damages for the libelous remark.

As Berlusconi prepared for elections in 1996, Dotti's name was removed from the list of candidates, and work at his law office dried up. After living through the media assault of 1996, Dotti began to rethink the implications of allowing the largest media owner to enter politics. "I now understand what it means to have three TV networks at your disposal in order to destroy your enemies," he told Turin's *La Stampa* in 1996. "Isn't it a little late to discover this after sixteen years as Berlusconi's lawyer?" Dotti was asked, to which he replied: "I admit I underestimated the problem."

Chapter Ten

BERLUSCONI'S DEAD— LONG LIVE BERLUSCONI!

1. DEFEAT

Berlusconi's dead!" I recall many Italians, particularly Italians on the left, saying in the spring and summer of 1996, after he had failed in his bid to return to power as prime minister in elections that April.

He had lost in a head-to-head contest with the less-than-charismatic Romano Prodi, a professional economist who mumbled and ate his words when he spoke and resembled, in the words of one commentator, a "*tortellino* with human features." The Fininvest networks had pulled out all the stops and Berlusconi had seemed omnipresent on the airwaves— but it hadn't worked.

Berlusconi's 1994 victory now seemed a curious anomaly—perhaps even a useful lesson. The center-left won in 1996 by copying many of his more successful tactics. They formed the broadest possible coalition, from the moderate center to the far left. They got behind a single candidate. And Prodi, as a centrist and a former Christian Democrat, positioned them to win over moderate and Catholic voters who had favored Berlusconi before. Prodi used his lack of glamour to project the image of a kind of Italian everyman. Instead of traveling in yachts and limousines like Berlusconi, he traveled by bus to small towns across Italy. Berlusconi had his soccer team, but Prodi was a cyclist, a sport with great blue-collar appeal in Italy. On weekends, he was filmed and photographed peddling uphill, mirroring the efforts of the average Italian workingman.

Italy was starting to seem like a normal country, in which right and left alternated depending on which put forward the stronger alliance, the more convincing program, the more appealing candidate. Berlusconi's dominance on TV hadn't won him the election; indeed, he and others concluded that it may have hurt him. "I did too much TV, and in the end some of those debates wound up being useless, excessive," Berlusconi told reporters the day after his defeat. "I want to disintoxicate myself from TV."[1]

To some, the 1996 elections proved that television does not win elections. It appeared to be the vindication of old-fashioned politics. Clearly, the greatest difference between 1994 and 1996 was the fact that Berlusconi could not count on the votes of the Northern League, which ran by itself and won 10.6 percent of the vote, most of which had gone to the center-right in 1994.

The real story of the 1996 election may not be why Berlusconi lost, but why he did as well as he did. Although running in a much weaker coalition, Forza Italia lost less than a percentage point, going from 21 to 20.6 percent of the vote. Given that Berlusconi's first government was widely viewed as a failure even by many on the right and that an enormous amount of evidence had surfaced in the previous two years about systematic, widespread corruption within the Fininvest empire, it is remarkable that Berlusconi held his ground and ran a highly competitive race in 1996.

With current and former employees running five of the six national networks, Berlusconi was heard twice as often as any other political leader, even though he was no longer the prime minister. Perhaps even more important, many major stories went unreported or unexplored. Despite all the disturbing revelations that had come out about Berlusconi and his inner circle in the previous year, his legal problems were not an issue during the campaign. In fact, Berlusconi made a point of choosing many of his most prominent defendant employees as candidates for parliament.

Marcello Dell'Utri, now on the brink of indictment for Mafia ties in Palermo, was put up for parliament, and so was Massimo Maria Berruti, the former Treasury Police inspector who had allegedly tried to silence his former colleagues with promises of money. Cesare Previti, despite emerging evidence of his paying off judges, also ran for office. The Northern League mocked Berruti's candidacy by making up a fake campaign poster with Berruti's photograph and the slogan: "Vote for me: I don't want to go to jail." The growing number of the "party of the indicted" seemed to be an obvious effort to gain them parliamentary immunity, which would keep them out of jail and thus reduce the chances that they might decide to testify against their old boss.[2]

But other than the Northern League, whose leader, Bossi, inveighed against the "*mafioso* of Arcore," Berlusconi's main competition, the center-left coalition, chose to avoid the subject of Berlusconi's legal problems. Its leaders were convinced that attacking Berlusconi was counterproductive. "It may even help him," Romano Prodi told me when I met him during the campaign. "Italy," he said, "is a country where the relationship between the citizen and the state is very fragile. People have enormous distrust of the government. And he is very good at playing the martyr."

The left was gun-shy after the Violante case of the 1994 elections, in which they had attacked Berlusconi's and Dell'Utri's ties to organized crime and that had seemed to backfire. As a result the Olive Tree coalition adopted a policy often referred to as "*buonismo*"—goodness. "We consciously made a point of avoiding polemics," Furio Colombo, a journalist who won a seat in parliament in his native city of Turin, told me. "We refused to say anything negative about our opponents, refused to respond to insults, avoided getting dragged into controversy by journalists, and continued talking about what we intended to do."

This may have been good campaign strategy, but the refusal to make an issue out of Berlusconi's criminal prosecutions meant that he has never had to pay any political price for a series of revelations that would have forced almost anyone else in any other society from public life.

2. BLUNDERS OF THE CENTER-LEFT

High on their election victory, the leaders of the center-left drew the unfortunate conclusion that Berlusconi's conflicts of interest and legal problems and the concentration of media in Italy were matters of secondary,
even trivial importance.

Had the Prodi government acted immediately after the 1996 elections,
when it enjoyed a considerable amount of consensus and credibility, it
could have passed a conflict-of-interest law—one that was broad and that
was directed not merely against Berlusconi personally. It could have abolished the phenomena of university professors' picking up a second salary
by serving in parliament or of judges' earning private consultant's fees,
politicians' holding seats in both the Italian and the European parliaments—
establishing higher ethical standards for itself as well as for the center-
right. The government could then have forced Berlusconi to choose once
and for all between his vast private business empire and public office. By
forcing its own constituents to make a sacrifice, the government would
have made clear to the public that conflict-of-interest rules are basic norms
of democratic governance and not simply weapons to be used against a
political opponent.

"That's an abstract problem that only interests you American moralists!" I recall one left-wing politician telling me when I stressed the
importance of conflict-of-interest and antitrust legislation. "Trust me:
Berlusconi's finished."

Massimo D'Alema, the leader of the Democratic Party of the Left,
had what he saw as a bigger, more important project in mind. As the behind-the-scenes architect of the center-left's electoral strategy, D'Alema
was justly proud of the election. Now, precisely because he perceived
Berlusconi to be weak, D'Alema saw this as a perfect moment to wring a
series of compromises from him on institutional reform. D'Alema's project was a perfectly defensible one: he hoped to get Berlusconi to agree
on a new electoral law that would reduce the number of smaller parties
and create a system closer to that of France or England. With this law,

D'Alema hoped to call for new elections and emerge as the head of a new and much stronger left-wing party, like Britain's Labour Party or France's Socialist Party. D'Alema proposed a bipartisan commission to work out the details of a new electoral law and made Berlusconi his principal interlocutor.

D'Alema saw Berlusconi as his principal ally in election reform because as the heads of the two largest parties, the two stood to be its main beneficiaries and together could muster the votes needed to pass any law. Privately, many on the left confessed that they wanted to prop Berlusconi up because they considered his junior partner in the center-right coalition, Gianfranco Fini, the more dangerous adversary.

The offer was like a life preserver for Berlusconi. He was in serious political trouble, with other members of his center-right coalition calling for a new leader. "The loss of his leadership worries me, it could block the creation of a democracy of alternating parties," D'Alema said in May, as the center-right was reeling from its election defeat. The investigations into Berlusconi's business dealings were picking up steam and with the center-left in power, he was fearful of having to sell one or two of his TV networks and losing the financing of state-owned banks to keep his financial empire afloat. D'Alema appears to have concluded cynically that Berlusconi's vulnerabilities would make him a perfect negotiating partner, prepared to agree to an overhaul of the electoral system in exchange for a kind of personal "safe-conduct."

Ironically, the leaders of the center-right now suddenly seemed to perceive how serious the problem of conflict of interest was. A number of them began to complain publicly that Berlusconi was being "blackmailed" by D'Alema and the left into making concessions because of his fears of winding up in jail or losing his TV stations. None of them, of course, had the courage to propose a tough conflict-of-interest law that would have forced Berlusconi to sell all his media holdings or get out of politics, and neither did the center-left.

To accomplish his grand political project, D'Alema was prepared to make concessions to the media magnate on the issues most dear to his heart—keeping his empire intact and reining in the prosecutors who were busy trying to send him to jail. The negotiations between D'Alema and Berlusconi, called the *inciucio* by many Italians, a slang term for a dirty deal, were an unmitigated disaster for the left and the beginning of Berlusconi's return to power.

The protracted D'Alema-Berlusconi dealings had various effects. They rescued Berlusconi from his political difficulties, recognizing him as the undisputed leader of the center-right. They legitimated his massive conflicts of interest and further habituated the Italian public to the bizarre anomalies of the Berlusconi phenomenon.

When Berlusconi appeared ready to sell his television empire to Rupert Murdoch, D'Alema and many of the left actually opposed the move, referring in flattering tones to Berlusconi's TV stations as "a national resource." At another point, D'Alema insisted that he trusted Italian television far more than the country's newspapers—a stunning observation for anyone who has watched Italy's broadcast news. The average Italian could well conclude, if Berlusconi's media monopoly was not a problem for his main political rival, why should it be for me?

Rather than reforming the state broadcasting system and forcing Berlusconi to give up part of his TV monopoly, the center-left did just as their predecessors had done, using the old patronage system to place their own people in key positions and to exert as much influence behind the scenes as possible. In short, rather than changing the rules of the game, they tried to out-Berlusconi Berlusconi, a game they were bound to lose. RAI is a large, staid, cautious institution, in which the news lineup was literally created with a stopwatch in hand, counting out sound bites by the second according to various parties' share of representation in parliament. The vestiges of this system were still very much in place, and the parliament had an "RAI oversight committee," whose center-right components would erupt in anger at the least deviation into partiality. The result is that in the ten years since Berlusconi entered politics, there has not been a single investigative report on Italian TV into the numerous charges of corruption in the Mediaset financial empire. Berlusconi's networks had no such reservations about appearing partisan. Trying to use RAI to counter Berlusconi's Mediaset was like pitting a house cat against a Doberman. It lowered the center-left to the same moral plane as Berlusconi and made the Italian public more cynical than ever about the commingling of media and politics.

In August of 1996, the Prodi government actually passed a special decree to prevent a partial breakup of the Berlusconi monopoly. In 1994, Italy's highest court had ruled that in order to make for greater pluralism in the TV market, Berlusconi would have to place one of his three national networks, Rete 4, on satellite to free up the broadcast frequency for another station. Fininvest estimated that the move would cost it hundreds of millions of dollars and significantly reduce the company's value. Berlusconi had succeeded in postponing the day of judgment for taking Rete 4 off the air and moving it to satellite, but after two years of stalling, the deadline was set for August 1996. At the last minute, however, the Prodi government passed a decree keeping Rete 4 on the air for another six months, while promising legislation to resolve the issue. When the legislation came it was another gift to Berlusconi: it postponed the moving of Rete 4 to satellite until 2003 and exacted a similar sacrifice from RAI. The third RAI network, the dreaded left-wing network, would have to give up all commercial advertising at the time that Rete 4 moved to satellite, potentially starving what was already the poorest of the three public channels.[3]

With guarantees that there would be no media antitrust legislation, and the generous cooperation of his creditors (some of which were state-owned banks), Berlusconi was able to take his company public, listing it on the stock exchange, solving all of his financial problems in a single stroke. The high price of the shares, determined in part by the favorable regulatory climate in which the company now operated, allowed Berlusconi to liquidate the debt that had almost crushed him, still retain a majority stake, and vastly increase his fortune.

3. THE DIRTY DEAL, PART II

Precisely as D'Alema was helping rescue Berlusconi, banking information began arriving from Switzerland and England that helped prosecutors piece together the offshore financial activity of Berlusconi's Fininvest. They discovered, for example, that not long after a court sentence that awarded 670 billion lire to the family of deceased bankrupt financier Nino Rovelli, Cesare Previti and two of his closest associates received an astonishing 67 billion lire in their secret Swiss bank accounts. Previti's share was 21 billion lire (about $15 million), about a third of this megapayment. The apparent relationship between the court decision and the payments; the arrival of a portion of this 67 billion lire in cash in Italy; phone records revealing an intense series of contacts between the defendants in the case around the time of the court decision; their close ties with the judges handling the case and the sudden enrichment of the judge writing the favorable sentence, who bought an expensive apartment for his daughter, in cash, shortly afterward—all this convinced the magistrates in Milan that Previti and his friends had helped to fix the case. Previti defended himself by insisting that the $15 million was a legal fee that was owed to him for the work of a lifetime, even though there was no documentation of any such work by Previti or his office for Rovelli or his company.

Even die-hard Berlusconi supporters found it impossible to defend Previti. "No lawyer in the world ever earned a legal fee of 21 billion lire, it's indefensible," said Carlo Taormina, one of the army of criminal defense lawyers in the Berlusconi camp and a candidate for parliament with Forza Italia. "Previti should resign from parliament in order to face the charges against him." Having worked in Rome, Taormina said it was well-known that Previti was in the middle of a world in which sentences were bought and sold. "What's coming to light is just the smallest part of the rot that has built up in the cesspool of the Rome Palace of Justice."[4] But in a few years, when Taormina became a member of parliament for Forza Italia and undersecretary of the interior, he would call for the immediate arrest of the magistrates who had presumed to prosecute Previti.

Even if the $15 million payment had been a legal fee, Previti would still have been guilty of a series of extremely serious crimes: defrauding the Italian state out of several million dollars in taxes that were due on the money he had socked away in the Swiss bank account he had always claimed didn't exist. But he knew that the statute of limitations had run out on tax evasion.

That Berlusconi's personal lawyer should be involved in these kinds of shenanigans, with many of these illegal foreign payments coming from the offshore accounts of Fininvest, did not give D'Alema pause about "reforming" the Italian state with Berlusconi. "With Berlusconi, we have to rewrite the rules of the State," he said. In July 1996, after many of the revelations about Previti were already public, D'Alema and Berlusconi agreed to open the bicameral commission on institutional reform. The fig leaf behind which Previti and Berlusconi were able to hide was the fact that, so far, none of the money that Fininvest had given Previti could be shown to have been directly and immediately passed on to judges. The money generally moved to other bank accounts and made its way back to Italy in the form of cash through intermediaries, making it difficult for magistrates to prove a direct, unassailable connection between Berlusconi, Previti and the suddenly enriched judges accused of corruption. (It would take another year for the magistrates in Milan to find their smoking gun: a payment of $434,404 that went from a Fininvest offshore account into one of Previti's accounts and into accounts of Renato Squillante, the very judge whom Stefania Ariosto said she had seen taking bribes.)[5]

When a law-and-order conservative in parliament, Elio Veltri, tried to propose a law that would have stopped the statute of limitations in cases in which prosecutors needed to apply to foreign governments for evidence (cases such as Previti's and Berlusconi's), he received some initial encouragement from some members of the center-left and was even granted a long interview about the bill on one of Berlusconi's networks main talk shows. The host promised to invite him back, but then a few days later he was stopped in the halls of parliament by Berlusconi, who chastised him, saying, "How can you, a good liberal, stay with these people here?" meaning the parliamentarians of the left. Veltri was never invited back by the Berlusconi talk show and any momentum for the legislation evaporated.[6]

Previti used his position in parliament to bring the trials against him to a virtual standstill. Although he had barely set foot in parliament during his first term as a legislator, he now insisted that he could not afford to miss a single sitting of parliament, making it extremely difficult to schedule trial dates for his cases in Milan. In 1997, when the magistrates asked parliament to waive Previti's parliamentary immunity and permit his arrest, a solid majority (341 against 248) refused to do so. Some eighty of the votes came from members of the center-left majority, while the legislators of the center-right were as compact as the old Soviet Politburo. Privately, some of the center-right parliamentarians expressed disgust at the vote, telling Veltri, "With evidence like this, anybody else would have been in jail," but when he asked them why they had voted to protect Previti, they looked at him as if he were mad: "Orders are orders."[7]

Despite this extraordinary situation, D'Alema pursued a bipartisan effort to reform the judiciary with considerable input from criminal defendants in a position to become primary beneficiaries of those same reforms. D'Alema and the center-left, together with Berlusconi and Forza Italia, worked out changes in the Italian judicial system that have made it almost impossible to prosecute crimes of political corruption. Ostensibly, the idea was to reform Italian justice along the lines of the American system, in which all evidence must be presented orally, giving the defense the opportunity to cross-examine all witnesses—what the Italians like to call "the Perry Mason system." But other aspects of the old system that crippled the functioning of trials were left in place. For example, the Italian system includes the right of witnesses not to testify, even in cases where self-incrimination is not an issue. Under the old system, this was not that big a problem, since written evidence—pretrial depositions or testimony from previous trials—could be used in place of a live witness. Under the new system, a witness to a crime can simply change his or her mind, decide—out of intimidation, corruption or friendship—not to appear in court and cripple a prosecution. Moreover, moving from a written to an oral system has made Italian trials much, much longer, but there was no provision made to change the country's statute of limitations. For offenses involving less than five years in prison, including most white-collar crimes, the prosecution has only five years from the time of the commission of the crime to win a definitive conviction. Since the Italian justice system provides for three levels of appeal, this places a notable burden on Italian prosecutors, but since much evidence could be submitted in written form, trials are much shorter. Now trials are much longer than before, but the statute of limitations has remained unchanged. Thus, a wealthy defender is almost guaranteed to win by running out the clock by filing time-consuming motions and pettifogging. Berlusconi himself and many in his entourage have overturned convictions by taking advantage of the statute-of-limitations law. The average trial went from 124 days in 1990 to 345 in 1997; while the average appeal went from 266 days to 573 days.[8] The overall result of these "reforms" is that virtually none of the thousands of defendants charged in the massive corruption investigations that began in 1992 and are known as Operation Clean Hands are in jail, and Berlusconi has been able to avoid any real accounting for the massive evidence of illegality discovered in his business affairs.

Berlusconi has often accused the prosecutors of Milan who initiated Operation Clean Hands as being *toghe rosse,* red-robed puppets in the hands of D'Alema and the former Communists. The action on judicial reform demonstrated just the opposite. As a lifelong professional politician, D'Alema resented the continual intrusion of the magistrates into the national life and felt that after shaking up the system a bit, they should return obediently to their place. He failed to understand that the investigations were part of an attempt to hold the Italian political class to the rule of law, not a political device that could be turned on and off. The result would be a reign of total impunity.

The investigations offered the hope that Italy might become a country of rules rather than one governed by personal connections and political might. Berlusconi represented the defeat of that hope, and D'Alema legitimated that position by using fundamental matters of principle, freedom of expression, conflict of interest and criminal justice as poker chips in his big negotiation with Berlusconi. The culmination of this was a meeting between D'Alema and Berlusconi that occurred over dinner on the terrace of the Rome apartment of one of Berlusconi's closest advisers. The press accounts of the meeting were full of the jovial good feeling that prevailed as the parties worked out the shape of Italy's future on a number of fronts. At a certain point, one of Berlusconi's aides scratched out a few details that had been neglected about changes Forza Italia wanted on criminal justice reform. And so, important principles of justice were negotiated away on a napkin by people who were not even members of the government.

D'Alema declared: "I don't care if Berlusconi wants the agreement on the reforms out of personal interest. If the interests of Mediaset coincide with those of the country, that's fine with me." What he failed to understand was the fact that Berlusconi's conflict of interest guaranteed that all the so-called reforms were tailor-made to suit his interests. And when he had obtained what he wanted, he reneged on the one reform that D'Alema really cared about: a new election law, modeled along the French system, that would have allowed for multiple political parties but provided a stable majority for the winning coalition.[9] Berlusconi had had D'Alema for dinner.

4. The Plot to Destroy Di Pietro, Part III

While the center-left was engaged in its prolonged campaign of *buonismo*, in the hope that the Berlusconi phenomenon would go away if it was ignored, Berlusconi himself felt under no such restraints toward those he regarded as his enemies.

Because Antonio Di Pietro had been absolved of any wrongdoing in the first round of cases brought against him by the prosecutors of Brescia, charges that he had extorted money from businessman Giancarlo Gorrini, he felt he was free to hold public office and accepted an offer from the center-left government to become minister of public works, an area where his experience in fighting corruption would be useful. But within a few months of his taking office, the Berlusconi machine appeared to be operating around the clock to destroy Di Pietro once again.

In late 1996, two police officers who had worked in the Milan Palace of Justice came forward with an extraordinary story: while working with the anticorruption pool, they had seen Antonio Di Pietro and his colleagues systematically plan to destroy Silvio Berlusconi. Di Pietro allegedly confided to one of the agents, "We've done in the Christian Democrats and the Socialists, now we have to get rid of Berlusconi and then I'll head the government."[10] The agents said they had heard the magistrates discussing their plans with left-wing politicians and they had seen them leaking the story of Berlusconi's indictment to the *Corriere della Sera*. And they claimed that Di Pietro had asked one of them to procure for him a visitor's pass to Palazzo Chigi, the prime minister's office, and to forge the words "Massimo Maria Berruti for Prime Minister Berlusconi." In short, the smoking gun that had appeared to tie Silvio Berlusconi to the attempts to silence the tax inspectors who had taken bribes from Fininvest was, according to this testimony, falsified evidence.

Before these accusations were out in the open, Silvio Berlusconi began to make sibylline references to "chilling news that he had become aware of . . . a mosaic of grave crimes."[11] He was also holding in his drawer his secretly taped confessions of Antonio D'Adamo that appeared to implicate Di Pietro in bribery.

Given the gravity of the new accusations, an investigation was immediately undertaken by the prosecutor's office of Brescia. Unfortunately for the two officers, their stories didn't hold up well. Neither had worked closely with Di Pietro or the pool, and an examination of their duties revealed that they would not have been in a position to do or see a number of the things they claimed to have done and seen. One of the agents, Felice Corticchia, had, in fact, been forced to leave the service because he had been caught going through a prosecutor's desk and was suspected of leaking confidential information to journalists. Their stories were flatly contradicted by the other police agents who were constantly at Di Pietro's side during the periods in question. Moreover, the visitor's pass that Berruti had used to visit Berlusconi was found to be authentic; the clerk on duty that evening recognized the handwriting as his own. The two agents were also contradicted by a witness they had said would be able to corroborate their stories, a young female journalist named Renata Fontanelli, to whom Corticchia had passed confidential documents during the early days of Operation Clean Hands. Corticchia, she said, told her that she would get a full-time job at Fininvest if she testified against Di Pietro. "He bragged that he had become rich because he was working for the Berlusconi group, which had given him the possibility of publishing two books, given him two consulting jobs and allowed him to become a screenwriter." He also insisted that he had met with both Emilio Fede and Berlusconi at his villa at Arcore.

Financial investigations showed that Corticchia had gone from being badly in debt, with banks threatening to seize his possessions, to suddenly having hundreds of thousands of dollars in the bank.

Given the evidence against them, the two agents pled guilty to defamation, but were given suspended sentences despite the gravity of the offense: inventing evidence that could have landed Di Pietro in jail and destroyed his career. The Brescia prosecutors never pursued the possibility that someone in the Fininvest group might have put these two officers up to the scheme, and given them the money that had suddenly rained down on them. Was there no relation between Corticchia's newfound wealth and his willingness to confirm what Berlusconi had been saying for years, namely that the Milan prosecutors had long been engaged in a ruthless political plot to destroy him?

There is an illuminating epilogue to the story. What does a police officer who is first removed from his position for rummaging through a magistrate's desk and then is found guilty of defamation do for work? In the case of Felice Corticchia, he found work as the head of security for the Fiera di Milano, Milan's principal convention center. The director of the convention center at the time was Flavio Cattaneo, who would be appointed director general of RAI under the second Berlusconi government. In the Italy of Berlusconi, loyalty is always rewarded.

The accusations of the former police officers may have missed their mark, but Berlusconi was still holding in reserve the secretly taped confessions of Di Pietro's old friend, Antonio D'Adamo. In late 1996, an investigator working on the case was quoted as saying: "We have incontrovertible proof against [Di Pietro]. . . . The only thing missing is the bank account number."[12]

In May 1997, Berlusconi and Previti came forward with the material they had gathered from D'Adamo purportedly showing that Di Pietro had accepted a massive bribe. The Berlusconi family's *Il Giornale* printed so many violently anti–Di Pietro stories, many of which were shown either to be libelous or undocumented, that Paolo Berlusconi eventually agreed to pay a large settlement to Di Pietro and the newspaper, almost incomprehensibly, after treating the ex-prosecutor as public enemy number one, suddenly published a huge two-page spread praising Di Pietro lavishly. It was part of the settlement of Di Pietro's libel suits, but one long story could hardly undo the work of years. The Jekyll-and-Hyde behavior was characteristic of the complete lack of journalistic scruples of its editor, Vittorio Feltri, who could publish one set of "facts" and their direct opposite in rapid succession without a moment of blushing.[13]

After four years of searching, the prosecutors were unable to show that Di Pietro had taken any money or acted improperly in his career as prosecutor, and he was absolved of all charges, but in the meantime he had been effectively neutralized as a political rival to Berlusconi, his public image badly eroded by almost daily attacks in the Berlusconi media. By the end, he was no longer any serious threat to the founder of Forza Italia. The role of Berlusconi in helping to gather evidence against Di Pietro— secretly tape-recording D'Adamo, appearing to put words in his mouth that would be damaging to Di Pietro, keeping the evidence under lock and key until a politically opportune moment—went virtually uncommented on in the Italian press. Equally unexplored was whether there was any connection among the fabricated story of the ex-police officer Corticchia, his visit or visits to Berlusconi, his frequent meetings with Emilio Fede and his sudden change of fortune from debt to prosperity. Ten years of relentless attacks had created a general impression among many voters that the prosecutors of political corruption were not much better than the people they were prosecuting.

5. "Beautiful. All the Candidates My Friends, All of Them Elected!"

While the Italian magistrature was uncovering some of the darker secrets of the Fininvest empire and the center-left was busy negotiating away the powers of the judiciary, there were many signs that the old organic relationship between the Mafia and political power in Sicily was reestablishing itself, with Berlusconi's Forza Italia as its principal interlocutor.

As early as the 1994 election, there had been a number of troubling signs. As Italian police tapped the phones or bugged the residences of Mafia suspects, they heard a surprising amount of election activity. Giuseppe Mandalari, a convicted money-launderer, who had been known for decades to Mafia investigators as the money manager of Totò Riina, the boss of bosses, was a whirl of election activity. "I have one thing to say to you: Forza Italia," he told a friend. "Berlusconi? I'm giving him a big hand because I've got an archive of all the Freemasons in Italy. Forza Italia is the one hope for Italy." Others did little to conceal their joy at the prospect that a Berlusconi government would finally stick it to the nosy prosecutors who had been making everyone's life impossible.[14]

A few days later, after Berlusconi's "Good Government" list had won fifty-four of the sixty-one seats at stake in Sicily, Mandalari was exultant: "Beautiful. All the candidates my friends, all of them elected!" This proved not to be an empty boast. In the days after the election, three newly elected members of Berlusconi's center-right coalition—two senators and a deputy of the lower house—called Mandalari to thank him for his support.

Mandalari's son's name turned up in Marcello Dell'Utri's office date book but Dell'Utri insisted that they had never actually met. Police found evidence that the Mandalaris had sent an emissary to the Rome office of Alberto Dell'Utri, Marcello's twin brother, who also worked for Berlusconi. Alberto Dell'Utri was out of the country at the time and the emissary, a big, tough-looking character named Salvatore Modica, left word that "I am here until Saturday, if there's the possibility of seeing him, it would be our great pleasure, but if I don't hear from him by Wednesday . . . I'll organize a demonstration against Berlusconi in Palermo." The demonstration never occurred. Instead, Modica, together with Giuseppe Mandalari, the convicted money-launderer, attended a rally in favor of Berlusconi's Forza Italia.[15]

In late 1995, police arrested Francesco Musotto, the president of Forza Italia in the province of Palermo, after learning that Leoluca Bagarella, a particularly bloody Mafia boss with numerous murders on his record (he was thought to have succeeded his brother-in-law Totò Riina as the boss of bosses of Cosa Nostra) had been given hospitality in Musotto's country home in Sicily while hiding out from Italian justice. The court decided that there was insufficient evidence to show that Musotto knew about Bagarella's presence at the family villa; his brother, however, was convicted. Rather than deciding that a man whose family had hidden a major Mafia fugitive might not be best suited to lead the largest party in the capital of the Mafia, Forza Italia decided to put Musotto up for reelection as a kind of martyr of the Italian justice system. He was triumphantly reelected.

Not all members of Forza Italia have been blind to this problem, but they have not fared well. In Catania, the second-largest city in Sicily, two local leaders of Forza Italia, Umberto Scapagnini and Antonio Fiumefreddo, fought a battle to rid the party of politicians with Mafia ties, checking with police before accepting candidacies and writing detailed reports about candidates who had been arrested or tried for serious crimes or had documented ties to organized-crime figures. But they received a cold reception within the party. One high-level party leader told them that they "had not understood the mentality of Forza Italia," and their activities were "contrary to the interests of the movement."[16] They were ostracized within the party and became the object of death threats. "Inside of Forza Italia in Sicily, there is no interest whatever in conducting a battle against the Mafia," Fiumefreddo said in May of 1996, in resigning from the party.[17]

In mid-1997, a court in Palermo ruled that there was sufficient evidence for Marcello Dell'Utri to stand trial for collusion with the Mafia. The documentation that prosecutors were required to submit to court outlined a twenty-five-year history of frequent and close contacts with organized-crime figures—wiretapped conversations, dinners, weddings—along with the testimony of more than a dozen Mafia witnesses that claimed that Dell'Utri was the Mafia's main contact with the new political establishment.

At a certain point, police followed Dell'Utri as he drove to a meeting with an organized-crime figure who was out of prison on furlough. The criminal, Giuseppe Chiofalo, was prepared to testify that a group of ex-Mafiosi who were witnesses against Dell'Utri had tried to convince him to make up damaging evidence about Dell'Utri and Berlusconi. The claim lacked any credibility. The criminal in question was from another region of Italy, had no connection to the Sicilian Mafia and to Dell'Utri's social circles. Since all the accusations about Dell'Utri came from gangsters from Dell'Utri's hometown of Palermo, and many had actually met him or were friends of his friends, it would make no sense to recruit a random criminal from another criminal organization from another region to join the supposed conspiracy to destroy Dell'Utri. Other prisoners in the same prison testified that Chiofalo and another prisoner were trying to recruit people to employ witnesses in order to get money and more lenient sentences with help from Dell'Utri and Forza Italia. When the police arrived at the gangster's home right after the meeting with Dell'Utri, they found 80 million lire (about $45,000) in cash; the briefcase that Dell'Utri had been carrying when he entered the house was empty. The gangster claimed that the cash came from the unregistered sale of an apartment, and Dell'Utri insisted he was only gathering evidence for his own defense, even though court rules specify that all gathering of evidence should be done by lawyers and investigators, not by defendants. It was at this point that prosecutors asked the Italian parliament to waive Dell'Utri's immunity, charging him with tampering with witnesses and evidence, and it was on this basis that parliament refused.[18]

6. A PACT WITH THE DEVIL?

Numerous Mafia witnesses—some of them Mafiosi who occupied positions at the top of the organization—testified that Dell'Utri had been the Mafia's contact person within Berlusconi's organization. Some spoke of a pact between Cosa Nostra and Forza Italia, saying that politicians in the party had promised to water down anti-Mafia legislation.

The Cosa Nostra and Berlusconi's party had common interests and a common enemy in the Italian magistrature. Many of Berlusconi's judicial reforms aimed at easing the plight of people accused of political corruption were equally helpful to many Mafia defendants. And given Vittorio Mangano's presence at Arcore and the previous investigations into both Dell'Utri and Berlusconi for their Mafia ties, it was natural to fear what might come out of Sicily.

Almost immediately after the 1994 elections, Domenico Contestabile, Berlusconi's choice for undersecretary of justice, proposed drastically modifying the witness protection program that had attracted so many new Mafia witnesses. And Berlusconi's minister of the environment proposed closing down the special island prisons, hated by the Mafia bosses, where the most dangerous subjects were kept in a condition of considerable isolation, far from their families and their criminal organizations. The minister insisted that his motivation was to make these beautiful places available to all Italians rather than waste them on prisons for convicted criminals. At the time, such a move was politically impossible; the memory of the countless Mafia assassinations of the 1980s and early 1990s was too fresh in the public mind. Moreover, the anti-Mafia legislation that Forza Italia was proposing to reform had produced extraordinary and documented successes: thousands of gangsters were behind bars, entire criminal organizations had been dismantled, and the murder rate for the entire Italian territory had been cut in half in about two years.[19] To have made major concessions to the benefit of Mafia defendants at that time would have been political suicide.

But Forza Italia did manage to push some reforms through when it was out of power. Between 1996 and 2001, creating an alliance with environmentalists and civil libertarians on the center-left, Forza Italia eventually got the island prisons of Pianosa and Asinara closed. "A historic mistake," says Ignazio De Francisci, one of Giovanni Falcone's deputies in the anti-Mafia pool of Palermo and more recently the chief prosecutor of Agrigento, Sicily. Forza Italia also rewrote the legislation for the "special prisons," so as to make life for the bosses much easier: they can now receive food from the outside, see relatives without Plexiglas barriers separating them, and have more time to socialize with other Mafia prisoners—all of which makes staying on top of Mafia business much easier.[20]

Similarly, Forza Italia was able to obtain a substantial revision of the witness protection program that has reduced the flow of new Mafia witnesses from a torrent to a trickle. There were some legitimate reasons to change the 1992 law: written in a time of emergency, when there were few cooperating witnesses, the new program offered generous benefits to Mafia turncoats. While this led to an unprecedented number of witnesses, the sincerity and reliability of the witnesses went down, authors of truly terrible crimes went free and some undeniable instances of abuse occurred—given maximum coverage in the Berlusconi-controlled media—discrediting the witness protection program in the public's eyes.

The new law regarding Mafia witnesses required them to serve much more time in prison, put their property at risk of confiscation, and reduced the amount of time they have to tell everything to investigators. Rather than occupying a sensible middle ground, many magistrates now feel that the program has become positively punitive, with the result that the last few years have seen extremely few new witnesses. From 1992 to 1994, there were one thousand new witnesses, Cosa Nostra was hemorrhaging members and the future of the organization was at risk. The bleeding has stopped.

Many of the reforms were the fruit of the cooperation between D'Alema and Berlusconi during the period of the bicameral commission, when the center-left sought to adopt a bipartisan approach to most issues. But the impetus for the reforms came from Berlusconi's Forza Italia. Mafia witnesses say that the organization wanted four things from the political system: the end of the special prisons; revision of the witness protection program; changes in the penal code to strengthen defendants' rights; and the elimination of life sentences for Mafia bosses. The Mafia ended up getting significant progress on three out of four issues.

As important principles were negotiated away on the terraces of Rome, D'Alema widened the chasm that exists in Italy between politics and government. His hyperactive and highly visible role took the spotlight away from the government. This was unfortunate because the center-left government contained many capable, hardworking ministers, and much good was done. Italy's ailing balance sheet was cleaned up, its economy returned to solid footing, and important concessions were won from unions and pensioners without dismantling many aspects of the country's social welfare state that most Italians were anxious to maintain. At the same time, basic services such as those of the post office and phone company were improved. There were few signs of the kind of corruption that plagued Italy's recent past.

The Italian public perceived this and when Prodi's coalition appeared ready to collapse in 1998, crowds of ordinary Italians actually demonstrated before parliament to protest. The sight of Italians protesting the fall of a government was a sign of genuinely positive change. But no crowd's exhortations could prevent the center-left from self-destructing. Not long after the failure of the bicameral commission, the neo-Communist party, Rifondazione Comunista, withdrew its support from the government of Romano Prodi. The end of the Prodi government was the beginning of the end for the center-left. Blame should be widely shared. The principal guilty one was the neo-Communist leader, Fausto Bertinotti, who withdrew the party's support from the government essentially because it was not sufficiently to the left. Prisoner of the fratricidal mentality of the old left, Bertinotti failed to understand that the current electoral system favored broad coalitions rather than ideological purity. Like Ralph Nader in the United States, Bertinotti has dedicated most of his energies to attacking his erstwhile allies of the center-left in order to increase his percentage of the vote by a point or two. Prodi, too, was excessively stubborn in refusing to negotiate to bring in new partners in order to save his coalition. D'Alema also deserves his share of responsibility. D'Alema's *inciucio* gave some credence to Bertinotti and the neo-Communists' claim that there was little difference between center-left and center-right, and it undermined Prodi's power. And while D'Alema helped get Prodi elected, he seemed to resent his success. One of D'Alema's close aides told me when Prodi was at the height of his popularity, "We elected Prodi but now he is getting all the credit." D'Alema, she said, was anxious to become prime minister himself. While it may be wrong to say, as many do, that D'Alema engineered Prodi's downfall in order to become prime minister himself, it is fair to say that he did not do everything he might have to keep Prodi in power, and he was happy for the chance to become prime minister in 1998.[21]

This played perfectly into Berlusconi's hands, allowing him to run not against a moderate economist who had been elected prime minister, but against an ex-Communist who had risen to power though interparty negotiations. Berlusconi won a huge victory in the European parliamentary elections of 1999 running against D'Alema and the Communists. In this election, D'Alema felt the full weight of having his former negotiating partner's media empire directed against him. Berlusconi's party bombarded the country with some 803 political advertisements broadcast on his three TV networks. The center-left took out no television ads of any kind. Since public TV in Italy does not broadcast political ads, the center-left was in the impossible position of either giving money to its opponent or doing without television advertising.[22]

Suddenly, the left began calling desperately for conflict-of-interest and antitrust legislation, but after four years in power, it appeared self-interested and hypocritical.

The left patched together a caretaker government headed by Giuliano Amato, a former Socialist prime minister, and headed toward the 2001 elections in complete disarray.

Again, by most objective measures, the center-left governed relatively well between 1996 and 2001. The government of Romano Prodi staked its reputation on being able to meet the economic criteria of the Maastricht Treaty that would make Italy eligible to join the single currency, the euro, together with the leading countries of Europe such as Germany and France. This meant that Italy would have to cut its budget deficit in half and bring down its rate of inflation to only 2 percent. Most predicted that this would prove impossible. Through a combination of tough austerity measures, a crackdown on tax evasion, and a one-time "Europe tax," the government pulled it off. At the same time, benefiting from the economic boom of the mid- to late 1990s, the Italian economy grew at nearly 3 percent a year and added more than a million jobs in five years—accomplishing what Berlusconi promised but failed to do when he was elected in 1994. Interest rates were cut nearly in half, and the stock market nearly doubled in value.

The government also simplified many bureaucratic procedures, made it possible to do on the Internet what in the past had taken hours of standing in line in government offices, and handed over a number of functions to local government that had previously been the province of the central government. Extremely difficult and economically depressed cities like Naples and Palermo were run by center-left governments and achieved remarkable turnarounds, recognized by local populations that rewarded them with reelections of nearly 70 percent of the vote.

"They did little, because they had a small and divided majority," said Indro Montanelli, looking back on the center-left-governments of 1996 to 2001. "But the little that they did was of a good quality. They didn't steal, they didn't raise their voices, they tried to reform this country that is allergic to reform. The ministers worked without spending their days on television. Certainly, they didn't try to punish or persecute the leader of the opposition, in fact they allowed him to do his business better than before. . . . It was they who helped him get his companies into sound economic shape."[23]

But much of this work was undermined by political infighting and public squabbling. Had the Prodi government remained in power until the recent elections it would have been the first time an Italian government had lasted an entire legislature, an impressive show of seriousness of purpose and desire for change. Instead, many voters felt betrayed. As one angry voter quoted by Turin's newspaper *La Stampa* put it: "I voted for a government headed by a centrist economist and then found myself with D'Alema, an ex-Communist, and then Amato, the former right-hand man of [Socialist leader Bettino] Craxi." The path was paved for Berlusconi's return.

Chapter Eleven

TRIUMPH

"Don't you understand? If something isn't on
television, it doesn't exist."
—*Silvio Berlusconi to Marcello Dell'Utri.*

1. AN ITALIAN STORY

In the early spring of 2001 twelve million Italian households opened their mail and found an envelope containing a biography of Silvio Berlusconi, called *Una Storia Italiana* (An Italian Story). It looked much more like a movie star fan magazine than a traditional political biography. Only 127 pages long, with about 20 percent text and 80 percent color photographs and banner headlines, it resembled the feel-good glossy publications sold at supermarkets like Berlusconi's own *Sorrisi e Canzoni* (Smiles and Songs), with a dash of *Famiglia Cristiana* (Christian Family), the Catholic Church's family magazine. Rather than having a single story that the reader has to follow, it offered a series of short articles and boxes with photographs, with headlines such as "Mamma Rosella: Always at Silvio's Side," images of Berlusconi's children: "The cubs grow up . . . ," "Feelings: To my father . . . dear, sweet Papa," "Silvio's little secrets," and a photograph of Berlusconi smelling a flower ("I've probably planted more trees than anyone who is not a professional horticulturist").[1]

Sent to almost half of all families in Italy, *Una Storia Italiana* was a direct mail campaign without precedent. Estimates of the cost of producing and sending the book to more than twelve million households vary from $25 million to $100 million.[2] The center-left, still in power as the election campaign of 2001 got under way, had banned all television advertising in an attempt to neutralize Berlusconi's vast advantage in media access and money. This was his answer.

Although widely ridiculed as a monument to kitschy bad taste and narcissism, *Una Storia Italiana* was an extremely shrewd piece of political marketing. It was a creative way around the television advertising ban but it was also a classic Berlusconi gesture, taking people by storm by doing something seemingly outrageous and unexpected, something on a scale that his opponents could never dream of and being everywhere at once.

At the same time Berlusconi blanketed Italy with the largest billboard advertising campaign the country had ever seen. Massive photographs of Silvio Berlusconi—looking younger, fitter and with more hair than he had had in years—stared down at tens of millions of Italians from virtually every town square and train station platform, and were strung across crowded streets. They were accompanied with simple but appealing slogans such as: "Less taxes for everyone." "Dignified pensions." "Safer cities."

In the campaign kit that every Forza Italia candidate received, the posters all bore the images of Berlusconi while leaving room to add the individual candidate's name. Candidates were strongly discouraged from putting their own photographs on their posters. The face of Forza Italia, from the Alps to the tip of the Italian boot, was Silvio Berlusconi's. In a country in which, since the end of Fascism, parties had always been more important than political leaders, this represented a degree of personalization of politics not seen since Mussolini's bust was omnipresent in every Italian town.

Una Storia Italiana contained almost no politics at all. It was designed and written like an entertainment magazine and featured a fairy-tale version of Berlusconi's life through a series of clichés meant to appeal to the lowest common denominator of the Italian middle and lower-middle class.

Una Storia Italiana had a dual aim. The first was to manage to make Berlusconi, the country's richest man, seem like a completely typical Italian, or at least an idealized archetype of the Italian everyman—from humble, working-class origins, ready to accept sacrifice, part of a strict but affectionate family, true to his word, devoutly loyal to parents, energetic, enterprising and even slightly mischievous but ultimately obedient to authority, both parents and Church. At the same time, the text needed to underscore that Berlusconi was exceptional, a superman in the making. "He is enterprising, sometimes hard-headed, but charismatic: in class, he is the leader," *Una Storia Italiana* tells us. As the story proceeds, behind all the apparent humility, the great man emerges. "He knows and recognizes all the species of trees, flowers and bushes. He likes to point them out with their botanical names in Latin. As an expert, he has been interviewed on numerous television programs."

The book had been carefully market-tested for its target audience, the mass of undecided voters who knew little about politics and cared even less. "The results were excellent," Luigi Crespi, the head of Berlusconi's polling company, Datamedia, told the *Corriere della Sera*. "At least one-third of respondents shifted from being 'don't knows' to center-right voters."[3]

But this final bit of electioneering—with the billboards and the biography—was just the end of a campaign that Berlusconi had been waging nonstop for two years. The television ban allowed Berlusconi to appear as something of a victim, when in fact it only applied to the last six weeks of the election period and Berlusconi had been running campaign ads during 1999 and 2000, allowing him to build up a huge lead in the polls. Six months before the elections, Berlusconi's own polling company, Datamedia, published in his family newspaper, *Il Giornale,* gave the House of Liberties (as Berlusconi dubbed his new coalition) a 59 to 33.5 percent lead over the fragmented center-left group.

Berlusconi repeatedly predicted the landside number of seats his party would take. "All the polls seem to suggest our victory is assured." His prophecies of certain victory were not just hubris, they were part of his campaign strategy. Despite his wildly optimistic public polls, real opinion research told Berlusconi that his lead was less formidable than he was letting on and likely to narrow considerably. The center-left had selected a candidate only a few months before the election while Berlusconi had been campaigning nonstop since 1998, in preparation for the European elections and the local administrative elections, which, like many midterm elections, serve as barometers of public mood and channels for expressing frustration with incumbent government. In fact, there were more potential center-left voters in 2001 than in 1994, and if it overcame its internal divisions, the left was in a good position to beat Berlusconi. His early lead depended on a large number of traditional left-of-center voters not voting this time around out of apathy and disillusionment. Berlusconi's predictions were shrewd "self-fulfilling prophecies," as several political scientists have noted in their analysis of the 2001 vote. Just as in 1994, he now used inaccurate poll numbers to great effect: broadcasting Datamedia numbers showing a landslide, which generated stories even in the non-Berlusconi press, sometimes casting doubt on those numbers but repeating them all the same. The vast majority of stories took for granted that Berlusconi was going to win—the only question was by how much. These polling stories, with their pessimistic predictions about the center-left's chances, had a lot to do with the increasing number of center-left voters who said they were planning on staying home on election day.

2. "Fit to Run Italy?"

But something unexpected happened on the way to Berlusconi's coronation. On March 14, 2001, Daniele Luttazzi, a popular comedian and TV talk-show host—a kind of combination of David Letterman and Howard Stern—violated what had been a sacred taboo since Berlusconi entered politics in 1994: he dedicated part of his program on RAI 2 to discussing the ties between the Sicilian Mafia and the Berlusconi group. Marcello Dell'Utri had been indicted four years earlier for suspected collusion with the Mafia, and thousands of pages of evidence—wiretapped conversations, depositions of witnesses, police reports—had been deposited in court and even published in book form. His trial had been conducted in open court and yet no one in Italian television had seen fit to dedicate a single program to the case. One might have thought that the organized-crime connections of the inner circle of the man who wanted to run the country would be a matter of considerable national interest, but no television station, public or private, had examined the story. When a small Milan publisher, Kaos, released two books on the case, one consisting of the prosecutors' evidence, the other a journalistic book examining Dell'Utri's Mafia ties, the books went virtually unreviewed. In 2001, just as the election campaign was getting under way, a prominent young journalist, Marco Travaglio, together with a member of parliament, Elio Veltri, published a third book on the case, *L'Odore dei Soldi* (The Smell of Money), outlining many of the Mafia charges against Dell'Utri and Berlusconi, together with numerous trial documents and transcripts. Although only one major newspaper dared to review it (the left-of-center *La Repubblica*) it began selling briskly, at the pace of a potential bestseller. Despite its success, the authors were never invited to talk about the book on television, greatly limiting its impact. Nearly all sixty million Italians watch TV, while the country sells only five million newspapers a day, proportionally much less than most European countries. A best-selling book might sell 50,000 or 100,000 copies, a tiny minority within a small minority of regular readers. As Berlusconi once remarked to Marcello Dell'Utri: "Don't you understand? If something isn't on television, it doesn't exist." By 2001, 77.4 percent got their information from television and only 6.4 percent from newspapers.[4] Control of television is tantamount to control of information as a whole.

Thus, after seven years of virtual blackout, millions of Italians were stunned to hear for the first time, in detail, for twenty-six minutes, about Vittorio Mangano, Berlusconi's Mafioso stable hand, Marcello Dell'Utri's numerous Mafia ties and the murky origins of Berlusconi's fortune. The effect was electrifying. The audience for the program jumped to record levels after the interview started, as hundreds of thousands of viewers started changing channels. One of them was Berlusconi, who was called by several friends to turn his channel to RAI 2. The broadcast was not especially fair or balanced. Luttazzi is a comedian and not a journalist, and so he did not seek out other points of view or push Travaglio to distinguish between the more speculative accusations (such as the charges, which had been dismissed by the courts, that Berlusconi and Dell'Utri were somehow behind the assassinations of two prominent Mafia prosecutors) and those that were well documented. Many were shocked and offended by Luttazzi's statement at the end of the interview: "At this point, I ask myself: what kind of country do we live in? Still, I want to thank you because in writing this book you've shown yourself to be a free man. And it's not easy to find free men in this piece-of-shit Italy of ours."[5] The director of the network, Carlo Freccero, told Travaglio that the interview had gone well but said he knew that his days as head of the network were numbered.

To judge from the reaction of the political world one might have thought that Italy had been attacked by a foreign power or that a major political figure had been assassinated. Almost as soon as the program went off the air, a leading figure for the postfascist party National Alliance and the president of the parliamentary committee overseeing RAI declared: "What went on the air this evening is without precedent in the history of television. Luttazzi's program must be shut down and Freccero removed from his position. [Roberto] Zaccaria and the whole leadership of RAI should resign."[6] Berlusconi rushed to Rome and held a meeting with the leaders of his main political allies. Some called on the president of the Republic to take immediate action. Others called for a special meeting of the oversight committee of RAI in parliament. The program, falling as it did during the election period, should have offered equal access to the other side; as a result RAI canceled Luttazzi's next show and offered his time slot to a reparatory program in which Dell'Utri would be given the chance to give his side of the story in a program moderated by a friendly journalist, Angela Buttiglione, the sister of a close ally of Berlusconi. (He refused the opportunity.)

The president of the Order of Journalists, Mario Petrina, raged against Luttazzi's program in the strongest terms possible. "I asked myself: Is this an entertainment or an information program? Neither one nor the other. It's the death of the rules of journalism, which require the chance of rebuttal."[7] The journalists' union tried to file charges against Luttazzi for acting as a journalist without being a certified as one. While Luttazzi certainly fell short of the best journalistic standards, surely the far bigger scandal was the fact that no member of the Order of Journalists at RAI had dared to take on what was clearly one of the most serious and important stories in the country, leaving the work to be done by a comedian–talk show host. Moreover, one-sided programs aired routinely on Italian television and passed without complaint. Every weekday since 1994, Vittorio Sgarbi, another nonjournalist, spoke for twenty minutes nonstop on Berlusconi's largest network, making wild and often entirely undocumented accusations against Berlusconi's enemies, without offering any possibility of reply. Sgarbi's show made the Luttazzi-Travaglio interview look positively tame, and it aired not once but hundreds of times.

Il Giornale published a poll claiming that Berlusconi's standing with voters jumped 5 percentage points, from 53 to 58, thanks to Luttazzi's program. But privately, Berlusconi was worried that RAI had slipped from his control. He was already furious because Enzo Biagi, perhaps Italy's most revered television journalist, had done an interview with Indro Montanelli in which Montanelli had compared the Berlusconi phenomenon to a dangerous disease to which Italy needed to develop immunity. He went on to call Berlusconi a pathological liar: "Berlusconi is a man with an entirely personal view of the truth, so that whatever he says is true. He tells lies, but he believes them." It was only a five-minute interview, but while Luttazzi normally had a smaller and younger audience of mostly left-of-center viewers late at night on RAI 2, Biagi was the soul of moderation, with a prime-time program on RAI 1, traditionally the most conservative of the state networks. Berlusconi declared that he and the members of his party would boycott all RAI broadcasts until they ceased these unfair attacks.

Two days after the Luttazzi broadcast, Michele Santoro, one of RAI's most famous television journalists, ran a program on Dell'Utri and the origins of Berlusconi's fortune. He invited Berlusconi and Dell'Utri, but they refused and Santoro had their point of view represented by the deputy editor of Berlusconi's newspaper *Il Giornale*. In the end Berlusconi could not stand to stay away and telephoned in during the live broadcast. Santoro told Berlusconi on air that he couldn't have it both ways, boycotting RAI, forcing his representatives to boycott RAI, and then calling up to interrupt the program and make speeches. Santoro said that he would be happy to listen to Berlusconi only if he lifted the boycott and agreed to enter into discussion like any other guest. When Berlusconi refused, Santoro said that he would have to hang up. Berlusconi, furious, snapped, "Santoro, you are a public employee!" "Yes, I am an employee of the public, but I am not your employee, Berlusconi."

The House of Liberties finally lifted the boycott on RAI programs and Marcello Dell'Utri agreed to appear on Santoro's program. When they appeared, Dell'Utri and the other pro-Berlusconi speakers received more than twice the air time of their critics, but Dell'Utri created a disastrous impression. At one point, in discussing his close encounters with the Mafia, he said, "The truth is, I'm a Mafioso . . . that is, I meant to say, I am a Sicilian."[8] At another point, someone said to Dell'Utri. "Technically, you are a convicted criminal, how can you be a candidate for the Senate?" Dell'Utri gave a disarmingly candid answer on air: that he had entered politics in order to obtain immunity against a prosecution he considered unjust.

The Berlusconi-owned media mounted a furious counterattack. Berlusconi's network Italia 1 dedicated a two-hour program to the four former Berlusconi employees (Montanelli, Travaglio, Luttazzi and Carlo Freccero, Luttazzi's producer, all of whom had worked for either *Il Giornale* or Berlusconi's TV stations) who "betrayed" their boss by criticizing him. As the program discussed their infamy, the caption "INGRATES" appeared at the bottom of the TV screen—to which Luttazzi responded: "Berlusconi finds it hard to understand that just because he has paid people doesn't mean he has bought them."[9]

Il Giornale published long attacks on Luttazzi, in which it included his tax returns and his home address. His apartment was broken into and robbed twice immediately thereafter.

On April 26, a little less than three weeks from the election, the serious-minded British newsweekly *The Economist* weighed in on the growing controversy, publishing a cover story entitled: "Fit to Run Italy?" After examining the many charges into Berlusconi and his group, the magazine answered the question with a resounding no:

> In any self-respecting democracy it would be unthinkable that the man assumed to be on the verge of being elected prime minister would recently have come under investigation for, among other things, money-laundering, complicity in murder, connections with the Mafia, tax evasion and the bribing of politicians, judges and the tax police. But the country is Italy and the man is Silvio Berlusconi, almost certainly its richest citizen. As our own investigations make plain, Mr. Berlusconi is not fit to lead the government of any country, least of all one of the world's richest democracies.[10]

The magazine went on to say that even if one decided to ignore the evidence of wrongdoing against Berlusconi, rounds of conflict of interest should disqualify him from holding office:

> Worth perhaps $14 billion, he is intricately involved in vast areas of Italian finance, commerce and broadcasting with ramifications into almost every aspect of business and public life; his empire includes banks, insurance, property, publishing, advertising, the media and football. Even during his ill-fated earlier stint as prime minister, in 1994, he issued an array of decrees that impinged heavily on his commercial activities. If he wins again on May 13th, he will control a good 90% of all national television broadcasting. He has made not the slightest effort to resolve this clear conflict.

The Economist ended by listing a series of questions that Berlusconi should be forced to answer before presenting himself to the electorate, questions forcing him to reveal the origins of his fortune, the identities of his early investors, the nature of his relationship with Marcello Dell'Utri, Vittorio Mangano and the Mafia. These were questions that any vigilant, independent newspaper serious about covering Italian politics should have been repeating again and again until they were answered, but which had been raised only very occasionally by a few isolated voices and never by a major, mainstream publication.

Within the establishment press, the editor of the *Corriere della Sera*, Paolo Mieli, had helped invent a position known as *terzismo* (literally "thirdism" or "the third position"): neither with nor against Berlusconi, conveniently abdicating any responsibility for adjudicating and weighing the relative truth-value of the competing claims of Berlusconi and his accusers, a kind of journalistic equivalent of Pontius Pilate's washing of his hands.

Berlusconi has long insisted that Italy's traditional financial and cultural establishment has always been against him. The most eloquent contradiction of this myth came immediately after the publication of *The Economist*'s declaration of Berlusconi's unfitness to hold office, which was seconded by foreign newspapers and magazines around the world. Gianni Agnelli, the chairman of Fiat, the incarnation of the establishment, the closest thing to royalty left in Italy, owner of the Turin newspaper *La Stampa*, and part-owner of the *Corriere della Sera*, came out in vocal defense of Berlusconi. "The thing that bothered me is that some foreign newspapers have made judgments about our possible future prime minister as if Italy were a banana republic," he said.[11]

Still ahead in the polls, but seeing his margin narrow day by day Berlusconi steadfastly refused to debate Francesco Rutelli. He was certainly aware that his image of great communicator had been dented by his not-so-successful debate with Romano Prodi in 1996. A head-to-head confrontation would have put them on the same plane and might have narrowed the gap further.

Berlusconi preferred environments he could control. He tried to negotiate a way onto Santoro's TV program *Raggio Verde* (Green Ray), to show he was not afraid to answer difficult questions, but he insisted on seeing the questions he would be asked in advance—an obvious violation of standard journalistic practice. Despite pressure from higher-ups at RAI, Santoro refused and Berlusconi stayed away.

Berlusconi found an extremely friendly home on RAI on Bruno Vespa's program *Porta a Porta* (Door to Door). Vespa was a journalist who in the pre-Berlusconi RAI days had not been ashamed to say that his professional compass was the Christian Democratic Party. In the Berlusconi era, it was no secret that his new professional compass was Berlusconi himself. Vespa received a second salary for a weekly column in Berlusconi's newsmagazine *Panorama* and made millions from books published by Berlusconi's publishing house Mondadori, which Berlusconi personally did much to publicize, appearing personally at Vespa's book launches, turning them into major public events which often resembled political rallies. A week before the election, Berlusconi appeared alone on Vespa's show to present his "contract with the Italians." Although largely a straight copy of Newt Gingrich's "Contract with America," it seemed like an intriguing novelty to an uninformed Italian public, very much in keeping with the businessman / prime minister. Instead of the detailed programs offered by the center-left, Berlusconi laid out five simple promises contained on one typed page, lined and formatted like a legal contract:

"1.) Reducing all taxes to 33 percent of income. 2.) A major reduction of crime. 3.) Raising minimum pensions to a million lire a month [about $462]. 4.) Cutting the unemployment rate in half and adding a million jobs. 5.) Starting 40 percent of a Ten year plan of great public works."

Berlusconi vowed that if he failed to keep at least four of the five promises, he would not run for reelection.

On May 13, Berlusconi's "House of Liberties" won, but by a much smaller margin than originally predicted. The vote in the lower house of parliament was 45.4 percent for the House of Liberties to 43.7 percent for the Olive Tree coalition. Berlusconi's private pollsters estimated that if the campaign had lasted another week or two, their man might have lost. Indeed if the far left party Rifondazione Comunista had not siphoned off 5 percent of the left-of-the-center vote, Berlusconi would have lost. But the nature of the Italian electoral law and the geographical distribution of the vote meant that Berlusconi had a majority in parliament of more than one hundred deputies, one of the largest majorities ever enjoyed by an Italian government. The alleged connections between Berlusconi, Dell'Utri and the Mafia certainly did not hurt their party in Sicily; on the contrary, the center-right won an astonishing sixty-one of sixty-one seats in parliament from the region, accounting for a large chunk of their margin of victory.

3. WHY DO PEOPLE VOTE FOR BERLUSCONI?

One could ascribe Berlusconi's 1994 lightning victory to the appeal of novelty, but by 2001 the Italian public had ample experience on which to base their judgment. They had seen that, contrary to his promises, he had not hesitated to pursue his personal business in office, short-circuited the court cases brought against him, and tamed the state broadcasting system that was also his chief economic competitor. They had seen initial charges of corruption borne out—what in 1994 were nothing more than alleged bribes were confessed to; an enormous system of hidden overseas bank accounts were uncovered; long denied under-the-table financing to Craxi was found and traced from one account to another. Rumors of Mafia ties had been corroborated by dozens of eyewitnesses, wiretapped conversations, and concrete signs of electoral support on the part of Cosa Nostra. If Berlusconi & Co. were as bad as this, how was it that millions of Italians continued to vote for him and his coalition?

The answer is complex. The collapse of the old parties in 1992–1993 left a void that Berlusconi ably filled. The Italian left, although it has governed in a moderate and responsible fashion, presents its own set of problems. There is a residual anti-Communism in the Italian electorate from forty-five years of the Cold War, which Berlusconi has done much to keep alive. Many Italians, rightly or wrongly, feel that the Italian left, which has governed many towns and regions for years, has occupied and abused political power—steering government contracts to friendly businesses—in ways that are as bad as the outright bribe-taking practiced by other parties. The old Communist Party took money from the Soviet Union for decades (although conservative parties and progovernment unions received money from the United States during the same period). The deep-seated cynicism of Italian voters, and the conviction that all parties have something to hide, led many to simply tune out the legal and ethical problems of Berlusconi.

For cultural and historical reasons, the conflict-of-interest problem has never been felt as important by most Italians. Conflicts of interest are pandemic in Italian life. Doctors in public hospitals—on the public payroll—steer patients to private clinics where they work or which they own. Lawyers, businessmen and journalists virtually never quit their original jobs when they win a seat in parliament and enjoy the very handsome salaries and perks that come with it. I remember how shocked I was, when I worked for Italy's largest book publishing house, Mondadori, in 1980, to discover that the head of our publicity office was also the chief literary critic of the company's weekly newsmagazine and that he enthusiastically reviewed the very books he was being paid to publicize. When the Mondadori-owned magazines ran a cover story on summer reading, they placed a stack of Mondadori books next to the person in the cover photograph (usually a topless woman, sunbathing). When I began reporting on Italian politics, I was surprised to find that the man I spoke to in the press office of the Christian Democratic Party in the morning could be found each afternoon at the newspaper *Il Tempo*, a theoretically independent newspaper. What was most surprising was that no one seemed to find these arrangements particularly surprising. So when Berlusconi took over Mondadori and *Panorama* and then used them for his political career, he was erasing boundaries in a system where they were already very blurry.

During the 2001 election, the *Corriere della Sera* published a poll showing that 62 percent of Italians surveyed were either indifferent to Berlusconi's conflict-of-interest problem (39 percent) or convinced that his personal interests "would meant he will govern the country better" (24 percent).[12]

Equally important is the nature of Berlusconi's supporters: they are drawn primarily from shopkeepers, small-business owners, self-employed people. In Italy, more than a third of the working population is composed of the self-employed—more than three times the ratio of Germany and Japan.[13] These were the bedrock of Berlusconi's support, while he did noticeably less well among business executives and rank-and-file employees in private industry. Italy has more than five million small businesses in a country of about 58 million people, nearly one business for every ten citizens, the highest per capita concentration of small businesses in the world. There are only 240 large corporations listed on the Italian stock exchange; the rest of the five million are privately held, almost entirely family-owned firms. The average size of an Italian business is 3.9 employees, about half the average size in Europe.[14]

Berlusconi's history of ignoring, skirting or flouting the law is not atypical of Italy's family-run businesses, many of which are deft at outwitting the country's legislature. One of the reasons that most businesses in Italy are reluctant to list on the stock exchange is their reluctance to open themselves to further regulation, oversight and transparency. Because it is virtually impossible to fire anyone in Italy, small-business owners routinely hire and fire people off the books. Italy leads Europe (and perhaps the world) in having some 90,000 laws in force (compared with 7,325 in France and 5,587 in Germany), as well as in lawlessness and tax evasion.[15] To conceal their wealth, the owners of car dealerships, appliance shops and many other stores routinely pay their shop assistants and cashiers less than the owners declare on their taxes.

Economically, the family business is both a blessing and a curse. The businesses are often extraordinarily nimble and hardworking, but the tiny number of publicly traded companies means that Italy has lagged far behind in fields such as computers and biotech research, which require significant investment and research. Berlusconi's Fininvest, although the second-largest company in Italy, was in 1994 still a family business and run very much like one. And so, although Fininvest was comparable in scale to giant companies like Fiat, Olivetti, Pirelli, and Montedison, it in some ways had more in common culturally with the small mom-and-pop businesses scattered throughout Italy. Berlusconi ran his business in a highly personalized fashion, placing his brother, son and daughter and most of his closest childhood friends in important positions in the company; he even made his tennis instructor an ad salesman at Publitalia. He ran Fininvest in a paternalistic fashion, and has a habit of giving his top managers (who are also close friends) millions of dollars in the form of personal "gifts," not company "bonuses."

The Italian economy is essentially divided in half between employees, whose taxes are deducted directly from their salaries, and the self-employed, who are much freer to cheat. Berlusconi did much better among the latter than the former. Because the self-employed routinely cheat the state and cook their own books, they view the much vaster imbroglios of the Berlusconi empire with less severity. Although most Italians cheered when police began arresting corrupt politicians in the Milan investigation known as Operation Clean Hands, a substantial part of the population was less thrilled when prosecutors and the government tried to apply the law to the general public with new severity. There was a major crackdown on tax evasion in 1993 and per capita consumption dropped by 2.5 percent. The investigation began to lose popular consensus not, as Berlusconi sustains, because he was singled out for persecution but because the new moralizing trend was applied so widely.

Reflecting on the declining support for Operation Clean Hands, former chief prosecutor Francesco Saverio Borelli said it began with the investigation into the bribes given to the tax inspectors. "When it became clear . . . that the problem of corruption in Italy didn't just regard the politicians, but large segments of society, the average citizen had the sensation that the 'moralists' of the Milan prosecutor's office were going to apply their cleaning tools to the entire surface of Italian life. . . . The average citizen lives through little expedients, favors, personal connections, 'tips,' in order to get by and to make up for the inefficiency of the public administration. At this point, people began to say, 'Enough, you did your work and got rid of the old political class that was sucking our blood, now let us live in peace.'"[16]

Thus, when Berlusconi began attacking the judiciary, he had a large and highly receptive constituency. He has loudly and repeatedly defended the morality of tax evasion. Berlusconi has declared that it is a matter of "natural law," that no one should ever pay more than a third of their income in taxes. "And so if you ask for fifty percent or more in taxes, it's unfair and so I feel morally authorized, if I can, to evade them," he has said. This is an extraordinary statement of principle from a man who has signed numerous laws requiring citizens to pay considerably more than 33 percent in taxes.[17]

The conflicts of interest, self-dealing and cronyism of Berlusconi make more sense when seen in the light of family business culture in Italy. In explaining over the years why he has not sold off his media empire, he has frequently said: "I can't, I have five children." To foreign observers this seems a preposterous statement—a prime minister ignoring the general good of the nation for his own family's interests—but it sounds less outrageous to the millions of Italians who own their own business and whose primary obsession is passing it on to their children.

Similarly, many small-business owners and home owners were no strangers to paying small bribes to keep from paying fines, so they were not so shocked at the notion that Berlusconi's companies had done so on a much larger scale. To some degree, in fact, it was reassuring. *"Berlusconi può occuparsi dei cazzi suoi, se mi lascia fare i cazzi miei,"* a Naples bar owner told me, a slightly more vulgar version of "Berlusconi can do what the hell he likes, as long as I can keep on doing what the hell I like."

The historian Paul Ginsborg has written about the continued centrality in Italian life of "amoral familism," a term coined in 1958 by the American anthropologist Edward Banfield to describe the behavior of the citizens of a small, impoverished Italian town where he did fieldwork. Banfield defined "amoral familism" as "the inability of the villagers to act together for their common good, or indeed, for any good transcending the immediate, material interest of the nuclear family."[18] The term went out of fashion for a while and has been widely criticized. Many scholars object to it as a kind of "essentialist" smear of Southern Italian culture and point out that the family nucleus plays an extremely positive role in many aspects of Italian life. Nonetheless, there is no denying that the family plays an unusually central role in Italian life. The percentages of Italians who live with their parents until marriage, and within the same building or within a few blocks of their mothers after marriage are extraordinary. The divorce rate (about 16 percent) is less than half that in France or Britain and less than a third of that in the United States. Eighty-three percent of Italian businesses are family-owned with fewer than fifty employees, in which family loyalty, patriarchal control and distrust of government are all central. Sociological research shows clearly that, when presented with a choice between following the law and protecting a friend or member of the family, Italians are much more apt to choose the latter than are most other Europeans.

When Berlusconi testified at Marcello Dell'Utri's trial for falsifying company receipts, he was asked by the court whether he knew that Dell'Utri was paying the workmen on his own country villa with money that had been siphoned from the company till, Berlusconi didn't bat an eyelash, insisting that it was a sign of Dell'Utri's great virtue: "Miranda [Dell'Utri's wife] complains because Marcello forgets to pay the workmen. I tell him, he's making me look bad . . . he doesn't pay attention to money, he lives for other things: family, books. I always tell him: 'Marcello, you're like Giorgio Washington, who cared too much about the interests of the state and let his own family go to ruin.'" (This might have been one of Berlusconi's made-up American allusions that he told his salesmen to use to impress people; George Washington lived and died a very wealthy man.) By falsifying receipts and paying for home improvements out of an illegal slush fund, Dell'Utri was just doing what Berlusconi would have wanted: looking after the family. The fact that Dell'Utri was breaking the law and was convicted of fraud does not appear to have bothered Berlusconi in the least.[19]

Suspicion of government is particularly high in Southern Italy, where standards of living and education are lower, the state has not performed particularly well, and people are more likely to fall back on informal networks, including, among many others, the Mafia. Forza Italia has won about 10 percent more of the vote there than in the rest of the Italy. "Berlusconi would not have won without Sicily either in 1994 or 2001," the sociologist Renato Mannheimer said.[20]

In Southern Italy, the informal or illegal economy is much greater than in the North. Some 70 percent of all new houses are built illegally, without a building permit, against zoning and building codes, sometimes on protected or even publicly owned land. In some cases, baroque permission processes make this necessary, essentially pushing people into illegal behavior. Mafia-owned construction firms often do the work, and home owners pay off local officials to look the other way, becoming accomplices to a corrupt system. There are some six hundred illegal constructions built on what is supposed to be archaeological land at the Valley of the Temples in Agrigento, one of the greatest sites of ancient Greek temples in the world. Every time bulldozers are called out to level the illegal buildings, crowds of angry people amass. Although they are illegal, a visual eyesore and ultimately a blight on one of the city's main money-making attractions, politicians win office defending illegal buildings.

In office, Berlusconi has gone out of his way to consciously serve this public. Both times he has become prime minister, his governments have immediately declared amnesties for tax evasion and for illegal buildings. When the first Berlusconi government prepared its first amnesty on illegal building there were an estimated 83,000 illegal buildings constructed—up from 58,000 the year before. Similarly, as Italy's Legambiente, an environmental group, estimated, the number of illegal buildings has jumped by 41 percent between 2001 and 2003.[21]

Chapter Twelve

ONE-MAN GOVERNMENT

1. FOXES IN THE CHICKEN COOP

On taking office in 2001, Berlusconi vowed publicly to resolve his conflicts of interest within the first one hundred days of office. Instead he created a government that was one enormous conflict of interest. Literally hundreds of members of parliament owed their livelihood to Berlusconi in one way or another—current and former employees of Publitalia and Mediaset, talk-show hosts and ad executives, several of Berlusconi's personal or corporate lawyers, consultants, journalists, business clients and those who held contracts as contributors to his vast galaxy of newspapers, magazines and TV stations.

Berlusconi's corporate tax attorney, Giulio Tremonti, was made the "superminister" for the economy and promptly passed an amnesty for tax evasion. Berlusconi insisted that Mediaset would not take advantage of the amnesty, but it did, saving 120 million euros in taxes it would have owed on the hundreds of millions of dollars in secret off-shore transactions it had hidden from the Italian state.[1]

The Italian postal service reached an agreement with Berlusconi's investment company (he owns about one-third of its shares) Mediolanum, so that ticket windows at every post office in every city and town down the boot of Italy could also serve as sales booths for Berlusconi's company's mutual funds, investment portfolios and other financial instruments. In this way, the massive resources of the Italian state meant to create a national postal service have been put at the disposal of the prime minister's business.

The parliament passed a new law on Italy's cultural patrimony that contained a clause that would allow property holders in Sardinia (of which Berlusconi was one of the most prominent) to develop coastland that had been protected as a national treasure. This would allow Berlusconi to move ahead with a plan he had been nurturing for nearly twenty years, a major real estate development on one of Italy's few protected pieces of coastline, and perhaps its most beautiful. Local authorities had been successful in blocking the project for years, but now, as head of the national government, Berlusconi was finally able to trump them. The Berlusconi government even snuck a little-noticed measure into a public works bill that overturned an old law dating from the time of Napoleon that prevented human burial outside of cemeteries. The measure would allow Berlusconi to realize his dream of eventually burying himself, his family and friends in the grand mausoleum at Arcore he had had built after he bought his villa.[2]

Berlusconi's undersecretary of interior, Carlo Taormina, saw no reason why he should not continue to represent organized-crime figures as a private attorney while the ministry where he supposedly worked full-time tried to investigate and arrest the associates of his clients. He would later react with indignation when it was suggested that he should not serve on the parliament's anti-Mafia commission while simultaneously representing Mafiosi in court.

Italy's national soccer league chose as its new president Adriano Galliani, even though he was also the president of A. C. Milan, Berlusconi's soccer team. The logic was fairly plain: rather than try to fight the gargantuan power of Berlusconi, why not try to harness it to our own benefit? Not surprisingly, it worked out mainly to the benefit of A. C. Milan and Mediaset. Galliani proceeded to negotiate a deal for the sale of television rights that greatly favored a handful of the largest teams, including his own, at the expense of the smaller ones. Another sign of the times, the

Berlusconi-controlled RAI, which had traditionally broadcast most of Italian soccer, chose not even to compete for the rights, leaving the field to Mediaset, which was able to choose exactly what it wanted, at the price it wanted, without having to worry about competition.

Throwing themselves into Berlusconi's arms wasn't an entirely mistaken move on the soccer club owners' parts. The Berlusconi government passed a law that helped bail them out of their financial difficulties, and get partial relief from their debts, a measure that A. C. Milan took advantage of as well. Berlusconi was both the salvation and the ruin of Italian soccer. He had driven up prices for star players, encouraging overspending by offering the El Dorado of infinite television revenue, using TV to increase the advantage of rich teams over poor ones—and then he was there at the end to help team owners out of their mess. As a result, they were all in his debt, and at his mercy, for saving them from disaster.

After nearly a decade of Berlusconi in public life, Italy had increasingly begun to resemble a kind of company town, where everyone works for the local factory, lives in company housing, buys at the company store and in which order is kept by the company guards. Berlusconi filled the average Italians' days from the morning newspaper to the nightly news. They bought their life insurance and mutual funds from his companies, they cheered for his soccer team, broadcast on his TV stations, surfed the World Wide Web on his Internet provider, watched movies produced by him in movie theaters owned by him, or rented them from the Italian franchise of Blockbuster video, also owned by him.

But nowhere was the conflict of interest more apparent than in the area of criminal justice, which was a principal focus of the new Berlusconi government's energies in its first months. Berlusconi's associates at greatest risk of winding up in jail (Cesare Previti, Marcello Dell'Utri, Massimo Maria Berruti) were elected so that they could enjoy parliamentary immunity from arrest and vote on legislation to water down the Italian penal code. Creating a conflict of interest within a conflict of interest, many of these defendant-parliamentarians were elected together with their personal criminal defense lawyers, so that whatever problems the parliamentarian-defense attorneys could not solve at trial they were able to legislate out of existence. For example, Berlusconi put his own criminal defense attorneys (Gaetano Pecorella and Niccolò Ghedini) up for seats in parliament and then had them appointed to the Justice Commission of parliament, with Pecorella, Berlusconi's lead attorney, becoming its president. Thus, as the new parliament began its work, Italy witnessed the curious phenomenon of having Berlusconi's lawyers flying back and forth between Milan and Rome—part of the week, they would be defending Berlusconi in a Milan courtroom, while the rest of the week they would be back in Rome drafting legislation that would help their clients get off the hook.

In this vein, under Pecorella's leadership, the Justice Commission decided to substantially decriminalize accounting fraud: as the United States was stiffening penalties for white-collar fraud in the wake of the Enron scandal, Italy was moving in the opposite direction. With the snap of a finger, several of the cases against Berlusconi and his closest associates simply disappeared. At the same time, the government passed a law that allowed people in his position to bring large amounts of money back into Italy without having to account for where the money came from and how it was earned, which, together with the tax amnesty, eliminated any tax risk for businessmen looking to recycle profits that had been hidden from the government—or Mafia money.

Berlusconi's position has proved simply invaluable in helping him beat the cases brought against him. For example, in 2001, Italy's highest court threw out the case against him for allegedly bribing the judges in the Mondadori takeover battle—a decisive event that gave Berlusconi a dominant position in book and magazine publishing to go with his TV empire—precisely because of his prominent political position. The court found Cesare Previti guilty, acknowledging that Berlusconi's lawyer had bribed judges on Berlusconi's behalf, but absolved Berlusconi because of "extenuating circumstances," namely "the prominence of the defendant's current social and individual condition [Berlusconi had become prime minister], judged by the court to be decisive." The message of the court sentence seemed to be: if you commit a serious crime, get yourself elected prime minister and you won't have to pay for it. Courts have used the formula of "extenuating circumstances" to absolve Berlusconi in six different sentences.[3]

The fact that the same magic was not enough to get some of his accomplices, in particular his attorney, Cesare Previti, out of trouble has represented a problem for Berlusconi. It was very difficult for the courts to ignore some of the evidence against Previti, in particular the $434,000 that moved from a Fininvest account into his Swiss bank account and into the bank account of Rome judge Renato Squillante. So the Justice Commission of the new Berlusconi parliament tried another approach, which made it much harder to acquire financial information from foreign countries. Applied retroactively, this might invalidate the banking information supplied by the Swiss government and used to convict Previti. In the wake of the terrorist attacks of September 11, 2001, when most other countries were trying to foster international cooperation to help trace money transfers of terrorist groups, the Italians were suddenly trying to out-Swiss the Swiss, the nation that had essentially invented bank secrecy, by claiming that Swiss standards were far too lax. Cesare Previti's lawyers immediately used the new law to try to throw out the incriminating documents from Switzerland and elsewhere. Swiss authorities reacted with indignation that the authenticity and validity of their documentation was being called into question, and the Italian courts refused to eliminate the banking data in the Previti case.

But determination is one of Berlusconi's and his closest associates' distinguishing traits and they were not to be discouraged. Previti, feeling the possibility of jail closing in on him, growled what appeared to be a menacing warning to the prime minister: "Silvio, they are going after me to get to you." Which many understood as saying something like: "If I go down, I may have to bring you with me." "Previti is blackmailing Berlusconi," former justice minister and Forza Italia senator Filippo Mancuso said plainly. Whether due to Previti's pressure or out of genuine conviction, the Berlusconi government then tried a new and extremely bold strategy to foil the magistrates of Milan. The new weapon was called the Cirami law, named after the little-known foot soldier of Berlusconi's coalition, Melchiorre Cirami, who proposed it. The law would allow criminal defendants to get rid of their prosecutors on grounds of "legitimate suspicion" that the entire prosecutor's office might have a bias against them. This was an extraordinary piece of new jurisprudence. Defendants already have the right to disqualify judges if they can prove they have it out for them. But while it is reasonable to expect neutrality from a judge, the idea of a neutral prosecutor was something new. It raised a series of startling possibilities: Could Mafia defendants disqualify "anti-Mafia prosecutors" on the grounds that they had passionately denounced the power of organized crime? If anticorruption prosecutors had written essays on the corrosive effects of corruption on Italian society, did that qualify as "legitimate suspicion" of bias? Nonetheless, the law was passed and immediately applied by Previti's lawyers in hopes of removing the Milan prosecutors from the cases in which he had already been convicted or from others that, after years of delay, were coming to trial—all would have to start over from scratch in another venue.

At a certain point, one opposition politician suggested that rather than destroying the whole Italian penal code the government should simply pass a law that exempted Berlusconi and a few others entirely from prosecution. The politician was joking, but this in fact was Berlusconi's next move. Noting that Italy was soon to assume the rotating presidency of the European Union for six months, Berlusconi's lawyers in parliament argued that it would be unseemly if the head of the Italian state were on trial for a serious crime while acting as the leader of Europe. The law was duly passed despite the usual demonstrations outside parliament. Thus Berlusconi's case was separated from Previti's. And although Previti ended up being convicted, Berlusconi's criminal record was technically kept immaculate.

A national politics built around one man and his business associates had the effect of reducing the Italian parliament to a useless vestigial organ like the appendix. There had always been a long tradition of internal dissent among Italian political parties, with the so-called *franchi tiratori* (snipers) voting against their own government on secret ballots. In Berlusconi's center-right, there is an astonishing degree of unanimity, especially on matters of personal interest to the leader himself. Many employee-parliamentarians don't even bother to show up for votes; the burdensome chore is sometimes done by worker-drones known as "piano players," who surreptitiously press several vote buttons at the same time. This was actually captured on Italian TV during the vote on one of Berlusconi's more controversial measures meant to help his trials in Milan, but no sanctions were taken. The practice of representative democracy had been reduced to an empty ritual.

This mortification of parliament has had its long-term effects. By the fourth year of Berlusconi's one-man-rule government, most deputies of Berlusconi's coalition simply stopped bothering to show up to work. In the spring of 2005, in the space of a single month, parliament failed on forty-five different occasions to muster the legal quorum necessary to hold a vote. Berlusconi did everything to try to induce his troops onto the floor of parliament. First, in good corporate fashion, he offered prizes and financial incentives for good voting records, and when this failed, he threatened, essentially, to fire his disobedient employee-parliamentarians by failing to make them candidates for the next round of elections if they didn't start showing up. "If a coach has players who refuse to enter the playing field on Sunday, what are you going to do, renew their contract?" said Berlusconi's minister for relations with parliament.[4]

2. Made-to-Order Legislation

One pressing threat for Berlusconi was a looming threat to one of Mediaset's television networks. In an effort to guarantee greater pluralism in the media, Italy's highest court had ruled back in 1994 that Mediaset (then still called Fininvest) would have to move one of its networks, Rete 4, to satellite in order to free up a major broadcasting frequency to make room for more competition. The Prodi government, in 1998 during the *inciucio,* in its desire to placate Berlusconi, had come to Rete 4's rescue, giving Mediaset five more years of time to "prepare" the network's move to satellite. The new deadline was December 31, 2003.

Soon, Berlusconi's minister of communications, Maurizio Gasparri, announced that there was urgent need of a new communications law—not in order to help Mediaset, he insisted, but to modernize Italy's media sector. The old limit of allowing one company to own only three national broadcast stations was clearly inadequate to the needs of the new digital age. In the future, there would be hundreds of channels, so why not let Mediaset keep its old three broadcasting channels and add several more? Such futurist talk ignored the simple realities of Italian television: there was no digital TV in Italy yet, not even cable TV and very little satellite TV. The market was still dominated by old-fashioned broadcast television stations, which were limited in number, and they are likely to dominate for at least the next several years. Moreover, as everyone in television knows, what matters is not how many channels you have but what share of the audience and advertising market you control. RAI and Mediaset control more than 90 percent of the audience and the advertising market, so that assigning a major network to another owner would not just free up a frequency, it would free up market share and hundreds of millions of dollars a year in advertising, making room for genuine competition. Conversely, if 90 percent of the analog market continued to be dominated by two companies, both, in effect, controlled by Berlusconi, the new digital market—when it came—would be dominated by the same players that controlled the old market. This was why the high court wanted to reassign a major broadcasting network: so a new player could enter the market and develop the expertise and the capital needed to compete in the digital market when it genuinely emerged.

Letting Mediaset retain Rete 4 would also leave it in perpetual violation of the law's 30 percent ceiling for the Italian media markets. But here, too, Gasparri had a futuristic answer. The 30 percent limit, he argued, was outmoded and needed to be redefined for the new age. The old legislation defined the media market as the combined market value of such conventional communication vehicles as television, radio, newspapers and magazines. What if, Gasparri argued, other media, like music, books, videos, DVDs, movies, billboard advertising and greeting cards, were considered as part of the same market as TV and newspapers? Suddenly, with the wave of a wand, the media market doubled in size from about $4 billion a year to $8 billion year and Berlusconi's share of it shrank miraculously from over 30 percent to under 20 percent. So a new law was proposed with what appeared to be a more stringent antitrust limit—no company could have more than a 20 percent market share—but which in fact allowed Mediaset to extend its grip over the media that genuinely matter in influencing public opinion: television, radio, newspapers and magazines.[5]

The logic was reminiscent of the trick used by the lawyer in Ignazio Silone's great antifascist novel *Fontamara*. In the novel, poor, illiterate farmers in the Abruzzi wake up one morning to find that the water from their stream, used to irrigate their fields, has been diverted by a shady businessman known as *l'impresario,* who has connections to the government. Faced with almost certain starvation, the peasants threaten to riot. A local lawyer, in the pocket of the *impresario*, calms them by offering a compromise: from now on, both sides will get three-quarters of the water and everyone will be happy. Since they know nothing of arithmetic, the peasants walk away relieved, only to discover later that the *impresario* is still taking most of their water. The Gasparri law is the digital equivalent of the *impresario*'s trick of the "three-quarters."

It is also typical of the Berlusconi style that, at least technically, Gasparri is not a member of Berlusconi's party, but of the National Alliance, the postfascist party. On his Web site Gasparri describes his "family and cultural background" as "one of unconditional loyalty to the state institutions and the Fatherland, the sense of Order." This means in plain Italian that he is from a Fascist background. Before entering politics, he belonged to neofascist youth groups and had a modest career writing for the neofascist newspaper *Il Secolo d'Italia.* It is characteristic of Berlusconi's Italy, that when there is dirty work to be done for which he could be accused of conflict of interest, he gets an ally from another party, usually the

National Alliance, to do it for him, so he can then claim that he knows nothing about such trivial matters as the future of telecommunications and the contents of the bill his government has crafted.

While Berlusconi insisted that the Gasparri law was not crafted for Mediaset's benefit, the money boys knew otherwise, as a report by Mediobanca in 2003 stated very clearly:

> We believe that Mediaset is the main winner, as: (i) the approval of the reform reduces the regulatory risk for the broadcaster. The reform supersedes both the decision taken by the Italian constitutional court, which obliged Rete 4 to switch to satellite broadcasting by the end of 2003, and the telecommunications authority's ongoing investigation into previous antitrust limits; (ii) the company has room to pursue new growth opportunities.

But Gasparri did not stop at the law that bears his name in his service to Berlusconi. Equally important, he prevented RAI from striking a deal that would have generated more than 800 billion lire ($500 million) it hoped to use to invest in new media ventures. RAI, following the general trend toward privatization, decided it no longer needed to own the actual broadcast towers it used to transmit its programs; it created a separate company for them called RAI Way and arranged to sell 49 percent of the new company to an American company called Crown Castle. The idea was to privatize nonessential assets in order to free up money to invest in new projects. Arguably, it was a shrewd move since it involved selling off part (not even a majority) of an old technology in order to finance investments in new ones. The BBC had done the same thing a few years earlier and many regarded it as a farsighted move that would prepare RAI for the inevitable switch from traditional analog broadcasting to digital television. But Minister Gasparri, the prophet of the digital age, minister of a government that preached the virtues of the private marketplace, blocked the partial privatization of RAI Way. If Gasparri had been sincerely interested in the development of the digital television market and in privatization, he would have given his green light to the move. But since Mediaset was itself preparing to enter the digital television market, a rich, aggressive RAI with money to spend and independent sources of revenue was a frightening prospect. A poor, cash-strapped RAI, forced to come to parliament tin cup in hand begging for handouts, was much more attractive to a government looking to exercise total control over state broadcasting.[6]

On top of everything else, the Berlusconi government gave a handsome subsidy to Mediaset in its digital TV venture. The government agreed to pay 75 percent of the cost of digital decoders Italians would need to get the newly offered service. With twenty-eight million Italian households, at a cost of about $75 per household, if half of the households got digital TV this amounted to a subsidy of about a billion dollars. Mediaset was ready, and announced its new "Happy Channel," offering what the Mediaset annual report describes as "optimistic/fun programs and productions"—theme music for the Berlusconi era.

3. *LAISSEZ-FAIRE*, ITALIAN STYLE

The blocking of the sale of RAI Way demonstrated that the Berlusconi government's commitment to a free-market Thatcherite economic agenda was mainly verbal, or limited to the few areas of the economy where the prime minister's business interests or that of other major constituents of the center-right coalition were not affected. An even more dramatic example of the anticompetitive practices of the Berlusconi government was the Telecom affair, in which a new competitor in the television market was strangled in its cradle.

In the waning days of the center-left government, when a Berlusconi victory appeared certain, and with it his effective occupation of all six major national TV networks, businessman Roberto Colannino had the idea of creating a "third pole," a second major private television company which would compete with both Mediaset and RAI. Colannino was at the time running Telecom, the privatized version of what used to be the national telephone company, one of the largest companies in Italy and one for which expansion into TV, in the age of cable and the Internet, was a natural move. Telecom bought out a TV station, Telemontecarlo, which was already a national network, but a very weak one with a market share that oscillated between 1 and 3 percent and which, unable to compete with the giants RAI and Mediaset, had been losing money for years. Colannino felt that with a major investment and new talent and programs, it could easily increase its market share and become profitable. The station was renamed La 7 (Seven), taking its place along the three RAI and three Berlusconi stations as the seventh national network. Colannino promised an investment of 500 billion lire (about $300 million) and signed up Fabio Fazio, one of Italian TV's top entertainment figures, to create an evening program along with Gad Lerner, who had headed one of the most successful and innovative news shows of the 1990s. Berlusconi's victory made the market niche for a "third pole" considerably more viable: with Berlusconi controlling both the three RAI networks and his own three channels, the appeal of a seventh, truly independent, network, was clear. Advertisers reacted with sufficient enthusiasm to guarantee the network 230 billion lire ($150 million) in advertising just to start with. Advertising time for Fabio Fazio's show alone was selling for 4 billion lire per episode. Part entertainment, part talk show, it would be competing with two programs that were central to Berlusconi's communications machine: *Maurizio Costanzo Show* on his own Canale 5, where he appeared instead of debating Francesco Rutelli on RAI, and his favorite RAI program, Bruno Vespa's *Porta a Porta* (Door to Door), in whose friendly environment Berlusconi had signed his "contract with the Italians."

The network was scheduled to start in the fall of 2001. Over the summer, the station did a couple of experiments in which it tried out some of the new programming. An entertainment show earned an audience share of 13.7 percent. Gad Lerner did a news special that won a 6 percent audience share, two to three times that of the usual share of the old Telemontecarlo. Since Colannino's business plan was to arrive at a market share of 5 percent after three years, which was the break-even point, the goal appeared entirely realistic.[7]

The project was extremely worrisome to the Berlusconi group. Colannino was thought to be close to Massimo D'Alema, the leader of Italy's
main opposition party. To the Italian right, La 7 looked like the left's effort to create its own network. The network did its best to dispel this notion, insisting that its goal was not to be an "anti-Berlusconi TV, but to be
the only TV not controlled by him." Indeed, one of its main news programs would team Lerner (who was considered to be a man of the left)
with a journalist very close to Berlusconi, Giuliano Ferrara, the former
official spokesman of the first Berlusconi government and editor in chief
of a newspaper, *Il Foglio,* owned by Berlusconi's wife, Veronica (in another circumvention of the law forbidding ownership of both television
stations and newspapers).

But in Lerner's view, La 7 was even more worrisome as an economic
competitor. "What really frightened Mediaset was that our advertising
manager, whose staff was all from Mediaset, had managed to break exclusive advertising contracts with some of Mediaset's biggest clients. Despite
all their talk about the private market, these people had been used to
working without competitors." It had been nearly twenty years since Berlusconi's TV empire had faced anything like real competition.[8]

In August of 2001, just before La 7 was scheduled to launch, the Pirelli
Tire Company took over Telecom and installed its chief executive, Marco
Tronchetti Provera, as the head of the new mega-conglomerate. The following month, the new management announced its intention to abandon
the idea of the third pole. The attack on the World Trade Center on September 11 had caused a major drop in advertising and they insisted that it
was the wrong time to launch a new network. Rather than compete with
RAI and Mediaset, they said, they would drastically scale back their am-
bitions, settling for the same 1 to 3 percent market share that their prede-
cessor, Telemontecarlo, had received. Even though advertising had been
sold and star performers hired, all the new programs were simply canceled. Fabio Fazio, the network's biggest star, offered to do the first program for free to show that the new model was economically viable.
Management refused and ended up paying Fazio some 38 billion lire

(about $25 million) *not* to do his show. Gad Lerner was given an 8 billion lire ($5 million) buyout package *not* to do his program.[9]

Although Telecom publicly insisted that its decision was not political, virtually everyone involved has admitted otherwise. Giuliano Ferrara, Berlusconi's former spokesman, said very candidly that Tronchetti Provera was told plainly to give up the idea of the third pole if he wanted a successful takeover of Telecom. Tronchetti Provera told friends that as long as the government set the telephone rates, it was impossible for him to risk displeasing Berlusconi. Telecom was extremely vulnerable to government pressure on several fronts. As the former national phone company, Telecom has retained the monopoly on the "last mile"—the physical phone connection that all other phone carriers must use to reach conventional land lines across the country. This monopoly position is extremely lucrative, and could be taken away at any moment by the government-appointed antitrust authority. Moreover, cellular phone rates are government-regulated in Italy, helping to determine the company's profit margins. That killing off the third pole was part of a larger deal with Berlusconi in exchange for being allowed to take over Telecom is clear from a few other deals that Tronchetti Provera did with the prime minister's companies during that same period. Shortly after taking over Telecom, the new management bought Edilnord, Berlusconi's real estate company. Having to operate in a genuinely competitive environment, Edilnord had not fared so well since Berlusconi's early deals and was actually losing money and seriously in debt. When Telecom took it off Berlusconi's hands for 460 billion lire (about $300 million)—estimated by some as two or three times its real market value—it seemed a gift. Why would a manufacturing and telecommunications company suddenly want to buy an ailing real estate business that had been struggling for more than a decade? Even more suspicious was a deal that the new Telecom made to buy out another losing property of the prime minister's. A few years earlier, Berlusconi's publishing company, Mondadori, thought that because of the deregulation of the telephone business, it would be a good idea to publish a competitor to the Yellow Pages called *Le Pagine Utili* (The Useful Pages). (The idea was apparently Marcello Dell'Utri's.) Unfortunately, it was a flop and Mondadori was now anxious to get rid of it or cut its losses and close it down. The company had absorbed 565 billion lire (about $350 million) in losses in five years. Mondadori offered *The Useful Pages* to Telecom, which, as the former national phone company, was already the owner of its chief competitor, the Yellow Pages, which was highly profitable. Telecom certainly had no need of a redundant, money-losing competitor, but Telecom bought Berlusconi's *Pagine Utili* nonetheless, for an astonishing 138 million euros (about $160 million). What made the deal even more suspicious was that Tronchetti Provera agreed to a curious condition: to pay Berlusconi's company a "penalty" of 55 million euros ($65 million) if the government's antitrust authority should reject the deal as being anticompetitive. When the authority, rather predictably, did exactly that, Telecom gave up its claim on the company and paid the 55 million euros without hesitation. In other words, Telecom paid 55 million euros to Berlusconi's company for exactly nothing. These are decisions that defy normal economic logic, but have a powerful political logic— helping the prime minister get rid of money-losing properties in exchange for being allowed to keep a lucrative monopoly.[10]

One last deal was in some ways the oddest of all. In the summer of 2003, through the Yellow Pages Telecom agreed to become an official "sponsor" of Berlusconi's soccer team, A. C. Milan, to the tune of 24 million euros. Since Telecom's new head, Tronchetti Provera, is an avid soccer fan and vice president of the other Milan soccer team, archrival Inter, this deal seemed nothing less than a kind of humiliating form of feudal vassalage, a declaration of total loyalty to the king.

Tronchetti Provera's generosity may not have been in vain. Telecom had made a major investment in Turkey that was at risk of going up in smoke. The Italians had spent 2.5 billion euros in buying the third-largest mobile phone company there and then spent the equivalent of another billion dollars improving the network and some 429 million dollars in a value-added tax. But the company's principal competitors, in defiance of national antitrust rules, refused to grant roaming rights, meaning the Italian-

Turkish company couldn't cover the whole national territory, greatly diminishing its appeal to customers. Silvio Berlusconi flew to Ankara and
personally met with Turkish prime minister Recep Erdoğan to resolve the
situation, which ended very favorably for Telecom; it was granted roaming rights and allowed to buy out the fourth-largest cellular phone company to become a true national competitor. The magazine *L'Espresso*,
which broke the story, estimated the value of the deal for Telecom at 2.3
billion euros (more than $2.6 billion). "Berlusconi's intervention was ex-
tremely useful because without it we would have had to leave Turkey."[11]

There is nothing wrong, of course, with an Italian prime minister
helping an Italian business. The problem is that when that prime minister is also the owner of the country's largest business empire, he is in a
position to profit mightily simply from doing his job. Because his interests
sprawl across so many different industries—from cellular phones and Internet providers, movie theaters and video rental companies, life insurance
and mutual funds, sports as well as the more famous media and publishing empire—he is in a position to benefit from or suffer from almost
any government action (lowering interest rates, raising interest rates, tax
write-offs, investment incentives) and almost any major move by other
large Italian corporations.

In order to curry favor with the prime minister, almost every major
company in Italy, as well as many ministries of the Italian government,
have shifted their advertising budget to favor Mediaset over both RAI and
other traditional advertising vehicles. Fiat in 2001—a year of crisis in
which the car company risked collapse—cut its advertising budget on
RAI by 9 billion lire ($6 million) but increased their ad spending on
Mediaset channels by 7 billion. The Nestlé food company cut its ad
budget for RAI by 9 billion lire and increased their spending on Mediaset
by 5 billion. Telecom removed 77.5 billion lire from RAI programs but
only about half that amount from the prime minister's networks. Companies that used to split their investments fifty-fifty between RAI and Mediaset now give about 60 percent of their ad budget to the prime minister's
networks.[12] Eighty-two companies stopped advertising in the newspapers,

costing the papers some 100 million euros ($125 million). At the same time, fifty-three companies increased their advertising on Mediaset by about 50 million euros. It was not purely a choice of TV over newspapers, for these same companies reduced their investments in RAI by 26 million euros.[13]

Whether these decisions were made spontaneously by the companies in hopes of currying favor with the prime minister or not hardly matters. The presence of this colossal double figure, the strongest man in both the private and public spheres, has the effect of violently distorting normal economic behavior.

4. WHAT'S GOOD FOR MEDIASET . . .

What the Telecom case shows is the way in which Berlusconi's presence in so many strategic industries makes a true liberalization of the market, constitutionally and physiologically, impossible. Berlusconi's desire to keep Telecom out of his primary business, television, makes him inclined to allow it to keep a quasi-monopolistic position in the phone business, and thus two crucial industries in the modern economy remain underdeveloped and under political control, with a stultifying effect on the economy as a whole.

Ironically, then, Italian business in the era of the entrepreneur–prime minister retreated from open-market competition and withdrew to the protected world of government-regulated industries. Thus, Pirelli, which had made most of its money from selling tires all over the world, took over Telecom. Fiat, which was steadily losing ground in the car market after trade barriers to selling foreign cars in Italy fell, bought out the former state chemical energy company, Montedison. Benetton, which had made its name and fortune selling chic and inexpensive clothes around the world, acquired the rights to operate the Italian national highway system. Gemina, which had been largely a media company, bought the concession to operate the Rome airport. Thus all of these famous Northern Italian industrial groups were forced to travel more and more often to Rome to maintain good relations with the government, on which they depended for their profit margins. The flight from the private to the government market was easily explainable. According to a report by Mediobanca, Italian companies competing in truly open markets had a profit margin of a mere 1.3 percent, while public service companies like those operating the highways and airports and providing water and energy had margins that were nearly three times as high. Public companies earned the most, with profit margins of 5.8 percent.[14] Berlusconi had little desire to force these companies out of the government nest and make them fly on their own wings. The myriad contacts between industry and government gave him instruments of influence and leverage that he had no intention of giving up.

The extreme inefficiencies of such a system explain, at least in part, why Berlusconi was unable to deliver on his promises of economic liberalization and why the Italian economy slowed down under his leadership. In 2002 and 2003, growth was only 0.4 and 0.3 percent, respectively, and even as the recovery took shape in much of the rest of the world, Italy grew by only 1.2 percent, still far below the rate of the rest of Europe. And in 2004, Berlusconi was forced to lower its growth projections from 2.1 percent to 1.4 percent. Italy's growth rate has been well below the norm for Europe and about half that of the United States. At the same time, average wages have actually gone down. Italy's share of world exports has continued to decline. Berlusconi's main strategies for stimulating the economy, such as tax amnesties that encouraged small businesses to continue cheating on their taxes, and government contracts and public works projects for large businesses that were in favor with the government, provided almost no incentive for technological innovation. Indeed, Italy is well at the bottom of major countries in Europe in corporate spending for research and development, government spending for scientific research, the number of scientific patents and the percentage of university graduates. In short, Italy is becoming a mediocre, provincial country.

Between 2001 and 2005, Italy dropped from fourteenth to fifty-third place in terms of competitiveness, according to the calculations of the Institute for Management Development in Geneva.[15] Transparency International, which measures corruption by questioning those who do business around the world, lowered its ranking for Italy from twenty-eighth to forty-first place, below African countries such as Namibia and Botswana. The organization Reporters Without Borders demoted Italy to a shockingly low fifty-third place among the world's nations for freedom of the press, behind Uruguay, Albania and Madagascar.

5. The Berlusconi Show

The economic establishment that supported Berlusconi in 2001 quickly began to regret its decision. As the CEO of one major corporation put it: "I supported Berlusconi because I thought he was pro-business. I didn't realize he was only pro his own business."

As thanks for his help during the election, Berlusconi agreed to appoint as foreign minister a man of Gianni Agnelli's choosing, Renato Ruggiero, a well-respected economist and former head of the World Trade Organization. For Agnelli, old and sick and the head of a declining automobile business, this was a last power play. Steering a respected economist and committed free-trader and supporter of the European Union to this key post was Agnelli's way of backing up his guarantee that Italy had not become a "banana republic" under Berlusconi. Quickly, however, Ruggiero (and Agnelli) discovered what anyone in the Berlusconi universe knows perfectly well: any real independence from the boss is not tolerated. When Ruggiero tried to rein in other members of the Berlusconi government who were interfering in foreign policy by engaging in xenophobic Europe-bashing, Berlusconi had him dismissed like an insubordinate employee. To many people's surprise, Berlusconi then insisted on making himself his own foreign minister. Irked by the notion that he needed to be flanked by a seasoned foreign policy specialist, Berlusconi wanted to show that there was nothing he could not do better than anyone else. "Since I didn't have much to do, someone thought I should do more. . . . I will bring to this ministry the culture of the trenches of the working world. . . . I am an expert in foreign affairs, I have had seventy-two foreign meetings, I've counted them, in these last months. . . . A fresh breeze enters Italian diplomacy: I am the right person in the right place."[16]

Addressing a group of diplomats at the Foreign Ministry, Berlusconi spoke to them as he might have the sales force at Publitalia. "As young diplomats, you've got to present yourselves well. Remember now: fresh breath and no sweaty palms!" Berlusconi transferred the corporate model to foreign policy, referring to Italy as Azienda Italia (Italy, Inc.) and telling the ambassadors that their job was to "sell shoes" (i.e., facilitate the sale of Italian products overseas) rather than to waste time on useless cultural programs.

But Berlusconi got off to a rocky start. Even before taking over the job of foreign minister, in the days immediately following September 11, he had caused an international ruckus by talking about the "superiority" of European civilization over Islam. He immediately claimed that he was misquoted and misinterpreted, a technique that he always adopted in Italy when he made mistakes, but which worked less well when reporters from around the world heard and recorded his remarks.

Gradually, the rest of the world would get to know the boyish charm and lighthearted style with which this man had won so many hearts in Italy. At an international summit in Spain, while posing with the other world leaders for a group photograph, he put up two fingers, making a pair of "horns" behind the head of the Spanish foreign minister, in Italy known as the sign of the cuckold. When foreign observers were scandalized by this puerile and disrespectful gesture, Berlusconi insisted he was only trying to create an atmosphere of friendly camaraderie at the summit. When addressing the Food and Agriculture Organization, he played the role of the Latin lover, thanking "all of you but in particular the beautiful female delegates." In a speech on Wall Street, trying to promote economic development in Italy, he listed "the beautiful secretaries" as one of the best reasons to invest in Italy—a speech that went over like a lead balloon in a world where even CEOs can be fired for violating company sexual harassment policies. He warmed up a foreign delegation from Turkey by telling them about "a marvelous Turkish girlfriend" he had had as a young man, not pausing to ask himself whether bragging about his sexual conquests would go over well with a delegation from an Islamic country. When a French newspaper asked him why he wasn't popular in France, Berlusconi disagreed by noting all the French women he had slept with: "I am very popular with the French people, you just have to count the number of French girlfriends I've had."[17]

When Berlusconi took over the rotating presidency of the European Union, he became known to the wider world for calling a German member of the European parliament a perfect "concentration camp kapo," after he had dared to ask a tough question about Berlusconi's control of the media. Here, too, Berlusconi insisted that he had been misunderstood and was only joking. And after the international criticism, a deputy minister of Berlusconi's government, a member of the xenophobic Northern League, responded by calling the Germans a bunch of dull-witted, beer-drinking slobs. This was imprudent on the part of a member of the government, as tens of thousands of Germans immediately canceled their plans to vacation in Italy. The minister was forced to resign.

Convinced that it was all a matter of misperception and bad press coverage, Berlusconi turned on the seductive charm for the foreign press as he had for the heads of state. Entertaining a group of foreign journalists at a government palace in Rome, Berlusconi suggested that "the ladies" might be interested in visiting a bathroom where Gary Cooper had "scrubbed the back" of some beautiful female guest. He proceeded to lead a group to see the part of the palace where the famous American actor had supposedly enjoyed a sexual conquest decades earlier.[18]

Toward the end of his presidency, Berlusconi hoped to get the other EU countries to sign a European constitution, crowning his six-month term with a major international triumph. It was already being billed as a miracle by the Berlusconi-controlled press in Italy. "If Berlusconi pulls off this miracle, he will enter history," Emilo Fede declared to the microphones of Berlusconi's Rete 4. The term "miracle" was used both to protect Berlusconi in case the negotiations failed, and to magnify his triumph if he succeeded. "It will take a miracle," Berlusconi said, "but I have some experience with miracles."[19] When talks stalled, Berlusconi startled the assembled heads of state by saying: "Let's lighten up the climate by talking about soccer and women. You, Gerhard," he said, turning to German prime minister Gerhard Schröder, "you've had four wives, what can you tell us about women?" The response was glacial silence. There would be no miracle.[20]

According to a member of his diplomatic team, Berlusconi tried to talk George Bush out of invading Iraq by telling him a humorous fable about a lion and a wolf. (The lion threatens to club the wolf, and even after the wolf offers to give up his prey the lion keeps beating him.) Berlusconi apparently practiced reciting the fable in front of the mirror for hours so that he could tell Bush the fable in his rudimentary English. When Berlusconi's aide asked if Bush had gotten the point of the fable, Berlusconi replied, "Yes, but he didn't laugh." Asked why he had felt the need to go along with the United States on the Iraq war when it was so unpopular in Italy, Berlusconi expressed a deep belief that going against the United States was political suicide.

Berlusconi's time on the international stage was generally perceived to be an embarrassment, raising the question: how could someone so shrewd and successful in some areas of his life be so apparently inept in another? Part of the answer is that Berlusconi, in the world arena, revealed his deeply provincial nature. Berlusconi after all had succeeded by getting the heads of pension funds drunk and telling dirty jokes. But his so-called "gaffes" are less incomprehensible than they might at first appear. Berlusconi, who, of course, is far from stupid, cares much less about the international public than his domestic audience. He knows that his political power derives from his electoral strength at home. Remarks like "Let's talk about soccer and women" play much better at home than overseas. The favorite topics of conversation in any café in a small town or working-class neighborhood in Italy are soccer and women, and so average Italians hearing his remarks react with a sense of identification. Berlusconi appears like a regular guy the average Italian male would love to buy a drink for in exchange for hearing about the sexual exploits of his favorite soccer star.

Berlusconi's foreign adventures also reflected the extremely protected environment that he had become used to. As the president of Fininvest/ Mediaset, he was never contradicted, and in the highly controlled world of the Italian press, he was never subjected to tough questioning. His press conferences were very few and always tightly monitored with only selected journalists chosen who were guaranteed not to rock the boat.

And Berlusconi did manage to form close ties with a number of leaders. He was a guest at the weddings of the daughters of both the Spanish president José María Aznar and the Turkish prime minister Recep Erdo-ğan, and in both cases he managed to use those ties to great benefit. Under Aznar, Spain relaxed its antitrust laws, allowing Mediaset to own a larger chunk of the Spanish channel Telecinco. And Erdoğan, at Berlusconi's urging, opened the doors in Turkey to Italy's Telecom. Vladimir Putin became a regular guest, with his family in tow, at Berlusconi's palatial villa in Sardinia. The need to guarantee the safety of so many foreign dignitaries allowed Berlusconi to invoke "national security" reasons for setting aside existing environmental laws and building a special submarine port and a huge faux ancient Greek ampitheater by the coast, the latter as a special favor to his friend Marcello Dell'Utri, a lover of ancient Greek tragedy.

What gradually emerged after a few years of Berlusconi was that there was no real program, no deep policy objectives, no real ideology other than a generic anti-Communism and a commitment to economic freedom—at least for himself. Indeed, the only real common thread to Berlusconi's economic, environmental, communications, criminal justice and foreign policies was Berlusconi himself and the need for more Berlusconi. He almost certainly believes, as he pursues his own interests, that what is good for Berlusconi and Mediaset is also good for the country. In fact, if only the rest of the country would let him have the power he wields at Mediaset, the rest of the country would be as rich and happy as the executives of Mediaset. What the country and the world needed was more Berlusconi, and by freeing him from his legal difficulties, by allowing Mediaset to grow larger and more profitable, by bringing RAI further under government control, by relaxing environmental laws and allowing him to build where he pleased, there would be more Berlusconi everywhere. Half-jokingly, Berlusconi once said that what Italy needed to solve its problems was thirty years of Berlusconi. By having Berlusconi as foreign minister and president of the European Union, the rest of the world would profit from more Berlusconi. His frustration and righteous anger at his critics and "enemies" stemmed from this deep conviction of his own goodness: why couldn't they understand that if they would stop criticizing him, he would make them rich, too? Even his best friend, Fedele Confalonieri, admitted, putting the best possible face on it, "The truth is that Berlusconi is not a politician. He is a Utopian. In another system, he could be an enlightened sovereign, but as a democratic leader he is something of an anomaly."[21] Or as Indro Montanelli put it, much less charitably: "Berlusconi? He's not a fascist, he's nothing. He imagines himself to be a cross between De Gaulle and Churchill and the problem is he believes it. . . . He is a little Perón who entered politics to defend himself, but now that the fear has passed, it's gone to his head."[22]

❦

Chapter Thirteen

THE PRESS TAKEOVER

1. TAMING THE PRESS

Not long after Berlusconi was first elected prime minister in 1994, his "image consultant," a woman named Mity Simonetto, appeared at the photo archives of the *Corriere della Sera* and demanded to see all the photographs of her client. She then selected and eliminated all the photographs of Berlusconi that she didn't like. The largest newspaper in Italy, supposedly one of the strongest bastions of independent thought in the country, allowed itself to be purged of any unflattering images of the prime minister.

The *Corriere* was hardly a stranger to political pressure. In the early 1980s, the secret P2 Masonic Lodge had the newspaper's owner, publisher and editor in chief on its list of members and helped move the paper toward the right. At various points, the Socialist Party and the Communist Party had exercised veto power, blocking candidates for editor whom they distrusted and promoting others in their place. But never (except during Fascism) had a political force ever exercised such power that it could ask for and receive the right to wipe the memory bank of history clean. "She had the permission of the ownership," Ferruccio De Bortoli, who was deputy editor at the time and later editor in chief, explained with evident embarrassment.[1]

The principal owner at the time was Gianni Agnelli and the Fiat car company, along with about twenty other major shareholders. By 2003, the publisher was Cesare Romiti, the longtime CEO of Fiat, who now found himself faced with pressure to perform the unpleasant task of firing De Bortoli, who in his six years as editor had incurred the wrath of Berlusconi and many in his inner circle. In particular, De Bortoli had refused to stop giving full coverage to Berlusconi's corruption trials in Milan. The stories were hardly sensationalistic or overtly anti-Berlusconi— they were soberly written in the classic court reporter's style—but the basic facts of the trial—evidence of bribery on the part of Berlusconi's corporate lawyer, Cesare Previti and various magistrates—continued to be a source of embarrassment to the prime minister and threatened to send Previti to prison. De Bortoli tried to placate the wrath of the Berlusconi camp by publishing interviews with the defendants and their attorneys, as well as letter after letter of protest. Most of the chief editorialists of the newspaper generally sided with Berlusconi, not contesting the facts of the cases, but arguing that the prosecutors should stay out of politics by not prosecuting major political figures. De Bortoli, however, also published opinion pieces that were highly critical of Berlusconi. The final straw came when he himself wrote a withering editorial, after the latest round of intimidation from Previti and Berlusconi's lawyers, in which he said that Berlusconi's lawyers would do well to serve the interests of the country rather than use parliament to draft laws on behalf of their client.

When the pressure to fire De Bortoli became truly insistent, Romiti and the other shareholders were not in a strong position to resist. They all had important business with the government and they knew that Berlusconi was a man who was willing to make good on his threats. When Umberto Agnelli, who had taken over the position of chairman of Fiat after his brother Gianni's death, spoke with Berlusconi about government help for the ailing car company, the prime minister reportedly replied: "Yes, we could do something, but you can be sure that the *Corriere* would rip the prime minister apart. . . . Certainly, that newspaper of yours is starting to be a bigger problem for you than it is for me." The message was clear: unless you change the *Corriere*'s editor we are not going to help you.

Other shareholders felt extremely vulnerable as well. There was Marco

Tronchetti Provera, the owner of Pirelli and Telecom, who had already killed off the idea of a third major television group rather than face a war with Berlusconi. There was Luciano Benetton, who after creating the successful international clothing business, had bought the government concession of the Italian national highway system. Fiat, once the colossus of Italian industry, was on the verge of bankruptcy and reduced to going cup in hand to Berlusconi and his "superminister" of the economy. And Romiti's own group, Gemina, itself in bad economic shape, owned the state concession for the country's airports, a business in which the government's goodwill was also essential.

When I went to see Romiti in December 2004, several months after De Bortoli had been replaced as editor, he warned me, "I am not going to tell you anything, but here's a story that might be a chapter of your book," and handed me a copy of that day's *Libero,* a daily newspaper close to Berlusconi. The paper contained an exclusive interview with Berlusconi that contained some rather menacing references to Romiti. Berlusconi complained about the fact that the *Corriere,* despite the defenestration of De Bortoli, had continued publishing critical pieces about him and revealed that a former president of the republic, Francesco Cossiga, had advised him to send an army of tax inspectors to the offices of Romiti and another owner of the *Corriere* to get them to shape up. "Cossiga continues to reproach me and pushes: 'Use your power!' . . . he's very detailed: fifty tax inspectors to Cesare Romiti's office and fifty tax inspectors to the offices of the Banca Intesa [another shareholder of Rizzoli known to have resisted pressures to replace De Bortoli]." . . . "But I said: 'Never, never! . . . I am a liberal prime minister.'"[2]

Handing me the story while refusing to discuss Berlusconi was Romiti's way of illustrating the kind of pressures and threats he and other economic players were under. At a certain point during our encounter, a friend and former Fiat executive turned up to see Romiti. Suddenly, the man turned to me and said: "You, who come from America, can you explain to me how it is that articles that are often harshly critical of Berlusconi appear in major newspapers like the *New York Times* and the

Washington Post when Berlusconi is a close friend of your government?" "It's simple," I answered, "it's called the free press." Obviously, even to this experienced corporate executive, the notion that a major newspaper would do something against its own government's will was incomprehensible. Romiti laughed and assured his incredulous friend that, unlike here in Italy, papers like the *Times* and the *Post* generally decided these matters for themselves.[3]

2. TAMING THE RAI

"Public television is entirely in the hands of the left," Silvio Berlusconi declared in January of 2002, six months into his second government. Having spent the first month in power passing criminal justice "reform" to short-circuit the various prosecutions against himself and his associates, and keeping a dangerous rival, Telecom, from entering the television market, Berlusconi turned to his dominant obsession: control of the press. For a media baron who believes that "everything is a matter of communication," this was, in his view, the mother of all problems.

Despite having won one of the largest and most stable majorities in Italian history, Berlusconi was still furious over the television coverage during the 2001 elections, calling the treatment he had received from RAI an attempted "coup d'état against democracy." He claimed that his private polls showed that unfavorable treatment on RAI had cost him seventeen points in approval ratings during the final weeks of the campaign.

"The RAI offensive ... destroyed my image," he declared.[4] In response to the growing drumbeat of attacks, the president of the state TV, Roberto Zaccaria, already near the end of his term, resigned, giving Berlusconi the opportunity to appoint a new board of directors.

What Berlusconi expected from the new board of directors of RAI he made clear in a diatribe he issued during a state visit to Bulgaria in April of 2002. He denounced the "criminal use" of the state TV during the 2001 elections, once again singling out three broadcasters in particular: Michele Santoro, Enzo Biagi and Daniele Luttazzi. He then issued what appeared to be a clear order to the new board of directors. "It is the precise duty of the new RAI leadership to make sure that this never happens again."[5] Within a couple of months, all three broadcasters mentioned by Berlusconi had their programs taken off the air.

The new board of directors changed the directors of the various nightly news programs. Clemente Mimun, a former Berlusconi employee and a right-wing appointee at RAI, was moved from head of news at RAI 2 to news director of the principal channel, RAI 1. The fact that Mimun, who was appointed to run *Tg2* (Telegiornale 2, Television News 2) when Berlusconi was prime minister the first time, had survived five years of center-left governments at the head of the second-largest news program is evidence that those governments did not conduct the kind of wholesale political purges that Berlusconi was undertaking.

Shortly after Berlusconi was reelected in 2001, Mimun demonstrated why he was a man who could be counted on. In July of 2001, Genoa hosted the G8 summit, a meeting of the heads of state of the world's great powers, which also attracted antiglobalization protesters from around the world. Although there was much concern about a repetition of the violence that had characterized the international summit at Seattle the year before, the Italian police still seemed badly prepared for the event. A twenty-three-year-old demonstrator was shot and killed, 280 people were arrested, and 231 were wounded. Responsibility for the violence was widely shared. Although the vast majority of the 200,000 to 300,000 demonstrators were peaceful, there were anywhere between 500 and 3,000 violent protesters who threw rocks and engaged in vandalism. Whether by design or inadequate means, the police chose not to go after the small contingent of highly visible violent demonstrators—in particular, the so-called Black Block, who wore black clothing and headgear—who proceeded to loot stores, break automatic teller machines, set cars on fire and attack both police and peaceful demonstrators. Perhaps because police were not able to retaliate against the more violent protesters, they took out their frustration by attacking some of the more peaceful ones, putting dozens in the hospital and arresting more than 150 people who were released immediately for lack of evidence.

A cameraman from *Tg2*, the nightly news program of RAI 2, managed to record a sequence of twenty minutes showing police beating up demonstrators. In one scene, police attacked a group of mostly very young girls, even though they had put their hands up and kept yelling that they were from a Catholic labor group. RAI 2, under the direction of Mimun, did not run the footage. Later, a journalist with RAI 1 made use of the film to great effect, winning a major journalistic prize awarded by the president of the Republic, Carlo Azeglio Ciampi (hardly a left-wing radical). Moving Mimun to RAI 1 would ensure that things of this kind did not happen any longer on the main state channel.[6]

While the rest of the world listened in amazement as Berlusconi insulted a German member of the European parliament by calling him a "concentration camp kapo," the viewers of Mimun's *Tg1* never got the chance. The sound track was replaced by a bland summary of the event. When Berlusconi addressed the United Nations to a semi-deserted hall, the producers of *Tg1* cut and spliced images of a large enthusiastic audience (taken from the speech of UN secretary general Kofi Annan) to create the impression of a rousing international success for Italy's prime minister.[7]

When the United States, with Berlusconi's reluctant backing, was getting ready to invade Iraq in 2002—an extremely unpopular move with more than 70 percent of the Italian public—rainbow-colored peace flags suddenly appeared in the windows of nearly every street in Italy. But when TV journalists proposed doing a story on the proliferation of peace banners—a topic in all the major newspapers—the idea was roundly rejected. The reason given was that "peace banners are sold by left-wing cooperatives."[8] Major peace marches involving hundreds of thousands, if not millions, of Italians were routinely not televised and RAI journalists were instructed to refer to antiwar demonstrators not as *pacifisti* (pacifists) but as *disobbedienti* (disobedients), the name of one of the more aggressive antiglobalization groups.[9]

Even reservations about the Iraq war among members of Berlusconi's coalition were censored, prompting Marco Follini, the head of a small Catholic party in Berlusconi's government, to refer to Mimun's RAI 1 as a "monument to servile behavior."[10]

Mimun and other senior producers at RAI began insisting that on all stories, particularly politically delicate ones, the center-right majority should always have the final word. In fact, Mimun established a formula that journalists sarcastically referred to as "the sandwich." Each story would begin with some action or statement by a member of the government, followed by a brief comment by someone in the political opposition, and concluded by a substantial rebuttal from a member of the government coalition: two thick pieces of bread with a slice of criticism between them.

During the first months of his government, Berlusconi alone took up an extraordinary 50 percent of the RAI newscasts, while the opposition on the first two RAI channels was reduced to 21 and 23 percent respectively. But study by the Observatory of the University of Pavia showed that the raw numbers on air time, while highly favorable to Berlusconi, told only part of the story. For one thing, Berlusconi's actions were generally recounted respectfully by political commentators of his own choosing. On the RAI 1's nightly news, 87.2 percent of the discussion about Berlusconi was conducted by one man, Francesco Pionati, a journalist from a Christian Democratic family with the deferential manner of a church sacristan.[11] Pionati had a talent for smoothing out the roughest edges. When the Berlusconi government defenestrated its chief finance minister, Giulio Tremonti, after a vituperative and highly public battle, Pionati told RAI viewers that "from sources close to Palazzo Chigi [the prime minister's palace] we have learned that the atmosphere is serene and constructive"[12]—a newscast worthy of Soviet television during the Brezhnev era. Pionati was so well liked by the prime minister that he received a second income from a column written for Berlusconi's weekly newsmagazine *Panorama*. Thus, in effect, Pionati received substantial sums of money from the principal person it was his job to cover. And discussion of Berlusconi on the largest national network was largely monopolized by a journalist who was essentially his employee.

By contrast, Berlusconi's opponent in the 2001 elections, Francesco Rutelli, had much less time to speak directly to the public, and commentary on Rutelli was frequently given by his own political rivals or critics. Thus even the meager amount of time given to the political opposition often consisted of negative stories about infighting and conflict among the parties and leaders of the center-left coalition.

A piece that ran on RAI 1 on February 18, 2004, was typical. The headline that opened the broadcast announced, "Berlusconi Attacks, Prodi Responds," but the story consisted of two minutes in which Berlusconi leveled a ferocious attack on Prodi, insisting that "out of a sense of decorum, he should resign" as president of the European Commission (Prodi's alleged offense, in Berlusconi's view, was speaking at a political rally for the center-left while occupying the presidency of the European Commission) without any reply from Prodi. Instead, a newscaster simply explained for a few seconds that Prodi intended to finish his term as EC president—the tiniest sliver of *prosciutto* in the sandwich. The segment then concluded with a statement from a spokesman for Forza Italia— quoted on camera—saying that the Italian people were interested in "concrete problems that the snobbish left doesn't understand." Berlusconi then asked whether it was proper to be the president of the European Commission and participate in a political rally, and finally Prodi (who was not given a chance to respond) was accused of worrying about abstract formal problems of no interest to ordinary Italian people. The journalists at RAI have come to refer to such a segment as a *panino blindato*—bulletproof sandwich.[13]

When RAI 1 did a story on the first year of the Berlusconi government, the headline promised a debate between left and right, but the actual story consisted of four interviews with members of the ruling coalition singing the government's praises, while the response of the opposition consisted of a brief statement read by a news commentator. What was completely absent was any attempt to do any real journalistic work—to list the principal promises made by Berlusconi during the election campaign and to assess, independently, the extent to which each had been maintained. But real journalistic work almost never happened anymore at RAI. In fact, Mimun's *Tg1* adopted the habit of no longer sending journalists to conduct interviews; they frequently sent only a cameraman and a sound person to hold the microphone in front of the politician to be interviewed. This is symbolic of the deterioration at RAI, journalism reduced to being the microphone to political power.[14]

3. "It's Up to Comedians to Say Serious Things"

On May 5, 2003, Berlusconi made a surprise appearance at the Milan courthouse where he was being tried for bribery. Although he had not bothered to attend court sessions until this point, he arrived at the end of the trial to make a "spontaneous declaration" to the court—something permitted by Italian law. Instead of a brief statement, as allowed to most defendants, the court let Berlusconi deliver a forty-minute harangue against the prosecutors of Milan. When he left the courtroom, a member of the public screamed out: "Buffoon! Respect the law! Go on trial! You'll end up like Ceauşescu!" Berlusconi, in a state of shocked rage, demanded that courthouse police officers arrest the man, as if he were the presiding judge rather than a criminal defendant—and they immediately did. That evening, the third RAI channel led its newscast with the embarrassing footage of Berlusconi and the protester.

When Berlusconi learned of the RAI 3 coverage, he was even more furious and insisted that the incident had been "an ambush planned evidently with the help of RAI 3." The new director general immediately ordered an internal investigation of the incident, interrogating the people involved and sequestering the footage. As it turned out, the cameraman who had taken the offending sequence was sent not by RAI 3, but by Clemente Mimun, the accommodating director of RAI 1. To save money, the three RAI networks commonly share footage of the same events. The cameraman had done only what every other cameraman there had done, which was film the prime minister as he left the courtroom. In short, there was no plot and the matter was dropped.[15]

Also to suffer for crossing the line was one of Italy's most popular comedians, Sabina Guzzanti. Guzzanti, who had been praised by Berlusconi in the past, was given a new show, *RaiOt*. On her first program, she appeared in a samurai costume in parody of Uma Thurman in *Kill Bill*, and made a series of biting attacks against Berlusconi and his company. She referred to the fact that Mediaset had kept Rete 4 on the air in direct defiance of the Italian Supreme Court. She explained that Italy had been ranked fifty-third in the world in terms of press freedoms. "You haven't heard it on our nightly news programs? Well, I guess if you had, we wouldn't be ranked number fifty-three." She recounted some of the history of Berlusconi's Mediaset, his friendship with Bettino Craxi and his membership in the P2 Masonic Lodge. "It's up to comedians to say serious things," she said, "since we have a prime minister who tells jokes."[16]

From a commercial point of view, the show was a total hit. On the smallest of the public networks, RAI 3, the show began at midnight with the network capturing only a 7 percent audience share, but as Guzzanti went on, the audience eventually broke 25 percent, making the third network, with its tiny budget and small audience, the biggest in the country for half an hour.[17]

But in the political world, all hell broke loose. Mediaset immediately filed suit against Guzzanti, and RAI suspended the program, insisting it needed to do so in order not to expose the company to any further legal risk. The only way that the network would agree to let Guzzanti keep her show was if she agreed to submit her program to the heads of the network a week in advance. It was, in effect, preventive censorship. She refused and the show was canceled, despite the extraordinary success of the first episode. Later, a court in Milan would dismiss the lawsuit brought by Mediaset, saying that Guzzanti's jokes were a legitimate form of satire. "They are not only socially relevant," the court wrote, but also "objectively true in their essential elements."[18]

RAI 3 is hardly a beacon of courageous or great journalism. It operates on a small budget, much smaller than the conservative networks RAI 1 and RAI 2, and often lacks the means to generate stories of its own. The news editors of the largest networks often decide which stories to cover and RAI 3 works with the footage they generate.

When it attempts to take genuine journalistic initiatives by doing its own stories, RAI 3 has faced threats and sanctions under the Berlusconi government. For example, when the accounts of torture during the American occupation of Iraq at the prison of Abu Ghraib began to emerge, journalists at RAI 3 began to explore an Italian angle to the story. They interviewed the widow of an Italian carabiniere who had been killed in Iraq, who claimed that her husband had seen Iraqi prisoners mistreated by American troops. Although she did not allege that Italians had been involved in torture, she did say that the Italian contingent knew about the situation and chose not to do or say anything about it. The interview, featured on *Tg3*, was greeted with howls of protest and furious counter-charges of defamation. The woman, clearly frightened by the fury she had created, backpedaled and insisted her words had been taken out of context. This only put gasoline on the fire, with numerous politicians, including deputy prime minister Gianfranco Fini, calling for the immediate resignation of the director of RAI, Antonio Di Bella. Entire programs on RAI were dedicated to excoriating the interview and Di Bella, with government ministers like Gasparri, calling for him not just to be fired from his job, but to be expelled from the journalists' guild as well.

Di Bella responded by making the entire, uncut interview available on RAI's Internet site, thus allowing viewers to judge for themselves. It was clear that rather than taking the widow's words out of context, RAI 3 had, if anything, cut some of her more inflammatory comments and presented a rather sober and balanced version of the interview. The parliamentary committee that monitors RAI was forced to absolve Di Bella of any wrongdoing. But the lynch mob atmosphere that followed the interview made it obvious to everyone the price to be paid for crticizing the regime.[19]

The prevailing view now was that state television had a duty to offer a vision of the world that was positive and reassuring. Plans for a live radio broadcast of a peace march were canceled because it would "disturb the tranquillity of the parliamentary debate" on the war.[20] "We talk a lot about shopping and consumption and of free time and little about the country's problems—a patina of carefree life which has little relationship to what is actually going on in the country," journalists from RAI 1 wrote in January 2004, in a letter of protest over the way the network was being run.[21] At the time, Italy was entering its third straight year of recession, the Christmas sales period had been a major disappointment and the topic on almost everyone's lips in Italy was the rising cost of living. Studies showed that consumer prices had in fact gone up by about 20 percent over the previous two years. Berlusconi oscillated between blaming the euro and insisting that it was simply a question of knowing the right place to buy things. His mother, he said, always knew at which market you could get the best prices. RAI showed images of full stores and ran stories about people using personal shoppers to help them make their holiday purchases. Perhaps needless to say, no stories ran examining whether and why the other countries that had converted to the euro had experienced a similar decline in purchasing power.

4. INDIRECT CONTROL

Despite having public TV firmly in his grasp, Berlusconi complained in November 2003 that "eighty-five percent of the press is against the government." Given that nearly 70 percent of the Italian public gets its news from television, which he controls almost entirely, Berlusconi's claim of being the victim of a hostile news media was baldly absurd even by his standards.

Only a tiny minority of Italy's newspapers could be described as "against" Berlusconi. Dozens of small and medium-sized provincial newspapers, such as *Il Giornale di Sicilia* and the *Gazzetta del Mezzogiorno* and the *Gazzettino* of Venice, while not owned by Berlusconi, are conservative and tendentiously pro-Berlusconi. There are the Rome papers *Il Messaggero* and *Il Tempo,* which are conservative papers close to other allies in Berlusconi's government. There are Catholic papers like *L'Avvenire* and *L'Osservatore Romano,* which are independent of Berlusconi but hardly hostile to him or his government, which has courted the Vatican on issues such as restricting artificial insemination to married heterosexual couples.

When Berlusconi is talking about the press being against him, he is really talking about the four largest daily newspapers that he does not control and that have some influence on public opinion: The *Corriere della Sera,* *La Repubblica* (which also owns a series of local newspapers), *La Stampa,* and the business newspaper *Il Sole 24 Ore,* which together sell about two million copies a day, about 40 percent of the total. Nonetheless, as the country's most respected papers, they have an influence well beyond their sales numbers in orienting government policy and public opinion.

Of these, only one major paper, *La Repubblica,* can be accurately described as anti-Berlusconi. The papers that Berlusconi really worries about are the *Corriere* and *La Stampa,* both of which have a generally moderate, middle- and upper-middle-class readership, made up of the kind of centrist voters who might be decisive in turning an election in favor of either left or right. Moreover, beyond their actual readership, they help create and orient public opinion in Italy's middle class as well as in political and industrial circles.

Although a fair amount of attention has been paid to Berlusconi's takeover of RAI, since it has occurred in front of the entire nation, his ability to influence, intimidate or tone down independent media that he does not control either through ownership or public office has often been overlooked.

During the late 1980s and early 1990s, when Gianni Agnelli was alive and well and the ownership group reasonably healthy, the *Corriere della Sera* had been relatively free from political influence. My father, Ugo Stille, who had been the editor of the *Corriere* between 1987 and 1992, told me that in his five years as editor he had never suffered any editorial interference. He sometimes received complaints from angry politicians, but with the backing of a strong owner, he was in a position to brush them aside. At this point, Agnelli, not Berlusconi, was the richest man in Italy and in a position to protect his editors. My father became extremely sick in February of 1992, the month that the corruption investigation known as Operation Clean Hands began, and ceded the reins of the paper to his deputy editor, Giulio Anselmi. Under Anselmi's direction, the *Corriere,* like most of the Italian press, greeted the investigation as the salutary housecleaning that Italy's corrupt political system needed. The political parties screamed bloody murder. "I'll have you thrown down the stairs!" Bettino Craxi, whose Socialist Party was most affected by the scandal, threatened Anselmi. The owners of the paper, including Agnelli's Fiat, were nervous about the direction of the corruption scandal, since their companies were also under investigation. To their credit, however, the owners did not prevent Anselmi from continuing his aggressive coverage of the corruption scandal. But when a new editor of the *Corriere* was to be named, Anselmi was passed over in favor of Paolo Mieli, who was then editor of *La Stampa*, the Turin newspaper that was directly owned by Fiat. Mieli's *Stampa* had also welcomed Operation Clean Hands, but managed to do so more cagily, without alienating those in power.

The corruption scandal, the weakness of Italy's great industrial groups and the entrance onto the political scene of Berlusconi gradually left the editors of Italy's main papers in a much more vulnerable position. Ezio Mauro, who took over the direction of *La Stampa* when Mieli went on to become editor of the *Corriere*, says that he, too, suffered no political interference—with one extremely notable exception. At the end of 1993, he was called into a meeting with Gianni Agnelli and Cesare Romiti. Romiti proceeded to tell Mauro that *La Stampa* should do whatever it could to prevent the left from winning and get the paper's roster of distinguished contributors to follow suit. Agnelli sat by in embarrassed silence. Mauro explained that he simply couldn't do that, that the journalists and editorial commentators of the paper were not privates in an army who could simply be ordered around. The discussion ended there, and it remained an isolated incident, but it was clear that the protection and independence that Fiat and Agnelli had been able to grant were diminishing. Fiat, at the time, had made a huge investment in a new ultramodern factory in the Southern region of Basilicata that depended vitally on an extremely generous government subsidy meant to encourage employment in the South.

Two years later, in 1996, Mauro went to become the editor in chief of

La Repubblica in Rome, leaving Fiat to choose a much more malleable editor. When Mauro was asked to suggest a successor, his first choice was Anselmi. "You should have seen the face that Romiti made," Agnelli told Mauro. Anselmi, although a political centrist who had successfully brought Rome's *Il Messaggero* back to health since leaving the *Corriere*, had made enemies by championing the cause of the corruption investigation in 1992. The owners chose instead Carlo Rossella, a Berlusconi journalist unlikely to cause similar problems. Rossella had been the deputy editor of Berlusconi's *Panorama* and had been made the head of news at RAI 1 when Berlusconi took power in 1994. Although Rossella was also on Mauro's short list, his selection over Anselmi guaranteed that *La Stampa* would not become a source of tension between the Fiat group and Berlusconi.

What this meant in practical terms, I learned by personal experience. In 1995, I was asked (when Ezio Mauro was editor) to become a regular contributor to *La Stampa*. I wrote mostly about American things, since I had returned to the United States, but in late 1996, after Rossella had become editor, I wanted to write a story about the role of the Mafia in Italian politics, a subject I had already written extensively about. Marcello Dell'Utri, Berlusconi's campaign manager and close friend, had just been indicted on charges of collusion with the Mafia, and the case had important political implications. I spoke with Rossella. "Good idea," he responded, "but let's wait and see if the case is actually sent to trial." In the Italian system, an indictment must be confirmed by a second, independent magistrate, who decides if the charges merit a trial. Knowing Rossella's background in the Berlusconi group, I was somewhat suspicious of his desire to put off the story. But, I thought, perhaps in his new position as the editor in chief of one of the country's best papers, he might adapt to his new circumstances. *La Stampa* was a newspaper with a great journalistic tradition, a history of excellent, scrupulous newsmen, good, clear writing, first-rate editorial writers, and commentators of the moral and literary stature of the novelist Primo Levi and the philosopher Norberto Bobbio. *La Stampa* had always been a moderate paper, but it had succeeded in a city that generally voted with the left by maintaining a highly independent spirit, and its contributors' views ranged across the ideological spectrum. Perhaps reinforced by this great tradition, Rossella would adopt an attitude of greater autonomy. When Dell'Utri's indictment was confirmed and he was scheduled for trial, I called *La Stampa* back and spoke to the deputy editor. He told me to go ahead with the story, only to call me back the next day and say, in a tone of great embarrassment: "The editor in chief doesn't want you to do that story on Dell'Utri. He's sued us over something else in the past and we don't want any more trouble." "If it's a libel suit you are concerned about," I replied, "you shouldn't be. I don't intend to mention any of the unproven allegations in the case. It will limit itself to listing the facts that have been agreed to by both defense and prosecutor. Dell'Utri has acknowledged meeting or being on friendly terms with a series of organized-crime figures or has been wiretapped having a series of discussions with various Mafia people. I will outline only these well-documented incidents and, without taking a position on whether this pattern of relationship constitutes a crime, ask a series of questions: 'Should a person with these personal connections be allowed to sit in parliament? Should he sit at the right hand of the most powerful person in the country, Berlusconi? Should he play a prominent role in the largest political party in Sicily?'" Needless to say, the editor did not want to run the story.

Thanks in part to his political reliability, Rossella went on to become the editor in chief of *Panorama*, Berlusconi's newsweekly. Here, he distinguished himself with an act of journalistic sycophancy that may go down in the annals of Italian journalism. When Berlusconi appeared in court in his Milan corruption trial, photographs of him all revealed his increasing baldness—a sensitive point with him. Rossella had the photograph that *Panorama* used digitally doctored so as to show the prime minister with a much fuller head of hair—something that caused Rossella to be denounced before the national Order of Journalists. And yet, when Berlusconi looked for a new news director of his largest TV network, Canale 5, it was to Rossella that he turned. That a man who conceives of the role of journalist as hairdresser to the prime minister should move from triumph to triumph—heading *Tg1*, *La Stampa*, *Panorama* and *Tg5*—gives one an idea of the abyss into which Italian journalism has fallen.[22]

"We had been a journalistic leader with Paolo Mieli and then with Ezio Mauro in covering first Tangentopoli and then the Berlusconi phenomenon," said Pino Corrias, who covered both stories for the Milan bureau of *La Stampa* and coauthored an early book about Berlusconi. "Politicians protested, but we had two editors who defended us—but with the arrival of Rossella all of that was silenced. Not only did we stop following judicial investigations with the same rigor, we stopped following Berlusconi as a cultural phenomenon—his anomalies, politics as spectacle, the comic aspects of Berlusconi—which is actually an important part of the whole thing. That way of writing about Berlusconi was now off-limits. Often the solution was just putting in a short wire-service story about Berlusconi rather than doing our own story. It was the safe way to do things. I left after 1999, when Marcello Sorgi became editor and I saw that the same servile attitude toward Berlusconi was going to continue."[23]

Even Sorgi's coeditor, Gianni Riotta, acknowledged that the paper had begun to pull its punches because of the enormous pressures on it. "Our solution to confronting the Berlusconi phenomenon was to be boring and safe," he said. "It wasn't that we didn't do stories, but we did them in a dull, gray way that wouldn't cause us problems. We realized that we couldn't do light, colorful, satirical writing anymore. If we did it about the right, there would be hell to pay, and as a matter of journalistic integrity, we didn't feel we could make fun only of the left, so we pretty much stopped doing any humorous writing."

The situation got worse after the triumph of Berlusconi in the 2001 elections. Sorgi told some of his closest associates, "These people are going to govern Italy for thirty years, we have to keep our heads down." Sorgi's name began to surface as a possible new president of RAI. The journalists' guild at the paper began to complain about the tendency to water down stories and headlines. When the governor of the Bank of Italy, Antonio Fazio, called Berlusconi's finance minister, Giulio

Tremonti, who was also Berlusconi's corporate tax attorney, an "expert in off-shore tax havens," it was the next day's featured quote in most newspapers, but was removed from the headline of the story in *La Stampa*.[24]

Editorial writers who were anti-Berlusconi were let go, often replaced by writers who were also contributors to *Panorama*. A paper that had been known for having some of the best commentators in Italy now shared much of its talent with the prime minister's newsmagazine, making it seem a weak satellite in the prime minister's orbit rather than the great independent newspaper it had often been. This, too, prompted a protest from the paper's journalists' guild: "For a paper, which, up until a few years ago, emphasized getting exclusive, original material, isn't there too much sharing of resources between *La Stampa* and *Panorama*? An attentive reader might detect an editorial line that is in line with that of a newsweekly that is part of a group owned by Silvio Berlusconi, head of the government."[25]

Dull and inoffensive, stripped of color and of most of its great writers, *La Stampa* is a shadow of its former self and, not surprisingly, readers have abandoned it in droves. In three years since Berlusconi's election, the number of copies sold dropped from 413,000 to just 364,000, a loss of more than 10 percent. "*La Stampa*, given the condition Fiat is in, is not in a position to criticize Berlusconi and this applies equally to many other newspapers," says Giulio Anselmi, who, besides having been deputy editor of the *Corriere*, has been editor in chief of *Il Messaggero* in Rome, the Italian wire service ANSA and the newsweekly *L'Espresso*, and is now editor of *La Stampa*. "Along with the newspapers he owns, there is a whole concentric circle of papers that he conditions heavily by direct and indirect means."[26]

As De Bortoli himself said, "The Italian press has undergone a genetic mutation. Journalism is seen as having a purely ancillary function to a political design. Papers like the *Corriere* and *La Stampa* have traditionally played a role as independent institutions, moderate but also as watchdogs, checks against government power, places of political and cultural encounter, where different views could clash and listen to one another. That has become much more difficult. Large industrial groups have always had the ability to influence and condition the media, but when one of those groups also runs the government, that brings about a real structural, genetic change."

Chapter Fourteen

BASTA CON BERLUSCONI! (ENOUGH BERLUSCONI!)

1. Too Much of a Good Thing?

On January 24, 2004, exactly ten years after Berlusconi's famous speech announcing his decision to "enter the playing the field," Forza Italia held a massive celebration to mark the tenth anniversary of its founding. Berlusconi's largest TV channel, Canale 5, interrupted its regular programming to provide two hours of coverage on Saturday night at prime time, dedicated almost exclusively to lavish praise of the great leader. The anniversary show was presided over by Gabriella Carlucci, a pretty blonde starlet who hosts one of Berlusconi's TV shows and is also a member of parliament. They replayed Berlusconi's historic speech, and Carlucci invited a group of young supporters ("our young blues," as she called them) onto the stage, to read aloud excerpts from the speeches of Berlusconi for more than twenty minutes. They constitute "a kind of secular creed for us," the starlet-parliamentarian explained.[1]

Then, to thunderous applause, as the hymn of Forza Italia played in the background, Berlusconi bounded onto the stage and read a long article by a priest-supporter who maintained that Berlusconi's decision to found Forza Italia was an "inspiration" guided by "the Holy Spirit." "From that point on," Berlusconi read, "I came to consider Berlusconi as a spiritual event. . . ." In a press interview, the secretary of Forza Italia said that his party was like "a small child whom Berlusconi had held by the hand," and would need the assistance of its founder for another thirty years. The great leader was not only irreplaceable but nearly immortal.

The tenth-anniversary program seemed the apotheosis of a great charismatic leader destined to rule for decades—in the tradition of Chairman Mao or Generalissimo Franco—but in reality, Berlusconi's poll numbers were sagging, dragged down by three years of economic stagnation and an unpopular war in Iraq. As his numbers dropped, Berlusconi's efforts to control the media grew more desperate.

Five months later, less than a week before the elections for the European parliament in June of 2004, Emilio Fede, anchorman of the nightly newscast on Berlusconi's Rete 4, appeared on air with a message board hung around his neck. The message board contained the text of a censure given out by the Authority for Communications: it stated that Fede's broadcasts had consistently violated the norms of "balance, objectivity, completeness and impartiality in newscasting." The Authority required that Fede read its censure on the air, which he did, while making it clear that he disagreed and was doing so as a kind of hostage. Shortly after reading the censure, the phone on Fede's desk rang and he began to carry on a phone conversation live on the air. "Oh, it's you, Minister, but aren't you with the government majority? Sorry, I can't talk to you."[2]

Fede didn't read the statistics from the agency's monitoring of his show over the previous six weeks that prompted the censure. Berlusconi or other members of his center-right coalition had occupied 61.6 percent of the air time on Fede's newscasts, and "institutional figures"—including ministers and other members of Berlusconi's government—accounted for 34.8 percent, leaving a mere 3.6 percent for the government opposition. In other words, in the six weeks leading up to a major election, candidates of the center-left had virtually no opportunity to speak on one of the country's leading nightly newscasts.[3]

And yet, just a few days later, the center-left registered a major election victory over Berlusconi's coalition in the European elections. This was followed by an even larger victory in a series of regional elections in 2005, in which the center-left won twelve out of fourteen regions up for grabs, seven of them changing hands from right to left. Berlusconi watched with a sense of helpless rage as Forza Italia's vote totals dipped well below 20 percent in most parts of Italy.

"It's a strange sort of regime in which you supposedly control all the information and yet the opposition is able to win just the same," says Paolo Mieli, former editor of both *La Stampa* and the *Corriere della Sera*, who has recently returned to editing the *Corriere*.

"Perhaps Berlusconi is not the evil genius everyone supposes," said Vittorio Sgarbi, the former attack dog of Berlusconi TV who now sits in parliament. (Although his 5 percent attendance record gives new meaning to this term.) "The paradox of the Berlusconi era is that he's spent all this energy trying to gain control of everything, especially the media, and it hasn't done him much good at all. The fact is that in government he's proved himself incompetent."[4]

Characteristically, Berlusconi blamed his defeats on the "equal time" law which forced him to share the stage (at least to some degree on the public networks) with both his opponents and the allies within his own government coalition. But, in reality, his own omnipresence during the past ten years may have gradually eroded the efficacy of his own media presence. There was a moment in October 2003 when the popular entertainment program *Domenica In* (Sunday In) conducted a game with its viewers called *Basta con?* (Enough of?) asking them to fax or e-mail a list of the things they had had enough of. To the surprise and embarrassment of the producers at RAI 1 (the biggest and traditionally the most conservative RAI network) at the top of the list—above Saddam Hussein, Osama Bin Laden and high taxes—was *Basta con Berlusconi!* (Enough Berlusconi!). Coming from the audience of such a popular entertainment program, it was an especially ominous sign, for this was the television public, Berlusconi's people, the backbone of his electorate.[5]

Berlusconi's media obsession may end up being both his greatest strength and his greatest weakness. His deep conviction that everything is a matter of perception made it difficult for him to grasp that it was important for him not just to *appear* to have done well, but to have actually governed well. The viewers of Berlusconi who had had enough of Berlusconi now placed him at the top of the category of politicians who talk a lot but do nothing, *i politici che dicono ma non fanno*. Media can help you get elected and even get reelected, but image alone, if it bears no correspondence to reality, is not enough. After ten years of videocracy, it would seem that Berlusconi's magic is finally wearing off.

Some interpret Berlusconi's recent failures to mean that, in the words of Paolo Mieli, "the Italian media and Italian democracy have held up pretty well. The fact that Berlusconi lost the elections for the European parliament and is, I believe, likely to lose the general elections in 2006 means that enough information has evidently gotten through to allow the electorate to form a negative view of him."

"I think that's nonsense," says Giulio Anselmi, an equally respected journalist, who has been the editor of the Rome newspaper *Il Messaggero*, ANSA, Italy's main wire service, and of *L'Espresso*, its second-largest weekly newsmagazine, and who is now editor of *La Stampa*. "People turned against Berlusconi not because they had enough information to allow them to change their minds, but because the things they were hearing and reading in the media were so much at odds with what they were experiencing—economic stagnation, rising prices—that they simply became fed up."[6]

By any objective measure, the performance of the Italian economy during Berlusconi's four years in office could only be described as poor. Between 2001 and 2004, the growth rate was close to zero and it actually began to shrink in 2005. Italy consistently trailed all the other major European countries in this period. More alarming was the fact that productivity in Italy was actually going down as labor costs went up. "For several years now, Italy has thus been losing price competitiveness within the euro-area.... Export volumes have fallen, and market shares in real terms have been eroded," noted a study by the Organization for Economic Co-operation and Development during the summer of 2005. *The Economist* began to refer to Italy as "the sick man of Europe."[7]

Some of this was not Berlusconi's fault. Traditionally, Italy's way out of economic distress had been to devalue its own currency, the lira, in order to make its own goods cheaper and more competitive, and indirectly to reduce wages. Locked into the single currency of the euro, the country could no longer use this strategy and so Italy's structural problems—high labor costs, an expensive pension system, government waste and inefficiency, the small size of its family-owned firms, the low levels of research, development and technology—became impossible to avoid.

These well-known obstacles had not prevented Berlusconi from promising a second Italian miracle, but he ultimately proved unable and seemingly uninterested in tackling these knotty problems. Rather than undertake structural reform, Berlusconi had resorted to quick-fix, one-time measures such as tax amnesties and the sell-off of state assets. "Ongoing reliance on such initiatives may undermine the government's revenue base in the longer term," a 2005 report by the investment firm Scotiabank noted. In fact, Italy's deficit increased by 30 percent under Berlusconi. The bond-rating company Standard & Poor's downgraded Italy's credit rating to AA-, putting it in a class with Portugal and Slovenia, two categories below the principal countries of Europe, forcing it to pay higher interest rates and placing a further drag on its economy. Italy had begun the 1990s neck and neck with Great Britain in its GDP and standard of living. The Italian economy grew half as fast that of the UK in the past decade. As of 2005, its economy was some 15 percent smaller.

Italy's tragic illusion—shared in different degrees by left and right—that Berlusconi's conflict-of-interest problem is a purely moral problem has caused millions of Italians to fail to understand the crippling effects it was bound to create for the Italian economy. Berlusconi's central position in so many key industries—television, telecommunications, publishing, the Internet, movies and entertainment, finance and investment, all integral to the postindustrial economy—has meant that a true liberalization of the economy was physiologically impossible even if Berlusconi had been a philosopher king and not a robber baron. It is human nature to pursue one's self-interest, and Berlusconi's dominant, in some cases monopolistic, position in so many important markets, has had a suffocating effect on the Italian economy. And of course Berlusconi is temperamentally much more a robber baron than a philosopher king. Although he supposedly has detached himself from his business affairs, those who know well say that in private he loves talking about business and is always on the lookout for business opportunities. In a meeting in 2005 with the businessman Carlo DeBenedetti, Berlusconi asked his arch-nemesis what projects he was working on. When DeBenedetti explained that he was creating a large investment fund for company turnarounds, Berlusconi immediately offered to invest hundreds of millions of euros. It would never have occurred to Berlusconi that there was anything wrong with a prime minister handing over hundreds of millions of euros to a man who is, among other things, the principal owner of two of the most important independent publications in the country, *La Repubblica* and *L'Espresso*. Berlusconi's proposed investment was wildly inappropriate on two grounds: it arguably would subtly condition one of the largest independent media groups in the country, and Berlusconi's role as prime minister might be decisive in helping many of the failing companies that the investment fund might be looking to turn around.

The heavy state involvement in the Italian economy offers an activist prime minister thousands of sticks and carrots to harm or help this or that interest. Berlusconi's controlling nature, his belief that he alone knows more about everything than his soccer coach, his foreign minister and his finance minister, and his natural instinct to reward friends and punish enemies, have meant that he would be very unlikely to push for real deregulation of the Italian economy.

Even the solidly right-wing American think tank the Heritage Foundation took a dim view of the Berlusconi government's performance: "Promised reforms have been postponed or forgotten. Serious structural problems . . . remain unaddressed. . . . The economy has underperformed the rest of the euro zone throughout the past half-decade . . . unemployment remains relatively high at 8.6 percent. Recent corporate accounting scandals will cost the state 11 billion euros, which numerically offsets the government's 2003 efforts to cut the budget deficit."

Italians had overlooked his checkered past, his conflicts of interest and his ethical deficits on the promise that he could deliver economic performance, and he had failed. Although Berlusconi continued to insist that the statistics were wrong; that Italy was moving from triumph to triumph, to most Italians Berlusconi began increasingly to appear like the emperor with no clothes. The self-described prime minister/center forward had scored no goals in four straight seasons.

So what, ultimately, is the meaning and lasting legacy of the Berlusconi phenomenon? Is Berlusconi a temporary anomaly—a reaction to the collapse of Italy's old parties in the early 1990s—or is he the harbinger of a new kind of media-based celebrity politics? Are Berlusconi's various conflicts of interest and his takeover of the media fundamentally innocuous since they do not appear to have brought him lasting success? Is the Berlusconi experience a lesson in the power of media politics or its limits? What is likely to be his lasting legacy, if any?

2. LASTING LEGACY

First, Berlusconi's political death has been declared numerous times and has always proved to be premature. Even if he does not continue as prime minister, he is likely to remain a powerful force for the rest of his days and well beyond.

Moreover, if Berlusconi's hold on power is more precarious, one should not forget the things his twelve years in politics has allowed him to accomplish. Already he has presided over the longest government in post–World War II Italian history and wrought a series of profound changes. While control of media cannot guarantee you lifetime tenure in office, it has allowed Berlusconi to win major battles on issues of great importance to him. In general elections, it is difficult to persuade voters that they are better off, if their pocketbooks and monthly budgets tell them that they are not. But on select issues that they may not understand well and don't have a personal stake in, people are much easier to manipulate. Berlusconi won the 1995 referendum that would have broken up his monopoly on private television in Italy because his media machine succeeded in convincing millions of Italians that the referendum would have effectively ended commercial television in Italy. The other side had almost no means of conveying its own message that it would have increased viewer choice by forcing Berlusconi to sell one or two of his networks to other private owners. By winning this battle he retained his ability to condition political life in many other ways.

If Berlusconi initially entered politics to save his media and financial empire and to defend himself against criminal prosecution, then his political career can only be judged a total success. But Berlusconi has achieved much more than that: he almost single-handedly derailed the national corruption investigation known as Operation Clean Hands; turned back the clock on the war against the Mafia; set a series of troubling precedents for mixing private and public affairs and created a politicized media that in many ways anticipated developments in the United States and elsewhere. His own particular combination of media, money, celebrity and political power may prove too highly personalized to be transferable, but he has experimented with a new formula of political power that could become the winning model elsewhere.

3. DERAILING OPERATION CLEAN HANDS

It is difficult to overstate the degree of power and popular goodwill the corruption investigation enjoyed in 1994 when Berlusconi "entered the playing field." Respect and trust in the magistrature was at record levels and Antonio Di Pietro, the symbol of the anticorruption forces in Milan, was the most popular person in the country—far more than Berlusconi himself. Similarly, between 1992 and 1995, prosecutors in Sicily and elsewhere had accomplished the seemingly impossible: they had arrested thousands of Mafiosi, including the boss of bosses, and helped bring the murder rate in a country of nearly sixty million people down by 50 percent. The Mafia seemed on its last legs and there was widespread public support for the war on the Mafia. When a man whose company was already under investigation entered politics, the immediate effect was to politicize criminal justice: any further effort to prosecute him or his associates would automatically be seen as a political attack.

In order to reverse the seemingly irresistible momentum of the investigation, Berlusconi conducted a scorched-earth campaign against the judges of Milan and Palermo that changed the Italian political landscape. The behind-the-scenes involvement of Paolo Berlusconi and Cesare Previti in initiating a secret investigation into Di Pietro and orchestrating his mysterious resignation was a major step in dividing the popular prosecutor from the rest of the office, a key step in tarring the anticorruption pool as left-wing. Berlusconi and his associates played key roles in a series of muckraking campaigns directed against Di Pietro, some of which were outright dirty-trick campaigns involving perjury and invented evidence, but all of which confused public opinion and left Di Pietro's image muddied. Years of nonstop attacks and unsubstantiated charges forced Berlusconi's daily newspaper, *Il Giornale,* to make a large financial settlement with Di Pietro and print a long piece retracting much of what the paper had written in the previous several years, but the effect of years of libelous stories about corruption charges and secret foreign bank accounts that were proven false outweighed the one-day retraction.

Italians became so used to the endless soap opera of Berlusconi's death struggle with the Milan prosecutors' office that they became inured to the unprecedented array of weapons available to a criminal defendant who was also the country's richest man, largest media owner, prime minister and head of its largest political party.

The control of hundreds of seats in parliament and thousands of key positions in the state bureaucracy, together with vast media power, meant that Berlusconi could actually manufacture pseudo-scandals at will. Thus, for example, a blistering exposé of supposed judicial wrongdoing would prompt Berlusconi's soldiers in parliament to call for a parliamentary inquiry or disciplinary proceedings against the judges. The Berlusconi media would then cover these events, quoting members of parliament or the government, which would give an appearance of substance and reality to their initial charges, which would lead to a new round of media stories and a new round of reactions from the political world—creating a perfect, self-perpetuating media machine, kept in constant motion through this feedback mechanism between Berlusconi's media employees and his political employees. The charges, almost invariably, would prove after a few weeks or months or years to have no substance—a fact that would go unnoticed in the Berlusconi press (and often in other press)—but the country would already have gone on to a new series of equally unfounded charges.

Berlusconi stunned the nation by holding a press conference in which he held up an electronic surveillance device that he said had been found in his personal residence. He railed against the "outlaw prosecutors" who were persecuting him. Both left and right denounced this outrage, which risked subverting Italian democracy. One Berlusconi ally called it worse than the Watergate scandal that brought down President Richard Nixon. A criminal investigation was initiated, and weeks later the investigation discovered that it was an old bugging device that had been placed in Berlusconi's home by his own security detail. The affair's innocuous end received far less press than its dramatic beginning in which the Italian public was put on alert that its constitutional order was at risk because of rogue prosecutors.[8]

At every opportunity, the Berlusconi press has sought to place prosecutors and the Berlusconi associates they have prosecuted on the same moral plane, on the cynical premise of *Tutti colpevoli, tutti innocenti* (If everyone is guilty, then everyone is innocent).

While virtually none of the thousands of charges made by Berlusconi and his media have stuck, the constant volley of charges and countercharges has taken its toll. The operating assumption of "Throw enough mud and some of it will stick" unfortunately works, particularly when you control so much of the media. And when the supposedly independent press has rarely dared to make a point-by-point comparison of how the charges made against Berlusconi and his associates have held up in comparison with those made toward his accusers, it is hardly surprising that a confused public has become essentially agnostic on the question of corruption and criminal justice, opting not to make it a factor in its electoral choices.

4. LOWERING THE MORAL BAR

Ten years of a prime minister who has continued to own a vast media empire while governing one of the largest economies in the world, and who has beaten back well-documented corruption charges with the help of the levers of government, has significantly lowered the moral bar—never especially high—in Italy. Although corruption has long been a feature of Italian political life, there were often at the top of the Italian political world figures of genuine moral stature—presidents of the Republic Luigi Einaudi and Sandro Pertini, prime ministers such as the Christian Democratic leader Alcide De Gaspari and Carlo Azeglio Ciampi, opposition leaders such as Palmiro Togliatti and Enrico Berlinguer. In the pre-Berlusconi past, in fact, it was virtually automatic that a high-level public official would resign if suspected of a serious crime—let alone if indicted or convicted—and wait until he had been cleared to return to public life.

Now, even trial convictions for fraud, bribery, extortion and collusion with the Mafia have not kept Berlusconi associates like Cesare Previti and Marcello Dell'Utri from holding public office or from playing prominent roles in formulating criminal justice policy. On the contrary, those most at risk of prison were put up for public office so that they could enjoy parliamentary immunity.

At a certain point, Dell'Utri, at a retreat meant for future candidates for Forza Italia, actually gave public lessons on how to beat the rap if you are accused of a crime. "First: never testify, always take advantage of the right against self-incrimination," he told the audience. "Second: never plea-bargain unless you are caught red handed. Third: don't miss any court dates, or the judge will feel slighted and the lawyer won't do his best. Fourth: follow your lawyer's advice only when he agrees with you." His fifth and most important principle elucidated the main strategy of all the Berlusconi defendants: "Let the case last as long as possible. . . . In desperate cases, that is to say, almost always, don't worry about the principal anomaly of trials: their interminable length. On the contrary, the rule is to make them last as long as possible. Because time is a gentleman, time makes for justice. . . . With time, lots of things can happen: the prosecutor or the judge might die, a witness might die, the atmosphere around the case might change. Things change."[9]

And so in Berlusconi's Italy, a man who has been convicted of several crimes but managed to spend only a very short time in prison gives lessons to the younger members of the country's largest political party in how to stay out of jail. The fact that criminal trials now last an average of twice as long as they did ten years ago is due in part to the legislative input of criminal-defendant members of parliament like Dell'Utri. As a result, Italy has a dysfunctional justice system, serving the double purpose of letting Berlusconi and his associates drag out their cases and avoid conviction and increasing the public distrust of the magistracy.

This attitude has seeped down and become increasingly widespread. In 2002, Italian police were tracking the activity of a Sicilian drug dealer and wiretapped him when he referred to a shipment for "the deputy minister." The police watched as an aide to the deputy minister of finance entered the ministry carrying an estimated twenty grams of cocaine. He was waved past security guards without inspection and handed off the drugs to someone inside. Various wiretapped conversations between the two main suspects convinced police that the recipient of the sizable drug buy was none other than the deputy minister of finance, Gianfranco Miccichè, a former Berlusconi employee and coordinator of Berlusconi's Forza Italia party in Sicily. In one call, Miccichè's aide, Alessandro Martelli, explained that he could pay back the supplier only after delivering the drugs to his boss. Moreover, it turned out that Miccichè had been a suspect years earlier in a cocaine trafficking case while he was an executive at Berlusconi's company Publitalia. He had defended himself by insisting that he was buying drugs exclusively for personal use, which was not a crime. Since the final delivery of the drugs was undocumented, it was impossible to make a case against Miccichè, but a normal sense of propriety would dictate that a man with a history of using cocaine, whose aide brings the drug into a government ministry for his boss, should not be a deputy minister and even less the head of the main political party in a place like Sicily, where these kinds of associations might make him eminently blackmailable. But the story was handled as little more than a brief local crime story, and Miccichè was never placed under any particular pressure to resign from either of his two prominent positions.[10]

In 2005, the minister of health of the Berlusconi government, Girolamo Sirchia, was found to have received tens of thousands of dollars in undeclared payments from an American pharmaceutical company. According to the former bookkeeper of the Italian affiliate of the company, the money was one of a number of kickbacks the company made to Italian doctors who ordered its blood transfusion equipment for their hospitals. The American company acknowledged making the payments to Sirchia but said they were consulting fees. The prosecutors actually found the cashed checks made out to the future minister, which were drawn on a Swiss bank by the German affiliate of the company. If the payments were for a legal consultancy, why were they made overseas and hidden from Italian authorities? The minister, in the face of the evidence, simply denied taking any money and remained at his post.[11]

"The general level of illegality in Italian life has increased," said Ferruccio De Bortoli, the former editor in chief of the *Corriere della Sera*, now editor of the financial newspaper *Il Sole 24 Ore*. "Since the prime minister's conflict-of-interest problem has gone unaddressed—in part thanks to five years of inertia on the part of the center-left—it has spread and impregnated every part of public and even private life. All kinds of things, passing laws on one's own behalf, illegality in public life, are now no longer even remarked upon, are no longer seen as unusual or pathological."

There was an opportunity, with the discovery of the system of corruption by the Clean Hands investigation, for Italy to become a nation of laws rather than a nation of men, where the strongest individual or clan was able impose his law on the lives of others. At the same time, in the period between 1992 and 1994, the Sicilian Mafia went through what was perhaps the greatest crisis of its long history, and even hardened investigators spoke about a possible end of the Mafia. Those dreams vanished with the election of a prime minister and his associates whose multiple legal problems were such that it was necessary to undo much of the criminal justice system to guarantee them impunity.

5. PARLIAMENT AS EMPTY SHELL

Besides greatly weakening the judiciary, Berlusconi has also gone a long way toward getting the power of the legislative branch. Berlusconi has made no secret of his desire to create a "presidential republic," endowing much more power in the executive branch and greatly reducing that of parliament. He rarely appears in parliament and has difficulty disguising his contempt for the people whom he got elected there. "I am the Prince Charming of the fairy tale, they were pumpkins until I turned them into members of parliament," he said. The secretary of Forza Italia once confessed: "I don't care whether we have a Nobel Prize winner as a candidate, what matters to me is having someone who will vote for a law without knowing anything about it."[12]

Deprived of any real function, in the absence of genuine debate among the members of parliament, Forza Italia has had great difficulty even getting its members to show up to vote, and so the parliament has frequently lacked the requisite quorum for voting. Members of Forza Italia were caught casting multiple votes for their absent colleagues, a scandal that Berlusconi dismissed as unimportant since "the real decisions are made elsewhere." Members of parliament who know they count for nothing and will be eliminated if they dare to challenge their leader on anything of importance fill an institution that risks losing any real meaning.[13]

Berlusconi is so much richer and more powerful than his colleagues in parliament that he is like Gulliver in the land of the Lilliputians. His money and his control of parliament are such that even those not in his own party, his potential rivals in the center-right majority, are in an unhealthily subordinate position to him. Umberto Bossi, the once proud and un-predictable head of the Northern League who brought down Berlusconi's first government, is now one of his most faithful allies after Berlusconi helped his party out of its financial difficulties. "My suitcase is always ready, but don't you understand that I'm a prisoner? A hostage?" he said, explaining why he remains firmly in the Berlusconi coalition.[14]

One of the most revealing examples of the distorted relations between government allies occurred shortly after the 2004 European parliamentary elections in which Berlusconi lost much of his support, and a few of his center-right allies began to find their courage and challenge his absolute control. Tired of being treated like flunkies and errand boys, they started demanding a more equal role in government. "The monarchy is over, the republic must begin," said Marco Follini of the Union of Christian Democrats, which had increased its share of the vote. Berlusconi reacted with ill-disguised rage: "Marco, you keep this up and you see how my TV stations will treat you in the coming days. . . . Don't pretend not to understand . . . I can see why you wouldn't understand given that you are very present on both the RAI and the Mediaset networks." When Follini pointed out that, as a matter of fact, he had been present for only forty-two seconds in the last month on the Berlusconi stations, Berlusconi said, "Don't be ridiculous, the truth is that on Mediaset no one ever attacks you." "I should hope not." "Well, if you keep it up, you'll see what happens." Follini replied, "I want to put it on the record that I've been threatened."[15]

Eviscerating both the judiciary and legislative branches of government, Berlusconi has introduced a different form of democracy—a kind of plebiscitary or direct democracy, in which a leader who has been chosen by the people should have the power and freedom to do as he pleases for the length of his mandate. When prosecutors have tried to hold him and his company responsible for alleged crimes, even some committed when Berlusconi was in office, he has frequently objected that they are trying to contravene popular will, overturn election results, conduct a coup d'état, as if election to office meant that one was no longer subject to the law. In similar fashion, Berlusconi has sometimes insisted that he should not be prosecuted because polls revealed the majority of Italians did not consider what he was being accused of a crime. Leaving aside the dubious value of his own polls on this matter, the results of which can be skewed by the wording of questions: the whole point of a legal system is to create a series of rules and protections that cannot be undone with each election, that protect minorities against the tyranny of the majority and hold everyone—even the richest, the most powerful and the most popular—to the same standards.

6. We Are All Berlusconi

Berlusconi may seem an extreme, at times even grotesque, figure, possible only in a society with no tradition of antitrust or conflict-of-interest laws, with a long history of political corruption and cynical toleration for rule-breaking. In fact, it would be a grave mistake to see him as an Italian anomaly, an example of typically Italian craziness like the traffic in Naples. Other contemporary figures, like Vladimir Putin in Russia, Hugo Chávez in Venezuela, Alberto Fujimori in Peru, have also developed forms of plebiscitary democracy, using popular elections to then change the democratic rules and diminish the powers of parliament and the judiciary and establish a kind of one-man rule. They have taken over their countries' media in order to speak directly to the people, over the heads of other branches of government or traditional forms of journalism that might serve as checks on their power.

The formula Berlusconi developed—money + media + celebrity = political power—is the winning formula in many advanced democracies, not least in the United States. With the dominance of television in politics, money has arguably never mattered more in our political life. The billionaire in politics—Ross Perot, Steve Forbes, New York mayor Mike Bloomberg—has become an unsurprising figure in American political life, multimillionaires able to finance their own campaigns are commonplace. New Jersey Democrat Jon Corzine, a former investment banker, spent $60 million of his own money getting himself elected to the Senate. Republican Mike Bloomberg spent $75 million to become the mayor of New York. The personal fortune allows an otherwise unknown person with little or no political experience to immediately dominate the political campaign by buying massive amounts of television time. These self-financed figures may, ironically, represent the public interest more than the politicians who must collect similar amounts of money from private donors and corporate interests. We have seen the extraordinary spectacles in recent years of checks from the tobacco industry literally being distributed on the floor of Congress and of lobbyists being called in to help write the legislation regulating their industries.

The emergence of a highly partisan broadcast media in the United States—the rise of Fox News, Sinclair Broadcast Group, many of the twenty-four-hour cable news programs—with their shouting, bullying, eye-gouging, mud-slinging verbal style is reminiscent of what the Berlusconi TV stations have been doing for years. The attack against John Kerry organized by the "Swift Boat Veterans for the Truth" resembled the kind of orchestrated polyphonic assault that the Berlusconi media machine so often practices. A nonstory—that John Kerry had fabricated the war record that had earned him numerous war medals in Vietnam—contradicted by all eyewitness testimony and documentary evidence, was kept alive on cable television for about a month during which time Kerry's sizable lead over George Bush evaporated. The mere existence of "charges," repeated in homes across America day and night, meant that Kerry's war record was suddenly "an issue" and his service in Vietnam, which should have represented a significant advantage over Bush's controversial time in the National Guard, suddenly became a liability. These media were not owned by Bush, but they behaved in ways much like the Berlusconi media in Italy. The concentration of major media into the hands of a few large, generally conservative corporations; the economic niche carved out by a new breed of high-testosterone right-wing TV and radio journalists; the need of twenty-four-hour cable to pump up the volume and keep stories alive and ratings up; and the clear intent of a couple of major media outlets like Fox News, Sinclair Broadcasting and Clear Channel to reelect Bush at any cost created a multiheaded beast that often behaved with the coordinated discipline of the Berlusconi juggernaut.

Berlusconi brought the permanent campaign to Europe, and Tony Blair appears to have done much the same. Venezuelan populist Hugo Chávez has his weekly TV show *Aló, Presidente,* and Vladimir Putin has secured the loyalty of all major Russian media. While more diverse, the U.S. media, especially television, has often seemed like a government mouthpiece. In the weeks immediately following the U.S. invasion of Iraq, it was close to impossible to hear any dissenting voices on American television. Nearly 30 percent of the U.S. population opposed the invasion of Iraq from the beginning, despite the instinctive tendency to support the government in a time of war and months of listening to the Bush adminstration argue in the strongest possible language for the urgent necessity of the invasion to protect us from future terrorist actions and even nuclear attack. And yet antiwar voices were only 10 percent of the voices heard on American television during the invasion and most of those heard opposing the war were foreigners, mainly Iraqis. Americans who disagreed with the invasion were only 3 percent of the on-air total, about one-tenth of the actual strength of those who opposed the invasion, and the result was an extremely distorted picture of the state of the nation and the internal debate on the war. Not surprisingly, Murdoch's Fox News was the most openly partisan, with 81 percent of its sources clearly prowar and only 1 percent against. But CBS—the network conservatives love to cite as the example of the "liberal" media—was not much different: 77 percent prowar, 3 percent antiwar. Dan Rather, the bogeyman of the American right, declared his bias without any hesitation: "When my country's at war, I want my country to win." Neil Cavuto, an anchorman for Fox, was even more emphatic: "Am I slanted and biased? You damn well bet I am."[16]

Given that a majority of the American people have now concluded that the invasion of Iraq was a mistake, perhaps less one-sided news coverage might produce a healthier, more open national debate, weighing carefully the pros and cons of war and the potential consequences of military occupation. Instead, the U.S. press, in some cases openly and unapologetically, turned into a cheering section for the invasion. "Navy SEALs rock!" Katie Couric told her viewers.

The parallels between Italy and the United States are not accidental: they have similar roots and arose for similar reasons. The 1980s—the decade of Reagan and Thatcher and, in Italy, Craxi—was a turning point in both the United States and Europe. It was the decade in which the post–World War II consensus around the welfare state began to crumble. Reagan declared that government was not the solution, it was the problem. Different countries looked to privatize and deregulate industries; the old manufacturing economy gave way to a postindustrial economy, unionized labor gave way to more flexible and precarious kinds of work. The Cold War ended and the twentieth-century political ideologies evaporated. Traditional, class-based mass parties atrophied and were replaced by a highly personalized form of politics, which was communicated largely through television. A culture of solidarity (the New Deal and the Great Society in the United States, the welfare state in Europe) was replaced by a new set of values based on personal initiative, success and wealth.

The deregulation of broadcasting played a significant role in these changes. Berlusconi understood that the introduction of commercial television, with its American soap operas, quiz shows and sitcoms, would reeducate a people who, over centuries of hardship, had been taught to save rather than spend. "We can do a lot to change the restrictive mentality of people, their vision of scarcity," he said, as he was helping to introduce commercial TV.[17] Berlusconi was convinced that his television could be the motor to a new kind of commercial capitalism, which would promote a more individualistic culture and diminish the hold that collective ideologies of solidarity (the Catholic Church, the Communist Party, the attachment to the welfare state) had on the population. Berlusconi was a major agent of these changes, and not just in Italy. "I was the missionary of private television throughout Europe," Berlusconi told me when I interviewed him in Rome in 1996. "I succeeded in convincing many state leaders that private television created greater liberty, increased competition with public television, helped industry and increased the level of democracy." The introduction of commercial television in societies where broadcasting had been a government monopoly not only meant changing the role of the state in society, but also introduced a new kind of culture into European life.

He was very much of a piece with 1980s culture in the United States. Ronald Reagan's chairman of the Federal Communications Commission, Mark Fowler, described television, "a toaster with pictures," as simply another household appliance. Similarly, Berlusconi understood that the key to commercial television was to create an effective vehicle to sell products. "We don't sell space, we sell sales" was one of his favorite slogans. This was a sea change from a society that regarded television as a public service to a purely money-making venture, and this involved substituting political values for commercial ones.

When researchers at the University of California Los Angeles began interviewing college freshmen in 1968, the students listed "acquiring a philosophy of life," as the number-one priority in their education, while they placed getting a good job and making money at the bottom. In the next twenty-five years, those values were turned upside down, with making money at the top and acquiring a philosophy of life at the bottom.

The shift could have many explanations—the end of the Vietnam War, the decline of the Cold War, the economic crisis of the 1970s and the increased cost of education—but the researchers were surprised to discover a powerful correlation between the amount of television students watched and the expression of materialistic priorities. They concluded that an increase in conservative and materialistic values was "associated with the number of hours per week that students watched television during the past year. . . . The more television they watched, the stronger the endorsement of the goal of being very well off financially, and the weaker the endorsement of the goal of developing a meaningful philosophy of life. While such correlations obviously cannot prove causation, they raise some interesting possibilities."[18]

In Italy, during this same period, Berlusconi and commercial TV had a radical effect on how people spent their time as well as how they thought.

Italian TV had only one channel until the 1960s and no color TV until 1977 and didn't even keep statistics on how many hours a week the average Italian watched TV. But after ten years of Berlusconi, in 1987, the average Italian was watching almost three hours a day (178 minutes). By 2002, in the age of Berlusconi, the time Italians spent in front of the television each day had reached an astonishing average of 235 minutes, with older people and housewives watching the most.

It was highly revealing that in the wake of the September 11 tragedy, President Bush urged Americans to "consume" and to travel, "visit Disney World and America's other vacation spots" rather than, say, calling on citizens to sacrifice or conserve energy in order to reduce our reliance on foreign oil. Berlusconi made a similar appeal to the Italian people in the midst of the post-9/11 recession. "Continue to spend and don't save money," he said. "Your salaries aren't going down; at worst, they'll remain the same. . . . All these rumors about the economy going badly, how many useless stomachaches they create. Don't read these stories." We have undergone a tectonic shift from a culture of sacrifice, public service and scarcity to one in which personal consumption is the highest form of patriotism.

As television triumphed over print, hundreds of newspapers closed and entertainment trumped information in the media that survived. From 1977 to 1987, *Newsweek* and *Time* reduced their public-policy-oriented covers from one in five to one in twenty. In the last quarter of the twentieth century, celebrity coverage, even at major news outlets like the *New York Times,* tripled, while hard news (which used to constitute the majority) was reduced to only a third of news coverage.

It is interesting to note that one of the best indicators of whether or not someone is a Berlusconi voter is how much television he or she watches. Those who watch the most television, especially on Berlusconi's channels, are those most likely to vote Berlusconi. The kind of programs they watch is also an excellent predictor of their voting patterns. Perhaps not surprisingly, the devoted viewers of *Who Wants to Be a Millionaire?* also tend to vote in great numbers for the billionaire prime minister.

Ironically, these teledependent voters also tend to be poorer and less

educated than most Italians. It is one of the telling contradictions of contemporary life that as modern media have become increasingly concentrated in the hands of a few fabulously wealthy individuals or companies,
the audience for broadcast television has gradually become poorer and
less educated. The right-wing politicians of the television age—whether
Ronald Reagan, Ross Perot, Berlusconi, or George W. Bush—are especially good at reaching this audience by projecting an interclass appeal.
While having radically different economic interests from those of their
voters and pursuing policies that are rarely in the economic interests of less-
educated working people, they have been extremely successful in adopting
a political language that has broad appeal across class lines through
generic expressions of religious faith, family, patriotism, and that projects
a strong, masculine image and speaks the clear, simple language of the
common man. By contrast, the politicians of the center-left, in the United
States as in Italy, have to fight off the perception that they are cultural
elitists who speak the effete language of university professors, trying to
explain the complexity of issues in long, difficult-to-understand sentences.
The right has succeeded in making class a matter of style rather than policy,
branding Democratic candidates like John Kerry as "out of touch" with
the American mainstream or referring to the opposition in Italy as *la sinistra
snob* (left-wing snobs). Both Berlusconi and Bush (like Reagan before
them) have mastered the art of populist rhetoric, walking and talking like
the common man while pursuing policies that are anything but populist.

Another crucial fact about Berlusconi's electorate that links him to his
American counterparts is that his voters express very little interest in or
knowledge about politics and have, perhaps as a result, a fundamental distrust of it. Many were unable to answer elementary questions about Italian politics or the nature of the political system. Many reported paying
little attention to the news and rarely discussing politics with friends and
relatives. This has something to do with the media environment of contemporary life.

"Newspapers are for the elite," Berlusconi declared in December 2003.
"No housewife reads the papers."[19] Unfortunately, his contemptuous re-

marks contain more than an element of truth. The percentage of Italians using television as their principal means of information shot up from 62.3 percent in 1990 to 77.4 percent in 2001, while those relying mostly on newspapers declined from 19.7 percent to only 6.4 percent.

Among this population of people who read little, know little and rarely discuss politics, there is a high level of distrust of and dislike for politics. It is an electorate ready-made for the rhetoric of antipolitics. Berlusconi inveighs against *il teatrino della politica* (the little theater of politics), against "professional politicians," "who have never worked a day inside a real company and do nothing but take taxpayers' money," who talk in "political speak." All this should be extremely familiar to anyone who has followed American politics over the past thirty years. Since Jimmy Carter and Ronald Reagan, every candidate of every party has tried to present themselves as an outsider running against Washington. The politics of antipolitics has spawned a proliferation of curious new hybrid figures—the actor-politician (Reagan, Schwarzenegger), the billionaire-politician (Perot, Bloomberg, Corzine, Forbes), even the professional wrestler-politician (Jesse "The Body" Ventura, who became governor of Minnesota). Berlusconi is a combination of them all, entertainer, celebrity, billionaire and media mogul. The success of celebrity tough guys like Ventura and Schwarzenegger appeals to the anger of the white working class and its alienation from the political system.

The deregulation of broadcasting—in the United States and Italy—has fit hand-in-glove with this trend, bringing about a balkanization of the media, the proliferation of dozens of channels, the loss of broad general channels that were designed to appeal to everyone. At the same time, the abandonment in the United States of things like the fairness doctrine and the equal time doctrine, the elimination of public interest requirements, paved the way for the highly partisan programming that dominates cable news today.

In the process, journalism as we know it has undergone a genetic mutation that has challenged and undermined the whole tradition of objectivity that was the foundation of American journalism. Of course, objectivity was a myth, but a useful myth that encouraged journalists to try to maintain a sense of fairness and balance, a healthy respect for the facts and a sense of obligation to report facts that ran counter to their most cherished views. Thus a liberal reader of the conservative *Wall Street Journal* might reject the views on the paper's editorial pages but still admire the superb reporting in its news pages. A conservative reader of the *New York Times* (or a far-left one, for that matter) might dislike the way the paper has handled various issues but can almost always build a counterargument from facts reported by the paper but perhaps given insufficient importance. The linchpin of modern journalism, as well as modern political discourse, is that "you have a right to your own opinions, but not to your own facts."

What both Berlusconi and the new right-wing press in the United States have done is to question and undermine the whole idea of "the facts." When Richard Viguerie, one of the founders of the new American right, was asked how conservative media could continue making the claim that Osama bin Laden supported John Kerry for president without citing any evidence to support it, he replied: "That's what journalism is. It's just all opinion. Just opinion."[20]

Berlusconi, Murdoch and others have forged a countermodel in which journalism is purely a political weapon, with any effort at fairness cast aside, except as smoke in the eyes of the ingenuous viewer. "Fact number one, France stabbed us in the back," Bill O'Reilly told his audience at Fox in a program over the split between the United States and Europe over the Iraq invasion. Of course, O'Reilly is entitled to his belief that France betrayed the United States by not backing the invasion (just as the French are entitled to believe they were merely exercising good judgment)—but neither are facts. And yet Fox insists on making Orwellian use of the language of objectivity by calling opinions facts and adopting the slogans "We report, you decide," "fair and accurate," while practicing the most wildly opinionated journalism possible. Journalists at Fox and Sinclair (as in Italy) are given orders from up top on what to cover and how to cover it: the news is meant to fit a political agenda.

Like Berlusconi, what the radical right in America has done is create its own facts. When I asked delegates at the Republican Convention in 2004 if they were troubled that no weapons of mass destruction had been found in Iraq, many of them replied: "They were there, but they sneaked them out of the country on trucks into Syria." When I asked what evidence they had of this, they simply replied: "We have our information, and you have yours." The fact that this claim had gone unreported (even by the Bush administration) was, to them, confirmation of its validity and of the malice of the liberal media.

Similarly, there are millions of Italians who firmly believe—because they have heard it repeated so often—that all of Berlusconi's legal troubles were the direct result of his entering politics, even though it can be demonstrated, facts and dates in hand, that several important investigations into his companies were well under way and executives of his companies had been arrested or indicted before he entered politics.

Bush and Berlusconi have both been enormously polarizing figures. Supporters and detractors of the two don't understand one another, have almost no common language, and live in completely separate information universes.

For years, conservatives in the United States have accused the left of "moral relativism," of denying the existence of a universal moral code, the "eternal verities" of traditional society. But it is in fact the new right who are genuine postmodernists and don't believe in any stable truth. "It's all just opinion," as Richard Viguerie put it.

Berlusconi—like the American right—has been extremely shrewd in polarizing both the media and the political realm. In Bush's world, you are either with him or with the terrorists. In Berlusconi's world, you are either with him or with the Communists. By immediately attacking any source that criticizes him, the information that source puts out becomes automatically tainted and suspect. In Berlusconi's Italy, raising issues that are in fact nonideological, like the conflict-of-interest problem, is made to seem a political attack that can be dismissed without examination. Thus even when the very moderate newspaper *Corriere della Sera* reported on Berlusconi's legal troubles or criticized specifics acts of the government, it was made into an enemy and its editor removed. In the United States, a report published by the *New York Times* can be dismissed as the product of the so-called liberal press. The notion has gained currency that the *New York Times* is to the American left what Fox News is to the right, when in fact they are entirely different.

What Berlusconi and the American right have done rather brilliantly is to eliminate the idea of any independent institutions that try to arrive at a set of agreed-upon facts—newspapers, courts, bipartisan commissions. Everything is politicized, so that the fact that a particular entity reached a conclusion that they regard as negative can be used to prove that that entity is "hostile," and therefore its conclusions can be disregarded a priori.

Although the American press has a stronger, healthier tradition of independence than the Italian press, we have begun to see here, too, some of the conflicts of interest and the blurring of lines between press and government that are so common in Italy. It came out in 2005, for example, that the Bush administration paid a prominent syndicated columnist $250,000 to sing the praises of Bush's main education program ("No Child Left Behind"). In the Florida of Governor Jeb Bush, one of the state's most prominent television journalists earned nearly a million dollars in consulting contracts from the same government agencies he covered as a journalist.[21] A Republican party operative was planted as an accredited journalist in the White House press corps, and called on frequently to ask questions sympathetic to President Bush.

Following their recent election victories, Republicans in the United States have been increasingly aggressive in promoting conservative views on public television. The head of the Corporation for Public Broadcasting, which is supposed to protect public TV from political pressure, has secretly hired consultants to monitor guests' political views, and pushed for openly conservative news programs even though studies he himself has commissioned show that a large majority of Americans find public television to be balanced and fair.

In perhaps the most troubling and systematic development, the Bush administration doubled the budget for public relations to more than $250 million and produced scores of videos that were carefully packaged to look just like television news segments. Stations across the country ran them unedited, without even explaining to viewers that they were government-produced videos rather than independent news stories. Whereas the traditional television networks were proud of their reporting and would never have aired material produced by someone else, local stations and low-budget cable outlets are only too happy to do so.

The Bush administration also produced what seemed like a news story, with a former TV reporter in the guise of a real TV reporter, that praised the benefits of the new prescription drug plan signed by President Bush just as he was hitting the campaign trial in 2004. "The segment," the *New York Times* reported, "made no mention of the many critics who decry the law as an expensive gift to the pharmaceutical industry. The Government Accountability Office found that the segment was 'not strictly factual,' that it contained 'notable omissions' amounting to 'a favorable report' about a controversial program." The "news segment" ran on three hundred stations and reached about a quarter of the U.S. population.[22]

After the photos of torture at the Iraqi prison of Abu Ghraib were published, the Defense Department created a news video that discussed the careful training of U.S. soldiers who guarded prisoners of war. "One of the most important lessons they learn is to treat prisoners strictly but fairly," the reporter said in the segment, which depicted a regimen emphasizing respect for detainees. A trainer told the reporter that military police officers were taught to "treat others as they would want to be treated." The account made no mention of Abu Ghraib or how the scandal had prompted changes in training at Fort Leonard Wood, and was run on news programs that made no mention that it was a government-produced video. We are not so far from the world of Berlusconi, marked by conflicts of interest, government pressure on state TV, and government-produced videos going straight onto the air.

The U.S. government has strict rules against conflicts of interest, and Vice President Dick Cheney reluctantly gave up part of his handsome golden parachute from the Halliburton Company, which would have given him a continuing share in the company's financial success. But these rules have not prevented large economic interests from shaping and in some cases actually writing legislation that concerns them. There is a constant revolving door through which government bureaucrats move almost immediately into lucrative jobs in the industries they were supposed to be regulating. It is reasonable to suppose that the knowledge that a modestly paid bureaucrat can instantly increase his income several fold by going over to the other side may affect the decisions he or she makes in office.

Vice President Cheney has refused to divulge who was present during the meetings of his energy planning committee because it was attended almost exclusively by industry figures with a strong interest in a progrowth and anticonservation energy policy. The no-bid contracts awarded to Cheney's former company, Halliburton, followed by evidence of massive overbilling on Halliburton's part, are not unlike many of the sweetheart deals between Berlusconi's companies and the Italian government. The numerous personal and financial ties between the Bush family and Saudi Arabia, a country that (unlike preinvasion Iraq) has in fact been a breeding ground for terrorism and has extremely close ties to Osama Bin Laden, is not so very far removed from the self-dealing and conflicts of interest of Berlusconi. Crony capitalism is not the exclusive realm of Italy.

With a more fragmented, partisan media, public trust in media has plummeted. Until the 1980s, a substantial majority of people trusted the news media. Now only about 35 percent of the American public does. That distrust is highest among those who read the least and are the least involved. A recent *USA Today* poll that showed dipping trust in media, showed, at the same time that among the "262 adults who said they had been part of a story covered by the media, the perception was far more favorable: 78% found the coverage had been accurate." Berlusconi's support is highest among those who watch the most television, read the least, are suspicious of both the media and politics. A population that is suspicious and relatively ignorant is relatively easy to manipulate.[23]

There are powerful correlations between high levels of television watching and low levels of voter turnout and other forms of civic and political participation. Our balkanized information environment reflects (or perhaps helps create) a society increasingly marked by economic class, with an active, very well informed, literate elite that knows how to get what it wants from government and gets it, and a much more passive, ill-informed majority that watches television, is suspicious of government and media, and feels that it is losing ground economically but isn't sure what to do about it.

George Bush beat John Kerry among white working-class voters by an astonishing twenty-three point margin. Average wages during the Reagan and two Bush administrations have fallen considerably for working class men without a college education. Their economic position has slipped both in absolute terms (declining wages) and in relative terms as the gap between rich and poor has reached a point not seen since the stock market crash of 1929. Their position has weakened largely for structural reasons—globalization, automation and deunionization: union membership has declined from about one-third of the U.S. labor force to a mere 12 percent. Republican administrations have openly favored economic policies beneficial to the very rich—eliminating estate taxes, cutting taxes on investment income—and hostile to working people: raising the minimum wage, extension of unemployment benefits in times of recession, programs to retrain workers in declining industries. And yet, working-class voters have turned against Democrats in part because they may figure that the Democrats, whatever their intentions, have been unable to reverse this deep structural decline. As a result, they appear to be deciding on how to vote based on noneconomic factors: the war on terrorism, gun control legislation, abortion, religion, gay marriage, the personal appeal of the candidate—issues fought on the symbolic level, where the right has proved extremely effective. As a typical Texas voter, a working-class man of forty-nine, told the *Washington Post*, Bush is "a man's man, a manly man," while describing Al Gore as a "little whiny baby."[24]

In virtually all American elections since the advent of television, the more "likable" candidate has ended up winning. Ronald Reagan's avuncular charm and celebrity aura allowed the Republicans to pass a harsh free-market agenda that they might otherwise have been unable to push through. Reagan's frequent misstatements, like Bush's mangled syntax and Berlusconi's gaffes, while making them the source of ridicule to intellectuals, are actually part of their interclass appeal. Voters surveyed consider Bush as more "like them," even though they have doubts about whether he has their best interest in mind.

In this highly depoliticized, apathetic environment, the democratic practice has become dangerously close to a formality. Voters are asked every four years (five in Italy) to vote in presidential elections. The candidate with the most money and the highest "likability" ratings in television focus groups generally wins. In the United States, mobilizing a mere 25 percent of eligible voters is enough to win the prize. But both Bush and Berlusconi have been able to use their elections as a mandate to push through agendas with which the majorities of both of their countries actually disagree.

The concentration of media, the decline of reading and civic participation, decreasing identification with political parties, the role of celebrity in politics, the appeal of antipolitics, declining unionization, and the rising gap between rich and poor are growing realities in many advanced capitalist democracies. They create new and troubling possibilities for governments that are run by and for the very few with an enormous media machine at their disposal, who need to win only a tentative nod of approval from an increasingly indifferent and ill-informed public every four or five years in order to continue with their business.

Thus, Silvio Berlusconi as a political figure may come and go, but the Berlusconi phenomenon is, in all likelihood, here to stay. He may appear at times a caricature, but in fact he is a reflection of ourselves in a fun-house mirror, our features distorted and exaggerated but distinctly recognizable.

AFTERWORD

It seems sadly fitting that Silvio Berlusconi's second government ended in a gigantic mess, an election whose result promises only to deepen the national sense of polarization, bitterness and paralysis. His rival, Romano Prodi, appears to have pulled out a narrow victory that will allow him to put together a shaky majority in parliament. The election was so close—the reported outcome changing repeatedly in the hours after the vote—that Berlusconi challenged its legitimacy and demanded alternately a recount and a place in a new, broad coalition that would include his party. The fact that Berlusconi's own government administered the elections did not prevent him from charging voter fraud, thereby scaring up ghosts of the disputed U.S. presidential election of 2000.

A weak government, presiding over a sharply divided country, will permit Berlusconi to continue to play an important role in blocking any measure that he opposes. His position is far stronger because of a recent electoral law passed in his government's twilight. A few months before the April 2006 election, the Berlusconi government—after studying polls that indicated the center-left would win a substantial majority in parliament with the country's winner-take-all electoral system—decided to overhaul this system and return to the proportional method that Italian voters had roundly rejected in a popular referendum in 1993. In the post–World War II period, the old, proportional system was thought to have encouraged a plethora of small parties, unstable majorities, short-lived revolving-door governments and endless horse-trading among coalition partners, all of which fostered corruption and lack of program-matic clarity. Berlusconi came to power for the first time in 1994 thanks to the new, majority-rule system, and he once declared that this majoritarian system was his "religion." But he lost his religion when studies showed his coalition doing better in early 2006 with the proportional system. At the very minimum, the center-right calculated, even if the center-left can-didates won, the proportional system would fragment their vote and leave them with a fractious, unstable coalition that could not govern without the center-right's help. In a moment of shocking candor, Berlusconi's minis-ter for reforms, Roberto Calderoli, admitted, "The election law? I wrote it, but it's a *porcata*"—a vulgar term that might be translated as "piece of crap." It was the move of a retreating army that decides to blow up the bridges, poison the wells, and sow the fields with salt in order to make life difficult for the conquerors.

Although a defeat, the April election results must count as a consider-able achievement from Berlusconi's point of view. A few months before the election, most polls showed him behind by eight to ten points, and even on the day of the vote, exit polls gave the center-left a comfortable margin of victory of four to five percent. Despite waging a lackluster campaign, the center-left appeared to enjoy one insurmountable advan-tage: extremely widespread dissatisfaction with the performance of the Berlusconi government. The latest economic numbers, which came out as the campaign kicked off, confirmed that Italy had experienced zero growth in 2005, the fifth straight year of virtual economic stagnation. In five years, the Italian economy grew by only 3.2 percent, the worst of all countries in the European Union and below half the average for the rest of Europe (7.1 percent). Italy's standard of living fell by seven percent between 2001 and 2006, and productivity by more than ten.

During the 2001 election campaign, while signing his "contract with the Italians" on national TV, Berlusconi made five specific promises to

Italian voters. If he failed to maintain at least four of the five, he said, he would not run for office again. Berlusconi honored only one of the promises fully (raising minimum old-age pensions to a million lire a month, or about $600), succeeded to only a small degree in two others, and failed entirely in the remaining two. (As far as the four other promises: Crime has gone up; taxes have barely budged; an estimated 600,000 jobs were created, instead of 1.5 million promised; and Berlusconi has initiated a mere fraction of the public works he said he would.) The tame journalists chosen to moderate two formal debates before the April elections were too polite to mention the contract, but the perception that Berlusconi failed to deliver on his promises was nonetheless deeply rooted, polls showed.

So how to explain the fact that Berlusconi's coalition was able to garner 49.7 percent of the popular vote—just 25,000 votes less than the center-left's 49.8 percent?

Officially, the election campaign began with the dissolution of parliament on February 10, but it really commenced a month earlier, with a massive media blitz by Berlusconi. On one typical night, he was on television virtually all evening, moving straight from one network's principal news talk show to an entertainment program where he spoke of the accomplishments of his soccer team. He spent a lot of time on subjects other than politics, quite aware that the undecided voters, those he was most concerned about reaching, said they disliked politics. And so to them he offered himself as the likable family man, trotting out his ninety-five-year-old mother and chatting about soccer, gardening and his sleeping habits. ("One night I sleep with Veronica, another with my two daughters, the third with [his son] Luigi, who tangles up his legs with mine.")

Playing good cop, bad cop, Berlusconi also orchestrated extraordinarily vicious attacks against his adversaries. In early January, the Berlusconi family newspaper, *Il Giornale*, published a series of stories alleging massive corruption among the leaders of the center-left. Specifically, the paper printed wiretapped phone conversations between Piero Fassino, leader of the Democrats of the Left, and Giovanni Consorte, the head of an insurance company made up of left-wing cooperatives, conferring about a bank takeover. "So, do we own the bank?" Fassino asked Consorte. There was no evidence of wrongdoing on Fassino's part, or of any money changing hands—Fassino was simply taking sides in the negotiations. Berlusconi himself had done as much or more for other players in the same takeover, meeting repeatedly with one financier who called a partner of his to explain that he was with the prime minister, who was doing everything he could to help them. This same financier now says that he paid bribes to Forza Italia politicians close to Berlusconi. But Berlusconi's conversations did not receive much attention in the Italian media. The notion of his acting improperly was not news, while unsavory behavior on the left allowed him to insist that members of the opposition were no better than he—were indeed worse, because they were hypocrites, claiming moral superiority while playing the same corrupt games.

Largely overlooked was the fact that the publication and leaking of these wiretapped conversations directly violated a law that Berlusconi himself had fought for and passed. Embarrassed again and again by revelations of wrongdoing in his company and his government, Berlusconi had supported a law strictly forbidding the wiretapping and the publication of wiretaps of members of parliament. Police were not allowed to wiretap a member of parliament even if, by chance, a dangerous criminal who was under surveillance happened to telephone a politician in the course of the commission of a crime. (There are numerous examples of Mafia members chatting with politicians that have been disallowed by the courts.) According to the new law, such wiretapped conversations were not to be transcribed and placed in the public record. The conversations between Fassino and Consorte, which existed only in audio form on a few CD-ROMs, must have found their way to Berlusconi's newspaper through a helpful hand in government—a gross abuse of power that Berlusconi had approved severe legislation to prevent. Such a leak on the eve of an election might itself, in a country with a genuinely free press, have become a major story and campaign issue.

Characteristically, Berlusconi's appearances on TV were almost always in situations where he didn't have to answer questions and where the interviewers were his own employees, who allowed him free rein. In one case, for a program on one of his networks, Berlusconi arrived with his own director, who arranged the set and worked out the questions with the show's nominal host.

In the first three weeks of January, Berlusconi appeared on television for a total of five hours and twenty-three minutes, while his opponent, Prodi, was on for only twenty-one minutes, more than a fifteen-to-one advantage in terms of airtime. Berlusconi used this advantage to set the terms of the debate for the campaign.

After parliament was dissolved and the election campaign officially began, Berlusconi's tactics seemed to change. In theory, all the national television networks—the public stations as well as Berlusconi's net-works—were to comply with "equal time" norms that guaranteed equal access to the principal candidates. Berlusconi's behavior appeared to grow more extravagant.

In response to criticisms of the modest accomplishments of his gov-ernment, he said, "Only Napoleon did more." On another occasion he stated, "Churchill freed us from the Nazis, Berlusconi is freeing us from the Communists." And then, as a grand finale, he referred to himself as "the Jesus Christ of politics," alluding to the patience and forbearance he displayed toward his enemies. Before an audience of devout Catholics, he vowed to abstain from sex until after the election. All this within one week.

These wild comments were much lampooned in the foreign press as further signs of Berlusconi's buffoonery. But the media missed the method in Berlusconi's madness. By traditional political standards, such statements would seem to be mistakes. In Berlusconi's world of celebrity politics, however, there is no such thing as bad publicity—it all translates into audience and ratings. And his media blitz of January and February helped him slash his center-left opponent's lead from eight percent to about three percent. If you look back over the front pages of the major opposition newspaper, *La Repubblica*, you will see that the most frequent word in its banner headlines between January and April 2006 is over-whelmingly "BERLUSCONI."

Essentially, Berlusconi has transformed Italian life into the world's longest-running reality television show: every day's lead news—flattering or unflattering, important or trivial—is about Berlusconi. The country has taken on the eerie quality of *The Truman Show*, the 1998 movie in which a television producer raises a child (played by Jim Carrey) in an artificial town that is nothing but an enormous stage set, which the boy (then the man) believes to be real. Viewers around the world, meanwhile, are glued to their sets watching his every action from childhood to maturity, twenty-four hours a day.

In the final month of the campaign, it seemed as if Berlusconi might stumble and fall. He did surprisingly poorly in the first of the two debates. Because he was behind in the polls, he reluctantly accepted strict U.S.-style rules for the debates, with thirty-second questions, limits of two and a half minutes for answers, and the cameras fixed in front of the two candidates. With both private and public TV in Berlusconi's hands, his opponent Prodi wanted to minimize the discretion of camera operators and producers. Used to holding forth at will, Berlusconi looked tense and angry, like a caged animal forced to respect the imposed rules. The man known as Mr. Television violated some of the most elementary rules of broadcasting. Inexplicably, instead of looking into the camera when he addressed his audience, he looked down and doodled on a piece of paper, leaving a very strange impression of distraction and unease. In a final three minutes in which he was allowed to make an appeal to voters, instead of explaining why people should vote for him, he complained bitterly about the rules of the debate, saying that within such limits he couldn't explain himself or complete a point. Thus he violated the cardinal rule of debating: basically he conceded publicly that he had lost the debate.

It looked as if Berlusconi was alone as never before and on the brink of catastrophic defeat. Many moderate and conservative institutions that supported him in 2001 had recently turned against him. Confindustria, the Confederation of Italian Industry, elected a new president, Luca Cordero di Montezemolo, who had been harshly critical of the government's economic policy, as had the newspaper that Confindustria owns, *Il Sole 24 Ore,* the country's leading business paper. In a highly unusual move, the *Corriere della Sera,* pillar of the Northern economic establishment, endorsed Prodi and the center-left, complaining that Berlusconi had governed chiefly for his own interests and done too little for the country. The Fiat-owned *La Stampa* changed editors and adopted a much more critical tone toward Berlusconi. Even two major allies, Gianfranco Fini, of the National Alliance, and Pierferdinando Casini, went out of their way to distance themselves from him. Fini said that Berlusconi was wrong to keep telling voters that everything was great, while Casini objected to his "monarchical conception" of their alliance. Berlusconi denounced the pair as rats jumping from a sinking ship.

In some ways, the situation of "everyone against Berlusconi," may have been rather congenial to him. It accentuated the *Truman Show* effect: everything was *still* about Berlusconi. And despite his being the head of the government and one of the main beneficiaries of the Italian political system over the past thirty years, Berlusconi has relished the role of the outsider who takes on the establishment. For years he has insisted that the *poteri forti,* the powerful forces of the Italian establishment, were against him, and now it was actually true.

After the first debate, his tone turned even angrier. "From this day forward, we change strategies. We go on the attack. . . . I will use all my ammunition in the last week of the campaign, when twenty-five percent of the undecided voters make up their minds." He began to do just that, walking off the set of a talk show on a RAI channel to make the point that the government channels were controlled by the Communists, not by him. At a Confindustria meeting, rather than use honeyed words to win over reluctant business leaders, he leveled a frontal assault of unprecedented ferocity. Among other things, he insisted that the growing array of forces represented a threat to Italian democracy. "The left with all its newspapers has invented an economic crisis that doesn't exist, in order to seize power. . . . The *Corriere della Sera, La Stampa, Il Sole 24 Ore, La Repubblica, Il Messaggero* . . . tell me this isn't a danger to democracy."

Looking more and more desperate, Berlusconi told stories about how the Communist Chinese "boiled babies" to use as fertilizer; he shouted obscenities at a protester, called Prodi an idiot, and remarked that he had too much regard for the intelligence of Italians to believe that they would be such *coglioni*—literally "testicles," roughly translated "dickheads"—to vote for the center-left. In his usual manner, Berlusconi at first denied that he had used the vulgarity, but when his comment was replayed on tape he insisted the left didn't know how to take a joke. Center-left voters began carrying signs announcing, "I am a *coglione*!"

At an appearance in Naples, Berlusconi's advisers told him to sound a more conciliatory note, but he could not restrain himself. "Do you want to be governed by people who idolize Stalin, Lenin, Mao and Pol Pot? Do you want to be governed by people who would remove crucifixes from classrooms? . . . In Holland the left kills disabled children, and in Spain it allows homosexuals to adopt babies!" A group of neofascist supporters yelled, *"Duce! Duce!"* And Berlusconi could not resist bringing out the c-word: "We will win because we are not *coglioni*!"

One might have thought that insulting half the electorate might backfire and alienate many moderate, undecided voters tired of the divisiveness of Berlusconi's Italy. How is it that a candidate with so many strikes against him was able to fight his opponent to a virtual draw?

One simple, though incomplete, explanation is Berlusconi's continued domination of television. Even with the "equal time" rules in effect, he and his center-right allies received about sixty percent of the coverage on the state channels; on the Berlusconi-owned channels, predictably, he received vastly more. His own stations, in flagrant violation of the Communications Authority rules, happily paid the modest fines and went on broadcasting as they saw fit. In an election as close as this, determined evidently by undecided voters who began paying attention to the campaign only at its end, this may have accounted for a decisive few percentage points.

Control of television is a necessary but insufficient explanation. It is equally true that Romano Prodi and the center-left failed to give Italians strong positive reasons to vote for them. They seemed to think it was enough not to be Berlusconi. Prodi, an economist and a former Christian Democrat with the unassuming and uncharismatic demeanor of a parish priest, tried to play to this sentiment, promising a more "serene" and "unified" Italy, and avoiding attacks on Berlusconi. In the first debate, in response to a question about Berlusconi's conflicts of interest, Prodi failed to cite any of the dozens of laws that were crafted expressly for his opponent's interests or from which his business has profited. He likewise failed to describe the disastrous economic figures of the Berlusconi years or to explain the comparatively better performance of his own previous government. Why should people vote for a candidate who can't give them good reasons for voting for him?

The fact that the Berlusconi–Prodi duel forced Italians to choose between the same tired old faces they were presented with in 1996 (when Prodi won) sent a depressing signal to many Italians eager for positive change. Both the left and the right conveyed the impression of a tired country in desperate need of fresh blood and new ideas to confront the serious problems of its relative decline. "Politicians are like detergents, they're all the same," one Roman shopkeeper told me recently. Not particularly persuaded by either side, Italian voters fell back on their traditional voting patterns, more or less equally divided between right and left.

Even in defeat, Berlusconi dominated and dictated the terms of the debate, and he may continue to do so for some time. And while he will probably remain in the opposition for the moment, he still has enormous power to condition or block the movement of the country—a nation of 58 million people held hostage to the interests of one man and his company. And so the Berlusconi Show rolls on.

NOTES

Introduction

1. Paolo Pagani, *Forza Italia: Come È Nato il Movimento Che in 5 Mesi Ha Cambiato la Politica Italiana* (Novara: Boroli, 2003), 33.

2. Ibid., 69.

3. Author interview in Alexander Stille, "The World's Greatest Salesman," *The New York Times Magazine*, March 17, 1996.

Chapter One. The Miracle Worker

1. Author interview.

2. Author interviews.

3. Stefano E. D'Anna and Gigi Moncalvo, *Berlusconi in Concert* (London: Otzium, 1994), 153.

4. Author interview.

5. Aldo Vincent, ed., *Il Libro Azzurro di Berlusconi: Battute, Aforismi, Opinioni, Barzellette* (Valentano: Scipioni, 2003), 26.

6. Author interview in Stille, "The World's Greatest Salesman."

7. *La Repubblica*, May 28, 2004.

8. Vincent, *Il Libro Azzurro di Berlusconi*, 25. http://www.vacasflacas.it/Pagina 016%20Pensierie%20e%20parole/Paroladipresidente.htm.

9. Pino Corrias, Massimo Gramellini, and Curzio Maltese, *1994: Colpo Grosso* (*Storie della Storia d'Italia*) (Milan: Baldini & Castoldi, 1994), 94.

10. D'Anna and Moncalvo, *Berlusconi in Concert*, 159.

11. Corrias, Gramellini, and Maltese, *1994: Colpo Grosso,* 93.

12. *La Repubblica,* April 11, 2001.

13. *Una Storia Italiana* (Milan: Mondadori, 2001), 6. Giuseppe Fiori, *Il Venditore: Storia di Silvio Berlusconi e della Fininvest* (Milan: Garzanti, 1995).

14. *Una Storia Italiana,* 13.

15. Ibid., 65.

16. Ibid., 10.

17. Ibid., 9.

18. Fiori, *Il Venditore,* 24.

19. Ibid., 27–28.

20. Ibid., 29–31.

21. Ibid., 32.

22. D'Anna and Moncalvo, *Berlusconi in Concert,* 183–85.

23. Corrias, Gramellini, and Maltese, *1994: Colpo Grosso,* 47.

24. Author interview.

25. Giovanni Ruggeri, *Berlusconi: Gli Affari del Presidente* (Milan: Kaos, 1994), 30.

26. Ibid., 31.

27. Ibid., 32.

28. Ibid., 34.

29. Ibid., 97.

30. Ibid.

31. Alessandro Gilioli, *Forza Italia: La Storia, gli Uomini, i Misteri* (Bergamo: Arnoldi, 1994), 98.

Chapter Two. The Thirteenth Guest

1. Fiori, *Il Venditore,* 67–68.

2. Procura della Repubblica di Palermo, Direzione Distrettuale Antimafia, *L'Onore di Dell'Utri: I Legami del Berlusconiano Marcello Dell'Utri con Cosa Nostra, nella Richiesta di Rinvio a Giudizio per Concorso in Associazione Mafiosa* (Milan: Kaos, 1997), 38–39.

3. Ibid., 91.

4. Ibid., 202.

5. Ibid., 87.

6. *Il Giornale,* March 15, 2001.

7. Maurizio Calvi, interview with Paolo Borsellino, *L'Espresso,* April 8, 1994.

8. Marco Travaglio, *Montanelli e il Cavaliere: Storia di un Grande e di un Piccolo Uomo* (Milan: Garzanti, 2004), 16.

9. *Il Giornale,* March 15, 2001.

10. Procura della Repubblica di Palermo, Direzione Distrettuale Antimafia, *L'Onore di Dell'Utri*, 33–34.

11. Ibid., 81.

12. Ibid., 45.

13. Ibid., 41.

14. Leo Sisti and Peter Gomez, *L'Intoccabile: Berlusconi e Cosa Nostra* (Milan: Kaos, 1997), 54.

15. Procura della Repubblica di Palermo, Direzione Distrettuale Antimafia, *L'Onore di Dell'Utri*, 68.

16. Ibid., 70.

17. Ibid., 85.

18. Calvi, interview with Paolo Borsellino, *L'Espresso*. Also found in Elio Veltri and Marco Travaglio, *L'Odore dei Soldi* (Rome: Editori Riuniti, 2001).

19. Procura della Repubblica di Palermo, Direzione Distrettuale Antimafia, *L'Onore di Dell'Utri*, 117.

20. Ibid., 85.

21. Ibid., 68–69.

22. The most detailed treatment of Berlusconi's early finances has appeared in Giovanni Ruggeri and Mario Guarino, *Berlusconi: Inchiesta sul Signor TV* (Milan: Kaos, 1994). For the Swiss connection, see Ruggeri, *Berlusconi*, 21–53, and Ruggeri and Guarino, *Inchiesta sul Signor TV*, 49–75.

23. Veltri and Travaglio, *L'Odore dei Soldi*, 100–135.

Chapter Three. Television (and Money)

1. Corrias, Gramellini, and Maltese, *1994: Colpo Grosso*, 71.

2. General background and many specifics about the history of Italian television can be found in Aldo Grasso, *Storia della Televisione Italiana: I 50 Anni della Televisione* (Milan: Garzanti, 2004).

3. Author interview.

4. Claudio Ferretti, Umberto Broccoli, and Barbara Scaramucci, *Mamma RAI: Storia e Storie del Servizio Pubblico Radiotelevisivo* (Florence: Le Monnier, 1997).

5. Grasso, *Storia della Televisione Italiana*, n.p.

6. Author interview.

7. Fiori, *Il Venditore*, 90.

8. Author interview.

9. Grasso, *Storia della Televisione Italiana*, xv.

10. Author interview.

11. D'Anna and Moncalvo, *Berlusconi in Concert*, 148.

12. Corrias, Gramellini, and Maltese, *1994: Colpo Grosso*, 153.

13. Fiori, *Il Venditore*, 93.

14. Author interview.

15. Vincent, *Il Libro Azzurro di Berlusconi*, 39.

16. Author interview.

17. Fiori, *Il Venditore*, 97.

18. Marcella Andreoli, Romano Cantore, Antonio Carlucci, and Maurizio Tortorella, eds., *Tangentopoli: Le Carte Che Scottano* (Milan: Mondadori, 1993).

19. Travaglio, *Montanelli e il Cavaliere*, 24.

20. Author interview.

21. Fiori, *Il Venditore*, 109.

22. For Berlusconi's involvement with the P2, see ibid., 45–63, and Ruggeri and Guarino, *Berlusconi*, 67–95.

23. Corrias, Gramellini, and Maltese, *1994: Colpo Grosso*, 71.

24. Fiori, *Il Venditore*, 60–62.

25. Ibid., 56.

26. Ruggeri and Guarino, *Berlusconi*, 10.

27. Ibid., 9.

28. Author interview.

Chapter Four. Professione: Amicizia *(Profession: Friendship)*

1. D'Anna and Moncalvo, *Berlusconi in Concert*, 82.

2. All quotations of Fabrizio are from author interviews.

3. D'Anna and Moncalvo, *Berlusconi in Concert*, 82–83.

4. Ibid.

5. Ibid., 67.

6. Ibid., 87.

7. Ibid., 68.

8. Corrias, Gramellini, and Maltese, *1994: Colpo Grosso*, 153.

9. D'Anna and Moncalvo, *Berlusconi in Concert*, 154.

10. Ibid.

11. Ibid., 263.

12. Ibid., 82–83.

13. Travaglio, *Montanelli e il Cavaliere*, 30–31.

14. Ibid., 39.

15. Ruggeri and Guarino, *Berlusconi,* 176.

16. Ibid., 180.

17. Travaglio, *Montanelli e il Cavaliere,* 24.

18. Ibid., 30–31.

19. Ibid.

20. Gianni Barbacetto, *B.: Tutte le Carte del Presidente* (Milan: Tropea, 2004), 139.

21. Ibid., 138–39.

22. Alexander Stille, *Excellent Cadavers: The Mafia and the Death of the First Italian Republic* (New York: Vintage, 1996), 204.

23. Gianni Barbacetto, Peter Gomez, and Marco Travaglio, *Mani Pulite: La Vera Storia da Mario Chiesa a Silvio Berlusconi* (Rome: Editori Riuniti, 2002), 259–60.

24. D'Anna and Moncalvo, *Berlusconi in Concert,* 174.

25. Corrias, Gramellini, and Maltese, *1994: Colpo Grosso,* 153.

26. D'Anna and Moncalvo, *Berlusconi in Concert,* 113.

27. Ibid., 75–76.

28. Barbacetto, *B.: Tutte le Carte del Presidente,* 139.

29. D'Anna and Moncalvo, *Berlusconi in Concert,* 37.

30. Ibid., 82–83.

31. Author interviews.

32. Corrias, Gramellini, and Maltese, *1994: Colpo Grosso,* 52.

33. Travaglio, *Montanelli e il Cavaliere,* 44.

34. D'Anna and Moncalvo, *Berlusconi in Concert,* 176.

35. Author interviews.

36. Barbacetto, *B.: Tutte le Carte del Presidente,* 138–39.

37. Procura della Repubblica di Palermo, Direzione Distrettuale Antimafia, *L'Onore di Dell'Utri,* 168.

38. *MicroMega,* 3 (2004), 88–89.

39. Ample account of Dell'Utri's affairs in Catania is given in Procura della Repubblica di Palermo, Direzione Distrettuale Antimafia, *L'Onore di Dell'Utri,* 211–37.

40. Ibid., 225.

Chapter Five. The Pax Televisiva *and the Expansion of Fininvest*

1. *Corriere della Sera,* November 10, 1986.

2. Fiori, *Il Venditore,* 127.

3. Testimony of Enrico Manca, Procura della Repubblica di Milano, N. 11749/97 R.G. notizie di reato/Mod. 21.

4. Tribunale Ordinario di Milano, N. RGNR 11749/9, Sentenza N. 11069/03, November 22, 2003.

5. For a full treatment of Berlusconi's investments in France, see Fiori, *Il Venditore*, 139–48.

6. *The Economist*, May 20, 1989.

7. *The Guardian*, August 6, 1990; on Berlusconi's illegal ownership, see *El País*, October 12, 1994.

8. Author interview.

9. Fiori, *Il Venditore*, 132–38.

10. D'Anna and Moncalvo, *Berlusconi in Concert*, 375.

11. Ibid., 373.

12. Ibid., 165.

13. Ibid., 138.

14. Ibid., 189.

15. Ibid., 146.

16. Ibid., 125.

17. Ibid., 143.

18. Barbacetto, Gomez, and Travaglio, *Mani Pulite*, 133.

19. Ibid., 403.

20. D'Anna and Moncalvo, *Berlusconi in Concert*, 143.

21. Barbacetto, Gomez, and Travaglio, *Mani Pulite*, 135.

22. Ibid., 403.

23. D'Anna and Moncalvo, *Berlusconi in Concert*, 143.

Chapter Six. Operation Clean Hands and the Entry into Politics

1. Federico Orlando, *Il Sabato Andavamo ad Arcore: La Vera Storia, Documenti e Ragioni, del Divorzio tra Berlusconi e Montanelli* (Bergamo: Larus, 1995), 94.

2. Travaglio, *Montanelli e il Cavaliere*, 59.

3. Barbacetto, Gomez, and Travaglio, *Mani Pulite*, 11–17.

4. Stille, *Excellent Cadavers*, 350–51.

5. Barbacetto, Gomez, and Travaglio, *Mani Pulite*, 32.

6. Travaglio, *Montanelli e il Cavaliere*, 51–52.

7. Ibid., 52.

8. Ibid., 53.

9. Orlando, *Il Sabato Andavamo ad Arcore*, 58.

10. Veltri and Travaglio, *L'Odore dei Soldi*, 72.

11. Barbacetto, *B.: Tutte le Carte del Presidente*, 320.

12. Veltri and Travaglio, *L'Odore dei Soldi*, 72.

13. Orlando, *Il Sabato Andavamo ad Arcore*, 98.

14. Travaglio, *Montanelli e il Cavaliere*, 59–60.

15. Veltri and Travaglio, *L'Odore dei Soldi*, 76.

16. Barbacetto, Gomez, and Travaglio, *Mani Pulite*, 132.

17. Orlando, *Il Sabato Andavamo ad Arcore*, 49.

18. Corrias, Gramellini, and Maltese, *1994: Colpo Grosso*, 51.

19. Ibid., 96.

20. Ibid., 94.

21. Ibid.

22. Author interview.

23. Orlando, *Il Sabato Andavamo ad Arcore*, 94.

24. Ibid., 98

25. Ibid., 96.

26. Ibid., 119.

27. Ibid., 113.

28. Barbacetto, Gomez, and Travaglio, *Mani Pulite*, 35.

29. Corrias, Gramellini, and Maltese, *1994: Colpo Grosso*, 50.

30. Orlando, *Il Sabato Andavamo ad Arcore*, 124–26.

31. Ibid., 129–30.

32. Ibid., 127.

33. Ibid., 120.

34. Pagani, *Forza Italia*, 69.

35. Ibid., 64.

36. Ibid., 19.

37. Travaglio, *Montanelli e il Cavaliere*, 86.

38. Ibid., 88.

39. Ibid.

40. Ibid., 89.

41. Ibid., 92.

42. Ibid., 93.

43. Ibid., 95.

44. Ibid., 99.

45. Orlando, *Il Sabato Andavamo ad Arcore*, 206.

46. Corrias, Gramellini, and Maltese, *1994: Colpo Grosso*, 57.

47. Pagani, *Forza Italia*, 19.

Chapter Seven. Berlusconi Enters the Playing Field

1. Silvio Berlusconi, "La Discesa in Campo," 1994. http://www.forza-italia.it/10anni/discesaincampo.htm.

2. Gilioli, *Forza Italia*, 189.

3. Ibid.

4. Berlusconi, *La Discesa in Campo*.

5. Ibid.

6. *Corriere della Sera*, January 27, 1994.

7. Corrias, Gramellini, and Maltese, *1994: Colpo Grosso*, 44.

8. *Corriere della Sera*, February 22, 1994.

9. Pagani, *Forza Italia*, 25.

10. Corrias, Gramellini, and Maltese, *1994: Colpo Grosso*, 32.

11. Author interview.

12. Pagani, *Forza Italia*, 20.

13. Ibid., 74.

14. Ibid., 65.

15. Vincent, *Il Libro Azzurro di Berlusconi*, 31.

16. Ibid., 30.

17. Pagani, *Forza Italia*, 61.

18. *Corriere della Sera*, February 1, 1994.

19. Gianni Statera, *Il Volto Seduttivo del Potere: Berlusconi, i Media, il Consenso* (Rome: SEAM, 1994), 118.

20. Ibid., 140.

21. Giacomo Sani and Antonio Nizzoli, *Quaderni di Scienza Politica*, 5, no. 3 (1997).

22. Giacomo Sani and Paolo Segatti, "Programmi, Media e Opinione Pubblica," *Rivista Italiana di Scienza Politica*, 26, no. 3.

23. Barbacetto, Gomez, and Travaglio, *Mani Pulite*, 212.

24. Ibid., 214.

25. *Corriere della Sera*, February 1 and February 12, 1994.

26. Barbacetto, Gomez, and Travaglio, *Mani Pulite*, 219.

27. Corrias, Gramellini, and Maltese, *1994: Colpo Grosso*, 67.

28. Barbacetto, Gomez, and Travaglio, *Mani Pulite*, 216.

29. *La Stampa*, October 28, 1995.

30. *La Repubblica*, April 29, 1994.

31. Procura della Repubblica di Palermo, Direzione Distrettuale Antimafia, *L'Onore di Dell'Utri*, 202.

32. *La Repubblica*, March 23, 1994.

33. Corrias, Gramellini, and Maltese, *1994: Colpo Grosso*, 89.

34. *La Repubblica*, March 29, 1994.

Chapter Eight. Berlusconi in Power

1. Mario Caciagli and Piergiorgio Corbetta, eds., *Le Ragioni dell'Elettore* (Bologna: Il Mulino, 2002), 172.

2. Ilvo Diamanti and Renato Mannheimer, eds., *Milano a Roma: Guida all'Italia Elettorale del 1994* (Rome: Donzelli, 1994), 42.

3. Caciagli and Corbetta, *Le Ragioni dell'Elettore*, 133.

4. Sani and Segatti, "Programmi, Media e Opinione Pubblica."

5. Elio Veltri, *Le Toghe Rosse* (Milan: Baldini & Castoldi, 2002), 71.

6. Enrico Marro and Edoardo Vigna, *Sette Mesi di Berlusconi* (Rome: Ediesse, 1995), 48.

7. Federico Orlando, *Fucilate Montanelli* (Rome: Editori Riuniti, 2001), 24.

8. Corrias, Gramellini, and Maltese, *1994: Colpo Grosso*, 80.

9. *La Stampa*, September 19, 1994. *La Repubblica*, September 20, 1994.

10. Author interview.

11. Veltri, *Le Toghe Rosse*, 27.

12. Barbacetto, Gomez, and Travaglio, *Mani Pulite*, 212.

13. Ibid., 220.

14. Gilioli, *Forza Italia*, 98.

15. Barbacetto, Gomez, and Travaglio, *Mani Pulite*, 229.

16. Ibid., 234.

17. Ibid., 236.

18. Ibid., 239.

19. Ibid., 244.

20. Ibid., 243.

21. Ibid.

22. Ibid., 245.

23. Ibid., 247.

24. Ibid., 252.

25. Ibid., 285.

26. Michele Caccavale, *Il Grande Inganno* (Milan: Kaos, 1997), 62.

27. Marco Travaglio, *Il Pollaio delle Libertà: Detti, Disdetti e Contraddetti* (Florence: Vallecchi, 1995), 53.

28. Caccavale, *Il Grande Inganno*, 96.

29. Ibid.

30. Giuseppe Ricci, *La Teledittatura: Il Berlusconismo: Neo-Civilizzazione Sociale e Consenso Politico* (Milan: Kaos, 2003), 121–22.

31. *MicroMega*, 4 (May 8, 2001).

Chapter Nine. Berlusconi out of Power: Counterpunching

1. *La Repubblica*, July 12, 1997.

2. Alessandro Corbi and Pietro Criscuoli, *Berlusconate* (Rome: Nutrimenti, 2003).

3. Vincent, *Il Libro Azzurro di Berlusconi*.

4. *Corriere della Sera*, June 30, 2001.

5. Caccavale, *Il Grande Inganno*, 104.

6. Ibid., 110.

7. Ibid., 106.

8. Orlando, *Fucilate Montanelli*, 30.

9. Caccavale, *Il Grande Inganno*, 108.

10. Barbacetto, Gomez, and Travaglio, *Mani Pulite*, 272.

11. Ibid., 318.

12. Ibid., 368.

13. *La Repubblica*, December 23, 1995.

14. Barbacetto, Gomez, and Travaglio, *Mani Pulite*, 526.

15. Ibid., 524–26.

16. Ibid., 524.

17. Ibid., 525.

18. Ibid., 401.

19. Ibid., 425.

20. Ibid., 426.

21. Ibid., 441.

22. Author interview.

23. Barbacetto, Gomez, and Travaglio, *Mani Pulite*, 446.

Chapter Ten. Berlusconi's Dead: Long Live Berlusconi!

1. For an account of the 1996 elections, see Alexander Stille, "Why the Left Won in Italy," *The New York Review of Books*, June 6, 1996.

2. Ibid.

3. *La Stampa*, August 27, 1996, and Roberto Zaccaria, *Televisione: Dal Monopolio al Monopolio* (Milan: Baldini & Castoldi, 2003), 25.

4. Veltri, *Le Toghe Rosse*, 132.

5. *La Repubblica*, October 4, 2002.

6. Veltri, *Le Toghe Rosse*, 110–113.

7. Ibid., 55.

8. Ibid.

9. Barbacetto, Gomez, and Travaglio, *Mani Pulite*, 489.

10. Ibid., 511.

11. Ibid., 514.

12. Ibid., 500.

13. *Corriere della Sera*, November 10, 1997.

14. Barbacetto, Gomez, and Travaglio, *Mani Pulite*, 223.

15. Leo Sisti and Peter Gomez, *L'Intoccabile*, 259–61.

16. *Il Manifesto*, May 23, 1996.

17. Ibid.

18. Camera dei Deputati, Domanda di Autorizzazione all'Esecuzione di Ordinanza di Custodia Cautelare, Doc. IV, N. 17, N. 17a., March 9, 1999.

19. Gilioli, *Forza Italia*, 106.

20. Author interview.

21. Alexander Stille, "Making Way for Berlusconi," *The New York Review of Books*, June 21, 2001.

22. Alexander Stille, "The Emperor of the Air," *The Nation*, November 29, 1999.

23. *MicroMega*, 4 (May 8, 2001).

Chapter Eleven. Triumph

1. All quotations here are from *Una Storia Italiana*.

2. *La Repubblica*, April 11, 2001.

3. *Financial Times*, April 14, 2001.

4. Caciagli e Corbetta, *Le Ragioni dell'Elettore*, 245.

5. Peter Gomez and Marco Travaglio, *Regime* (Milan: Rizzoli, 2004), 30.

6. Ibid., 31.

7. Ibid., 33.

8. Ibid., 102.

9. Ibid., 38.

10. *The Economist*, April 26, 2001.

11. *Corriere della Sera*, May 4, 2001.

12. *Financial Times*, March 11, 2001.

13. Caciagli e Corbetta, *Le Ragioni dell'Elettore*, 140.

14. Paul Ginsborg, *Italy and Its Discontents: Family, Civil Society, State, 1980–2001* (London: Allen Lane, 2001), 56–58.

15. Ibid., 217.

16. Barbacetto, Gomez, and Travaglio, *Mani Pulite*, 686.

17. *La Repubblica*, February 18, 2004.

18. Ginsborg, *Italy and Its Discontents*, 97.

19. Barbacetto, Gomez, and Travaglio, *Mani Pulite*, 508.

20. Author interview.

21. *La Repubblica*, April 2, 2004.

Chapter Twelve. One-Man Government

1. *La Repubblica*, December 30, 2002.

2. *Avvenimenti*, January 2004.

3. Ennio Remondino, *Senza Regole* (Rome: Editori Riuniti, 2004), 64.

4. *La Repubblica*, March 3, 2005.

5. Zaccaria, *Televisione*, 32–36.

6. Federico Orlando, *Lo Stato Sono Io: L'Ultimo Governo della Guerra Fredda* (Rome: Editori Riuniti, 2002), 35–37.

7. Gomez and Travaglio, *Regime*.

8. Author interview.

9. Travaglio and Gomez, *Regime*, 369.

10. Ibid., 370.

11. Ibid., 372.

12. Remondino, *Senza Regole*, 80.

13. *La Repubblica*, February 7, 2004.

14. Roberto Petrini, *Il Declino dell'Italia* (Rome: GLF Laterza, 2004), 18.

15. Ibid., 14.

16. Vincent, *Il Libro Azzurro di Berlusconi*, 71.

17. *La Repubblica*, November 13, 2002. *Corriere della Sera*, October 20, 2005. Corbi and Criscuoli, *Berlusconate*, 95–96.

18. *International Herald Tribune*, July 14, 2003.

19. *La Repubblica*, December 12, 2003.

20. *La Repubblica*, December 3, 2003.

21. Corrias, Gramellini, and Maltese, *1994: Colpo Grosso*, 94.

22. Ibid., 57.

Chapter Thirteen. The Press Takeover

1. Author interview.

2. *Libero,* December 27, 2005.

3. Author interview.

4. Gomez and Travaglio, *Regime,* 125.

5. Ibid., 380.

6. Ibid., 256.

7. Ibid., 260.

8. This and a host of other examples were collected by the union of journalists at RAI in a document known as the "Libro Bianco sulla RAI" (White Book on RAI). It is reprinted in large part in Gomez and Travaglio, *Regime,* 284–313. This particular incident occurred during a broadcast of February 4, 2003.

9. "Libro Bianco sulla RAI," March 7, 2003.

10. Gomez and Travaglio, *Regime,* 250.

11. Osservatorio di Pavia, "Chi Parla dei Leader: Gli Alter di Berlusconi e Rutelli nei Telegiornali." http://www.osservatorio.it/interna.php?m=v&section=analysis&idsection=000003&pos=0&ml=f&wordtofind=rutelli.

12. RAI 1, February 18, 2004.

13. Gomez and Travaglio, *Regime,* 252.

14. Ibid., 253.

15. Ibid., 262–63.

16. For an account of Guzzanti's program, see *La Repubblica,* November 17, 2003.

17. Gomez and Travaglio, *Regime,* 170.

18. *La Repubblica,* January 31, 2004.

19. *La Repubblica,* May 14, 2004.

20. Gomez and Travaglio, *Regime,* 348.

21. Ibid., 271–72.

22. *La Repubblica,* July 23, 2004.

23. Author interview.

24. Letter of the editorial committee of *La Stampa* to Marcello Sorgi, January 28, 2004.

25. Ibid.

26. Author interview.

Chapter Fourteen. Basta con Berlusconi! *(Enough Berlusconi!)*

1. http://www.forza-italia.it/10anni/decennale.htm.

2. *La Repubblica*, June 11, 2004.

3. Ibid.

4. Author interviews.

5. *La Repubblica*, October 6, 2003.

6. Author interviews.

7. *La Repubblica*, March 1, 2004. *The Economist*, April 1, 2004. Organisation for Economic Co-operation and Development, "Economic Survey of Italy," 2005. http://www.oecd.org/document/61/0,2340,en_2649_201185_34752381_1_1_1_1,00.html.

8. Barbacetto, Gomez, and Travaglio, *Mani Pulite*, 498–99.

9. *La Repubblica*, December 1, 2002.

10. *La Repubblica*, July 29, August 9 and 13; and September 2, 2002.

11. *La Repubblica*, February 2, 4, 7, and 12, 2005.

12. Orlando, *Fucilate Montanelli*, 30.

13. Gomez and Travaglio, *Regime*, 295.

14. *La Repubblica*, January 28, 2004.

15. *La Repubblica*, July 12, 2004.

16. Steve Rendall and Tara Broughel, Fairness & Accuracy In Reporting, "Amplifying Officials, Squelching Dissent," *EXTRA!*, May/June 2003. http://www.fair.org/index.php?page=1145.

17. *Fahrenheit 9/11*, directed by Michael Moore. Transcript at: http://www.script-o-rama.com/movie_scripts/f/fahrenheit-911-script-transcript.html.

18. Higher Education Research Institute, University of California, Los Angeles, *The American Freshman: National Norms for Fall 2000* (Los Angeles: HERI/UCLA, 2000).

19. *La Repubblica*, December 11, 2003.

20. Interview with Richard Viguerie, *NOW with Bill Moyers*, December 17, 2004. http://www.pbs.org/now/transcript/transcript351_full.html.

21. On reporter Mike Vasilinda's financial relationship with the state of Florida, see: http://www.heraldtribune.com/apps/pbcs.dll/article?AID=2005503260408.

22. *The New York Times*, March 13, 2005.

23. David T. Z. Mindich, *Tuned Out: Why Americans Under 40 Don't Follow the News* (New York: Oxford University Press, 2005), 28–33.

24. *The Washington Post*, April 26, 2004.

BIBLIOGRAPHY

Abruzzese, Alberto. *Elogio del Tempo Nuovo: Perché Berlusconi Ha Vinto*. Genoa: Costa & Nolan, 1994.

————, Vincenzo Susca, and Franco Ferrarotti. *Tutto È Berlusconi: Radici, Metafore e Destinazione del Tempo Nuovo*. Milan: Lupetti, 2004.

Amadori, Alessandro. *Mi Consenta: Metafore, Messaggi e Simboli: Come Silvio Berlusconi Ha Conquistato il Consenso degli Italiani*. Milan: Scheiwiller, 2002.

Andreoli, Marcella, Romano Cantore, Antonio Carlucci, and Maurizio Tortorella, eds. *Tangentopoli: Le Carte Che Scottano*. Milan: Mondadori, 1993.

Andrews, Geoff. *Not a Normal Country: Italy After Berlusconi*. London: Pluto, 2005.

Barbacetto, Gianni. *B.: Tutte le Carte del Presidente*. Milan: Tropea, 2004.

————, Peter Gomez, and Marco Travaglio. *Mani Pulite: La Vera Storia da Mario Chiesa a Silvio Berlusconi*. Rome: Editori Riuniti, 2002.

Benedetti, Amedeo. *Il Linguaggio e la Retorica della Nuova Politica Italiana: Silvio Berlusconi e Forza Italia*. Genoa: Erga, 2004.

"Berlusconi, Silvio." *Current Biography Yearbook*, vol. 55. New York: H. W. Wilson, 1994.

Berlusconi, Silvio. "La Discesa in Campo." 1994. http://www.forza-italia.it/10anni/discesaincampo.htm.

Blondel, Jean, and Paolo Segatti. *Italian Politics: The Second Berlusconi Government*. New York: Berghahn, 2003.

Bocca, Giorgio. *Piccolo Cesare*. Milan: Feltrinelli, 2002.

Bufacchi, Vittorio, and Simon Burgess. *Italy Since 1989: Events and Interpretations*. New York: St. Martin's, 1998.

Bull, Martin J., and Paolo Bellucci. *The Return of Berlusconi*. New York: Berghahn, 2002.

Caciagli, Mario, and Piergiorgio Corbetta. *Le Ragioni dell'Elettore*. Bologna: Il Mulino, 2002.

Calvi, Maurizio, interview with Paolo Borsellino. *L'Espresso*, April 8, 1994.

Caniglia, Enrico. *Berlusconi, Perot e Collor Come Political Outsider: Media, Marketing e Sondaggi nella Costruzione del Consenso Politico*. Catanzaro: Rubbettino, 2000.

Catalogo Generale dei Fascicoli d'Archivio. Gropello Cairoli: Mafia Connection, Biblioteca e Centro Documentazione, 1992.

Corbi, Alessandro, and Pietro Criscuoli. *Berlusconate*. Rome: Nutrimenti, 2003.

Cordero, Franco. *Le Strane Regole del Signor B*. Milan: Garzanti, 2003.

Corrias, Pino, Massimo Gramellini, and Curzio Maltese. *1994: Colpo Grosso (Storie della Storia d'Italia)*. Milan: Baldini & Castoldi, 1994.

D'Anna, Stefano E., and Gigi Moncalvo. *Berlusconi in Concert*. London: Otzium, 1994.

Darraj, Susan Muaddi. *Silvio Berlusconi: Prime Minister of Italy (Major World Leaders)*. Broomall, PA: Chelsea House, 2005. http://www.loc.gov/catdir/toc/ecip052/2004025073.html.

De Angeli, Floriano. *Archivio Berlusconi, Cuccia & Co*. Gropello Cairoli: Mafia Connection, Biblioteca e Centro Documentazione, 1994.

———. *Berlusconi 1: Gli Inizi Misteriosi, i Compari della P2, gli Amici di Tangentopoli, i Soci Ambigui, i Collaboratori Chiacchierati*. Gropello Cairoli: Mafia Connection, Biblioteca e Centro Documentazione, 1993.

———. *Le Connections con Mafia e Massoneria: Guida all'Archivio*. Gropello Cairoli: Mafia Connection, Biblioteca e Centro Documentazione, 1994.

Devescovi, Francesco. *Principi di Economia della Televisione*. Milan: Guerini, 2003.

Diamanti, Ilvo, and Renato Mannheimer, eds. *Milano a Roma: Guida all'Italia Elettorale del 1994*. Rome: Donzelli, 1994.

Ferrari, Giorgio. *Il Padrone del Diavolo: Storia di Silvio Berlusconi*. Milan: Camunia, 1990.

Ferretti, Claudio, Umberto Broccoli, and Barbara Scaramucci. *Mamma RAI: Storia e Storie del Servizio Pubblico Radiotelevisivo*. Florence: Le Monnier, 1997.

Fiori, Giuseppe. *Il Venditore: Storia di Silvio Berlusconi e della Fininvest*. Milan: Garzanti, 1995.

Forconi, Augusta. *Parola da Cavaliere*. Rome: Editori Riuniti, 1997.

Froio, Felice. *Il Cavaliere Incantatore: Chi È Veramente Berlusconi*. Bari: Dedalo, 2003.

Gambino, Michele. *Il Cavaliere B.: Chi È e Che Cosa Vuole l'Uomo Che Sogna di Cambiare l'Italia*. Lecce: Manni, 2001.

Ghezzi, Paolo. *La Voce di Berlusconi: Vittorio Feltri e Il (Suo) Giornale*. Turin: Sonda, 1995.

Gilioli, Alessandro. *Forza Italia: La Storia, gli Uomini, i Misteri*. Bergamo: Arnoldi, 1994.

Ginsborg, Paul. *Italy and Its Discontents: Family, Civil Society, State, 1980–2001.* London: Allen Lane, 2001.

———. *Silvio Berlusconi: Television, Power and Patrimony.* London: Verso, 2004.

Gomez, Peter, and Marco Travaglio. *Bravi Ragazzi: La Requisitoria Boccassini, l'Autodifesa di Previti & C.: Tutte le Carte dei Processi Berlusconi–Toghe Sporche.* Rome: Editori Riuniti, 2003.

———. *Lo Chiamavano Impunità: La Vera Storia del Caso SME e Tutto Quello Che Berlusconi Nasconde all'Italia e all'Europa.* Rome: Editori Riuniti, 2003.

La Grande Truffa: Previti, Berlusconi e l'Eredità Casati Stampa. Milan: Kaos, 1998.

Grasso, Aldo. *Enciclopedia della Televisione.* Milan: Garzanti, 2002.

———. *Storia della Televisione Italiana: I 50 Anni della Televisione.* Milan: Garzanti, 2004.

Gray, Susan, Elena Filippini, Stefano Tealdi, Jamie Rubin, Mishal Husain, and Jay O. Sanders. *Wide Angle: The Prime Minister and the Press.* New York: WNET, 2003. Videorecording.

Guarino, Mario. *Fratello P2 1816: L'Epopea Piduista di Silvio Berlusconi.* Milan: Kaos, 2001.

———. *L'Orgia del Potere: Testimonianze, Scandali e Rivelazioni su Silvio Berlusconi.* Bari: Dedalo, 2005.

Helfand, William H., and donor. *Berluschenol: 85 G di Barzellette sulla Politica.* Rome: Arti Grafiche La Moderna, 2003.

Jones, Tobias. *The Dark Heart of Italy.* New York: North Point Press, 2004.

Lane, David. *Berlusconi's Shadow: Crime, Justice and the Pursuit of Power.* London: Allen Lane, 2004.

Lehner, Giancarlo. *Storia di un Processo Politico: Giudici Contro Berlusconi: 1994–2002.* Milan: Mondadori, 2003.

Lombardi, Gian Valerio, and Luciana Acquafresca. *Governo Berlusconi: Sette Mesi di Attività (11 maggio–11 dicembre 1994). Vita Italiana, nos. 8–12, August–December 1994.* Rome: Presidenza del Consiglio dei Ministri, Dipartimento per l'Informazione e l'Editoria, 1994.

Lucidi, Marcantonio. *Le Mani sulla Cultura, Berlusconeide.* Rome: Malatempora, 2002.

Madron, Paolo. *Le Gesta del Cavaliere: La Prima Biografia Completa di Silvio Berlusconi.* Milan: Sperling & Kupfer, 1994.

Montanelli, Indro, and Mario Cervi. *L'Italia di Berlusconi, 1993–1995.* Milan: Rizzoli, 1995.

Mutarelli, Donato. *Silvio Berlusconi e il Senso dell'Estate: Lo Strabiliante Rapporto del Cavaliere di Arcore con la Politica, i Partiti, le Istituzioni.* Milan: ASEFI-Terziaria, 2003.

Orlando, Federico. *Fucilate Montanelli.* Rome: Editori Riuniti, 2001.

———. *Il Sabato Andavamo ad Arcore: La Vera Storia, Documenti e Ragioni, del Divorzio tra Berlusconi e Montanelli.* Bergamo: Larus, 1995.

————. *Lo Stato Sono Io: L'Ultimo Governo della Guerra Fredda.* Rome: Editori Riuniti, 2002.

Pagani, Paolo. *Forza Italia: Come È Nato il Movimento Che in 5 Mesi Ha Cambiato la Politica Italiana.* Novara: Boroli, 2003.

Parola del Presidente. (http://www.vacasflacas.it/Pagina016%20Pensieri%20e%20parole/Paroladipresidente.htm)

Pasquino, Gianfranco. *Dall'Ulivo al Governo Berlusconi: Le Elezioni del 13 Maggio 2001 e il Sistema Politico Italiano.* Bologna: Il Mulino, 2002.

Petrini, Roberto. *Il Declino dell'Italia.* Rome: GLF Laterza, 2003.

Procura della Repubblica di Palermo, Direzione Distrettuale Antimafia. *L'Onore di Dell'Utri: I Legami del Berlusconiano Marcello Dell'Utri con Cosa Nostra, nella Richiesta di Rinvio a Giudizio per Concorso in Associazione Mafiosa.* Milan: Kaos, 1997.

Ricci, Giuseppe. *La Teledittatura: Il Berlusconismo: Neo-Civilizzazione Sociale e Consenso Politico.* Milan: Kaos, 2003.

Ricolfi, Luca. *Dossier Italia: A Che Punto È il "Contratto con gli Italiani."* Bologna: Il Mulino, 2005.

Ruggeri, Giovanni. *Berlusconi: Gli Affari del Presidente.* Milan: Kaos, 1994.

————, and Mario Guarino. *Berlusconi: Inchiesta sul Signor TV.* Milan: Kaos, 1994.

Sani, Giacomo, and Antonio Nizzoli. *Quaderni di Scienza Politica,* 5, no. 3 (1997).

Sani, Giacomo, and Paolo Segatti. "Programmi, Media e Opinione Pubblica." *Rivista Italiana di Scienza Politica,* 26, no. 3.

Sisti, Leo, and Peter Gomez, *L'Intoccabile: Berlusconi e Cosa Nostra.* Milan: Kaos, 1997.

Statera, Gianni. *Il Volto Seduttivo del Potere: Berlusconi, i Media, il Consenso.* Rome: SEAM, 1994.

Stille, Alexander. "The Emperor of the Air." *The Nation,* November 29, 1999.

————. "Making Way for Berlusconi." *The New York Review of Books,* June 21, 2001.

————. "Why the Left Won in Italy." *The New York Review of Books,* June 6, 1996.

————. "The World's Greatest Salesman." *The New York Times Magazine,* March 17, 1996.

Una Storia Italiana. Milan: Mondadori, 2001.

Sylos Labini, Paolo. *Berlusconi e gli Anticorpi: Diario di un Cittadino Indignato.* Rome: GLF Laterza, 2003.

Travaglio, Marco. *Montanelli e il Cavaliere: Storia di un Grande e di un Piccolo Uomo.* Milan: Garzanti, 2004.

————. *Il Pollaio delle Libertà: Detti, Disdetti e Contraddetti.* Florence: Vallecchi, 1995.

Veltri, Elio. *Le Toghe Rosse.* Milan: Baldini & Castoldi, 2002.

————, and Marco Travaglio. *L'Odore dei Soldi.* Rome: Editori Riuniti, 2001.

Veltroni, Walter. *Io e Berlusconi (e la RAI).* Rome: Editori Riuniti, 1990.

Vespa, Bruno. *Il Cavaliere e il Professore: La Scommessa di Berlusconi, il Ritorno di Prodi.* Rome: RAI-ERI, 2003.

Vincent, Aldo, ed. *Il Libro Azzurro di Berlusconi: Battute, Aforismi, Opinioni, Barzellette.* Valentano: Scipioni, 2003.

Zaccaria, Roberto. *Televisione: Dal Monopolio al Monopolio: La Legge Gasparri Azzera il Pluralismo ed È Pericolosa per la Democrazia.* Milan: Baldini Castoldi Dalai, 2003.

INDEX